IN DEFENSE OF
NATURAL THEOLOGY

A Post-Humean Assessment

EDITED BY

JAMES F. SENNETT
AND DOUGLAS GROOTHUIS

InterVarsity Press
Downers Grove, Illinois

InterVarsity Press
P.O. Box 1400, Downers Grove, IL 60515-1426
World Wide Web: www.ivpress.com
E-mail: mail@ivpress.com

InterVarsity Press® is the book-publishing division of InterVarsity Christian Fellowship/USA®, a student movement active on campus at hundreds of universities, colleges and schools of nursing in the United States of America, and a member movement of the International Fellowship of Evangelical Students. For information about local and regional activities, write Public Relations Dept., InterVarsity Christian Fellowship/USA, 6400 Schroeder Rd., P.O. Box 7895, Madison, WI 53707-7895, or visit the IVCF website at <www.intervarsity.org>.

Design: Cindy Kiple
Images: David Hume: Image Select / Art Resource, NY
galaxy: Ian McKinnell / Getty Images
leaf: David Trood Pictures / Getty Images

ISBN-10: 0-8308-2767-6
ISBN-13: 978-0-8308-2767-1

Printed in the United States of America

Library of Congress Cataloging-in-Publication Data

In defense of natural theology: a post-Humean assessment / edited by
James F. Sennett and Douglas Groothuis.
    p. cm.
Includes bibliographical references and index.
ISBN 0-8308-2767-6 (pbk.: alk. paper)
1. Hume, David, 1711-1776. 2. Natural theology.3.
Religion—Philosophy. I. Sennett, James F., 1955 II. Groothuis,
Douglas R., 1957-

B1499.R45I5   2005-06-03

210'.92—dc22

                        2005012139

P	19	18	17	16	15	14	13	12	11	10	9	8	7	6	5	4	3	2	1
Y	20	19	18	17	16	15	14	13	12	11	10	09	08	07	06	05				

*"There has been much too much
genuflecting at Hume's altar."*

JOHN EARMAN

CONTENTS

1

INTRODUCTION

Hume's Legacy and Natural Theology

James F. Sennett and Douglas Groothuis

For well over two hundred years the intellectual defense of theism in general and Christianity in particular has been practiced beneath the looming shadow of the eighteenth-century Scottish philosopher David Hume.[1] It is no exaggeration to say that, from his day to ours, the vast majority of philosophical attacks against the rationality of theism have borne an unmistakable Humean aroma. Virtually all topical introductions to philosophy contain sections on the existence of God that quote or borrow extensively from Hume and his successors.[2] Typically when Christian philosophers attempt to offer sophisticated defenses of the faith, they are met with a rather condescending dismissal along the lines of, "Oh, well, we all know that Hume refuted such

---

[1] In this volume we are using the term *theism* in the sense most prevalent in contemporary philosophy of religion to define the conviction that there exists a unique personal omniscient, omnipotent, morally perfect creator and sustainer of the universe. This definition is narrow enough to distinguish it from supernaturalistic notions, such as classical polytheism, Aristotle's Prime Mover or the disengaged creator of eighteenth-century deism, but broad enough to include virtually all specific views employed in the Judeo-Christian-Islamic tradition. While some philosophers doubt the coherence of such a conception (see, e.g., R. Douglas Geivett's chapter in this book), this notion of theism has served well as a first approximation, and it is in this sense that it is employed throughout this volume, unless otherwise noted.

[2] See, e.g., Simon Blackburn, *Think: A Compelling Introduction to Philosophy* (Oxford: Oxford University Press, 1999), pp. 159-82. Blackburn acknowledges Hume's *Dialogues Concerning Natural Religion* as "the classic philosophical analysis of traditional theological arguments" (p. 159) and quotes quite extensively from them and other Humean sources throughout his treatment. He is also not shy about his conviction that Hume's criticisms remain unrefuted to the present day.

naiveté long ago."[3] Christian philosophy at the beginning of the twenty-first century is swimming upstream against a stiff and unrelenting dogmatic current we like to call "Hume's legacy." Neo-Wittgensteinian philosopher of religion D. Z. Phillips took the legacy to be so firmly established that he rejected entirely the notion that God's existence can be inferred from the world. Instead, he opted out of the epistemic justification game entirely and offered a nonrealist account of "religion without explanation."[4]

The historical and philosophical origins of Hume's legacy lie throughout the Humean corpus. Hume's empiricist philosophical system is complex and intricate, and his views on theism follow quite naturally and predictably from his broader philosophical perspective.[5] The specific details of his attack, however, lie predominately in two locations: sections 10 and 11 of *An Enquiry Concerning Human Understanding* and the whole of his *Dialogues Concerning Natural Religion*. In the former he is concerned explicitly with the question of miracles. In the latter he addresses many of the critical issues at the foundation of what philosophers and theologians call "natural theology" (NT)—the attempt to provide rational justification for theism using only those sources of information accessible to all inquirers, namely, the data of empirical experience and the dictates of human reason.[6] In other words, it is defense of theism without recourse to purported special revelation.

The last forty years have brought a marvelous resurgence in academic philosophical research and publication among Christian scholars. This resurgence has been inspired by the exemplary work of such contemporary giants as Alvin Plantinga, Nicholas Wolterstorff, William Alston, Robert and Marilyn Adams, William Lane Craig, and others, and has been bolstered by the establishment of organizations like the Society of Christian Philosophers (and its journal *Faith and Philosophy*) and the Evangelical Philosophical Society (and its journal *Philosophia Christi*). Hundreds of Christian philoso-

---

[3]Such dismissive attitudes sometimes show up in the most professional circumstances. Several years ago I (James) was presenting a paper on the distinction between providence and miracle at an American Philosophical Association meeting. During the Q&A, a prominent philosopher from a well-known research university commented, "I don't know why you're worrying about this stuff, anyway. Hume settled these issues centuries ago, and any talk of miracle is nonsense. I don't understand why they even allow papers like this at the APA." I'm still not too sure why he bothered to come to my presentation.
[4]D. Z. Phillips, *Religion Without Explanation* (Oxford: Basil Blackwell, 1976), esp. pp. 9-25.
[5]This point is demonstrated well in the present volume in chapter 2 (by Terence Penelhum) and chapter 4 (by Keith Yandell).
[6]And so the term "natural theology" is actually a misnomer. The enterprise, so conceived, is an exercise in philosophical, not theological, inquiry.

phers have undertaken to apply the very best tools of contemporary philosophy to the questions surrounding the claims of traditional Christianity. Very large research programs in religious epistemology, the coherence and implication of the divine attributes, the evidences for the resurrection of Jesus, the relationship between theology and science, and many other areas are currently being developed with impressive and exciting results.

Firmly ensconced in the middle of this revival are renewed interests in both miracles and NT. These investigations are using many new developments in science, theology and philosophy to make new and intriguing cases for the justification of theistic and Christian concepts and beliefs. Nonetheless, at every turn contemporary Christian philosophers are met with the dominating influence of Humean ideas, which are often taken as sacrosanct and impenetrable, and as undercutting the whole idea of Christian philosophy or rational defense of theistic concepts. There is great need in the Christian philosophical literature for a direct confrontation with Hume's legacy and a convincing demonstration that the Humean attacks do not sound the death knell for Christian philosophical inquiry.

A huge step in this needed confrontation was taken in 1997 with the publication of a collection of new essays by prominent Christian philosophers boldly titled *In Defense of Miracles*.[7] While not specifically touted as a response to Hume's legacy, the arguments throughout the book are clearly (and often explicitly) aimed at Hume's concerns and the heritage they have spawned. And it is less than serendipitous that the book's first chapter is a reprint of the aforementioned section 10 of Hume's *Enquiry*. Concerning Hume's influence the editors say, "There is a notable tendency among contemporary critics of miracles to rehabilitate arguments first launched by Hume over two centuries ago."[8]

The same can be said concerning critics of NT. The most prominently launched attacks against the whole idea of NT, as well as the most common criticisms of traditional arguments like the teleological, cosmological and ontological arguments, are directly reminiscent of those presented in the *Dialogues*. These include (but are by no means limited to) the following charges: (1) the idea of God does not stop the regression of cause and effect; (2) the idea of matter is just as capable of stopping the regression as that of

---

[7]R. Douglas Geivett and Gary R. Habermas, eds., *In Defense of Miracles: A Comprehensive Case for God's Action in History* (Downers Grove, Ill.: InterVarsity Press, 1997).
[8]Ibid., pp. 18-19.

God; (3) if the universe appears designed, it appears *badly* designed; (4) the kind of evidence typically offered for theism cannot in principle support such a conclusion; (5) theism, as a nonempirical, nonanalytical thesis, cannot be justifiably believed or established by argument; and (6) the catch-all criticism, called in this volume "Hume's stopper," that (even if sound) the NT arguments do not prove enough—they do not prove the existence of the God of theism. We assert without fear of contradiction that one will be hard pressed to find an attack on NT at an introductory or advanced level that does not make substantive use of one or more such Humean criticisms.

OUR DEFENSE OF NATURAL THEOLOGY

So we offer the present volume as a direct confrontation with Hume's legacy concerning NT.[9] This confrontation takes place on two levels. In the four chapters of part one the general Humean program is explained and challenged. In chapter two noted Hume scholar Terence Penelhum[10] offers an overview of the most important and influential Humean teachings on religion from the *Enquiry* and the *Dialogues,* as well as Hume's *Natural History of Religion.* Chapter three is the book's lone contrarian contribution. We hear from Todd Furman, a philosopher with strong Humean sympathies, about what he sees to be right about Hume's attacks on NT. Furman notes three basic fallacies in NT reasoning that Hume identifies and that seem to creep up at every turn in attempts to defend the classical arguments.[11] In chapter

---

[9]While this book is not a sequel to, nor in any way officially connected with *In Defense of Miracles* (excepting a common publisher and a few common authors), the editors nonetheless wish to acknowledge their indebtedness to that very fine volume as (a large part of) the inspiration for this one. We have chosen the title of our work, in part, in honor of the groundbreaking and beneficial work of Geivett, Habermas and their contributors.

[10]See, e.g., Terence Penelhum, *Philosophers in Perspective: Hume* (New York: St. Martins, 1975); *David Hume: An Introduction to His Philosophical System* (West Lafayette, Ind.: Purdue University Press, 1992); and *Themes in Hume: The Self, the Will, Religion* (Oxford: Clarendon, 2003).

[11]Both the Penelhum and Furman chapters contain sections on miracles. Although this volume contains no direct rebuttal of Hume's assault on miracles, it seemed appropriate to include these sections in order to give the reader a well-rounded view of Hume's concerns about theistic belief. In the case of Penelhum's chapter, the section demonstrates the uniformity of epistemological concerns Hume has with all matters religious. In the case of Furman's chapter, the section shows the similarity between Hume's arguments against NT and his arguments against miracles. Furman understands Hume to be identifying the same kinds of fallacies in theistic reasoning in both areas. Therefore, many of the rebuttals of Hume's attacks on NT in this volume can be applied via analogy to his attacks on miracles. For specific and detailed theistic response to Hume's legacy regarding miracles, the reader is referred to Geivett and Habermas, *In Defense of Miracles.*

four Keith Yandell, a specialist in Hume's views on religion,[12] explains and criticizes the philosopher's empiricist and verificationist commitments and then offers a general rebuttal of the Humean reasoning parsed out by Penelhum and Furman. Here Yandell speaks specifically to the implications of Hume's empiricism for the ontological and cosmological arguments. Finally, James Sennett argues in chapter five that the all-purpose "Hume's stopper" objection mentioned above is not the universal NT solvent that many philosophers—even many Christian philosophers—imagine it to be.

In part two nine different NT arguments are defended against the criticisms of Hume and Humeans. These include first of all classic arguments that are directly attacked by Hume. Douglas Groothuis addresses the cosmological argument in chapter six. He divides that argument into what he calls its vertical and horizontal versions, and argues that both versions escape Hume's stopper (though the latter fares better than the former) and carry metaphysical implications that strongly suggest the God of theism as the "causally necessary being" required to explain the universe's existence. In chapter seven Garrett J. DeWeese and Joshua Rasmussen offer a defense of the widely discussed *kalam* cosmological argument against Humean objections involving causality, the principle of sufficient reason, and Hume's stopper. And James Madden addresses the teleological argument (or argument from design) in chapter eight, which he likewise divides into two versions—a classical one and a modern one. Madden holds out little hope for the classical version, but argues that the modern version, inspired by the kind of scientific research utilized in the so-called intelligent design movement, does show promise for overcoming Humean obstacles.[13]

Also addressed in part two are NT arguments that are not dealt with explicitly by Hume, but which nonetheless bear directly on key Humean doctrines and themes, and for which Humean objections are not difficult to construct. These include the fine-tuning version of the teleological argument, which Robin Collins addresses in chapter nine. Collins is the leading propo-

---

[12]See, e.g., Keith Yandell, "Miracles, Epistemology, and Hume's Barrier," *International Journal for Philosophy of Religion* 7 (1976): 391-417; "Hume's Explanation of Religious Belief," *Hume Studies* 5 (1979): 94-109; and *Hume's "Inexplicable Mystery": His Views on Religion* (Philadelphia: Temple University Press, 1990).

[13]However, Madden's conclusions are significantly more guarded than those of most authors in part 2.

nent of this argument.[14] Here he offers us the latest development in his on-going defense of the thesis that the so-called anthropic coincidences, those many precisely calibrated features of the physical universe that are individually necessary for the production of life, combine to offer a powerful, Hume-resistant theistic argument. In addition, Collins offers a rebuttal of the classic Hume-inspired "Who designed God?" objection to the teleological argument, fueled by fine-tuning reasoning. In chapter ten Paul Copan defends the moral argument by showing that Hume's views on morality, which would not support a moral argument for theism, are seriously flawed. Vastly superior is the approach taken by Hume's contemporary countryman Thomas Reid. And Reid's highly plausible theory of morality lends itself quite naturally to an argument for theism. Keith Yandell returns in chapter eleven to defend the argument from religious experience by showing that, despite widely held assumptions to the contrary, there is nothing in Hume's doctrine concerning the nature of experience that precludes experience from constituting evidence for the existence of God.

The book's final three chapters address more contemporary NT arguments that postdate Hume's treatments, but to which Humean criticisms nonetheless can be and often have been applied. In chapter twelve Victor Reppert presents the latest installment in his ongoing defense of C. S. Lewis's argument from reason—the argument that human rational capacities are only adequately explained via a theistic hypothesis.[15] In particular, he defends the argument against two Humean objections: what Theodore Drange calls "the inadequacy objection" (the view that appeal to the God of theism to explain human rationality in fact explains nothing) and Hume's stopper. Chapter thirteen is a defense by J. P. Moreland of the closely allied argument from consciousness. Moreland sees the best expression of a Humean attack on this argument in John Searle's account of consciousness, and shows this account,

---

[14]See, e.g., Robin Collins, "A Scientific Argument for the Existence of God: The Fine-Tuning Design Argument," in *Reason for the Hope Within*, ed. Michael J. Murray (Grand Rapids: Eerdmans, 1999), pp. 47-75; "God, Design, and Fine-Tuning," in *God Matters: Readings in the Philosophy of Religion*, ed. Raymond Martin and Christopher Bernard (New York: Longman, 2002), pp. 119-35; and "The Evidence for Fine-Tuning," in *God and Design: The Teleological Argument and Modern Science*, ed. Neil Manson (New York: Routledge, 2003), pp. 178-99.
[15]See, e.g., Victor Reppert, "The Argument from Reason," *Philo* 2 (1999): 33-45; "Reply to Parsons and Lippard on the Argument from Reason," *Philo* 3 (2000): 76-89; "Several Formulations of the Argument from Reason," *Philosophia Christi*, n.s. 5 (2003): 9-34; and *C. S. Lewis's Dangerous Idea* (Downers Grove, Ill.: InterVarsity Press, 2003). The clearest statement of Lewis's original argument appears in *Miracles: A Preliminary Study* (New York: Macmillan, 1978), pp. 12-24.

along with other prominent nontheistic accounts, to be woefully inadequate, leaving ample room for a theistic explanation of consciousness to win the day. In the last chapter Douglas Geivett presents a new version of the cumulative case argument that skirts Humean objections and culminates not merely in theism, but specifically in *Christian* theism. Geivett's path to a defense of Christianity lies through a demonstration that the form of theism Hume objects to is actually inconsistent with Christianity, and therefore his criticisms are inapplicable to philosophical defense of the latter. Because of its utilization of many different NT strategies in the development of a cumulative case and its move beyond the defense of theism to the defense of Christianity, Geivett's chapter serves as a fitting capstone and conclusion to the collection.[16]

The aforementioned revival in Christian philosophy has been quite fruitful in bringing the very best developments in contemporary philosophy to bear on the defense and explication of theism and Christianity. For instance, many philosophers have utilized modal logic and possible worlds semantics to offer enlightening accounts of and impressive arguments for many Christian concepts and doctrines. Likewise, contemporary discussions in epistemology and the nature of human knowledge have been brought to bear on the concept of religious knowledge and the possibility of rational religious belief. The chapters in this volume are, in most cases, designed to follow this trend. They apply the best in contemporary philosophical advancement to the defense of the NT enterprise in general and to specific arguments in particular. The resulting message, and thesis of the book, is this: *Natural theology is alive and well in contemporary philosophy; the supposed Humean refutation of the enterprise is a myth whose exposure is long overdue.*

HUME'S LEGACY AND CONTEMPORARY PHILOSOPHY

Two facts of contemporary philosophy leave Hume's legacy open to vigorous attack. The first concerns the revival in NT study mentioned above. This revival has largely concerned what we might call "modest NT." Contempo-

---

[16]The astute reader will notice the absence of a chapter on the ontological argument. This seemingly glaring omission, spawned by editorial necessities and concerns for space, can nonetheless be justified by two facts: (1) Hume never explicitly addresses the ontological argument, but rather incorporates his concerns about necessary existence into his discussion of the cosmological argument, which does receive ample attention in these pages; and (2) two chapters in part one address explicitly and in some detail a Humean treatment of the ontological argument. These include Todd Furman's defense of a Humean attack in chapter three and Keith Yandell's rebuttal of such an attack in chapter four. Fans of Anselm's jewel should find plenty to satisfy their thirst in those discussions.

rary philosophers of religion seldom claim a NT argument *proves* or **demon-strates** the existence of God, or even that it offers *overwhelming* evidence for it, such that no person aware of the argument's implications could rationally reject its conclusion. (In fact, contemporary philosophy has shown that it is unlikely that *any* major metaphysical theory can be proved in this fashion.) Rather, using the recognition in contemporary epistemology that epistemic rationality and justification are concepts that admit of degree and person-relativity, proponents of NT seek to show that these arguments can supply a significant level of epistemic pedigree to the theistic or Christian beliefs of many people. While this conclusion is less grandiose than that espoused by many NT advocates of the High Middle Ages or the Enlightenment, it is nonetheless a significant and powerful one, and puts the lie to Hume's legacy, which perpetuates the myth that rational religious belief is impossible for any intellectually aware individual.

The second fact that renders Hume's legacy vulnerable is the general anti-skeptical attitude that pervades contemporary philosophy. An extreme epistemological humility dominated the early twentieth-century in the guise of logical positivism and its relatives. This Hume-inspired quasi-skepticism called into question many of the great ideas of Western thought, relegating to the philosophical scrap heap such venerable notions as substance, the self, moral realism and all things religious. However, time and scrutiny proved this philosophical clean sweep to be implausible, equivocal, necessarily inconsistent in application and referentially incoherent. In its wake has arisen a general philosophical demeanor much more charitable and generous to traditional philosophical and even commonsense concepts, often assuming that such are coherent and referential unless proved otherwise. The game then becomes finding the correct analysis for or account of the concept's application, rather than the desperate struggle to legitimate its employment at all.

Although Hume scholars debate the extent (if any) to which Hume can be labeled an epistemic skeptic, there can be no doubt that serious skeptical concerns dominated his thinking. Hume was extraordinarily modest and cautious in the kinds of knowledge he would deem possible or even likely. His doubts about causation, the unity of the self and inductive reasoning are legendary, and it is safe to say that he was no friend of common sense or traditional philosophy. And, as we have already intimated, Hume could be considered the patron saint of logical positivism. Contemporary philosophy's repudiation of the skeptical inquiry of the latter can legitimately be read as a fundamental dissociation with the hermeneutic of suspicion of the former. Only in its application to religious concepts, it seems, is a Humean distrust of the basic categories of human experience warranted today. But of course such a double standard, properly exposed to the light of metaphilosophical awareness, cannot hope to survive. The chapters in this book demonstrate on many levels that the current philosophical willingness to bracket skeptical suspicions and grant audience to venerable concepts can only benefit the case for theism and illuminate once more the unjustifiable nature of Humean skeptical assumptions.

CLOSING REMARKS

We recognize that the subject matter of this volume will appeal to a wide variety of readers, not simply to professional philosophers and theologians. Therefore, we have tried to walk a very narrow line between accessibility and sophistication. The result is a collection of chapters with a rather wide range of "user friendliness" and appeal. Some chapters (e.g., those by Furman, Copan and Reppert) are very accessible to any educated reader and do not require much philosophical background at all. Others (e.g., those by Moreland, Yandell, and DeWeese and Rasmussen) are quite sophisticated and require a good bit of awareness of philosophy for full appreciation. None are what could fairly be called "popular" presentations—all require at least a student's level of philosophical and theological awareness. Nonetheless, we believe that they will reward careful reading and scrutiny and will be worth whatever time and effort is required to follow them.

For those not practiced in the reading of philosophy, one word of caution is warranted. Philosophical writing is often highly dialectical, engaging in an ongoing conversation with imagined interlocutors who might question or attempt to rebut the position being offered. Philosophy professors often encounter students who complain that the reading material is inconsistent or contradictory, arguing for or asserting on one page what it argues against or denies on the next. Such students fail to recognize that dialectical material frequently switches voices, and that philosophers often speak on behalf of those who will question or disagree with what they are saying. Those unfamiliar with this rhetorical technique must be especially careful to be aware of markers in the text that will note changes in voice, perspective or point of view. Students often find it helpful to imagine the presentation as a discussion among various parties, and to be careful to note which party is speaking at each point in the dialogue. But whatever approach works, it is absolutely imperative throughout this book that the reader stay aware of the differing positions that may be represented.

Finally, we must say a word concerning the target of this collection. There is a debate in contemporary Christian philosophy over the efficacy of NT and its place in a Christian apologetic.[17] This debate centers around the research program in religious epistemology dubbed "Reformed Epistemology" (RE) by its founder, Alvin Plantinga.[18] RE is the view that Christian belief can be, and often (perhaps typically) is, *properly basic*—epistemically justified without evidence or argument. Some (though by no means all) proponents of RE disparage NT as unnecessary at best and somehow deficient or inappropriate at worst. While all the contributors to this volume would no doubt take umbrage with this sentiment, it is important to note that RE is not the target of our efforts, nor is any alternative attempt to defend the rationality of Christianity. Ours is a dispute with agnostic and atheistic philosophy inspired by Humean empiricism, not any form of Christian philosophy.

---

[17]See, e.g., the discussions in Steven B. Cowan, ed., *Five Views on Apologetics* (Grand Rapids: Zondervan, 2000).

[18]Plantinga's program is presented, developed and defended in many publications. The most complete presentation of its earlier formulation is in "Reason and Belief in God," in *Faith and Rationality: Reason and Belief in God,* ed. Alvin Plantinga and Nicholas Wolterstorff (Notre Dame, Ind.: University of Notre Dame Press, 1983), pp. 16-93. Plantinga's fully mature explication of Reformed Epistemology is presented in *Warranted Christian Belief* (New York: Oxford University Press, 2000).

PART ONE

HUME ON NATURAL THEOLOGY

2

HUME'S CRITICISMS
OF NATURAL THEOLOGY

Terence Penelhum

𝔅

In this chapter I describe Hume's objections to the enterprise of natural theology. This is a narrower purpose than that of describing his wider views on religion, although I shall not avoid straying into those when this narrower purpose can be served by commenting on them. Religion was a profoundly important part of the general culture into which Hume was born, and of the literary culture of which he became such a prominent adornment; he was concerned throughout his career with understanding it and evaluating its place in both human society and in the world of letters. This concern was all the greater because of the fact that he did not share in the religiousness of those around him and was keenly aware of his difference from most of his friends and acquaintances in this respect.

THE HISTORICAL CONTEXT OF HUME'S CRITICISMS

Natural theology has a long history. It can certainly be traced back to classical times, for example, to the *Laws* of Plato, or to Cicero's *On the Nature of the Gods,* which was a model for Hume's *Dialogues Concerning Natural Religion.* Most find it convenient, however, to think of it as having been given its traditional role and character by Aquinas. Aquinas held that some of the truths that it is necessary for us to accept for our salvation can be shown to be true by reason alone, even though God has chosen to reveal them, so that those not able to learn of them in this way can nevertheless be aware of them. Such truths are those of God's existence, his omnipotence and perfection, his eternity and simplicity, and his providential governance of the world. These do not suffice for salvation, however, and so other truths are revealed to us that reason could not learn independently, such as the triune nature of God and the incarnation. Even though these latter truths cannot be learned by unaided human reason, it is still rational to believe them, since there are independent evidences of their truth, such as the miracles and prophecies that attest the authority of the church that proclaims them to the world. They also derive their rational plausibility from the prior fact that God's existence and perfection can be known to reason, and would lead us to expect human history to contain additional signs of his goodness such as these.[1]

By Hume's day the English debate about the rationality of faith was still in its deistic phase, in spite of Joseph Butler's arguments against deism in the *Analogy of Religion*.[2] The deists accepted at least some of the traditional arguments of natural theology, but rejected the claims of revelation. While the orthodox tradition deriving from Aquinas maintained the rational continuity of belief in God and belief in the Christian revelation, the deists separated them, holding that the God who had created the orderly world that Newton had described would not need to intervene in its workings by performing miracles, and could make his moral demands known through the workings of the individual conscience, without the aid of sacred books or priestly utterances. "Natural religion" was enough, and revealed religion was archaic and unnecessary.

Deism was the cultural manifestation of the century's revulsion against sectarian division and "enthusiasm," and although it has faded from the religious scene, it is important for us to recall that it did not represent (or did not see itself as representing) a rejection of religion, but merely a rejection of those features of religion that had led to so much suffering and warfare in the generations before. Furthermore, science, that is Newtonian (and pre-Darwinian) science, was not seen as a threat to religion, but as a body of knowledge that helped to establish its foundations. This latter opinion was shared by the deists and their orthodox opponents; they parted company over the claims of revelation and church tradition. Hume's arguments were to undermine them both.

---

[1]St. Thomas's position on these matters is stated in chapters 1-8 of book 1 of the *Summa contra gentiles*. See Thomas Aquinas *Summa contra gentiles*, trans. Anton C. Pegis (New York: Doubleday, 1955).

[2]On deism, see Peter Byrne, *Natural Religion and the Nature of Religion: The Legacy of Deism* (London: Routledge, 1989). On Butler's response to it, see part 2 of Terence Penelhum, *Butler* (London: Routledge, 1985).

HUME'S *ENQUIRY CONCERNING HUMAN UNDERSTANDING*

Hume's earliest published writing on religion is to be found in sections 10 and 11 of the *Enquiry Concerning Human Understanding*. This was published in 1748, and consisted of essays that were, for the most part, recastings of material Hume had included in books one and two of his earlier work, *A Treatise of Human Nature*. This was published in 1739 and 1740, but the lack of interest in it prompted Hume to present its main positions in what he judged to be a more palatable and elegant form. The *Treatise* did not contain any sections devoted to religion, although we learn from Hume's correspondence that this was because he removed some material, now thought to have been an earlier version of his arguments about miracles, in order to make it easier to obtain the approval of Joseph Butler. The *Enquiry* contrasted with the *Treatise* in this respect, and what we find there is of the greatest importance for our present theme.

Section 10 of the *Enquiry,* titled "Of Miracles," is probably Hume's most well-known essay, and it has prompted a great number of replies ever since its appearance.[3] Since it does not deal with any part of the traditional subject matter of natural theology, I will deal with it only briefly here. It is not Hume's most careful work, and its precise intent is disputed. Its tone is sarcastic and hostile, but in spite of this it is best read not as an attempt to show that there cannot be any miracles (which would be a very un-Humean piece of negative dogmatism), or even as an argument that there have in fact been none (although Hume clearly thinks this). We must take Hume's stated conclusion very seriously, namely, that "no human testimony can have such force as to prove a miracle, and make it a just foundation for any system of religion" (EHU 10.35; SBN 127).[4] This is a conclusion about *testimony*—that it can never be good enough to prove a miracle. Hume assumes that, if it could, it would establish the truth of the religion to which the miracle belongs. Hume confines himself to the question of how we ought to respond to what others tell us about miracles, and never says anything directly about how we should respond if we think we have witnessed one ourselves.

The essay reaches its conclusion by a set of arguments that is in two parts.

---

[3]See chapter 1, note 11, on page 12 of this volume.
[4]References in this chapter to Hume's *Enquiry Concerning Human Understanding* (EHU) are to the section and paragraph numbers in the Oxford Philosophical Texts, ed. Tom L. Beauchamp (Oxford: Oxford University Press, 1999), followed by the page number in Hume's *Enquiries Concerning Human Understanding and Concerning the Principles of Morals,* ed. L. A. Selby-Bigge, 3rd ed., with revisions by P. H. Nidditch (Oxford: Clarendon, 1975) (SBN).

The first part offers a very general argument about evidence, miracles and natural laws. "A wise man," says Hume, "proportions his belief to the evidence" (EHU 10.4; SBN 170). When we are told of some alleged event, wise judgment requires two things. First, we have to consider the likelihood of the event that is reported to us: has such a thing happened often, or occasionally, or never? Here we must be guided by past experience. Our experience may be too limited to guide us well; Hume tells the story of an Indian prince who had never seen water turned to ice and would not believe stories involving freezing. If our experience is mixed, and events of the reported sort have sometimes happened and sometimes not, we will, if we are wise, feel uncertain, and think there is only a limited degree of probability that what we are told is true. Sometimes we have what he calls "infallible experience," which has always been one way, and then we can suppose that we have a "proof" that the event will indeed have happened, or that it will not have. But in addition to considering the likelihood of the sort of event reported, we have also to estimate the quality of the testimony we have. Here also we depend on experience to guide us: are our witnesses truthful, informed or competent, and are their memories of the event recent ones?

These considerations may conflict. In particular, we may find ourselves in a situation where we have high quality testimony to an event that experience tells us will not have happened. This (again if we are wise) will lead to suspended judgment (or "counterpoise"). But suppose the event reported is not merely marvelous or extraordinary, but miraculous. This, says Hume, means that it is, or was, "a violation of the laws of nature." In such a case past experience will be entirely against it. This will provide not a mere probability, but a proof against its reality. But suppose the testimony in its favor is impeccable. Then we would have "proof against proof," and of course we should withhold our verdict. So we should only accept testimony to a miracle if the falsehood of the testimony would be more miraculous than the event related—that is, never.

This argument, which is original to Hume, tells us that if we have impeccable testimony to a miraculous (as distinct from a merely remarkable) event, we should suspend judgment about it. The second part of the essay, which is not original in the same way, contains a number of arguments to show that the actual testimony to miracles is not impeccable at all. The witnesses who testify to miracles have never been of such quality that their testimony should outweigh our proper hesitations; far from being wise in their attitude to prodigies, human beings have a lamentable tendency to long for wondrous events and to welcome signs of them; reports of miracles come from "ignorant and barbarous nations," not sophisticated and informed ones; and the miracle-stories of one religion count against the miracle-stories of other religions. So the actual testimony to the miraculous that is available to us is of low quality and does not even justify us in suspended judgment.

These arguments in the second part of the essay are of a sort that would have been familiar to those who had followed earlier English debate about miracles, which Hume joined quite late. The argument of the first part is original to him, and amounts to an insistence that the evidence of miracle testimony has to be weighed against the uniform past experience in favor of the natural law that the miracle, had it occurred, would have violated. It is natural to respond that Hume has ignored the weight that would lie on the side of miracle testimony if one had established the reality of a God who was responsible for all natural laws. Hume is, on this matter, siding with the deists who denied that the creator of natural law could ever have occasion to arrange violations of it. But he does not himself, of course, use any argument based on such considerations, and only insists that if an event would contravene natural law, no testimony could ever suffice to establish that it had occurred. The fact that he presents this argument before he enters any discussion of natural theology indicates that he considers this point to be decisive even if some form of natural theology has been agreed to be successful.

Even though he sides with the deists in section 10, he turns with total negativity in section 11 to consider the theological premises that they and the orthodox shared. Although this essay is much less often studied than "Of Miracles," it is of much greater philosophical importance. It also leans more heavily on the details of Hume's theories of causation.

There is a striking difference in tone and procedure between the two sections. "Of Miracles" is aggressive and sarcastic and has caused much offense to some of its readers. Hume could write it in this way because he was contributing to a familiar debate that had already contained hard-hitting writings by others. Section 11, however, enters territory that is more dangerous for Hume, and he resorts to careful indirection in presenting his arguments. The *Enquiry* was written in the aftermath of an unpleasant controversy that had led to Hume's failure to gain an academic appointment at the University of Edinburgh.[5] The fact that the *Treatise* had not contained any overt discus-

---

[5]On this lamentable episode, see chapter 12 of Ernest Campbell Mossner, *The Life of David Hume* (Oxford: Clarendon, 1970).

sion of theological themes had not prevented Hume's contemporaries from judging him to be an antireligious thinker and concluding he was spiritually unfit to teach the young. He saw himself as a victim of superstition, but he also saw the need for circumspection in the presentation of the opinions that he no longer felt willing to excise from his work. A careful reading of section 11 makes it clear that it is a devastatingly negative treatment of the matters with which it deals.

Section 11 is titled "Of a Particular Providence and of a Future State."[6] It begins with a supposed conversation between the author and a friend "who loves sceptical paradoxes." This friend tells him that philosophy has itself to blame for being subject to attack by the forces of superstition. It has brought this fate upon itself by seeking to base religion upon reason, instead of leaving it as a matter of custom and tradition as it was in the classical world. To support this claim, he imagines Epicurus defending himself before the people of Athens against the charge that his alleged atheism is dangerous to public morality. (That atheists were a moral danger was a commonplace of religious controversy in Hume's time that had only recently been questioned by Bayle.)[7]

Epicurus insists that he has no less reason to support the moral traditions of his society than his religious critics do. His critics have departed from the religious traditionalism of their forefathers by attempting to establish religious doctrines by rational argument. The argument they have used (the one that Hume's immediate forebears and contemporaries used) is based on the orderliness and the beauty of the natural world, which they maintain (in disagreement with Epicurus) cannot be due to chance, but must be the result of intelligent design. Let us, says Epicurus, concede this for the sake of argument. What has the argument shown? It has shown that the order and beauty of our world have been caused by a power or powers that are great enough to produce them. What such argument does not do is show that this power is any greater than that. One cannot, in other words, infer from this evidence that Jupiter is almighty or morally perfect—only that he is mighty enough and good enough to produce the world we see, with all its limitations. Such an argument cannot, therefore, show that the world was at one time wholly perfect and free from evil and fell from that state, or that this

---

[6]Hume originally titled it "Of the Practical Consequences of Natural Religion"—a more revealing title. The message of the section is, of course, that there are none.

[7]Pierre Bayle, *Various Thoughts on the Occasion of a Comet (1682)*, trans. Robert C. Bartlett (Albany, N.Y.: SUNY Press, 2000).

life will be succeeded by another that will be free of the pains and evils that attend the present one; for such conclusions depend on mounting up to Jupiter and ascribing to him powers that are greater than those needed to produce our cosmos as we find it. These conclusions may indeed be true, but the argument cannot establish them.

If this is recognized, then the practical consequences of "natural religion" (that is, religion that is confined in its content to those doctrines that natural reason can establish) will be no different from the practical consequences of a metaphysic like that of Epicurus. Epicurus holds, he says, that virtue is the most rewarding form of life, and he bases this claim upon the observation of human society. Since the only theology that reason can establish is one that limits the deity's powers to those sufficient to cause the world we live in, it is this same observation that has to be used by the rational theist to determine the profitability of virtue. Claims about the afterlife cannot be added to this evidence without going beyond what natural theology can establish. So the moral importance of natural theology is zero.

Hume now imagines an objection to the position that the friend has put into the mouth of Epicurus. Surely we often infer, quite soundly, that an effect has a cause greater than that which would suffice to produce it? If we see a half-finished building, do we not correctly infer that it is the work of a builder who can, and will, complete it and eliminate its temporary shortcomings? If we see the print of a foot in the sand, do we not correctly infer that its owner had another foot? The friend responds that in cases such as these, we can properly infer powers in the cause greater than those needed to produce the observed effect, because we have independent evidence of those powers in their past exercise: we have seen builders complete half-finished buildings and have seen walkers with two feet rather than one. But in the case of the whole cosmos, which is necessarily a unique effect, we cannot draw upon such prior experience and are not entitled to a parallel inference.

In his essay on miracles, Hume did not need to lean on his prior analysis of causation beyond insisting that an event covered by a natural law has to have been part of a uniform past sequence that has had no exceptions. In section 11, however, Hume draws much more on the detail of his causal theories. He appeals to the maxim "that where any cause is known only by its particular effects, it must be impossible to infer any new effects from that cause." He concludes the section by drawing on a principle that is quite fundamental in that analysis, a principle that does not merely cast doubt on the

details of claims about the divine purposes in nature, but on the argument
that had been thought, both by the deists and the orthodox, to establish that
agency itself.

The principle is the one that Beauchamp and Rosenberg have described
as embodying a "Copernican revolution" in philosophical thought about
causation: that in describing one object, agent or event as the cause of another, one is identifying the earlier member of a regular sequence that has
always led to the same later one.[8] Since there are no intrinsic connections
between causes and effects, only experience can teach us what causes what,
and it does this by presenting us with regular sequences. To say that A is the
cause of B is to say that objects, agents or events like A have always been
followed by objects, agents or events like B. In the final paragraph of section
11 Hume, in his own person, gently suggests that this undermines natural
theology altogether:

> It is only when two species of objects are found to be constantly conjoined,
> that we can infer the one from the other; and were an effect presented, which
> was entirely singular, and could not be comprehended under any known spe-
> cies, I do not see, that we could form any conjecture or inference at all con-
> cerning its cause. (EHU 11.30; SBN 148)

The universe is the alleged effect in this case, and the deity is its alleged
cause, and both are "singular and unparalleled." Hume leaves his friend to
ponder on the implications of this principle, but they are obvious. The section has led us from an argument that Hume thinks shows us that natural
theology is of no moral relevance to one that shows it to have no proper
basis in causal reasoning. It is not surprising that such a radical conclusion
has been expressed by using palliative devices, but I do not myself think
that the sheer negativity of Hume's position in the *Enquiry* is ever seriously
modified in his later writings.

HUME'S *NATURAL HISTORY OF RELIGION*

The *Enquiry* leaves us with deep questions about the very possibility of natural theology being able to establish the perfection of God. The deists and
the orthodox had shared the assumption that it could do, and had done, this,
and disagreed over whether the divine perfection precluded or required
God's intervention in nature in the form of prophecies or miracles. Hume's

---

[8]Tom Beauchamp and Alexander Rosenberg, *Hume and the Problem of Causation* (New York:
Oxford University Press, 1981).

next major writing on religion was *The Natural History of Religion,* published in 1757.[9] This short treatise is not about natural theology at all, but its importance for an understanding of Hume's views about natural theology is considerable. Hume opens it with an important distinction between the question of religion's "foundation in reason" and that of its "origin in human nature." *The Natural History* is to be about the latter.

The former is put aside by Hume with the following comment:

> Happily, the first question, which is the most important, admits of the most obvious, at least the clearest, solution. The whole frame of nature bespeaks an intelligent author; and no rational enquirer can, after serious reflection, suspend his belief for a moment with regard to the primary principles of genuine Theism and Religion. (NHR 21)

An unguarded reader might suppose that Hume is here restating the very consensus that he had gone to such pains to undermine in the *Enquiry.* In a sense he is, but the patent insincerity in his statement of it needs no emphasis, and he is clearly paying prudent lip-service to that consensus in a work that is devoted to another topic.

In the briefest outline, Hume's account of the origin of religion in human nature goes as follows. Religion is originally polytheistic (a claim that undermines the common view among the orthodox that human beings were originally aware of the one true God and lost this awareness because of the Fall). It originated because people were beset by calamities such as disease and storms and accidents, and wanted to understand them and (if possible) prevent them; they resorted to personalistic explanations of them that enabled them to propitiate the spirits that they thought had caused them. Hume's central contention here (at least for our purposes) is that actual religion, as opposed to the religion of philosophers, came about because humans were anxious in the face of special and extraordinary calamities, not because of any consciousness of the orderliness and law-abidingness of nature.

Polytheism, though a form of superstition, is not the most dangerous form of religion, because it consists of an essentially commercial relationship between people and their gods, who are local and restricted in their powers.

---

[9]The edition I use in this chapter is that of H. E. Root (Stanford, Calif.: Stanford University Press, 1957), hereafter references given in the text with NHR. The importance of the *Natural History* is recognized by Keith Yandell in Keith Yandell, *Hume's "Inexplicable Mystery": His Views on Religion* (Philadelphia: Temple University Press, 1990).

Their devotees do not, for the most part, intrude their claims upon the territory of other deities. But in time polytheism has given place to monotheism. This has come about because of the inner logic of worship, which encourages devotees to exaggerate both the powers and the moral qualities of their gods. The monotheist considers his god to be supreme in both power and holiness, and to demand absolute and worldwide obedience, which includes inner submission and the suppression of all forms of independent thought and feeling. It therefore leads to self-deception and the corruption of reason, the latter taking the form of the subordination of philosophical thought to the demands of religious factionalism.

The key claim here (again for our purposes) is the fact that Hume has offered an account of how monotheism has actually arisen that gives no place at all to the awareness of natural order or any other of the intellectual factors that generate natural theology. It rather suggests an explanation of why it is, in Hume's view, that when philosophers come to be sensitive to these considerations, they are so quick to assume that the deity that explains them is the all-perfect God of the Christian tradition and not some lesser creative mind.

HUME'S *DIALOGUES CONCERNING NATURAL RELIGION*, PARTS 1-8

I turn now to *The Dialogues Concerning Natural Religion.* This is a great and subtle work that, for all its surface clarity, demands many readings and defies proper summary.[10] It was published posthumously in 1779 by Hume's nephew, since Hume was dissuaded from publishing it during his lifetime by some of his friends, notably Adam Smith. The importance of this fact for the interpretation of Hume's opinions is not easy to determine, especially since the decision to keep it unpublished seems to have been one that Hume made reluctantly. The work seems to have been at least largely written at about the same time as the *Natural History* and to have been fre-

---

[10]The edition of the *Dialogues* that I have used in this chapter is that of Norman Kemp Smith (Edinburgh: Thomas Nelson, 1947; reprint, Indianapolis: Bobbs-Merrill, 1980), hereafter cited in text with DNR. The most accessible edition, excellently edited, is that of J. C. A. Gaskin (Oxford: World's Classics, 1993), which also includes the *Natural History* and *Enquiry 11.* There is first-class commentary in the edition of Nelson Pike (Indianapolis: Bobbs-Merrill, 1970), in J. C. A. Gaskin, *Hume's Philosophy of Religion,* 2nd ed. (London: Macmillan, 1988), and in Yandell, *Hume's "Inexplicable Mystery."* The literature on the *Dialogues* has been immeasurably enriched by the recent appearance of William Lad Sessions, *Reading Hume's Dialogues: A Veneration for True Religion* (Bloomington: Indiana University Press, 2002). I have attempted to comment on these matters myself in chapters 9-11 of Terence Penelhum, *Themes in Hume* (Oxford: Clarendon, 2000).

quently revised, but not in any fundamental way.

The title tells us that the conversations in it are about natural *religion,* that is, about that form of religion that can be based on what natural reasoning can tell us about God and his relationship to ourselves. This is important to bear in mind in judging Hume's views; but most of the argument is about natural *theology,* namely, the attempt to establish the truths on which the practice of natural religion would depend. The exception here is the twelfth and final part, whose meaning has been by far the most controversial among scholars.

In electing to use the dialogue form, rather than arguing in his own person as he normally does, Hume is able to convey messages that it would have been impossible or imprudent to convey directly. There are three protagonists in the discussions: Cleanthes, who argues for a natural theology based upon the argument from design; Philo, described as a "careless skeptic," who raises objections and difficulties; and Demea, who represents "rigid orthodoxy," and also presents an a priori argument for God that is in a quite different category from the argument championed by Cleanthes. The whole set of conversations is supposedly reported by Pamphilus, a young pupil of Cleanthes, to his friend Hermippus. At the close Pamphilus awards the palm to Cleanthes, which for some time encouraged readers to think Cleanthes represented Hume's own views in the last resort. Had this been true, Hume would have changed his mind substantially from the position in the *Enquiry.* But most scholars now agree, following Norman Kemp Smith, that if any single protagonist represents Hume himself, it must be Philo, who has by far the most to say and is by far the most fertile in ideas and controversial suggestions. I do not myself think that the *Dialogues* represents any substantial change in Hume's position on these themes since the *Enquiry,* although the increase in detailed support for his position is immense. It is in the arguments of Philo that we find the most profound challenges to natural theology that rational theists have had to encounter.

Since Philo is identified at the outset as a skeptic, part 1 is devoted to the implications and relevance of skepticism for the topics to be discussed. While some suppose that in the course of the work Philo takes up attitudes that reflect a more radical Pyrrhonian stance, the position he presents in part 1 seems to be the same as that espoused by Hume in section 12 of the *Enquiry* under the name of "mitigated" or "academic skepticism." On this view, developed by Hume through the first book of the *Treatise* and revised somewhat in the *Enquiry,* skeptical doubts cannot be refuted by philosophical means, but are defeated in practice by human nature, which ensures we hold the fundamental beliefs on which common life depends. The encounter with skeptical doubts, however, quite properly chastens us from indulging in metaphysical speculations and should encourage us to confine our philosophical activities to the systematization of the beliefs of common life and the deliverances of natural science.

In part 1 of the *Dialogues,* Philo and Demea begin by agreeing with each other on the limits of human reason, which Philo says cannot deal with themes like "the origin of worlds." The implication would seem to be the fideistic one that religious beliefs should be a matter of faith and not of reason, and Cleanthes intervenes to criticize the skepticism on which such fideism seems to depend. He says that the doubts of Pyrrhonian skeptics are beyond the normal capacity of human nature, a view that Hume has argued in his other writings. Philo concedes this, but continues to maintain that if philosophical reasoning is not restricted to matters of common life, we shall find "we have here got quite beyond the reach of our faculties." Cleanthes, preparing the way for his own natural theology, replies that such apparently arbitrary limits on human reasoning would prevent the sort of intellectual achievement that Newtonian science embodied, since this is also far beyond the ken of most of us. This is not answered by Philo immediately, but the reason surely is that the lengthy arguments that are about to begin are intended to test Cleanthes' claim and to vindicate (or, if Cleanthes triumphs, to refute) Philo's view that reason is not able to establish conclusions that transcend matters of common life.

The *Dialogues,* therefore, will not depend on assuming Hume's mitigated skepticism, but will test it. The argument for God that Cleanthes will present is one that claims to proceed in a manner that has been vindicated by the successes of the natural sciences. If Cleanthes is right, God's existence can be shown by a scientific form of argument. If Philo is right, the argument Cleanthes offers is not good science, but bad science, and scientific reasoning will have been shown to have the more pedestrian limits that Hume's mitigated skepticism imposes upon it.

In part 2, Cleanthes states his argument. If we look around the world, he says, we shall find that it is one vast machine, "subdivided into an infinite number of lesser machines." These machines are adjusted to each other with amazing accuracy, and the adaptation of means to ends that they show "resembles exactly, though it much exceeds, the productions of human contrivance." Given this resemblance between the effects, we can infer that the causes are also similar, and that the Author of nature is somewhat similar to the mind of man, though "possessed of much larger faculties." He concludes: "By this argument *a posteriori,* and by this argument alone, we do prove at once the existence of a Deity, and his similarity to human mind and intelligence" (DNR 43).

So the argument that the *Dialogues* will consider is one that is based on experience and not on a priori reasoning (a feature that Demea immediately protests) and starts from the perception of nature as a system ruled by Newtonian mechanics. Philo immediately responds by concentrating on how such an argument fares when judged as a scientific argument. He begins, that is, with aspects of the argument that are discussed at the end of section 11 of the *Enquiry.* The issue that dominates that section's opening passages, namely, the practical implications of natural theology, is left for treatment until the end of the *Dialogues,* when the scientific credentials of Cleanthes' argument have been assessed.

Philo immediately assesses them negatively, along lines that *Enquiry* 11 has led us to expect. First, the argument Cleanthes has presented depends on an analogy between the universe and human artifacts. Analogical arguments depend for their cogency on the closeness of the analogy to which they appeal. The analogy between the universe and the products of human contrivance is at best a vague one, and certainly not close enough to warrant the conclusion that it has a similar cause. Cleanthes responds that the adjustment of means to ends throughout nature is a close enough likeness for his purpose. Philo's second objection is that the experience to which Cleanthes appeals shows us that "thought, design, intelligence" is only one of the "springs and principles" of the universe. Cleanthes is asking us to infer from the fact that what experience has shown us to be a cause of features of some parts of the world is the cause of the whole world: "From observing the growth of a hair, can we learn anything concerning the generation of a man?" (DNR 147). Third, experience only shows us that some phenomena are the result of the workings of intelligence, not that all are; many seem to be the result of quite different factors. Last, our knowledge of causes and effects comes from observing sequences in which objects of one kind are succeeded by objects of another kind. So a causal argument is only sound if we can point to sequences among species, or classes, of objects. In the present case, we have no such basis of inference, as the universe is unique, and does not belong to any class. (When cosmologists talk of comparisons between worlds, they are comparing different planets or stars within the whole universe, not comparing the universe in its totality to another.)

Cleanthes offers a strange reply in part 3. He asks Philo to imagine two cases. The first is that of a loud and melodious voice coming from the clouds, expressing a wise message. The second is that of a great library in which the books propagate like vegetables or animals. In the first case, we would all immediately infer the message came from a great and wise mind, even though this conclusion would violate the causal principles that Philo has just expressed. In the second, no one would hesitate to agree that the first book or books in the library came from an intelligent source, even though all the subsequent steps were wholly natural and nonintelligent ones. Cleanthes says that these imaginary examples show that Philo's objections cannot wholly remove the effect of the argument from design; to see this we have only to consider the human eye, which makes us think at once of the "idea of a contriver."

The form of these responses from Cleanthes is the subject of considerable disagreement among scholars, partly because Philo is said to have no answer to them. One interpretation of them is that they represent an appeal to a direct apprehension of design that does not depend on the appeal to the analogy of human artifacts. If this is how Hume intends them, it is clear that although he must be conceding the appeal of the argument and recognizing that objections to it do not seem to remove that appeal in the minds of its readers and hearers, he must also be reiterating, and not modifying, Philo's claim that the version Cleanthes has originally presented depends on an analogy that is ineffective, since the imagined cases do not owe any appeal they have to that analogy, which Cleanthes himself admits would not tell us how to respond to them.

At this stage, Demea objects to the thinking of both his fellow discussants by pointing out that they are both content to liken the mind of God to those of human beings, and that their God is too small—a point that is confirmed by Cleanthes when he says, early in part 4, that a mind that is infinite, immutable and simple (possessed, that is, of the attributes ascribed to God in classical theology) is "no mind at all." His anthropomorphism is now seized upon by Philo, who points out that if the divine mind is similar in some respects to human minds, it might, for all we know to the contrary, depend for its character upon a physical body, as human minds do, and be itself the result of prior causes, as all the other minds we know are. In part 5 Philo pursues further the inconveniences of the analogy on which Cleanthes' argument rests. He suggests that since an effect needs only a cause adequate to produce it, not a cause that could have produced something greater, the divine mind does not have to be considered infinite or perfect, since human minds are neither, and indeed the world we know might have been the result of the work of a number of creative minds, rather than one, and these creative minds might be subject to the limits of mortality as we are.

In the next three parts Philo pursues three other possibilities. Each depends on noticing that the comparison of the world to an artifact is not the only analogy that could yield a story of its origin. The world could reasonably be compared to an animal organism, whose parts work together and whose life seems self-sustaining; this analogy could lead to the theory that God is not distinct from the world as theism teaches, but is the indwelling soul of the world. Again, a biological model in cosmology could suggest that the world came into being through some analogue of animal or vegetable generation, rather than through the workings of an external mind. In both these cases, Philo is merely insisting that Cleanthes' analogy is not the only one that could lead to a theory of the world's origin, and that the field of speculation is wide open. His third suggestion is that the world has come together by chance, as the ancient Epicureans like Lucretius maintained. Once the fortuitous assemblage of atoms had come about, the order that it had accidentally come to exhibit might have survival value, so that the order that so impresses us might merely be what sustains the world in being, without the world having come into existence in the first place because of it. (It has been pointed out more than once that this suggestion is an interesting anticipation of the doctrine of natural selection, applied to the cosmos as a whole rather than to particular species.) All these suggestions show that the analogy Cleanthes has drawn at the outset between the world and machines is a weak one that not only leads to theoretical inconveniences, but also is not obviously better than alternative analogies that have even more heterodox results.

HUME'S *DIALOGUES CONCERNING NATURAL RELIGION*, PARTS 9-11

In part 9 Demea tries to cut off these difficulties by presenting an a priori argument for God's existence. If successful, it would of course evade all the difficulties that Cleanthes' argument has generated. The argument Demea offers is in fact the version of the cosmological proof that had been used not long before by Samuel Clarke.[11] It depends on the principle of sufficient rea-

---

[11]For a full discussion of this argument, see William L. Rowe, *The Cosmological Argument* (Princeton: Princeton University Press, 1975).

son, which asserts that there must be a reason for everything. (Hume had in fact questioned the standing of this principle in the *Treatise* 1.3.3.) Since everything has a cause, which in turn has a cause, there must be some end to the infinite regression of explanations, at least in the sense that there must be a reason for the existence of the whole series of which individual causes and effects are members. We must therefore come to rest in the existence of a necessary being, the reason for whose existence lies within himself, and who "cannot be supposed not to exist without an express contradiction" (DNR 189).

Hume gives the refutation of this argument to Cleanthes. He begins by saying that "there is an evident absurdity in pretending to demonstrate a matter of fact, or to prove it by any arguments *a priori*" (DNR 189). Taken alone, this is a mere reassertion of the position known as Hume's Fork: the claim that demonstrable truths are restricted to "relations of ideas" and that matters of fact can only be known through experience. What follows immediately, however, may well be regarded as an argument to support this claim, rather than as a simple deduction from it. Cleanthes continues, "Nothing is demonstrable, unless the contrary implies a contradiction. Nothing, that is distinctly conceivable, implies a contradiction. Whatever we conceive as existent, we can also conceive as nonexistent. There is no being, therefore, whose nonexistence implies a contradiction. Consequently, there is no being, whose existence is demonstrable" (DNR 189). This is a model of clear and crisp statement, but the very brevity of this exchange emphasizes that the *Dialogues,* like section 11 of the *Enquiry,* is concerned with one particular form of natural theology, namely, that form of the design argument that had become popular and commonplace in the wake of Newtonian mechanics—a form that assumed a purely mechanical cosmos, devoid of final causes, which derived any meaning it might have from outside itself.

It is to this form that the argument returns in parts 10 and 11. In part 9 Philo and Cleanthes had sided together against the a priori argument of Demea. In part 10 it is the turn of Philo and Demea to isolate Cleanthes when the discussion turns to the implications of evil for natural theology. They compete with each other in emphasizing the depth and variety of evil and suffering in the world: Demea because he no doubt wishes to emphasize how deeply our world needs redemption, and Philo because he wishes to make clear how much of an obstacle its evils present to any attempt to base theism on an argument from experience. Cleanthes responds to their gloomy consensus by denying things are so bad. Rejecting Demea's appeal to revealed knowledge of compensatory joys "in other regions, and in some future period of existence," he insists things are better than he and Philo have said, in the here and now (DNR 199). "The only method of supporting divine benevolence (and it is what I willingly embrace) is to deny absolutely the wickedness and misery of man. . . . Health is more common than sickness: pleasure than pain: Happiness than misery" (DNR 200).

Philo responds with a key speech. He denies the plausibility of what Cleanthes has said, but does not insist upon it; he points out that even a preponderance of good over evil in the creation looks impossible to reconcile with perfect power and wisdom and goodness in God. But even here he makes a concession, in order to reinforce a critical difficulty. Perhaps it is possible, he says, to reconcile the evils in our world with the infinite power and goodness of God, but Cleanthes must do better than this. Cleanthes has argued that the evidence in our world proves that we are the creatures of a deity with these attributes. Mere compatibility is not enough for this: the infinite power and goodness of God have to be inferred from the evidence, which does not, of itself, suggest any such conclusion. Philo then makes a vitally important statement. Hitherto, he says, he has been raising mere "cavils and sophisms" in the face of the evidence for design on which Cleanthes has relied. But now he claims to "triumph" against him. The fact of even moderate evil in our world shows that Cleanthes cannot prove the infinite power and goodness of God on the basis of the evidence itself.

In part 11, after Cleanthes has fallen back on saying that he will abandon the claim that God is infinite in power and goodness, and claim only that God is very powerful and good, Philo, who does almost all the talking for the rest of the book, presents his own account of what the observation of the evils in the world actually suggests about any creative power or powers that have produced it. He selects four ills that beset "sensible creatures." The first is the fact that action has to be stirred by pain as well as by pleasure. The second is the fact that the law-abidingness of nature, which is often said to be the reason for some of its inconveniences, might from time to time be subject to interventions by a benign deity without our noticing, yet seems never to have been. The third is that creatures may be endowed with enough powers for their survival and adaptation, but only minimally; it is too easy to think of improvements in natural endowments that would transform the quality of their lives for the better. The fourth defect in our world is that the "springs and principles" on which our lives depend, such as wind and rain and heat, are so often lacking in "due proportion." Each of these features is something that is regularly quoted by thinkers like Cleanthes as showing divine benevolence and power, but in each case it is also a source of suffering. This fact may have a deep explanation in each instance, but the facts as we find them suggest more natural explanations than that of infinite, or even very great, divine power and goodness. The most natural, in Philo's view, is that the "first causes of the universe" have "neither goodness nor malice" (DNR 212).

HUME'S *DIALOGUES CONCERNING NATURAL RELIGION,* PART 12

At this point the discussion of the merits of Cleanthes' form of natural theology is really at an end. But of course one part remains, and it is the part that has generated the most perplexity among scholars. For our present purposes it is not really necessary to enter into the controversies that part 12 has aroused, for the very reason that what is at issue within it is not the merits of natural theology, but the nature and status of natural religion. Natural religion is that form of religion whose tenets can be supported by reason alone, so what is at issue here is the same question as that which Hume brought before us in section 11 of the *Enquiry*: what are the practical implications of the natural theology whose merits, or defects, we now have before us? In my view, the answer Hume gives to the question here is the same one he gave in section 11, and the years between publication of the two works do not represent any change in his opinions.

Demea has left the company, and Philo and Cleanthes are more free to express themselves with candor—or so Philo indicates. He talks throughout in a way that has puzzled many readers, but which he has already signaled at the close of part 10: he says that in spite of all the objections he has raised to Cleanthes' argument, "no one has a deeper sense of religion impressed on his mind, or pays more profound adoration to the divine Being, as he discovers himself to reason, in the inexplicable contrivance and artifice of nature" (DNR 214). As he proceeds to elaborate his supposed confession, however, it becomes clear that what he assents to is the view that the intelligence behind nature has a "remote inconceivable analogy" to human intelligence—an insipid view that is further qualified by saying that "we have reason to infer that the natural attributes of the Deity have a greater resemblance to those of man, than his morals have to human virtues" (DNR 219). Cleanthes senses no irony in this apparent agreement, but worries instead that Philo's "abhorrence of vulgar superstitions," which he has contrasted with "true religion," might have unfortunate moral consequences, since "[r]eligion, however corrupted, is still better than no religion at all" (DNR 219). The two now argue about the degree of difference there is between "true" religion and "religion as it has commonly been found in the world," with Philo emphasizing their distance and Cleanthes expressing alarm that Philo's "zeal against false religion" will undermine his "veneration for the true" (DNR 224).

What true religion amounts to is something on which they agree, their common view having been stated by Cleanthes at the outset:

> The proper office of religion is to regulate the heart of men, humanize their conduct, infuse the spirit of temperance, order and obedience; and as its operation is silent, and only enforces the motives of morality and justice, it is in danger of being overlooked, and confounded with these other motives. When it distinguishes itself, and acts as a separate principle over men, it has departed from its proper sphere, and has become only a cover to faction and ambition. (DNR 220)

In other words, though Cleanthes himself seems not to see this, it is in practice featureless. It is therefore the right and proper expression of the state of mind of anyone who accepts the conclusion of the natural theology to which Cleanthes' original argument has by now been reduced, which is stated by Philo in his final speech: "that the cause or causes of order in the universe probably bear some remote analogy to human intelligence" (DNR 227). To this the enquirer can do no more than "give a plain, philosophical assent to the proposition, as often as it occurs." His final advice is this: "To be a philosophical skeptic is, in a man of letters, the first and most essential step towards being a sound, believing Christian" (DNR 228). So Philo, having reduced natural theology to this vague consciousness of cosmic order, and having made clear that its practical import is the same as that of sound secular morality, leaves the scene with a warning that any more positive view of the speculative power of natural theology can only detract from the purity of the featureless religiosity of the informed believer.

I have doubts whether Hume himself can be said with any confidence to ascribe even to Philo's "attenuated deism," as Gaskin has described it. But there is little doubt that Hume could live in practice with those whose religion had as little content as this, and saw Philo's arguments as correctives to any inclination they may have had to subscribe to more. In an age where atheism was felt by most to be unthinkable, this toothless theism would have to do.

SOME CONCLUSIONS

There is no doubt that Hume's criticisms of natural theology are by far the most substantial in the English language and have been equaled in importance, if at all, only by those of Kant, who was aware of Hume's contributions. In taking the measure of the arguments of either of them, one must take account of the relationships of what each says about this theme to the rest of his philosophical system. I conclude with a few reflections on this in Hume's case. Hume is a highly systematic philosopher, and his views on the multitude of topics on which he writes are closely integrated. We must avoid assuming, however, that rejecting his opinion on one theme will expose fatal weaknesses in his views on another.

Let us begin with Hume's skepticism. While the conclusions of Hume's philosophy of religion are those we would expect from someone who adopts his mitigated skepticism, and while Philo's position at the outset of the *Dialogues* is a statement of that skepticism, the arguments Hume puts into his mouth in that work do not depend upon it. On the contrary, they are rather to be seen as his most extended attempts to show its truth. By showing the weaknesses of an argument that is supposed to establish a conclusion of the greatest cosmic importance, and to establish this conclusion from experience, Hume thinks he has shown that our understanding cannot be expected to lead us to truth if it exceeds the limits of that experience. But the very complexity and detail of the arguments of the *Dialogues* show that he is arguing from Cleanthes' failures to the wisdom of skeptical restraint, not the other way about.

It can reasonably be argued, however, that Hume's general epistemological stance determines the selection of the form of natural theology that he subjects to detailed analysis. Both in the *Dialogues* and in section 11 of the *Enquiry,* it is the mechanistic form of the argument from design that Hume examines with care, just because it seems to conform to standards of enquiry that he endorses in his theory of knowledge. It was an argument that was endorsed by deists and orthodox alike, and his selection of it could be justified on that ground alone. What he considers he has shown by the end of the *Dialogues* is that, by the standards of enquiry he has endorsed, the argument fails. It is bad science.

It is an argument that makes no use of the notion of final causes. Even though the phrase appears from time to time, what is at issue is always the beneficence of an order supposedly imposed upon a mechanistic, Newtonian universe from outside, not any form of inbuilt teleology. Part 9 of the

Dialogues does of course contain a brief discussion of a classic a priori argument, and it seems clear here that Hume does appeal to his own epistemological thesis that no matter of fact can be proved in such a fashion. Even here, however, he offers a supportive case that does not merely lean upon this thesis.

The one place where Hume does simply apply arguments from elsewhere to his examination of natural theology—drawing from the closing passage of *Enquiry* 11—is in Philo's opening salvo in part 2 of the *Dialogues,* where he questions our ability to speculate profitably about the cause of the universe on the ground that our knowledge of causes must always be based upon experience of repeated sequences of events of certain kinds. A rejection of his critique here requires us to question his veto on the extension of causal reasoning to a unique case. It is not self-evident, however, that someone wishing to extend causal reasoning to the universe as a whole must abandon Hume's account of causation altogether merely in order to dispense with this restriction that he infers from it.

3

IN PRAISE OF HUME

What's Right About Hume's Attacks on Natural Theology

Todd M. Furman

𝔇

There are plenty of critics of natural theology, but the arguments of David Hume seem to be the most disturbing. There is a reason for this. Hume does not just nitpick the details and tactics of the arguments of natural theology. Hume simultaneously and stealthily illustrates how the arguments, at a larger level, are disingenuous. That is, Hume illustrates how the arguments of the eager-believer are not the sort of arguments a truly unbiased investigator would or should find convincing.

For instance, at a critical moment in the cosmological argument, it is deduced that there must be some ultimate cause that is necessarily existent. Of course, the eager-believer leaps from this deduction to the conclusion that this ultimate cause could only be the God of the Judeo-Christian tradition. But an unbiased investigator realizes that there are other possibilities that must be considered and eliminated before one gets to the desired God—that the material universe itself could be the necessarily existent being, to use one of Hume's examples. Hence, the eager-believer and the arguments of natural theology simply "preach to the choir."

In what follows, some of Hume's attacks on the arguments of natural theology will be surveyed. The focus, however, will not be to defend Hume's technical criticism of the arguments of natural theology against all comers, past and present. Rather, the spotlight will be on the big picture, illustrating how Hume shows that the arguments of natural theology—at least those of his contemporaries—are not, at the macro level, the sort of arguments an unbiased investigator would or should find convincing. Speaking broadly, we shall see that Hume accuses the eager-believer of sinning in her quest for the truth in one or more of the following ways: (1) the theist offers evidence that is categorically inappropriate for the desired conclusion; (2) the theist begs the question; or (3) the theist concludes more from her argument than she is entitled to.[1]

For the sake of clarity, I will refer to the first sin as the "evidence error" and the third sin as "jumping the gun." The second of our three sins is a bit more complicated. When someone makes an argument and, implicitly or explicitly, assumes the point in question, it is normal to say that she has begged the question. Therefore, I will refer to this straightforward way of committing the sin as "begging the question." But there are at least two indirect ways in which proponents of natural theology might beg the question. First, whenever eager-believers employ evidence or premises that are (ultimately) known—and could only be known—through revelation, they are guilty of begging the question indirectly, since there can only be revelation if God in fact exists to give it. I will call this sort of question begging the "revelation ruse." Second, whenever proponents of natural theology employ an argumentative premise without justifying it, they are again guilty of begging the question indirectly, since one will likely only agree with the premise (without quibble) because one understands it to lead to the desired conclusion. I will call this sort of question begging the "presumptive premise." For example, suppose one argues as follows: (1) a fetus is an innocent person; (2) it is wrong to kill innocent persons; (3) abortions kill innocent persons—fetuses; therefore (4) abortions are wrong. This argument commits the sin of presumptive premise inasmuch as premise 1 is argumentative and it is offered without justification.

Now that we understand the various sorts of possible sins against objectivity that Hume identifies, we are ready to survey his exposure of the eager-believer's biased quest for the truth.

ONTOLOGICAL ARGUMENTS

Consider a token version of the ontological argument (OA):

    O1: If an object X cannot be conceived of without attribute Y, then X
             has attribute Y.

---

[1] I will not quibble with those who would argue that any one of these *different* sins is merely a different side of the same coin.

O2:   God cannot be conceived of without the attribute of necessary existence (otherwise God, by definition a perfect being, would be less than perfect).

O3:   Therefore, God must have the attribute of necessary existence. That is, God exists.[2]

When Hume focuses his energies on the tactics of OA he denies the second premise, O2. Using his famous distinction between *matters of fact* and *relations of ideas* (EHU 15)[3] Hume argues along the following lines. God's existence—whatever attributes he might have—is a question concerning a matter of fact. Hence, we can always *imagine* this matter of fact to be either true or false. That is, it is possible to imagine that there is no instantiation of the idea of God—a being with the attribute of necessary existence (DNR 55).[4] But O2 claims otherwise. Therefore, O2 is false and OA fails as a proof of God's existence.

This criticism seems to me to be right on target, but never mind that. There is a bigger problem with the overall strategy of OA to explore here. Ontological arguments are generally construed as a priori arguments. To use Hume's terminology, ontological arguments are a particular strategy for proving God's existence—a matter of fact—using premises that express relations of ideas. But relations of ideas can prove nothing about whether or not a matter of fact such as *God exists* is true (DNR 55). Gaskin paraphrases Hume's argument as follows:

---

[2]Norman Malcolm has identified two different versions of the ontological argument in Anselm's original offering from the *Proslogion*—one focusing on existence per se, and the other focusing on *necessary* existence. See Norman Malcolm, "Anselm's Ontological Arguments," *Philosophical Review* 69 (1960): 41-67; reprinted in Alvin Plantinga, ed., *The Ontological Argument: From St. Anselm to Contemporary Philosophers* (Garden City, N.Y.: Doubleday, 1965), pp. 136-59. Clearly the token I offer here is of the latter version. It is appropriate to center our attention here for two reasons. First, and more important, it is this version that seems most relevant to Hume's attacks. Keith Yandell, for instance, concentrates completely on the necessary existence version in his answer to Hume's criticisms of the ontological argument (see "David Hume on Meaning, Verification, and Natural Theology," chapter 4 of the current volume). Second, it is this version that has been the locus of the revival in the defense of the ontological argument among philosophers of religion since Malcolm's landmark paper. Without a doubt the high water mark of this revival is the modal version of the argument presented by Alvin Plantinga in *The Nature of Necessity* (Oxford: Clarendon, 1974, 1989), chap. 10.

[3]References to Hume's *Enquiry* are given in the text with EHU, and this chapter uses *An Enquiry Concerning Human Understanding* and *A Letter from a Gentleman to his Friend in Edinburgh*, ed. Eric Steinberg (Indianapolis: Hackett, 1977).

[4]References to Hume's *Dialogues* are given in the text with DNR, and this chapter uses *Dialogues Concerning Natural Religion,* and the posthumous essays, *Of the Immortality of the Soul,* and *Of Suicide,* ed. Richard H. Popkin (Indianapolis: Hackett, 1980).

No assertion is demonstrable unless its negation is contradictory. No negation of a matter of fact is contradictory. All assertions about the existence of *things* are matters of fact. Therefore no negation of an assertion that some *thing* exists is contradictory. Hence, there is no thing whose existence is demonstrable.[5]

Hume is essentially accusing the theist and ontological arguments of committing the evidence error, offering evidence that is categorically inappropriate for the desired conclusion. The evidence concerns relations of ideas, and the conclusion—God exists—concerns a claim that is a matter of fact, an empirical claim, a claim that requires empirical evidence for any sort of justification it might ever have.

COSMOLOGICAL ARGUMENTS

Consider the following version of the cosmological argument (CA):

C1: Whatever exists must have a cause or reason for its existence.

C2: Therefore, all that exists now must have a cause or reason for its existence.

C3: To explain all that exists now, we must either (a) make use of an infinite regression of causes or (b) have recourse to some ultimate cause that is necessarily existent.

C4: But (a) is not reasonable because the regression of causes is left uncaused or unexplained.

C5: Therefore, to explain all that exists now, we must have recourse to some ultimate cause that is necessarily existent.

C6: And only God could be this necessarily existent cause.

C7: Therefore, God exists.

Hume identifies several technical problems with CA. First, he denies that one could ever be sure that C1 is true.[6] Therefore, even if CA goes through to C7, there is no real force behind this conclusion. Second, Hume questions the legitimacy of C6 and the move, therefore, from C5 to C7. And finally, Hume denies C4.

The real sins of the theist are to be found in Hume's second and third complaints, so let us begin to expose the sins of the eager-believer by considering Hume's second complaint in some detail. Let us suppose that CA

---

[5]J. C. A. Gaskin, *Hume's Philosophy of Religion* (New York: Barnes & Noble, 1978), p. 66.
[6]David Hume, *A Treatise of Human Nature*, 2nd ed., ed. L. A. Selby-Bigge and H. Nidditch (Oxford: Oxford University Press, 1978), pp. 79-80. Hereafter cited in the text as THN.

goes through to C5. As I said, it is the move from C5 to C7 that Hume questions, the move from the fact that there must be something that is necessarily existent—and therefore eternal—to the claim that that thing must be God. In the *Dialogues* Cleanthes asks, "Why may not the material universe be the necessarily existent Being, according to this pretended explication of necessity?" (DNR 56).

Hume's point is that God is certainly one candidate for the *something* that is necessarily existent. But is it not also possible—asks the unbiased investigator—that *matter itself* is necessarily existent and eternal? Unless this possibility is eliminated by argument, one cannot move from C5 to C7 without jumping the gun because C6 begs the question by being a presumptive premise.

Of course there are contemporary arguments that purport to demonstrate that the move from C5 to C7 is legitimate, on the grounds that science has demonstrated the physical impossibility of the eternal existence of matter—the material universe.[7] Hence, I need to explain briefly why Hume and contemporary Humeans will find such arguments lacking. The arguments are based on the application and extension of cause and effect reasoning to matters that are in principle unobservable (e.g., the beginnings of the universe). For Hume, cause and effect reasoning per se is, at best, less than perfectly reliable (THN 73-84)—how much more so its extension to matters we can never hope to observe for ourselves. All such arguments, therefore, fall well short of *absolute* or *demonstrative* proofs. Hence, theists will always be jumping the gun when moving from C5 to C7 because C6 will always be in doubt to some degree—even if it is not a presumptive premise.[8]

---

[7]See, for example, William Lane Craig, *The Kalam Cosmological Argument* (New York: Barnes & Noble, 1979), and Craig's many other works on the subject. For an explication of big bang cosmology and its temporal implications for matter, see Steven Weinberg, *The First Three Minutes: A Modern View of the Origin of the Universe*, 2nd ed. (New York: Basic Books, 1993).

[8]Some may consider such a refutation to prove too much. It may appear to question not only C6, but the whole of scientific reasoning, wedded as it is to inductive extensions of cause and effect reasoning to unobserved phenomena. But it is a major plank in Hume's important contribution to philosophy that he cautions us against glib inductive moves. His often unnerving demonstrations of the ultimate precariousness of such reasoning bids us approach with trepidation. And there is, he seems to warn us, a definite limit to the distance we can move from what we know by direct observation. And this journey all the way back to the dawn of physics certainly seems well beyond that border.

Besides, cosmology is by no means an exact science, and at times borders on pure speculation. As Nobel Laureate Lev Landau once noted, "Cosmologists are often in error, but never in doubt." Moreover, many theories are currently available that would preserve the eternality of matter in some form or another: quantum fluctuation models, oscillating universe models and the like. The temporal nature of matter is by no means a closed question, and there is plenty of skeptical wiggle room for Hume and contemporary Humeans.

Let us now turn to Hume's third technical complaint against cosmological arguments, his denial of C4. To gain an understanding of this complaint, suppose that we let everything that exists, B, at the present time, t, be represented by B_t. To explain the existence of B_t causally, we might refer to everything that existed at some prior time, B_{t-1}. And we might represent the matter this way:

$B_{t-1} \rightarrow B_t$ (i.e., "B_{t-1} causally explains B_t"). And to causally explain the existence of B_{t-1}, we might refer to B_{t-2}; and to causally explain the existence of B_{t-2}, we might refer to B_{t-3}, and so on, and so on, ad infinitum. Hence our picture of the universe might look something like this:

$$\ldots \rightarrow B_{t-2} \rightarrow B_{t-1} \rightarrow B_t \rightarrow B_{t+1} \rightarrow B_{t+2} \ldots$$

Let us call this collection of causal explanations "the chain of being." C4 tells us that our picture of the universe cannot be right since it leaves the existence of the chain of being causally unexplained. But this charge rests on a colossal mistake, says Hume. The chain of being is nothing more than a mental construction to represent the conjunction of all of the causal links leading to B_t. Hence, if one can explain the existence of each link in the chain, one has de facto explained the entire chain. Moreover, each link can be explained by its temporal antecedent. Hence, there is nothing left to be explained regarding the existence of the chain of being (DNR 56).

Of course, the theist usually concedes everything that Hume argues here, but the eager-believer continues to complain as follows. "Yes, to ask for *a causal explanation* for the existence of the chain of being, above and beyond a causal explanation of each link, is a mistake. But, it is still fair to ask *why* the chain of being exists at all when it might not have existed. It is still fair to ask why there is something rather than nothing. There must be an answer to this question, and the only possible explanation that avoids an infinite regression of explanations is God. Therefore, God exists."

In response, Hume argues that we cannot prove that whatever begins to exist must have a cause of existence (THN 79-80). In other words, he returns to his worries over C1. Since we cannot *know* or *prove* that everything must have a cause, it seems, ipso facto, that we cannot know or prove that there must be a reason for everything that exists. Hence, if the theist merely insists that everything that exists must have a cause or explanation, then the theist is clearly guilty of employing a presumptive premise. Why must everything have a cause? Must there be a reason for everything?

In order to avoid employing a presumptive premise, the theist may—and

often does—argue that Hume is wrong in doubting C1. But in these arguments, as Hume points out, the theist begs the question in a major way.

For instance, the theist may claim that Hume's rejection of C1 leads us
straight into one of two logical absurdities. Either *some existent things
caused themselves* or *some existent things were caused by nothing*. But the
first of the alleged absurdities can only be arrived at by a reassertion of C1—
if the cause does not come from without, it must come from within (since
there must always be a cause). And the second is simply a denial of C1, and
therefore only absurd if C1 is so obvious as to be denied only on pain of
absurdity—which it is not. Explicating the first of these points, Hume writes:

> Every thing, 'tis said, must have a cause; for if anything wanted a cause, *it*
> wou'd produce *itself*; that is, exist before it existed; which is impossible. But
> this reasoning is plainly unconclusive; because it supposes, that in our denial
> of a cause we still grant what we expressly deny, viz. that there must be a
> cause; which therefore is taken to be the object itself; and *that,* no doubt, is
> an evident contradiction. But to say that anything is produc'd, or to express
> myself more properly, comes into existence, without a cause, is not to affirm,
> that 'tis itself its own cause; but on the contrary in excluding all external
> causes, excludes *a fortiori* the thing itself, which is created. An object, that ex-
> ists absolutely without any cause, certainly is not its own cause; and when you
> assert, that the one follows from the other, you suppose the very point in ques-
> tion, and take it for granted, that 'tis utterly impossible any thing can ever be-
> gin to exist without a cause, but that upon the exclusion of one productive
> principle, we must still have recourse to another. (THN 81-82)

Hume has caught the theist begging the question in order to avoid the use
of a presumptive premise.

Now, for the sake of argument, and in order to expose further sins against
an unbiased quest for truth, let us grant the theist the notion that everything
that exists must have a cause or reason behind its existence. Is it not fair
then to ask for the reason why God exists? The standard answer to such a
question is simply to assert that God explains himself. But isn't this response
obviously question begging by employing a presumptive premise? To avoid
begging the question, an explanation of how God explains himself, the reason he exists, is in order. But how is this to be done without sin?

I suppose that one might try—borrowing from the ontological argument—to cash the idea out as follows. God explains his own existence inasmuch as it is not possible for the creator of the universe, God, not to exist
(otherwise God would be less than perfect). But it is unclear how we could

know that the creator of the universe, God, actually possesses the attribute of necessary existence without committing the revelation ruse, since, as we have already seen, it is always possible to imagine that there is no instantiation of the idea of God, a being with the attribute of necessary existence.

An alternative strategy, then, is this. One might claim that God explains himself, his existence, inasmuch as he is *eternal*—never mind whether or not his existence is necessary. For the sake of argument, suppose that it makes sense to say that God explains himself, his existence, by virtue of the fact that he has existed forever. The first question to ask is this: Without committing the revelation ruse, how do we know that God is eternal, that God has existed forever? Or, to drive the point home in another way, we might ask: If God is allowed to explain his existence by virtue of the *supposition* that he is eternal, then why cannot matter explain itself by virtue of the supposition that *it* is eternal? Unless such a possibility is excluded by argument, the theist cannot move from C5 to C7 without jumping the gun.

But further, suppose that we allow God to explain his own existence—by virtue of being eternal—but do not allow matter to explain its own existence—by virtue of being eternal. In this case, we might be able to move from C5 to C7 and reach the conclusion that God exists. But what exactly does C7 prove, assuming that it proves anything at all? Strictly speaking, CA proves that *something* eternal exists, something that is the ultimate reason behind the existence of the universe. But this does not get us the God of the Judeo-Christian tradition. The unbiased investigator must admit that the argument does not prove the existence of an omnipotent, omniscient or omnibenevolent God. Of course, the theist does conclude all of these things about God. Hence, the theist is clearly guilty of jumping the gun.

TELEOLOGICAL ARGUMENTS

The teleological argument (TA) comes in two basic forms: deductive and inductive. Let the following arguments serve as our tokens:

TD1: The universe possesses the attributes of order and purpose.
TD2: The only thing that could have caused such a state of affairs is God.
TD3: Therefore, God exists.

TI1: It has been observed that objects that possess order or purpose—e.g., a pocket watch—have artificers.
TI2: It has been further observed that these artificers must, by neces-

sity, be smart enough and powerful enough to have conceived of
and produced the artifacts.

TI3:   The universe is like a pocket watch in that it possesses both order
        and purpose.

TI4:   Therefore, the universe must have an artificer smart enough and
        powerful enough to have conceived of the universe and to have
        produced it.

TI5:   The only being smart enough and powerful enough to have con-
        ceived of and produced the existent universe is God.

TI6:   Therefore, God exists.

Essentially, the deductive form of TA (TAD) is asking us to deduce a
cause—God—from an effect: the existence of an ordered and purposeful
universe. And this might be reasonable if we had multiple experiences with
gods and ordered and purposeful universes that seemed to suggest that the
former are the causes of the latter. But we have no such experiences because we are dealing with a unique effect—the one and only universe that
we have ever experienced. To think that we could deduce the cause of a
unique effect is foolishness. We do not have the proper sort of evidence.
Hence, TAD is guilty of the evidence error. Hear Hume on the matter:

> It is only when two *species* of objects are found to be constantly conjoined,
> that we can infer the one from the other; and were an effect presented, which
> was entirely singular, and could not be comprehended under any known *spe-
> cies,* I do not see, that we could form any conjecture or inference at all con-
> cerning its cause. (EHU 101-2)

One might acknowledge Hume's point and try to save the argument as
follows. "True, the universe is a unique effect, but there are similar effects—
ordered and purposeful artifacts—to be found in the universe, and we know
that artificers cause these effects. Hence, by analogy, we know that a great
artificer is the cause of the universe." But to argue this way is to abandon
TAD for the inductive form (TAI) and, as we shall see, TAI has its own set
of problems. For now, let us back up a bit and overlook the fact that TAD
is attempting to deduce the cause of a unique effect. What, in general, can
be deduced about causes from their supposed effects?

The short answer is this. We can reasonably attribute nothing more to a
cause than that which is minimally sufficient for the realization of the effect
(EHU 93-94). The upshot of this point is that the god that we reach in the
conclusion TD3 falls far short of the God of the Judeo-Christian tradition.

For example, the great artificer of TD3 need not be one individual. The great artificer need not continue to exist after the initial creation and activation of the universe. It is also true that the great artificer need not be omnipotent, omniscient or omnibenevolent. Hence, anyone who concludes these things from TAD would be guilty of jumping the gun.

Now, to expose further sins of the eager-believer, let us move to a completely new line of attack employed by Hume against teleological arguments. Notice that premises TD2 and TI5 claim that God is the only possible explanation for the existence of our ordered and purposeful universe. But Hume can think of at least three counterpossibilities. Hence, unless these possibilities can be eliminated by argument, the eager-believer is guilty of jumping the gun again.

First, consider

M: Matter has the intrinsic property of (unconsciously) arranging itself into ordered and purposeful structures.

M seems logically possible. Hence, there is no necessity in postulating the existence of God in order to explain the existence of an ordered and purposeful universe (EHU 17-18). Of course, one might want some positive reason for believing that there is some actual substance to M beyond mere logical possibility before one abandons TD2 and TI5. This brings us to Hume's second reason for doubting TD2 and TI5.

There is evidence all around us for believing that ordered and purposeful objects can be produced without the oversight of an intelligent artificer. Take, for example, a tree. We take it that trees are ordered and purposeful objects and yet they are produced by other trees—nonintelligent artificers, as it were (DNR 46-47). The obvious and instantaneous reply of the theist is to suggest that the only reason that something such as a (nonintelligent) tree is able to produce another (ordered and purposeful) tree is because God, the master artificer, created trees in the first place. But such a reply clearly begs the question (DNR 46-47).

And if we really want to be ugly about the matter, we can note that God, supposing that he exists, is himself an ordered and purposeful object. Hence, by the reasoning implicit in TA there must be an artificer responsible for the existence of God. Similarly, this artificer will need an artificer, and so on, and so on, ad infinitum. It seems that the theist could only stop the regression at the theistic God either arbitrarily (in which case he employs a presumptive premise) or by appeal to revelation (in which case he commits the revelation ruse). Hume rightly asks, then, why we should not simply stop the regression (one step earlier) at M instead of God (DNR 47).

Finally we come to Hume's third reason for rejecting TD2 and TI5. We all recognize that Darwinism represents a direct challenge and counterpossibility to TD2 and TI5. So, until the Darwinian thesis can be ruled out, we cannot reach our conclusions, TD3 and TI6, with any sort of confidence. But what exactly does all this have to do with Hume, since Hume's *Dialogues* predate *The Origins of Species* by some eighty years? In a brilliant passage, Hume foreshadows a Darwinian position and its devastating impact on teleological arguments for God's existence (DNR 51-52).

Of course, many contemporary theists are wont to reconcile the Darwinian thesis with the existence of a Judeo-Christian God.[9] And we assume that this reconciliation or compatibility is feasible. But one must not forget the damage that has been done here. As long as the Darwinian possibility (sans theistic assistance) is not refuted, TD2 and TI5 remain unfounded bravado—presumptive premises—and the eager-believer jumps the gun when concluding that the Judeo-Christian God is responsible for the order and purpose found in the universe.

One might respond by arguing that God's hand is required to drive the Darwinian bus—to guide and implement the forces of natural selection such that we were able to arrive at our present position. But it is by no means obvious that the Darwinian bus needs a driver, and there are plenty of scientists and philosophers who have argued that it does not. Hence, to tack God on to the Darwinian picture, without good reason, is ad hoc. Of course, the theist may assert that revelation tells us that God necessarily belongs in the picture, but then he is guilty of the revelation ruse.

"By Wondrous Signs": Miracles

In this final section I would like to consider Hume's discussion of the existence of miracles[10] as a means of illustrating the further sins of the eager-believer, as identified by Hume. Consider this first approximation of an argument from miracles (MA):

MA1:   A miracle has occurred.

MA2:   If a miracle has occurred, then God exists.

MA3:   Therefore, God exists.

---

[9]See, for example, Howard van Till et al., *Portraits of Creation: Biblical and Scientific Perspectives on the World's Formation* (Grand Rapids: Eerdmans, 1990). Nor is this view unique to theists; see Michael Ruse, *Can a Darwinian Be a Christian? The Relationship Between Science and Religion* (New York: Cambridge University Press, 2001).

[10]See chapter 1, n. 11.

Whether MA could possibly work as a proof of God's existence depends, in part, on how one defines a miracle. And since Hume's interest in miracles concerns their role as possible evidence for God's existence, he insists on a definition that affords us a prima facie reason for believing in the existence of God given the existence of a miracle. Hence, Hume says:

> A miracle may be accurately defined, *a transgression of a law of nature by a particular volition of the Deity, or by the interposition of some invisible agent.* (EHU 77)

Let us refer to miracles so defined as *Humean miracles*. In addition, so that we have a clear picture of what Hume is driving at, let us remind ourselves of what a law of nature amounts to for Hume. According to Hume, a law of nature is nothing more than a regularity or uniformity observed in nature that admits of no observed exceptions (THN 1-25). Hence, if we experience a Humean miracle, a violation of a law of nature, then we have a prima facie reason for believing that some god or other exists.

Notice that we qualified, or limited, what we could conclude from the existence of a Humean miracle to the existence of *some god or other.* While a Humean miracle gives us a prima facie reason for believing that some sort of divinity exists, the miracle may or may not point to the god of a particular religious tradition as the culprit. Hence, anyone who concludes that a particular god existed based on the existence of a Humean miracle is guilty of the evidence error and jumping the gun.

In an attempt to repair MA let us make the following distinctions. Let us use the form *God-type-X-miracle* to refer to Humean miracles that point directly to God-X as the instigator of the miracle. Let us call those miracles that suggest the handicraft of a god, but no god in particular, *ambiguous miracles*.

Now consider two revisions of MA (MB and MC):

MB1:   There is a person (S_1) who believes that she has experienced a God-type-X-miracle.

MB2:   If S_1 believes that she has experienced a God-type-X-miracle, then S_1 has (probably) experienced a God-type-X-miracle.

MB3:   If S_1 has (probably) experienced a God-type-X-miracle then God-X (probably) exists.

MB4:   Therefore, (S_1 knows) God-X (probably) exists.

MC1:   There is a person (S_2) who is justified in believing that S_1 claims that she has directly experienced a God-type-X-miracle.

MC2:   If S_2 is justified in believing that S_1 claims that she has directly experienced a God-type-X-miracle, then a God-type-X-miracle has (probably) occurred.

MC3:   If a God-type-X-miracle has (probably) occurred, then God-X (probably) exists.

MC4:   Therefore, (S_2 knows) that God-X (probably) exists.

In the *Enquiries* Hume seems primarily concerned with whether or not reports of the resurrection could serve as a good reason for believing in the God of the Christian tradition.[11] Hence, Hume's remarks are primarily directed at arguments like MC, and I plan to explain and assess these remarks. However, I will also try to extrapolate from Hume's remarks concerning MC-type arguments and come to some determination concerning the viability of MB. In fact, to best understand Hume's argument against MC-type arguments, we will begin our discussion by considering MB.

Suppose that S_1 believes that she has experienced an ambiguous miracle or a God-type-X-miracle. To what extent should S_1 believe that she has actually experienced a miracle? For example, suppose S_1 directly witnesses another individual—who claims to be God—command a piece of lead to levitate in midair and then, after several seconds, and on command, fall to the ground. What should S_1 think about what she has seen? On the one hand, S_1 should believe that she has just witnessed a Humean-miracle because it seems as if she has just witnessed a violation of the laws of nature. But since our senses are not foolproof, S_1 must balance the evidence for her miraculous experience against any possible evidence to the contrary and make a judgment about what to believe based on the weight of the one side versus the other (EHU 73-74).

So, again, what should S_1 think? In order for her to even conceptualize what she has witnessed as a Humean-miracle, S_1 must necessarily have a stack of experiences telling her that such things—pieces of lead levitating—do not happen. Hence, on balance, she should not believe that she has seen what she thinks that she has seen—she should not trust the anomaly over the rule. Hence, if the eager-believer places her faith in the miracle as evidence of God, she is guilty of jumping the gun. It is more reasonable for S_1 to believe that she has experienced an illusion—a Penn-and-Teller-miracle, as it were—or that she is hallucinating (EHU 76-77).

---

[11]See Gaskin, *Hume's Philosophy of Religion,* pp. 102-12.

There are, however, a couple of possible objections to address here, focusing on Hume's notion of a law of nature. First, one might note that any observed exception to a currently accepted law of nature could always be incorporated into a new law of nature. Hence, no observation could ever count as a violation of a law of nature. Ipso facto, no observation could ever count as a Humean-miracle. As such, Hume has unfairly denied the logical possibility of a miracle. Second, given Hume's conception of laws of nature, if a particular miracle were ever repeated (and let us suppose them to be actual acts of God) then we would be forced to incorporate these repeated anomalous observations into a new law of nature that recognizes and incorporates this newly discovered regularity of nature. Hence, we would thereby strip these genuine miracles of their rightful status as miracles.

These objections may indicate a possible problem with Hume's notion of a law of nature, but they do not undermine his critique of MB or absolve the eager-believer of her sins. It is true, given Hume's account of laws of nature, that Hume could always commandeer any violation of a law of nature into some more sophisticated law of nature, thereby eliminating the very possibility of miracles, but he does no such thing. For the sake of argument, Hume lets the anomalies/miracles stand as possible violations of the existing laws of nature. He then asks whether we should believe that the anomalies/miracles (or even *repeated* anomalies/miracles) actually occurred, or accept the great amalgam of experiences that we have suggesting that no such things ever occur. The answer is obvious.

To be clear, Hume is not arguing that miracles cannot, or do not, occur. Rather, he simply claims that it is unreasonable to believe in them, even if we think that we have seen one with our own two eyes, because the entirety of our experiences (save this one) tells us that the sort of event that we think we have seen does not actually happen. Hence, to believe in God based on a miracle is to jump the gun.

So what about MB? Can secondhand knowledge of Humean miracles serve as good evidence for believing in God? If firsthand experience of a Humean miracle is not good enough evidence for believing in God, then the case for God based on secondhand reports of miracles is necessarily weaker. For example, suppose that S_1 reports to us that he has experienced, firsthand, a loved one being restored to life by a person claiming to be God. Should we believe S_1's report?

First, the content of the report gives us a prima facie reason for rejecting the report, since what S_1 reports to have happened contradicts what experience indicates as possible. In fact, the more amazing the miracle reported, the more reason we have to doubt the report (EHU 76). Hence, if we did accept the report of the miracle as evidence of God, we would be guilty of jumping the gun. And second, since reports or testimony are—for numerous reasons—unreliable in and of themselves, the weight of the report is diminished again, and the balance of evidence shifts further against the report of the miracle to such a degree that belief in the report is unreasonable (EHU 77). That is, MB2 is false.

Of course, Hume has allowed for the logical possibility that "the testimony be of such a kind, that its falsehood would be more miraculous, than the fact, which it endeavors to establish" (EHU 77). But in Hume's mind there have never been such reports. So no one has ever had reason to believe in God based on an argument such as MC; this includes reports of the resurrection of Jesus (EHU 78).

Of course, what Hume believes here is exactly what members of various (and mutually exclusive) religious traditions deny. So, for the sake of argument, let us suppose that the reports of God-type-X-miracles are everything one could want a report to be—the testimony of a number of people of unquestioned good sense, and so on. And let us suppose, then, that the reports of God-type-Y-miracles that believers in God-Y base their belief on are everything one could want a report to be—the testimony of a number of people of unquestioned good sense, and so on. In this case, we have two MB-type arguments concluding that God-X and God-Y exist. But if we suppose that God-X and God-Y are not just different, but mutually exclusive as well, then the competing arguments lay waste to each other, leaving belief in God-X and God-Y unjustified. And since this situation seems to be analogous to our situation in the real world—competing secondhand claims of miracles indicating the existence of mutually exclusive Gods—we have no right to believe in any particular god over another based on reports of a miracle. And when the eager-believers do, they jump the gun. Hume closes his case as follows:

> [I]n matters of religion, whatever is different is contrary; and that it is impossible the religions of ancient ROME, of TURKEY, of SIAM, and of CHINA should, all of them, be established on any solid foundation. Every miracle, therefore, pretended to have been wrought in any of these religions (and all of them abound in miracles), as its direct scope is to establish the particular system to which it is attributed; so has it the same force, though more indirectly, to overthrow every other system. In destroying a rival system, it likewise destroys the

credit of those miracles, on which that system was established; so that all the prodigies of different religions are to be regarded as contrary facts, and the evidences of these prodigies, whether weak or strong, as opposite to each other. (EHU 82)

CONCLUSIONS

So what have I accomplished here? I have explained some of Hume's technical criticisms of some of the major arguments of natural theology that were in circulation in his day. I have not, however, attempted to argue that these objections still prove lethal to contemporary defenses of these arguments. Instead I have attempted to show how some of Hume's technical objections to these arguments raise a larger question—namely, were the arguments of natural theology the kinds of arguments that a truly unbiased investigator should have found convincing? And I answer, "No, they were not." The arguments ultimately sinned against an unbiased quest for the truth by resting on inappropriate evidence, or by begging the question, or by concluding more than they should. I leave it to the reader to ponder whether or not contemporary defenses of theistic arguments, such as those represented in the second section of this book, can overcome these big-picture problems raised by Hume.[12]

[12]I would like to thank my colleagues Hanno Bulhof and Stephen Hanson for their helpful comments on earlier drafts of this chapter. I would also like to thank the editors of this volume, James F. Sennett and Douglas Groothuis, for their helpful comments on earlier drafts of this chapter and for their faith in me to carry out this assignment.

4

DAVID HUME ON MEANING,
VERIFICATION AND NATURAL THEOLOGY

Keith Yandell

David Hume, it is still widely believed, sounded the death knell for natural theology. He wrote and published such works as *A Treatise of Human Nature, The Natural History of Religion, Dialogues Concerning Natural Religion* and *An Enquiry Concerning Human Understanding.*[1] Monotheistic religion was Hume's chosen target. Once he had launched his attack, attempts to offer rational justification for theistic religious belief were exposed as abject failures. Ever after, the choices were fideism (embracing theistic belief in the recognized absence of any good reason to do so) or agnosticism (suspension of judgment) or atheism (sheer disbelief). So the story goes. In what follows we will look again at the foundations of Hume's supposedly devastating critique.

HUME'S SUPERIORITY TO MANY LATER CRITICS

Plato long ago ventured the sad opinion that "the many believe by chance"—that most of us believe as we do in the absence of anything like good reasons for doing so. He at least was evenhanded—his remarks con-

[1]The *Treatise* was published in 1739 and 1740, reprinted in 1888, then reprinted by Oxford at the Clarendon Press in 1978. Quotations here are from the second edition, edited with an analytical index by L. A. Selby-Bigge and notes by P. H. Nidditch. This chapter will cite this edition in the text by THN followed by the page number(s). The *Natural History* was printed in 1757, and it and the *Dialogues* were reprinted in *Hume on Religion*, ed. Richard Wollhiem (New York: Meridian, 1963). The *Dialogues* were printed in 1779 and reprinted in Indianapolis by Bobbs-Merrill Press in 1962, edited by Norman Kemp Smith. This chapter will cite this edition in the text by DNR followed by page number(s). The *Enquiry Concerning Human Understanding* was printed in 1748 and reprinted with Hume's *Enquiry Concerning the Principles of Morals* by Oxford at the Clarendon Press in 1975 with, again, an analytical index by L. A. Selby-Bigge and notes by P. H. Nidditch.

cerned both the irreligious and the religious. Freudians, among others, added to Plato's pessimism the assertion that theists believe because thinking that God exists makes them feel better about living in an otherwise cold and emotionally dismal universe. (The degree to which Freudian doctrine itself passes muster under careful critique is itself an interesting question.)[2] Such secular patter has long been recognized as thin stuff. If one wants to play the "let's belittle those who disagree with us" game, one can do it from a theistic perspective, too. The idea of there being a final judgment, where we are held responsible for the way in which we have lived, is not one that everyone finds encouraging. The idea of having been created by an omnipotent and omniscient being who providentially governs the world does not lend support to our being the captains of our fate and the masters of our souls. (Neither does the large population of hospitals and nursing homes; usually cited as part of the problem of evil, they challenge the perspective for which human beings are autonomous agents fully in charge of their own destinies.) The notion that we are sinners who need to repent and receive divine forgiveness fits ill with pride. Disbelief is at least as easily explained by reference to what we want to be true as is belief. In any case, it is only time to appeal to psychological explanation of a belief if and when it has been established that there are good reasons for thinking the belief to be false, or at least that there aren't any good reasons for thinking the belief true. Freud was notoriously neglectful regarding this task. It is to Hume's credit that he attempted to show that theistic belief enjoys no rational support before (or at least along with) his efforts to account for the rise of theistic belief in what he took to be the absence of evidence or reasons in its favor. He faced the question of evidence and argument straight on rather than taking cheap shots in the absence of careful argument.

TWO STAGES IN HUME'S STRATEGY

His approach to natural theology came in two stages. The first was an attempt to show that the core claims of theism—that God exists, is omnipotent and omniscient, is morally perfect, created the world and the like—are neither true nor false. Like *Eggly wissity wafflebrews*, they are only nonsense disguised as sense. One argument for this conclusion was based on a theory of the meaning of words. Another concerned the meaning of whole sen-

---

[2]See Paul Vitz, *Faith of the Fatherless: The Psychology of Atheism* (Dallas: Spence, 1999) and *Psychology as Religion: The Cult of Self Worship*, 2nd ed. (Grand Rapids: Eerdmans, 1994).

tences. Respectively, these are *concept empiricism* and *verification empiricism*. We will explore them both in detail in the next section. Hume used these views as sticks with which to beat his opponents into submission. Once he had done this to his own satisfaction, he quietly put them away and developed his own views, which fared no better by his concept empiricist and verification empiricist criteria than did the views he opposed. (I say that this is what he did, not that he was himself aware of his doing so.)

The other part of his critique was more subtle and interesting, and more in line with Hume's reputation as a figure to be reckoned with. Hume's concern in this second stage was to show that there is no good reason to accept theistic belief. This was part of his overall skepticism, but it has a distinct flavor all its own. His general skepticism concerned such beliefs as *There exist mind-independent and enduring spatial objects, Mind-independent causal connections hold between events,* and *I am a mental substance that has essential properties and retains numerical identity over time.* He held that these beliefs are the products of the operations of natural propensities and automatically operate when elicited by experiences that we all have, leading to uniform beliefs on these matters on the part of everyone. He also held that neither immediate sensory experience, nor introspective experience, nor proper inference from such experience, gave the slightest evidence for the truth of these beliefs. He held them to be *natural beliefs,* beliefs the possession of which is caused by beings with our nature having the sensory and introspective experiences of the sort we in fact have. The prospects for knowing that this theory of how our belief-formation works is correct, if we have to do so within a properly Humean skeptical account of our range of knowledge, are depressing indeed—they rank somewhere around the prospects our seeing the number seven do a waltz.

Commonsense Beliefs

The whole idea of explaining commonsense beliefs as natural beliefs—beliefs produced in us because we have natural propensities to form them when we have sensory and introspective experiences that we all have—supposes that there is an *us* to have such a nature, that we know what that nature is, that we know what sorts of sensory and introspective experiences we have, and the like. But given Hume's theory of what we can know (on which we can't know that there are mind-independent physical objects, enduring self-conscious minds and causal connections), we can't know that there is any such *us,* let alone know what the nature of persons is, that certain experiences cause us to form commonsense beliefs, or the like. Hume's natural-belief account of commonsense beliefs requires us to know, or have reason to believe, the very sorts of propositions that led Hume to offer the theory in the first place. The idea was to explain belief in there being mind-independent things in space, enduring self-conscious minds, and causal connections in a way that did not require that these beliefs be true or that there be any evidence for them. Then the explanation appeals to causal connections between sensory and introspective experiences that any minds have, and the belief-forming propensities those minds also have, such that commonsense beliefs result.

It is telling that belief in the existence of other minds does not appear among the commonsense beliefs whose occurrence Hume is trying to explain in a way that does not require them to be true or have evidential support. Hume's explanation needs the belief that there are minds other than one's own, and that belief fares no better on Hume's account of what we can know than do the commonsense beliefs whose occurrence he is endeavoring to explain. To put it bluntly: if for skeptical reasons we can't know or have reason to believe that there exist bodies, one's own enduring mind, or causes, then for skeptical reasons we can't know or have reason to believe that there are minds other than one's own that have certain sorts of propensities and are causally impacted by certain sorts of experiences that they have. The skepticism that puts commonsense belief outside the range of knowledge and evidence puts the data the explanation endeavors to account for and the assumptions that the explanation makes also outside the range of knowledge and evidence. This is a deep and, so far as I can see, unsolvable difficulty in Hume's philosophy for which there is no remedy other than to grant that the explanation, as it stands, is a failure.

BELIEF IN GOD

Hume treated the belief that God exists in a manner different from the way he treated commonsense beliefs. His view was that theistic belief, when it arises, is also produced by propensities. But these propensities do not operate in everyone, and when they do operate they do not produce uniform beliefs. For example, they may yield polytheism rather than monotheism. Further, these propensities conflict with one another in the sense that they tend to produce incompatible beliefs, and their operation, in conjunction with the more approved propensities concerned in the production of the uniform commonsense beliefs noted above, weakens what unity there is to human nature. If one divides thinkers into two camps—those who think that theistic belief is a necessary condition of robust human flourishing and those who think theistic belief is a sign of human floundering—Hume clearly belongs to the latter camp. But all this rests on a theory of belief formation that cannot be justified on Humean terms. Further, any such theory is needed only if there isn't any evidence for theism in the first place. Further still, one can offer a theory of belief formation according to which theists know that God exists, so long as theism is true, even if there isn't a whiff of evidence for theism. Alvin Plantinga's Reformed Epistemology is just such a theory.[3] But what interests us here is why Hume thinks that there are no reasons to accept theism.

There is another way in which Hume treats theistic belief differently from the manner in which he treats the other beliefs about which he is skeptical, and this is the important part for our purposes. He considers the arguments for theistic belief—the arguments of natural theology—in this manner: he claims that even if his general skepticism is mistaken, those arguments fail. Specifically, he contends, even if we knew that there are enduring self-conscious minds, mind-independent objects in space, and mind-independent causal connections among events, we still could not offer good arguments for the truth of theism. He thus intends his critique of natural theology to be logically independent of his general skepticism and to be sound even if his skepticism is utterly mistaken. We turn now to stage one of Hume's attack on natural theology. It has two parts: concept empiricism and verification empiricism.

THE FIRST STAGE OF HUME'S STRATEGY: MEANING AND VERIFICATION

Concept empiricism. Empiricist theories of meaning, or their modern roots, can be found in Hume's *A Treatise of Human Nature.* There he suggests views that, in more contemporary language, can be put as follows. Suppose, as Hume thinks is true, that the constituents of sensory experience are to be found in observable qualities and that the descriptive predicates of our language are names of these qualities. Such qualities are colors, shapes, sounds, tactual sensations, odors, tastes and the like. The terms that name such qualities, let us say, are *content terms*—terms like "red," "round," "a ringing noise," "rough," "smoky" and "sweet." (That these terms alone, with-

---

[3]Alvin Plantinga, *Warranted Christian Belief* (New York: Oxford University Press, 2000).

out nouns, could possibly make up our language is, to put it mildly, problematic; so is the idea that any term that designates a physical object can be defined by reference only to such terms.) According to concept empiricism, such terms are all the indefinable content terms of our language. There are also *logical connectives,* such as *and, or, therefore, entails* and the like. There are also *quantifiers* like *all, some* and *none,* and there is *negation.* Such logical terms, let us say, are *structure terms,* and they are all the indefinable structure terms that there are. (Actually, some of these structure terms can be defined in terms of others, but that does not matter here.) These predicates, connectives and quantifiers, plus negation, are the foundation of our language; in a different metaphor, they are its building blocks.[4]

Given this germ of an idea, one can then suggest what we will call *minimal concept empiricism:* for any concept C that it is alleged that we have, either C is the concept of an observable quality, the concept of a structure term, or else C is definable without remainder by the use of (indefinable) concepts of observable qualities and/or structure terms; *if not, we lack the alleged concept.*

One who accepts minimal concept empiricism will have to admit that *God exists* cannot be expressed within its limits. God isn't a collection of sensory qualities, however complexly related to one another they might be. No astute theist ever claimed otherwise. So one has to choose between the alternative that minimal concept empiricism is true and the alternative that one can have a concept of God. The Hume of stage one takes the former stance.

It isn't generally a refutation of a view V that one can think of some other view V* such that, if V* is true, then V is false. (In fact, for any view V, if one can think of V, one can think of not-V, and this fact does not typically provide the faintest reason for rejecting V.) Just because one can think of a view, namely, minimal concept empiricism, that entails that *God exists* is not either true or false, this isn't the slightest reason to think that *God exists* is neither true nor false. More important is that in fact minimal concept empiricism is not true. Consider the claim *Hume thinks that there is no such proposition as the one theists typically express, and atheists typically dissent from, when they assert that God exists* or *Hume is inclined to accept something like min-*

---

[4]For purists in Hume interpretation, with whom I have much sympathy, I note that Hume says little about the structure terms and mainly treats them as conceptual manna fallen from heaven into our minds. What he does say about their origins is embarrassingly bad and I leave it alone here.

imal concept empiricism. These aren't propositions according to minimal
concept empiricist criteria. The concepts they use are meaningless on its
terms. Neither the concept of *being minimal,* nor of *being a concept,* nor of
being an empiricist, nor of *expressing something,* nor the concept of a *being
a theory,* nor of *having meaning,* can be defined in the only manner allowed by minimal concept empiricism. A minimal concept empiricist cannot, if her view is true, so much as say *I am a minimal concept empiricist*
and thereby say anything that is true or false.

Things may look better if we consider what we can call *not-so-minimal
concept empiricism*—a view that says our language contains terms that refer
to *observable objects,* terms that refer to the observable properties *of such
objects,* and structure terms as well. On this view, not only quality-words but
also thing-words like "table," "tree" and "tea cup" are meaningful. Given this
germ of an idea, one can then suggest not-so-minimal concept empiricism:
for any concept C that it is alleged that we have, either C is **the concept of
an observable object,** *the concept of an observable quality, the concept of
a structure term, or else C is definable without remainder by the use of (indefinable) concepts of observable objects, the concepts of observable qualities
and/or the concepts of structure terms; if not, we lack the alleged concept.*
Here, we can risk simply repeating ourselves. Consider the claim *Hume
thinks that there is no such proposition as the one theists typically express,
and atheists typically dissent from, by asserting that God exists* or *Hume is
inclined to accept something like minimal concept empiricism.* These aren't
propositions according to not-so-minimal concept empiricist criteria. Neither
the concept of *being minimal,* nor of *being a concept,* nor of *being an empiricist,* nor of *expressing something,* nor the concept of a *being a theory,*
nor of *having meaning,* can be defined in the only manner allowed by not-
so-minimal concept empiricism. A not-so-minimal concept empiricist cannot, if her view is true, so much as say *I am a not-so-minimal concept empiricist* and thereby say anything that is true or false.

Such theories as these contain a theory of language (essentially, that the
meaning of descriptive terms derives solely from their experiential referents)
and a theory of experience (essentially, that experience is sensory experience). They hold that the constituents of sensory experience are sensory
qualities (construed as concrete particulars that compose the mind or as items
residing in mind-independent objects). One can broaden the theory of meaning by widening the range of what is allowed to count as experience. We can
add concepts of *psychological states.* Consider, for example, *still-less-minimal*

concept empiricism, which tells us that *for any concept C that it is alleged that we have, either C is the concept of an observable object, the concept of an observable quality,* **the concept of a psychological state,** *the concept of a structure term, or else C is definable without remainder by the use of (indefinable) concepts of observable objects, observable qualities, psychological states and/or structure terms; if not, we lack the alleged concept.*

Here the idea is that we experience pains, fears, hopes, desires, pleasures and the like, and that terms referring to them also are meaningful. But we still haven't gotten to the point where terms like *theory* or *meaning* or *concept* can be meaningful if the theory we are offered is true (of course *true* isn't meaningful on this account either, nor is *account*). Sadly, a still-less-minimal concept empiricist still can't, on her own terms, tell us that she is a still-less-minimal concept empiricist. Her view, on the grounds that she has chosen, is ineffable—on her chosen turf, she has no view to hold.

We do manage to believe some things and not others, to make inferences, offer arguments, frame hypotheses, assess theories, remember events and the like, as well as managing to be aware of ourselves as doing these things. We have lots of sorts of *epistemic states*—states involving knowledge, belief, inference, and so on. One could then offer a *much-less-minimal concept empiricist* view that goes as follows: *for any concept C that it is alleged that we have, either C is the concept of an observable object, the concept of an observable quality, the concept of a psychological state,* **the concept of an epistemic state,** *the concept of a structure term, or C is definable without remainder by the use of (indefinable) concepts of observable objects, observable qualities, psychological states, epistemic states and/or structure terms; if not, we lack the alleged concept.*

Hume, for example, thought that minds are properly thought of as composed of psychological and epistemic states, where these states are themselves basic metaphysical units, the irreducible atoms of the mental world (he called them "simple impressions and ideas"). Others have thought that minds themselves are basic metaphysical units—they are simple in the sense of not being composed of other more basic sorts of things (Plato and Descartes and Reid, for example, thought this). If the latter view is right, you can't have the concept of *there being a psychological or epistemic state* in the absence of having the concept *some mind's being in a psychological or epistemic state;* indeed, on the latter view, the first of these descriptions is simply a more abstract way of describing what obtains if there is something to which the second description refers.

On the *much-less-minimal concept empiricist* view, things get less clear but more generous. We can now form the idea of a being that has belief states and has only true belief states (the concept of a belief is the concept of a state that has content that is either true or false). We can have the idea of an omniscient being—a being that, for any belief state whose content is true, this being has or is in that belief state. At this point, the motivation behind concept empiricism (which was to commit all metaphysics, includ-ing all theology, "to the flames") has been left far behind; nothing of the sort would follow from much-less-minimal concept empiricism being true. It plainly isn't true, however; the concept of truth itself, the concept of a quark, the concept of it being wrong to torture for pleasure and the like, are not concepts of observable objects, observable qualities, psychological states, epistemic states or structure terms. More carefully: one who claims to have the concept of an epistemic state implicitly claims to have the con-cept of truth, which isn't the concept of an observable object, an observ-able quality, a psychological state, an epistemic state, or a structural con-cept, or definable in terms of these. Yet we have these concepts. True or not, this view doesn't really give us any account of how our epistemic states get the content that they have. Further, it puts no constraint on what such content may be. Much-less-minimal concept empiricism, inadequate as even it is, at least seems to allow one to say that she holds the theory of much-less-minimal concept empiricism.[5] But much-less-minimal empir-icism also won't serve to rule out our having the concept of God unless it does so by, say, not allowing us to have the concept of truth. But then of course the theory is false for that reason, and so is no barrier to our having the concept of God.

The conclusion of the matter is this: by the time we come to a theory of meaning that has enough plausibility to make it possible for us to say that we have it, we have far exceeded Hume's favored account; and by the time we get to a theory of meaning that is not subject to clear and decisive coun-terexample, we have a theory of meaning that allows *God exists* to be mean-ingful.

There are, of course, other ways of trying to develop some sort of con-cept empiricism that retains the motivation of the earlier hopeless versions. But there isn't any reason to think that they will fare any better than these

---

[5]Unless it is prevented from allowing this because to hold a theory is to think the theory true, since *true* isn't among the concepts that it allows. (Strictly, of course, belief also requires assent.)

versions. It is time to turn to a different strategy, that of *verification empiricism*.

Verification empiricism. This view, as it develops, in effect takes a different view of what the basic unit of meaning is. For Hume, as concept empiricist, the basic unit of linguistic meaning is a descriptive word, and the basic unit of nonlinguistic meaning is the mental impression or idea to which the descriptive word refers or that it names or (in more typical Humean phrasing) "corresponds to" or "is associated with." For the later logical positivists, the unit of linguistic meaning is the sentence. Further, the criterion for being meaningful was changed. It now becomes, not reference to sensory experience—to objects or constituents thereof—but verification or falsification by sensory experience. For concept empiricism, the meaningfulness of a *descriptive word* is obtained by its referring to or naming or corresponding to something observable; for verification empiricism, the meaningfulness of a *declarative sentence* is obtained by its being verifiable and/or falsifiable by the existence of something observable. (For a sentence to be verified or falsified is presumably for what it expresses, or what one expresses by asserting it, to be verified or falsified.)

At least on one reading, the Hume of the *Treatise* is also a verification empiricist.[6]

The modern roots of verification empiricism are in Hume's *Treatise* where he informs us that there are two sorts of statements, *matters of fact* and *relations of ideas*. A relations of idea statement has this defining feature: the ideas it expresses are necessarily connected; their denials are formally contradictory. Strictly, there are two kinds of relations of ideas statements: true ones (whose denials are contradictory) and false ones (which are themselves contradictory). Thus both *There are no married bachelors* and *There are married bachelors* are relations of ideas statements, the former being true and the latter being false. (Hume seems to have thought of necessary falsehoods as meaningless, which would preclude their being false, and

---

[6]The later logical positivists (who flourished in a period that began around the early 1930s and continued through at least the late 1950s; philosophical migraines can last a long time) in effect took Humean verification empiricism and put it through the technical apparatus of Russell and Whitehead's *Principia Mathematica,* one of the great works on symbolic logic. Some later work in philosophy (later than the late 1950s), as well as some work in what said it was theology, was done in the shadows cast by logical positivism, and its after-effects are still being felt. For some of the many varieties of logical positivism, whose manifesto is A. J. Ayer's *Language, Truth, and Logic* (New York: Dover, 1946), see Keith Yandell, *Basic Issues in the Philosophy of Religion* (Boston: Allyn and Bacon, 1971).

hence is a mistaken way to think of them.) So we can put the idea this way: *S is a relations of ideas statement if and only if either S or not-S is of the form P and not-P.*

A matter of fact statement, in contrast, does not have a formally self-contradictory denial. Thus *There are green skunks* and *There are no green skunks* are both matter of fact statements and neither is of the form *P and not-P*. Further, both statements concern the existence or nonexistence of observable items and the observable properties of such items. *S is a matter of fact statement if and only if S asserts the existence of some observable object or ascribes an observable property to an observable object.*

Besides its distinction between relations of ideas sentences and matters of fact sentences, verification empiricism requires some doctrine of experience, some account of the sorts of facts that are available to us in experience. If confirmation of *there is a God* is available in experience—if God can be experienced[7]—then verification empiricism will allow the claim that God exists to be verifiable at least in principle, which is all that the view requires in order for a sentence to be a statement (i.e., to be meaningful, or to be either true or false). The doctrine of experience typical of verification empiricism limits experience to one or more of the following: sense data (private states of consciousness with sensory content), sensory perception (seeing, hearing, etc. some mind-independently existing observable object) and introspection (awareness of one's inner states). This brief account of what verification empiricism typically allows to count as an experience lacks full clarity.[8] But this account seems sufficient for present purposes.

Now we can state verification empiricism as follows: For any alleged statement S, S is meaningful (i.e., is either true or false) if and only if S is a relation of ideas statement or a matter of fact statement. Only sensory and introspective experience count as observation. The doctrines that there are only matters of fact and relations of ideas statements, and that sensory and introspective experience exhausts our range of experience, constitute verification empiricism. Verification empiricism faces devastating problems.

---

[7]See Keith Yandell, "David Hume, Experiential Evidence and Belief in God," chapter 11 in this volume.

[8]Among the matters not discussed here are the following: Is one's awareness of one's own epistemic states to count as experience? What exactly is the range of introspective experience? Are we directly aware of physical objects?

Some of these problems can be illustrated from Hume's other views. Hume claims that persons are simply bundles of conscious states at a time and sequences of such bundles over time. This isn't a relations of ideas statement (or, in later language, a tautology—a statement true in virtue of the meanings of the words it contains). Nor is it an observation statement. Even if all we introspectively observe is conscious states (and that is controversial), Hume needs the claim that *All we are is open to introspection* and that is neither a relations of ideas nor a matter of fact statement—it isn't true by definition or observably confirmable. Put another way, Hume needs to infer from *All introspection reveals is momentary states* to *All we are is momentary states*. To make the inference sound, he also needs *Everything we are is revealed in introspection*. This last claim is neither a relation of ideas nor a matter of fact statement. So Hume's own claim that persons are simply bundles of conscious states at a time and a sequence of such bundles over time is meaningless on his own verificationist terms. This is so even if, say, William James (and Descartes, Husserl and many others) are wrong in holding that "The universal conscious fact is not 'Feelings exist' or 'Thoughts exist,' but 'I think' and 'I feel.'"[9]

A devastating criticism can be put simply and without reference to Hume's other views. The principle of meaning that constitutes Hume's verification principle is that *For any alleged statement S, S is meaningful (i.e., is either true or false) if and only if S is a relation of ideas statement or a matter of fact statement*. But this statement itself is neither a relation of ideas nor a matter of fact statement. Hence on its own terms it is meaningless. So we need not discuss it; on its own terms, there is nothing to discuss, and if there is a view here to discuss, that is sufficient for the view being false. We may turn then to the second stage of Hume's attack on natural theology.

THE SPECIFIC ATTACK ON NATURAL THEOLOGY

Natural theology is the attempt to provide good reasons for thinking that God exists. Hume's concern with natural theology centers on considering some of the classic arguments, offered as premises that one could know to be true without already having to believe that God exists and from which *God exists* could be derived. One who reads these lines from Hume might think that Humean philosophy and natural theology might be friends after all.

---

[9]William James, *The Principles of Psychology* (New York: Dover, 1918), 1:226.

"Whatever ideas are adequate representations of objects, the relations, contradictions and agreements of the ideas are applicable to the objects, and this we may in general observe to be the foundation of all human knowledge" (THN 29). The ontological argument endeavors to show that *God does not exist* is necessarily false, and hence that its denial is necessarily true. The cosmological argument endeavors to show that if there are dependently existing things, then there must be an independently existing thing which, in virtue of its existing independently and its being the source of dependently existing things, is God. These arguments purport to deal with ideas that are adequate representations of the relevant objects and relations, and so to be applicable to those objects and their relations. So far, the natural theologian may sit happily at Hume's philosophical table.

Hume and the ontological argument. Hume, however, offers two suggestions that are distinctively unfriendly toward the ontological argument (OA). One is his famous dictum that "Whatever we can conceive the existence of, we can conceive the nonexistence of." Since this is precisely what the ontological arguer claims that we cannot do regarding God, there plainly is disagreement here.[10] So we must ask whether Hume has any reason for his counter-ontological-argument claim.

Not surprisingly, he does. He has two suggestions in this regard. One goes like this:

> There is no impression nor idea of any kind, of which we have any consciousness or memory, that is not conceived as existent. . . . The idea of existence, then, is the very same with the idea of what we conceive to be existent. To reflect on any thing simply, and to reflect on it as existent, are nothing different from each other. That idea, when conjoined with the idea of any object, makes no addition to it. Whatever we conceive, we conceive as existent. Any idea we please to form is the idea of a being; and the idea of a being is any idea we please to form. (THN 66-67)

While in fact not every idea that we have is an idea of a being, let's restrict Hume's claim to ideas that are ideas of beings, roughly of things or sub-

---

[10]The wonder is that this is often spoken of as Hume's *refutation* of the OA. That seems a bit quick—*rejection*, yes; but *refutation?* All the objection amounts to is this: Hume says regarding the claim that God cannot be so much as conceived not to exist that it is false. If that is all that is needed for refutation, refutation is a cheap and pointless exercise. One can refute any claim C by just saying *C is false*. So let's do it here: Hume's claim that *Whatever we can conceive the existence of, we can conceive the nonexistence of* is false. This, of course, is not the way of true philosophy.

stances.[11] He isn't saying that to form an idea of some X is to think that X exists—that the authors of fairy tales, for example, as well as their readers, either don't understand these stories or believe that they are the literal truth. He is saying this: that to form the idea of a troll is to form the idea of a troll *as trolls are if there are any trolls*. To form the idea of a cow is to form the idea of a cow *as it is if there are any cows*. To form the idea of an X is to form a concept that fits any X there may be at least better than it fits anything else. That, or something much like it, seems to be Hume's claim. One thus cannot form the idea of a nonexistent X. That would be an idea of X *as it would not be if it existed,* and such an idea wouldn't be an idea of X at all. Maybe this is what Hume has in mind in his somewhat puzzling comments. Perhaps, so understood, he is right. Even so, one can form a logically consistent idea of the proposition *X does not exist* for things that cannot exist, but won't be able to form a logically consistent idea of the proposition *X does not exist* for anything that cannot fail to exist. The dispute between Hume and the supporter of the OA is over whether there is, or even can be, anything that cannot fail to exist. Even if Hume is right that one manages to conceive of something only insofar as one manages to conceive of it *as it is if it exists,* it does not follow that, for anything that we can conceive the existence of, we can also conceive the nonexistence of it. It does not follow that there is nothing that cannot fail to exist. There may be something that a concept will fit only if it is a concept of something that cannot fail to exist.

It is worth noting that many philosophers think that there are abstract objects—numbers, propositions and the like. Such objects are thought of as enjoying necessary existence—as existing in all possible worlds. Few philosophers think that Hume showed that there cannot be any such things as abstract objects. I agree that he did not. But then he equally did not show that there cannot be a necessarily existing God.

Another way of taking Hume's argument, not incompatible with the way just described, is to view him as denying that we have the general notion of *existence* as opposed to the more concrete notion of *the-existence-of-so-and-so.* Semantically, the implication is said to be that *"existence" is not a*

---

[11]This passage claims too much too quickly. Suppose I form the idea of the exclusive *or*—the idea that is defined as follows: "or" is being interpreted exclusively if and only if any proposition of the form *P or Q* is true just in case exactly one of the propositions is true. This is an idea that one can form but it doesn't really seem to be the idea of a *being.* It isn't the idea of some item's existing, and so it seems a counterexample to Hume's claim that every idea that we form is the idea of a being.

predicate. Metaphysically, the corresponding claim is that *existence is not a property.* This does seem to be at least part of Hume's view. But suppose he is right. The OA requires, metaphysically, that *necessary existence* be a property. When we turn to the niceties of formal logic, it requires that we use modal logic—the logic of necessity, possibility and contingency—to properly express the full claim that God exists. But nothing that Hume says even begins to show that these views are mistaken. One may hold, for example, that *necessary existence* and *contingent existence* are properties and agree with Hume that we have no general notion of existence—i.e., of *existence, neither necessary nor contingent.* This is a contradictory concept, one that cannot possibly fit (be true of) anything. Talk of what exists, at the most abstract level, is talk of everything that has contingent existence (that both exists and can fail to exist) and of everything that has necessary existence (that both exists and cannot fail to exist). Hume has done us a real service by pointing out that the idea of just plain existence—that is, simple existence, neither necessary nor contingent—is nonsense. Now, since Hume did not think that there *is* any such concept as necessary existence, this would be inaccurate as a serious reading of Hume. However, the point is that the one who offers the OA can simply waive the question as to whether existence is a property, and its semantic and conceptual kin.

At this point, we reach another Humean suggestion, namely, that the notion of logically necessary existence is deeply flawed; indeed, it is strictly nonsense.

> Nothing is demonstrable, unless the contrary implies a contradiction. Nothing that is distinctly conceivable implies a contradiction. Whatever we conceive as existent, we can also conceive as not existent. There is no Being, therefore, whose non-existence implies a contradiction. Consequently, there is no being whose existence is demonstrable. I propose this argument as entirely decisive, and am willing to rest the entire controversy upon it. (DNR 1890)

Hume's claim here can be put in various ways, none of which is satisfactory. Here are four typical ways of putting Hume's central relevant claim:

1. *No necessary truth is existential.* An existential proposition is true only if something exists—namely, what it claims to exist.[12] Claim 1 is obviously false: *There is a successor to (the number) 1* is both necessary and existential.

---

[12] Strictly, only if what constitutes its truth condition exists.

2. *All necessary truths are hypothetical in structure and hence do not assert the existence of anything.* For a proposition to be hypothetical in structure is for it to be of the form *If P then Q*. Propositions that are hypothetical in structure are not existential propositions; asserting them is not asserting that something exists. Claim 2 is obviously false. *There are many prime numbers between 1 and 1,000* is a necessary truth, but it is not hypothetical in structure.

3. *All existential statements are contingent.* Contingent statements express propositions that are not necessary, and existential propositions are true only if what they claim exists does exist. Claim 3 is obviously false. See the examples used in 1 and 2.

4. *All categorical (nonhypothetical) statements are contingent.* Claim 4 is obviously false. See the examples used in 1 and 2.

By now we have investigated, so far as I am aware, all of the Humean arsenal against the possibility of there being a successful OA. Hume has not shown that there cannot be an argument that shows God to be a necessarily existing being.[13]

Hume and the cosmological argument. One version of the cosmological argument (CA) begins with the fact that there are things that exist that might not have existed—you, the moon and the tallest tree in Montana, for example. These items also possibly depend for their existence on other things.[14] Call these sorts of thing *fragile beings*—it is possible that they never have existed, and they can exist dependent on something else. Then the CA appeals to one or another version of the principle of sufficient reason. The relevant version of the CA, given how we have begun, is this: *If there exist things that might not have existed and possibly depend for their existence on other things, then there exists something that cannot depend for its existence on other things, on which these fragile things depend.*[15]

---

[13]For a recent famous and widely discussed version of the OA, see Alvin Plantinga, *The Nature of Necessity* (New York: Oxford University Press, 1974, reprint 1989), chap. 10.

[14]One reason for its being possible that they exist dependently is that they *do in fact* exist dependently.

[15]There are other versions of the CA. One again begins with the existence of fragile beings (this is the starting point for CAs). It then claims that there must be a beginning to the existence of such things—that such things cannot always have been around. But if they cannot always have been around then they must be caused to exist by something, and that something cannot itself be a fragile being. I have never been able to see that the essential premise of this sort of argument—the premise that says that there just can't always have been fragile beings—is

This version of the CA entails the claim that *Whatever is possibly depen-dent is actually dependent*. One might try to make do simply with the claim that you, the moon and the tallest tree in Montana all in fact depend for ex-istence on other things, as indeed they do. But the moon and the tree and your body (which I think is not identical to you, but that is another story) are made of little physical things, and they are in their turn made up of still smaller physical things. Suppose we get to the smallest physical things there are. Are they dependent on one another for existence? That, I take it, isn't something philosophical reflection can tell us; for that information we must turn to the physicists. But an astute cosmological arguer won't rest her po-sition on what the answer to that question turns out to be. She will claim that whether the smallest physical items depend for existence on one an-other or not, they all share two features: it is possible that they never have existed, and it is possible that they exist dependently on something else. Therefore, she will hold, they do depend for existence on something of which it is not true that it could even possibly depend for existence on something else. The claim that whatever can depend for its existence on something else does so depend isn't another premise that the CA requires. It is something that itself follows from the principle of sufficient reason which is the main and most interesting premise of the argument.

Hume is not exactly a supporter of the principle of sufficient reason that the CA requires. The CA needs a premise that precludes something simply popping into existence uncaused. Hume does not actually think that *this* is possible. Strictly, his view is that he doesn't think it is possible and he doesn't have any good reason whatever for this belief. He thinks that there are causal connections and this is one of the natural beliefs that are pro-duced in us for which we have no reason or evidence whatever. But we be-lieve them anyway. Belief in mind-independent causal connections, on Hume's view, is something we are condemned to by our natures in the ab-sence of rational support.

But, in another mood, Hume writes concerning the items that we expe-rience that they are

> in themselves totally distinct from one another, and have no union but in the
> mind which observes them. . . . Necessity, then, is the effect of this observa-
> tion, and is nothing but an internal impression of the mind, or a determination

---

something that we are justified in accepting. So I will leave this version of the CA alone here.
For a treatment of this version, and references to others, see chapter 7 in this volume.

to carry our thoughts from one object to another. (THN 165)

On one reading, the claim here is that the concept of *necessity* is an invention of ours, and *that nothing in mind-independent reality corresponds to that concept*. Not only is our belief in causal connections without evidence; it is plainly false, as is our belief in necessity.

One question is: how does Hume know this? *Existing independently* isn't an observable property of a perception. It isn't a formally necessary truth that every noncomposite thing (which is what Hume has in mind here) exists independently. The claim that some such item exists dependently is not a formal contradiction. We can't offer an inductive argument for the claim. For one thing, we can't confirm by observation the premise we would need—namely, that *Relative to independent existence, unobserved things are like observed things.* That premise, too, is not a formally necessary truth.

For another, we don't have the data to make the inductive inference from, namely, a cluster of cases in which we have observed items to possess an existence independent of anything else. On Hume's view, we haven't observed their dependence (we can't observe this sort of thing). But not observing dependence is not at all the same as observing independence. That necessity is simply and always a product of the mind—a feature we mistakenly think applies mind-independently to some things—is not a claim that Humean resources can ground.

Further, necessity and possibility necessarily go together. What exists necessarily is just what does not possibly not exist, and what does not possibly not exist is just what exists necessarily. If necessity is mind-dependent, then so is possibility. Then, on the present reading of Hume, you don't actually have the property of *possibly not existing* and the proposition *It is possible that you never have existed* is not true. But, on the view being offered, this isn't because you exist necessarily, or have the property of necessary existence, or because the proposition *You exist* is necessarily true. It is because the very notion of necessity has no application outside the context of relations of ideas statements.[16]

Nonetheless, Hume thinks each simple perception actually has independent existence of everything else. So his view entails that it is possible that

---

[16]Consider the following question: Have I better reason to think (1) that it is logically possible that I never have existed (that the world could have existed without me) or (2) that Hume is right that necessity is an artifact of our thought and speech? I take it that I have vastly better reason to think it is logically possible that I never have graced the world by my presence.

each simple (noncomposite) perception exists independent of everything
else. It entails that it is not necessary that a perception depend for existence
on anything else. To this extent at least, his own views require that possibility and necessity are mind-independent features of the world. His claim,
then, can only be that necessity has only negative application to the world—
that nothing exists with necessity or necessarily only exists if it is caused to
exist by something else. The claim that nothing can have necessary existence we considered when we discussed Hume's dismissal of the OA; his
case for that claim is a failure for reasons detailed there. What remains is the
idea of *something necessarily existing dependently if it exists at all*. On
Hume's view, this concept perfectly fits complex perceptions—they exist, if
at all, only dependently on their component perceptions. So the idea itself
is not inconsistent. It is only inconsistent that simple perceptions can exist
only dependently if they exist at all. Further, Hume is of two minds about
even that. Sometimes he says that a simple perception exists dependent on
its being a constituent of a mind, and he seems to think of this as a necessary
feature of simple perceptions. Then the concept of *something necessarily existing dependently if at all* will, on Hume's own account, fit (be true of) simple perceptions—it will apply to the world in a way not merely invented by
us.

A brief review may be helpful here. Hume writes concerning ideas that
are adequate representations of what they are ideas of:

> The plain consequence is, that whatever *appears* impossible and contradictory
> upon the comparison of these ideas, must be *really* impossible and contradic-
> tory, without any farther excuse or evasion. (THN 29)

Hume thus sanctions in very forceful terms the inference from *Proposition P is contradictory* to *It is impossible that things are the way that P represents them*. At least negative necessity—contradictoriness—is *not* a mind-
dependent feature of things. Further, the idea that positive necessity cannot
be a feature of anything has already been discussed in our treatment of
Hume's objections to the OA.

Strictly, the CA does not focus on the concept of a being that exists necessarily, but on the notion of a being of which it is true that *Necessarily, if
it exists, it exists independently*. But Humean strictures on the concepts concerning any sort of necessity will be no more effective against this notion of
necessarily independent existence than they were against the notion of necessary existence itself. Finally, Hume himself sometimes thinks that there are

things that are necessarily fragile, as the CA claims. It is from this claim that the CA begins. The CA proponent will claim that Hume has misapplied the notion of something that can only exist independently if it exists at all. This notion does not fit (is not true of) simple perceptions. Perceptions themselves are fragile beings. Sometimes, Hume himself agrees (when he argues that perceptions are mind-dependent). Then the CA proponent will contend that there is something else that the concept of necessary nonfragility fits.

There is still the objection that the passage quoted above (from THN 165) refers to causality, and it denies that there can be causally necessary connections. This is correct, and it is relevant to the CA in that this argument requires the idea that a dependently existing thing necessarily causally depends on an independently existing thing.[17] So it is not necessity in general, but necessity in connection with causality that is relevant here. We will deal with this claim after first disposing of a red herring.

One consideration that has had some influence can be dealt with quickly. Hume writes:

[A]s the ideas of cause and effect are evidently distinct, 'twill be easy for us to conceive any object to be non-existent this moment, and existent the next, without conjoining to it the distinct idea of a cause or productive principle. (THN 79)

Hume proposes, in effect, that we can imagine a scene without a red ball in it, and then we can imagine a red ball just popping into existence. But "nothing we imagine is absolutely impossible" (THN 32). Popping into existence is coming into existence uncaused, and so being independent at least regarding origin (but then why not also regarding continuing to exist?). The problem here is that the story told is too indeterminate to bear the weight of the argument that rests on it. Hume supposes that the label under the image should be *Uncaused red ball* or *Uncaused event of red ball beginning to exist*. But nothing whatever in the imagined scene rules out as equally appropriate titles *Red ball whose cause is not presented* or *Event of red ball being caused to exist by unrepresented cause*. Since nothing in the imaginings votes for one set of labels rather than the other, it is fallacious to infer that the possibility of the imaginings justifies the claim that things can just pop into existence.

---

[17]The idea is not that an independently existing thing necessarily causes a dependently existing thing—concretely, that God necessarily causes the world. That the world necessarily depends on God if it exists does not entail that necessarily, God creates the world.

We may now return to the notion of causal necessity. Hume writes:

> The efficacy or energy of causes is neither placed in the causes themselves,
> nor in the deity, nor in the concurrence of these two principles, but belongs
> entirely to the soul, which considers the union of two or more objects in all
> past instances. 'Tis here that the real power of causes is placed, along with
> their connection and necessity. (THN 166)

Hume's view here is radical. There isn't any causality in the world; there
is just a tendency on our part to associate some experienced items with others when those items in fact have no intrinsic connections among themselves. What we call causal connections are simply psychological associations that correspond to no mind-independent relations in things. So far as
causal necessity goes, anything can cause anything and anything can be
caused by anything. Interestingly, one who offers the CA need not deny that
this is so *among dependently existing things.* Granted, philosophers who accept some version of the principle of sufficient reason are unlikely to take
this view. But they could do so and offer the CA without being logically inconsistent. All they need insist on is that dependent things cannot exist without there being an independently existing thing that causes them. The CA is
concerned with the relation of all the fragile things there are to a being that
is not fragile.

Another Humean claim is that *Whatever begins to exist has a cause of existence* is not a formally necessary truth—its denial is not formally contradictory. Nor is it something we can know by generalization over cases; we cannot properly reason from case after case of things that begin to exist having
a cause of existence to the conclusion that *Whatever begins to exist has a
cause of existence.* That inference would require us to know something like
Relative to coming into existence, nature is uniform or *Relative to things
coming into existence, the future will be like the past,* and those propositions
are neither necessary truths nor derivable from observational premises without assuming their own truth (or that of something no better off than they
are).[18] Nor, on Hume's view, have we any cases of observing something being caused to exist as opposed to something merely being preceded by
other things. Not even observing that a certain sort of thing is *always* preceded by another sort of thing counts as observing the later thing to have
been caused by the earlier thing. Hume writes:

---

[18]Hume claims, rightly as it seems to me, that the attempts he was aware of to prove the claim
Whatever has a beginning has a cause were failures.

[T]here is nothing in any object, considered in itself, which can afford us a reason for drawing a conclusion beyond it. (THN 139)

That is, for any item X that we experience, no inference from *X exists* to *Y exists* is justified, including the inference to *Some Y exists that causes X to exist*.

Here, I take Hume to be right so far as he goes. On the terms of what sort of justification a Humean can appeal to, we cannot justify the claim that things that can depend for their existence on something else do so depend. One can't justify the claim that things that do depend for their existence on something else must, individually or as a class, depend for existence on something that cannot exist dependently. Hume, then, in the *Dialogues*, does not base his objection to natural theology on our not being able to know that an event always has a cause. He is content to assume that this is true, and to argue that one event can be caused by another without end—that a past series of dependent events can go on forever and that a simultaneous series of dependent beings can exist without having a last member. (Another possibility is that the simultaneous series be circular.) But here, too, he denies that core claim of the CAs—the principle of sufficient reason on which the argument relies.

The Humean strategy assumes, however, that there are no informally necessary propositions. Such propositions lack formally self-contradictory denials. A simple example of an informally necessarily true proposition is *If Tom frowns then his frown has shape*. This proposition cannot be false but its denial is not of the form *P and not-P*. There are more interesting examples: *If P is a necessarily true proposition then it is also necessarily true that P is a necessarily true proposition* and *Nothing that is a person always lacks the capacity for self-consciousness*. Candidates for being informally necessary truths, insofar as they are philosophically interesting, tend to be more controversial than the claim about Tom's possible frown. The CA proponent will, of course, propose *If there are fragile beings, then there exists something that cannot depend for its existence on other things, on which these fragile things depend* as an informally necessary truth. She will claim the same for its entailment that *Whatever exists and is possibly dependent is actually dependent*. She need not claim to be able to derive her version of the principle of sufficient reason from something more clearly true than it is, though she might welcome such a proof were it provided.

Hume did not consider the idea of informally necessary truths, though his division of all statements into relations of ideas statements and matters of fact statements was intended to rule out anything like informally necessary truths. That division turned out to be utterly indefensible (not that this fact prevented later philosophers from reviving it). So it cannot serve as a basis for denying that there are informal necessities. In the absence of a good reason for doing so, a Humean also has not ruled out a successful version of the CA.

While there are various versions of the CA, and each version raises interesting and controversial issues worth discussing, it is possible here only to say a couple of things about how the sort of version we used as our sample version of the argument will go. First, it is neutral about how long fragile beings have existed and about how many of them there are. Consider the collection of all fragile beings that ever exist; call it "fragility." Fragility itself might not have existed, and it depends for its existence on the existence of its members, so that both they and it are possibly dependent things. This will be so regarding fragility if there have always been an infinite number of fragile beings or if there is only one and it came to be just last Tuesday. Given the principle that whatever exists, but might not have existed, exists dependently and (the proposed informally necessary truth that) *If there are fragile beings, then there exists something that cannot depend for its existence on other things, on which these fragile things depend for existence,* it follows that there exists something that cannot depend for its existence on other things. Call that being *the Independent One.* Our reason for thinking that the Independent One exists is that it caused the existence of fragility. So it must have the power to do that—to make it the case that things that would not otherwise exist actually do exist. So it must be a creator, strictly speaking—a being with the power to make things without using previously existing materials. A being that can do this is omnipotent. If a being is omnipotent, then it is also omniscient. An omniscient being must be self-conscious and alive. By now we have the notion of an omnipotent, omniscient, self-conscious, living creator, and we are in the neighborhood of theistic belief.[19]

The aim of this all-too-rapid movement of thought is to make three points. First, the strategy of the CA is to link up the notion of a *being that exists and cannot depend for existence on something else* and the notions of

---

[19]For further development of and argument for very similar points concerning the CA, see Douglas Groothuis, "Metaphysical Implications of Cosmological Arguments," chapter 6 in this volume.

at least some of the properties traditionally ascribed to God (*omnipotent, omniscient, creator*)—to argue that there is a being that exists and cannot depend for existence on something else and that such a being must have theism-relevant properties, independent of its having created anything (though the *evidence* that there is such a being comes from creation). The success of the argument depends on making these connections, or something in their conceptual neighborhood, well. Note that a being that exists and cannot be dependent on anything else for its existence need not be a logically necessary being, and that it cannot itself be caused to exist (then it would depend on something else for its existence.) Second, note that such a being must be causally active if its existence is to explain the existence of fragile beings. The success of the argument also depends on making connections between the powers a nonfragile being must have if it causes fragile beings—on making clear that such a being must (again) have theism-relevant properties. Finally, note that, even if the argument fully succeeds, it is an argument for theism, not for Christianity rather than (say) Judaism, Islam or Hindu monotheism. It is always a mistake to claim that an argument proves more than it does. Even as a fully successful proof, a version of the CA will yield what we might call generic monotheism.[20]

CONCLUSION

I have argued here that Hume in fact did not kill natural theology—he did not show that the natural theological enterprise of trying to give proof or evidence for the belief that God exists is a hopeless endeavor, beyond the realm of possibly justified effort. Those conclusions do indeed follow from various views that he held. But there is no good reason to hold those views, and very good reason to reject them. The idea that Hume dealt a deathblow to natural theology is sheer fiction. The degree to which natural theology succeeds is the degree to which its arguments are valid, have true premises and are persuasive to their auditors. Hume's critique does not show what that degree is—it will have to be decided on its own merits.[21]

---

[20]For an argument beginning with cosmological considerations and moving beyond a generic theism to *Christian* theism, see R. Douglas Geivett, "David Hume and a Cumulative Case Argument," chapter 14 in this volume.

[21]Hume's *Dialogues* focuses in detail on the argument from design, or teleological argument. I have discussed his treatment of this topic in considerable detail in *Hume's "Inexplicable Mystery": His Views on Religion* (Philadelphia: Temple University Press, 1990).

5

HUME'S STOPPER AND THE
NATURAL THEOLOGY PROJECT

James F. Sennett

𝕯

A common response to natural theology arguments is to offer a rebuttal that I call "Hume's stopper."[1] It goes something like this: "Well, even if this argument is sound, it doesn't prove theism, since the 'god' required by [fill in the argument du jour] is a far cry from the elaborate deity envisioned by traditional theism." That is, one does not need to postulate a full-blown omnipotent, omniscient, morally perfect creator and sustainer of the universe in order to satisfy the requirements of the argument (a first cause, a designer, etc.). In short, Hume's stopper is the accusation that any natural theology argument, even if sound, simply does not prove enough.

So, for example, Michael Martin rejects William Lane Craig's famous version of the first cause argument[2] on the grounds that it "shows [at the most] that some personal agent or agents created the universe," and that "the creator or creators of the universe [need not be] greater than the universe itself."[3] And in critique of Bruce Reichenbach's cosmological argument he charges,

> Clearly the correlation of the attributes of a necessary being and the attributes of God does not make the probability of the hypothesis that God exists more

[1]This chapter expands and generalizes many ideas originally presented in "Stopping Hume's Stopper: A Rejection of a Traditional Attack on Natural Theology," *Stone-Campbell Journal* 5 (2002): 207-16. I have adopted and adapted some portions of that paper in several sections of this chapter. I am grateful to the editor of the *Stone-Campbell Journal* for permission to incorporate them here.
[2]William Lane Craig, *The Kalam Cosmological Argument* (London: Macmillan, 1979).
[3]Michael Martin, *Atheism: A Philosophical Justification* (Philadelphia: Temple University Press, 1990), p. 103.

probable than the contradictory hypothesis. After all, the correlations established are compatible with many rival hypotheses. Besides the alternative one of a completely evil necessary being, there is, for example, the alternative hypothesis of a necessary being that is neither completely good nor completely evil. Why should we not suppose that these rival hypotheses are more probable than the hypothesis that God exists?[4]

Employment of the stopper is not limited to atheistic philosophers. John Hick criticizes all versions of the design argument with the assertion that "the appearances of nature do not entitle us to affirm the existence of *one* God rather than many; . . . nor of a wholly *good* God; . . . nor . . . of a perfectly *wise* God or an unlimitedly *powerful* one."[5] And William Wainwright charges, "Even if the design argument is successful, it shows only that the world is rooted in mind and reflects its purposes. It doesn't show that this mind is omnipotent, omniscient or perfectly good. The evidence may not even show that there is only one divine mind rather than several cooperating designers. Hence, the design argument doesn't establish God's existence."[6]

This objection is at least as old as Hume.[7] In part 5 of the *Dialogues Concerning Natural Religion,* Philo complains to Cleanthes that the design argument does not show God to be infinite, perfect or even one. In a famous passage Philo muses over other possible explanations for a designed universe:

This world, for aught [Cleanthes] knows, is very faulty and imperfect . . . and was only the first rude essay of some infant Deity, who afterwards abandoned it, ashamed of his lame performance; it is the work only of some dependent, inferior Deity; and is the object of derision to his superiors; it is the production of old age and dotage in some superannuated Deity; and ever since his death, has run on at adventures, from the first impulse and active force, which it received from him.[8]

---

[4]Ibid., p. 142.
[5]John H. Hick, *Philosophy of Religion,* 3rd ed. (Englewood Cliffs, N.J.: Prentice-Hall, 1983), p. 26; emphasis his.
[6]William J. Wainwright, *Philosophy of Religion,* 2nd ed. (Albany, N.Y.: Wadsworth, 1999), pp. 50-51.
[7]Hume's stopper is a species of (though—I think—not coextensive with) the epistemic "sin" that Todd Furman labels "jumping the gun." See chapter 3 of the present volume.
[8]David Hume, *Dialogues Concerning Natural Religion,* ed. Norman Kemp Smith (Indianapolis: Bobbs-Merrill, 1947), p. 169. All subsequent quotations from the *Dialogues* in this chapter will be from this edition and cited by DNR and page number(s) in the text.

Pamphilus tells us that Philo delivered these remarks "with an air of alacrity and triumph" (DNR 166). And the glee in his voice has echoed through the denouncements of countless philosophers over the last two and a half centuries. So natural theology, it seems to many, dies the death of a thousand disqualifications.

It is the purpose of the present volume to explore what the editors have called "Hume's legacy"—the general mood of skepticism concerning natural theology that permeates much of philosophy of religion in the wake of Hume's criticisms. I consider Hume's stopper to be a major plank in Hume's legacy. While it may be argued that it is not altogether proper to credit this objection to Hume,[9] it is clearly in the spirit of Hume's legacy and often emerges from quotations of or allusions to the above *Dialogues* passage and others similar to it.[10] Undoubtedly, a refutation of the stopper's power will go a long way toward accomplishing the purpose of this volume—to show natural theology to be alive and well in the wake of Hume's legacy.

In this chapter I provide just such a refutation. That is, I offer a detailed answer to Martin's fair and important question quoted above: "Why should we not suppose that these rival hypotheses are more probable than the hypothesis that God exists?" My answer begins with the identification of an important assumption that Hume's stopper makes, which I will call "the ignorance assumption." I will then argue that the ignorance assumption is unjustified, and that without it Hume's stopper cannot survive as a legitimate complaint against any standard natural theology argument.[11] I conclude,

---

[9]As both Terence Penelhum and John Castelein have argued in independent correspondence. Penelhum notes that the objection was raised before Hume by both Aquinas and Pascal. Castelein correctly points out that the objection is more accurately labeled "Philo's stopper," since it is not altogether clear throughout the *Dialogues* just who is speaking for Hume—and it is likely that his voice is in the mouths of different interlocutors at different times. However, David O'Connor has recently joined the growing number of Hume scholars who argue that, while Hume's voice is indeed heard from time to time in each of the main characters, it is overwhelmingly prominent in Philo. See *Hume on Religion* (London: Routledge, 2001), pp. 214-16. For an argument that Cleanthes is the primary Humean, see Nicholas Capaldi, "Hume's Philosophy of Religion: God Without Ethics," *International Journal of Philosophy of Religion* 1 (1970): 233-40. See also n. 11 below.

[10]See, for example, William Rowe, *Philosophy of Religion: An Introduction*, 2nd ed. (Belmont, Calif.: Wadsworth, 1993), pp. 51-52.

[11]In private conversation Todd Furman offered one other reason why "Hume's stopper" may not be a legitimate name for this objection (see n. 9 above)—namely, that Hume never intended the point to stop anything. The stopper may be read throughout the *Dialogues* as simply a point of logic and clarification about what the arguments as they stand prove, and what work they leave undone. That is, Hume may be read as claiming that the traditional arguments at best get us to Martin's question, and it is now up to theistic philosophy to offer a

therefore, that Hume's stopper does not deserve anything like the attention and endorsement it has received in the history of natural theology.

Two last introductory points need to be made. First, I referred above to "standard natural theology arguments." What I have in mind is any of the arguments that one might find discussed in a reputable philosophy of religion textbook or a detailed study of natural theology. This includes the classical cosmological, teleological and moral arguments, as well as many of their contemporary expressions. It also includes many of the arguments arising from contemporary science, such as the arguments from consciousness and fine-tuning. All of the arguments represented in part two of this volume qualify as standard. The ontological and cumulative case arguments are special instances, since they focus on a wide variety of divine characteristics, rather than on a single characteristic, as do most of the rest. However, this makes them less, not more, susceptible to the stopper. The more theistic characteristics an argument supports, the less effective the claim that some other entity might fill the argument's bill.

Second, there is a subtle oxymoronic irony to Hume's stopper. The same argument is granted as sound and yet charged with a serious logical infelicity. This strange situation arises from the fact that natural theology arguments are thought of as arguments for the truth of theism, when in reality they are typically arguments for some significantly more modest claim—usually that a being (or beings) with a given characteristic exists (or has existed). Nonetheless, the arguments are traditionally treated by their proponents as reasons to accept theism. Indeed, it is this ambiguity that fuels the stopper. The charge is that, even if the argument in question fulfills its specific purpose—proving the existence of a being with a given characteristic—it does not fulfill its broader purpose of proving the truth of theism.

To keep these specific and broader aims clearly before us, let us distinguish between the *minimal form* of a standard natural theology argument and its *extended form*. We can represent the minimal form thus:

P1:   Phenomenon X requires an entity with characteristic A.

---

defensible answer to that question. While Hume (like Martin) would likely be quite skeptical regarding the possibilities for such a defensible answer, he does not, by employing the stopper, mean to suggest that it is impossible. If this is the case, then the present chapter can, ironically, be considered a *continuation* of the Humean project, rather than a rebuttal of it. Furman may well be right. (My history of interaction with him on Hume interpretation leads me to suspect that he is.) But again I choose to retain the moniker "Hume's stopper," since it is clear from its employment by philosophers of religion that it is most widely viewed as a reason to abandon natural theology, rather than a corner to be turned in its development.

C1:   Therefore, an entity with characteristic A exists.[12]

The extended form adds to the minimal form the further premise and conclusion:

P2:   The God of theism has characteristic A.

C2:   Therefore, the God of theism exists.

The inference from C1 and P2 to C2 is clearly invalid, and only under the strictest of conditions could an argument of such form be inductively strong. Yet it seems that natural theology arguments can only work as defenses of theism if they employ this extended, unjustified form. Hume's stopper, then, can be understood as the charge that the soundness of the minimal form does not entail or even suggest the soundness of the extended form.[13] Put in this way, the stopper seems virtually indisputable. Nevertheless, I intend to dispute it vigorously.

THE IGNORANCE ASSUMPTION AND ALETHIC EVALUATION

In the argument from design discussed in parts 4 and 5 of Hume's *Dialogues,* Cleanthes makes much of the principle of proportionality between cause and effect in order to argue that the design present in the universe must result from an intentional mind, just as design we find in physical artifacts results from intentional mind. However, Philo insists that this principle entails that Cleanthes "must renounce all claims to infinity in any of the attributes of the Deity" inferred by the design argument (DNR 166). The design in physical artifacts does not trace back to an infinite mind; hence, Cleanthes cannot assume that the design in nature does either.[14] Philo goes on to assert that Cleanthes cannot make any claims for perfection in this deity for the same reasons. Moreover, there is no reason to assume that the designer is the omnipotent theistic God who spoke creation into existence once for all. Given that designed artifacts are inevitably the result of a long, slow process of attempt, rejection and improvement, it follows that "many worlds might

---

[12]For sake of simplicity, I will omit the understood qualifiers "entity (or entities)" and "exists (or has existed)."

[13]Though many natural theology arguments are best expressed in inductive forms, I will (for the sake of simplicity) speak only of an argument's soundness, understanding this as metonymous for "soundness or cogency."

[14]Prior to his charge, Philo extracts from Cleanthes the concession that the latter knows of no minds other than those "like the human." This is a subtle move, emphasizing the fact that the shift from human to divine mind is an enormous leap, straining the bounds of legitimate analogical inference, which is nonetheless required if Cleanthes' argument is to succeed. See O'Connor, *Hume on Religion,* pp. 110-12.

have been botched and bungled, throughout an eternity, ere this system was struck out" (DNR 167).

This line of objection is a clear application of Hume's stopper. It is charged that the design argument fails as a proof of theism, since the soundness of its minimal form would fall well short of proving the existence of so great and complex a being as the God of theism—that is, it gives no reason to accept the soundness of the argument in its extended form. Moreover, Philo's retort seems irrefutable to many, atheist and theist alike. This is (at least partly) because Philo employs a presupposition in his refutation that is prima facie quite plausible and would find widespread endorsement among critical thinkers. I label this presupposition "the ignorance assumption," and explicate it thus:

IA: In assessing the strength of the conclusion of an argument, it is inappropriate to take into account any information not explicitly or implicitly contained in the premises of the argument.

A couple of explanatory notes are in order. First, I do not mean by *strength* the technical notion that word invokes in its usage in inductive logic. I intend IA to be applicable to inductive and deductive arguments alike, and use the word *strength* simply to refer to the appropriateness of the conclusion, given the structure and content of the argument at hand. Second, I do not mean for the expression "explicitly or implicitly contained in the premises" to have the formal force that it would have in discussions of deductive validity. I mean simply that a conclusion is proper only if it is supported in a recognizable way given only the premises and any applicable rules of deductive or inductive logic. In other words, no substantive "hidden premises" are allowed.

I have labeled the principle in focus "the ignorance assumption" because it asserts that we must, in assessing the conclusion of an argument, presume ignorance of any information not available to us via the premises. Even if we are aware of relevant information beyond those parameters, we cannot legitimately incorporate it into our deliberations. To do so is to consider "facts not in evidence" as it were—a seemingly obvious faux pas of any legitimate critical thinking exercise.

I have appealed to the jurisprudential concept of "facts not in evidence." However, while such relevant information is legitimately excluded from a court of law, the exclusion is for reasons that are not applicable to the arena of pure critical debate. These venues have different goals. The goal of criminal justice is not simply (nor even primarily) the discovery of truth. It is, rather, the enactment of justice, which includes proper consideration of the rights of the accused and the rules of evidence. The accomplishing of this goal often requires the exclusion of relevant information in order to preclude prejudicial tainting of the jury, benefit to the prosecution deriving from a violation of the defendant's constitutional rights, or other miscarriages of justice.

The goal of critical debate, on the other hand, is simply the ascertaining of truth. The parties in such a debate have no rights that need to be protected against full disclosure of all elements relevant to the discovery of truth. Furthermore, prejudice is avoided by eschewing emotional appeals and other fallacies—not by cordoning off information that bears on the truth to be sought. Hence, an appeal to "facts not in evidence" has a rather odd ring in critical debate, since such facts are by stipulation relevant to the conclusion sought, and therefore vital to the single goal of truth detection. As intuitively obvious as it may have first appeared, there seems to be something fundamentally inappropriate about IA.

This tension over IA can be resolved by noting that there are two distinct levels on which an argument can be evaluated. On the one hand, it can be evaluated as a piece of pure logical reasoning. Here the question to be answered is simply how well the argument adheres to the recognized canons of deductive or inductive logic. Let us call this the *logical* evaluation of an argument. On the other hand, an argument can be evaluated as an aid in discovering truth concerning the question in focus. Let us call this the *alethic* evaluation of an argument.[15] It is important to note that the evaluations of a single argument on these two levels may differ wildly. An argument may fail miserably as a piece of pure logical defense of its conclusion, while nonetheless spurring us forward by great leaps toward discovering whether or not its conclusion is in fact true.

The ignorance assumption is applicable only to the logical evaluation of an argument. Here the "facts not in evidence" must be precluded, since the

---

[15]From the Greek *alētheia,* "truth." Michael Sudduth has suggested in private correspondence that alethic evaluation is simply a broader form of logical evaluation—that the difference here is one of degree only, not of kind. After all, he notes, even alethic evaluation will rely heavily on deductive and inductive criteria. This is, of course, true. However, I am not ready to concede that all epistemic criteria reduce to logical criteria. That is, I believe that epistemic justification is a broader notion than logical support. Therefore, I want to leave open the possibility (even, I think, the likelihood) that a positive alethic evaluation may invoke justificatory data that are not reducible to deductive or inductive argument. In short, if epistemic justification is bigger than logic (and I believe it is), then alethic evaluation is bigger than logical evaluation. These issues are, of course, much too detailed to be anything but mentioned here.

purpose just is to determine the extent to which the premises (alone) support the conclusion. However, when the goal becomes not the assessment of an argument but the unhindered quest for truth, we cannot legitimately bar the door through which an argument beckons us, simply on the charge that the premises tell us nothing about what lies beyond it. The claim of Hume's stopper can now be spelled out much more explicitly as comprising the following claims:

1. Even if the minimal form of a natural theology argument deserves a positive logical evaluation, its extended form does not.

2. This poor logical evaluation of the extended form entails a poor alethic evaluation of the extended form as well.

This second claim is false, and in its falsehood lies the key to stopping Hume's stopper. The stopper is assumed to arrest the natural theology project because the (admittedly) negative logical evaluation of the extended form arguments is mistakenly understood to support a negative alethic evaluation of them as well. In the remainder of this chapter I will argue that, despite their negative logical evaluation, the (extended form) standard natural theology arguments possess alethic power that Hume's stopper offers no muscle against.

The "Candidate Gods" Approach

I love the game of chess. And while my play does not come close to that of fellow philosopher and contributor to this volume Victor Reppert, I have spent countless hours of sheer pleasure studying and playing the game of kings. One very important concept that any chess player must learn is the notion of the "candidate move." At any given point in a game, there may be dozens of legal moves one might make. Of those, there are only a handful—perhaps no more than four or five—that are prima facie sensible. These are the player's candidate moves. Each one must be considered in turn to determine whether its prima facie sensibility survives *ultima facie,* and then to determine which of these constitutes the best move, given the position on the board.

The thought process taking one first to the candidate moves and then to the best move requires a great deal of cognitive consideration. First, it calls for *analysis* of the present board position. Analysis includes important chess concepts like king safety, piece deployment and cooperation, space control, material balance and pawn structure. But such analysis is seldom sufficient.

In fact, it is analysis that typically produces the list of candidate moves, and it hardly ever aids in narrowing them down. The player must go beyond analysis to *calculation*. This is the process of determining the opponent's candidate responses to each of one's candidate moves, the candidate counterresponses, and so on to a point where the situation resolves itself. The player must then be able to visualize the resulting position on the board and analyze it in much the same way as the original position was analyzed. It is impossible to progress from candidate moves to best move without being able to foresee and analyze the most likely outcomes of the candidate moves.

However, even calculation, essential as it is to good chess, is only a necessary condition for move selection, not sufficient. The final ingredient is *evaluation*. At any given time in the game, a good player has a *plan*—a tactical or strategic goal one is working to accomplish. The determination of which candidate move is best often hinges on the extent to which each move furthers that plan. Judging this extent is the task of evaluation. Still, even the current plan is subservient to the overall goal of any game—securing victory or avoiding loss.[16] It does no good to select a move that accomplishes a given plan (winning a pawn, say, or securing an open file with one's rook) if the resulting position gives the opponent an obvious win.[17] So evaluation works on two levels: the current plan and the overall goal. And evaluation on both levels requires more than analysis and calculation. It requires a vast storehouse of knowledge concerning what kinds of board positions typically do and do not lend themselves to accomplishing certain kinds of goals. It requires a deep understanding of the ramifications a position may have many moves later in the game. It requires an intuitive feel that can only be developed and honed via careful study and frequent play.

So let us recap this overview of one of the most fascinating aspects of the world's most fascinating game. Simple analysis typically produces nothing more than a list of candidate moves. But the objective is not the production

---

[16]These are not the same goal. Players often find themselves in positions where victory is beyond reach, but continue playing with the aim of achieving a draw.

[17]At a recent tournament a young novice showed me with great glee a game he has just played against an expert level player in which the novice worked a combination that resulted in winning his opponent's rook for a bishop (a maneuver in chess known as "winning the exchange"—generally a very strong advantage). Of course, the achieved position was one in which the expert forced checkmate in the next three moves (in fact, he never even recaptured the bishop after it took his rook)—a fact which seemed not to diminish the novice's delight one iota!

of such a list. It is the selection of the best move. To accomplish that objective, the player must move beyond the minimum information provided by the analysis and consider a great deal of information provided by the further steps of calculation and evaluation.

It is probably clear by now that I am setting up an analogy. At the end of the last section I distinguished between the logical evaluation and the alethic evaluation of an argument. These different approaches have different goals, and these different goals necessitate consideration of different bodies of information. The results of applying the two approaches to a given natural theology argument are analogous to the results of applying the two tasks of analysis and move selection to a given chess board position.

Analyzing a chess position is analogous to logically evaluating the minimal form of a natural theology argument. Even with a positive evaluation, one can do no better than produce a list of "candidate gods," any one of which is prima facie as plausible as any other. It is this realization that leads the critic to conclude that the corresponding extended form is ludicrous—it appears to select one candidate from the list in a totally arbitrary and unjustified manner. And it is here that Hume's stopper has its force. Given only the premises and logical structure of the minimal form argument, there is no justification for moving beyond this candidate list to the selection of one as the best candidate for fulfilling the role required (designer, first cause, ground of morality, etc.). Just as simple analysis cannot narrow down a list of candidate chess moves, so logical evaluation cannot narrow down a list of candidate gods.

But like analysis, logical evaluation is only a means to an end. It produces a list of candidate gods, and simple consideration of the argument's logical merits cannot give us reason to go beyond this list. But there are other tools—there is more information to be considered. There are the "facts not in evidence," legitimate and necessary in our quest for truth. So, just as narrowing the candidate moves to the best move in chess requires much more than the information provided by the analysis, so moving from the candidate gods suggested by the minimal argument to the theistic God proclaimed by the extended argument requires much more than the logical evaluation of either argument.

But—and here is the key point of the analogy—if the consideration of this further information results in the selection of the best chess move, then that process vindicates not simply the calculation and evaluation, but the analysis as well. The analysis is a successful piece of analysis, even if it does not produce (on its own) the best move. So also going beyond the list of candidate gods and considering additional information to select the best god—if a successful endeavor—vindicates the original minimal-form natural theology argument that produced the candidate gods. It is a successful piece of natural theology, even if it does not produce (on its own) the best god. A positive alethic evaluation of the extended argument will vindicate the minimal argument—it does not, on its own, need to narrow the candidate gods down.

This analogy then raises two questions. First, what are the candidate gods suggested by standard natural theology arguments? Second, can the case be made that the theistic God is the best candidate? Answering these two questions is the burden of the next three sections of this chapter.

THE CANDIDATE GODS

What I am calling the "candidate gods" approach, then, consists of two steps: (1) constructing a list of candidate gods to satisfy the requirements of the minimal form of a given natural theology argument; then (2) utilizing the "facts not in evidence" to conduct an alethic evaluation of the extended form of the argument, thereby paring down (if possible) the candidate gods list to the best god for the job. It is my contention that the candidate gods approach is the proper way to formulate judgment on the ultimate alethic success of an extended-form natural theology argument.

After all, the search for truth does not take place in a vacuum, a sterile laboratory or the unavoidably restrictive confines of a criminal court. A standard natural theology argument is not a "whodunit" mystery to be solved using only the information provided in its formulation. Rather, the argument shows the need for an entity displaying a given crucial property. When we ask the question, "What or who might that entity be?" there is nothing in the canons of rationality or fair discourse that limits us to the entailments of the thought process that got us to the question. To switch analogies, once the resumés of the job applicants are submitted, *all* information in those resumés becomes relevant. The rational thing to do is hire the most highly qualified candidate—not simply one who can do the job. This is the unique strategy of the "candidate gods" approach.

So who are the candidate gods? There is, of course, the God of theism. I will divide the other options into two exclusive groups: the gods of other religious traditions, and what we might call "gods without portfolio"—divinities not touted by any religion but certainly within the realm of epistemic possibility. The whimsical fancies of Philo's imagination enumerated in the quotation in the first section of this chapter are prime examples of such stipulated deities. The strategy for the theist is now clear. Given this list of candidate gods, it must be argued that the God of theism is the best move, the best applicant for the job. The next two sections will argue that the theistic God is preferable as the entity satisfying the need revealed by a standard natural theology argument—preferable first to the gods of other religions, and then to the gods without portfolio.

THEISM AND OTHER RELIGIONS

I will begin with the more difficult case to make: that theism is a preferable alternative to other established religions. My case here is threefold: (1) the enormous philosophical scrutiny under which theism has been placed compared to other world religions; (2) the amount of natural theology work theism does; and (3) the non–ad hoc nature of theism.

First, I submit that no other religious tradition has undergone the philosophical scrutiny that theism has. The only traditions that come close in terms of philosophical heritage are certain strains of Hinduism and Buddhism. However, those philosophical traditions have been intentionally and understandably sympathetic to the relevant worldviews, and little in the way of confrontive challenge to fundamental claims or basic apologetic argumentation are to be found there, at least not much analogous to the rigorous analytical framework of Western thought's encounter with theism.

True, the sympathies of the Western intellectual tradition were firmly with theism throughout the Middle Ages, but the situation is disanalogous to that of Hinduism and Buddhism for at least two reasons. First, even in the officially safe confines of scholastic philosophy, rigorous challenges to and careful philosophical explications of the most fundamental theistic claims still abounded. The constant charges of heresy and official banning of books throughout this period are sufficient testimony to the constant presence of academic challenge to dearly held beliefs. Second, we have not been anywhere near the relative security of the High Middle Ages for many centuries. The challenges to theism just since the Enlightenment have easily outpaced the scrutiny afforded any other tradition through its entire existence. (It should be noted, given the theme of the current volume, that much of the very best this scrupulous attack has offered is a product of Hume's legacy—not just in reference to natural theology, but on many other levels, e.g., miracles, the nature of the soul, the case for naturalism, etc.)

Yet throughout two millennia of critical examination and over two hundred years of top flight antagonistic criticism, there have not arisen refutations sufficient to compel all thinking people to reject them. Indeed, at every historical period there have been innumerable scholars, fully appreciative of the best criticism of theism their day had to offer, who nonetheless retained their conviction and offered defensible responses to the criticism. This history of survival and thriving in the face of intense criticism sets theism apart from all other world religious traditions.[18]

Here I must be clear about what I am and am not saying. I am not saying that other religions are irrational or that one cannot rationally reject theism in favor of some alternative view. I am not even saying that one cannot rationally reject theism in favor of atheism. What I am saying is that, after many centuries of debate, it is possible for one to consider fully the very best criticisms that have been offered and still rationally accept theism. Furthermore, no other religion has even *undergone* such scrutiny, much less survived it.

I turn now to my second reason for the preferability of theism over its rival world religions. One of the most remarkable features of traditional theism is the fact that it can be used to answer so many classical philosophical problems without significant alteration. So, for example, in the version of the cosmological argument known as the contingency (or Thomistic) argument, the existence of contingent beings is seen to require the existence of at least one necessary being. Theism provides such a being. Also, in the first cause argument, the fact of cause/effect chains seems to require an uncaused cause to escape an embarrassing regression. Theism has long held that God is uncaused (or perhaps self-caused). The design argument requires an intelligence sufficiently knowledgeable and sufficiently powerful to call the complexities of the physical universe into existence. Theism comes readymade with a God who displays both omniscience and omnipotence. And so on throughout the standard natural theology arguments. Theism provides a tidy answer to a wide range of metaphysical questions. When one tradition answers so many different questions, the virtues of metaphysical parsimony and explanatory simplicity give us great reason to prefer it to its alternatives.[19]

---

[18]Indeed, it sets *Christian* theism apart. The tradition of scholarly scrutiny just elucidated is almost exclusively a Christian phenomenon. In fact, much of the most scrupulous apologetic work done by the Scholastics was in direct response to the work of Muslim scholars. Nonetheless, I will in the text retain the general focus on theism, since my point is only that the natural theology project does make a case for the truth of theism, despite Hume's stopper.

[19]This raises the question of whether or not my approach is simply a version of the cumulative case argument. See the "Three Objections" section below.

This preference is undergirded by the fact that no other religious tradition can provide a concept of deity that so neatly dovetails with the problems of philosophy. Granted, this may partly be a result of the point argued above that no other religious tradition has undergone the philosophical scrutiny theism has. Nonetheless, theism is able to boast a "theological solutions to philosophical problems" track record unique in the annals of world religions. Besides, it seems clear that many of the problems theism so neatly responds to *could* not be similarly answered by other traditions. For instance, the design argument clearly requires a god (or gods) with intention, will and intelligence—which entails personality. William Lane Craig and J. P. Moreland have both argued impressively that the first cause argument also requires a personal god.[20] Any tradition for which deity is impersonal will not fill either bill.

It is often suggested by apologists that the theistic notion that God is both personal and infinite sets the tradition apart from every other religious tradition in history.[21] So, for example, the gods of the Western polytheistic pantheons were personal but finite, while the gods of Eastern pantheism are either personal and finite or impersonal and infinite. Whether such a distinction is ultimately helpful or not, it is quite arguable that the unique character of God as conceived in the Western theistic tradition is a necessary condition for the virtually effortless way in which it answers the continual challenge of philosophical problem after philosophical problem. It is, therefore, not surprising that no competing conception of deity is so fruitful.

This leads to my third point in favor of theism over the gods of other religions. Theism answers this variety of philosophical conundrums with little if any alteration of the basic mold within which it has been cast for many centuries. There is no ad hoc flavor to theism's solutions. Theism is what it is, independent of the metaphysical considerations that give rise to these problems, and many have accepted theism without any knowledge of or concern for said problems. Theism was not created or altered significantly in order to

---

[20]J. P. Moreland, *Scaling the Secular City: A Defense of Christianity* (Grand Rapids: Baker, 1987), pp. 41-42; William Lane Craig, "Philosophical and Scientific Pointers to *Creatio ex Nihilo*," in *Contemporary Perspectives on Religious Epistemology,* ed. R. Douglas Geivett and Brendan Sweetman (Grand Rapids: Eerdmans, 1992), pp. 185-200, esp. pp. 197-98.

[21]This point has worked its way into contemporary evangelical apologetics primarily via the work of Francis Schaeffer. Schaeffer particularly employs the implications of the infinite/personal conception of God in his apologetic trilogy *The God Who Is There* (Downers Grove, Ill.: InterVarsity Press, 1968), *Escape from Reason* (Downers Grove, Ill.: InterVarsity Press, 1968) and *He Is There and He Is Not Silent* (Wheaton, Ill.: Tyndale House, 1972).

solve them. It is there, doing lots of work in lots of areas and lots of lives, *and* it happens to handle quite neatly many perplexing problems of philosophy.

This is not to say, of course, that theism has not evolved or expanded in its understanding of God's qualities as a result of its encounter with such problems. But making the implications of a theory explicit or committing it to one of a number of alternatives with which it was previously consistent is hardly the same thing as making up out of whole cloth doctrines or dimensions of doctrines that did not exist or suggest themselves prior to consideration of certain puzzles.

THEISM AND THE UNKNOWN GODS

I turn now to the claim that theism is preferable to the gods without portfolio—i.e., the claim that it is more rational to assume that the God of theism is the "best move" than to assume that it is some god or gods hitherto unimagined in the history of religious conviction. I will consider two subcategories of such undocumented deities: those such as Philo imagines in the quotation early in this chapter, which I will call the "Keystone gods," and those virtually manufactured out of consistent characteristics, which I will call the "generic gods." Prominent among this latter type is that god who possesses precisely and only those characteristics needed to fill the bill of the natural theology argument in focus, which I will call the "minimal god."

The Keystone gods stumble over each other in Philo's imagination like so many of their namesake oafs in a Mack Sennett silent short. They include a toddler deity for whom this universe is but so much modeling clay clumsily constructed and long forgotten, an imbecile god whom compatriots laugh into scorn for his feeble creation efforts, and an elderly divinity whose best creation days are far behind him. Moreover, only space considerations and the threat of dialectical overkill halt Hume's speculations. It is clear that such superhuman buffoons could be manufactured *ad infinitum aut ad nauseum,* whichever comes first.

But why shouldn't these products of Hume's fancy be just as seriously considered as the theistic God when shopping for the best solution to a natural theology puzzle? Well, to begin with, because they are so obviously just that—products of Hume's fancy. Neither Philo nor Cleanthes nor Hume nor any reader over the past two hundred years has ever seriously considered the suggestion that the world was created as the initial feeble effort of a god not yet out of diapers or any such thing. These suggestions are, and were clearly intended to be, nothing more than rhetorical mockeries.

But, one might protest, this is precisely the point. The Keystone gods are clearly not the right solution to the mystery in question, yet we have every bit as much reason to think they are as we do to think that the theistic God is. My point is that we do *not* have every bit as much reason. I refer to the discussion above. The theistic God has behind it an impressive history of weathering intellectual scrutiny, solving philosophical problems and under-girding rational worldviews. This God was not manufactured in idle specu-lation over a curious philosophical riddle. In contrast, the Keystone gods are the very essence of ad hoc solutions—so much so that not even their inven-tors take them seriously.

Here we see the power of the candidate gods approach in full force. Re-member that our task is the *alethic* evaluation of a standard (extended form) natural theology argument, not its *logical* evaluation. Were we interested only in the latter, the Keystone gods alternative would carry much more weight. Granted, most natural theology arguments give little if any reason *as exercises in pure logic* to prefer the theistic God to any of his boorish competitors.[22] However, when our quest is for truth, we are permitted—even required—to look beyond the confines of the argument at hand to ask what broader reasons there are to choose among the candidates. Armed with this panoramic perspective, the choice between the God of theism and the gods of slapstick is a philosophical no-brainer.

Besides all this, any Keystone gods hypothesis is subject to that most feared of contemporary postulation pummelers, Ockham's razor. Given the long, rich history of the theistic tradition and its widespread success in of-fering defensible responses to many historical problems of philosophy, the conjecture of a Keystone god with no other dialectical purpose to serve than the filling of a slot already tailor-made for the God of theism smacks of the most egregious of philosophical profligacy. If ontological parsimony is a theoretical virtue at all, there can be no serious consideration of such obvi-ous ad hoc solutions.[23]

---

[22]I offer this concession for the sake of argument. However, at least two of the authors in this volume argue that standard natural theology arguments can be seen as supporting a much more robust picture of God than is often thought—even without the gracious aid of my stopper refutation! See chapter 6 by Douglas Groothuis on the cosmological argument and chapter 8 by James Madden on the teleological argument. Furthermore, as I mentioned at the beginning of this chapter, the cumulative case and ontological arguments are special cases.

[23]I do not mean to suggest that theism is a theory or a hypothesis in the scientific sense. This is, of course, a matter of great debate. However, even if one denies the theoretical status of

I turn now to the generic gods—conceptions of divinity manufactured by the piecing together of consistent characteristics into a deity that would clearly answer the call of the natural theology argument on trial. Martin proposes such generic candidates in his responses to Craig and Reichenbach quoted at the beginning of this chapter. He speaks of "some personal agent or agents" who need not be "greater than the universe itself," of "a completely evil necessary being" and of "a necessary being that is neither completely good nor completely evil." But these gods seem to have nothing to offer above their Keystone counterparts, other than a certain lack of farcical genesis and a more appropriate concentration on the functionality of the concept in solving the philosophical puzzle at hand. But the constructions are clearly ad hoc, clearly without prior problem-solving pedigree, clearly subject to dialectical elimination by the swift application of Ockham's mighty razor.

One interesting generic god strategy would be to start piecing together a composite deity using consistent properties that would solve a wide variety of problems that creep up in philosophy. The only problem is that such an exercise would likely produce a composite sketch so reminiscent of the God of theism as to convince any impartial jury of the identity. This would be, to say the least, an embarrassing result for the antagonist of theism, and an impressive victory for the legitimacy of the candidate gods approach.

So what about the minimal god? Perhaps this is the appropriate response, given the minimalist empiricist spirit that motivates Hume's legacy. Perhaps the most rational response to the alleged soundness of a (minimal form) standard natural theology argument is to postulate a god that is nothing more than the argument requires. So, for example, perhaps the best candidate for the first cause argument is a god that is nothing more than an ultimate cause—a cosmic jumper cable that sparks the battery of reality into existence, but serves no other purpose thereafter. Isn't the only god permitted by the first cause argument one so small in scope and influence as to make an eighteenth-century deist blush?

By this point my response should be easily anticipated. The minimal god fares no better than the Keystone gods or the generic gods when the standard to which the candidates are held is upgraded from that of logical eval-

---

theism, it is nonetheless clear that there are concepts utilized in theory evaluation that are also useful and even vital to the evaluation of theism. See James F. Sennett, "Theism and Other Minds: On the Falsifiability of Non-Theories," *Topoi* 14 (1995): 149-60. This whole issue of *Topoi*, edited by Paul Draper, is dedicated to the question "Is Theism a Theory?"

uation to that of alethic evaluation. The minimal god is clearly ad hoc and carries no other credentials than its ability to solve a given philosophical problem. If anything, it is *more* ad hoc than the others, since the only dialectical function such speculation could ever hope to perform is the solving of the single problem on the table. Furthermore, to cover the gamut of natural theology issues, a whole stable of minimal gods would be needed, since many different problems are uncovered by the various arguments. This is a clear violation of the ontological parsimony so deeply cherished by post-Enlightenment thinkers, a wide-open target for Ockham's razor, and a betrayal of the minimalist sentiments appealed to above.

AND THE WINNER IS . . .

So we seem to have our winner. Analysis, calculation and evaluation have done their work, and the task of move selection is accomplished. It is possible that other candidates could be offered, but it is hard to see how any could escape the criticisms raised against the gods without portfolio here considered.

The history of theism and the history of other world religions is not going to change. Even if antagonistic philosophical scrutiny of other traditions develops and grows, it will be centuries before they produce any kind of dialectical pedigree worthy of comparing to that of theism. The ad hoc and prodigal nature of the gods without portfolio option likewise seems closed to critical alteration. The histories of competitive religious traditions are what they are. The histories of the stipulative deities aren't what they aren't. They have no history, no philosophical lineage, no reason at all to consider them in the face of living, vibrant candidates. Unless someone begins the Infant Deity Cult soon, that, too, is unlikely to change.

THREE OBJECTIONS

Before closing, I want to consider three important objections to my "candidate gods" approach to natural theology: (1) the charge that this is nothing but the cumulative case argument in new garb; (2) the charge that this is not really natural theology, but somehow exceeds the acceptable boundaries of such an enterprise; and (3) the charge that I have not included the null hypothesis among my candidates.

The idea behind the cumulative case argument is that the various natural theology arguments can be combined into a single case for theism. Like my own argument, the cumulative case argument typically utilizes the correlation between the characteristics of the theistic God and the wide ranging problems raised by the various natural theology arguments, combined with the concept of ontological parsimony, to make its case. So it is easy to understand why one might think that my refutation of Hume's stopper amounts to nothing more than a rehashing of this argument.

I must admit that I am undecided myself about whether or not the candidate gods approach constitutes a cumulative case argument. However, I believe that, regardless of the answer, the approach still represents a defensible refutation of the stopper. In the first place, I am not as convinced as many philosophers of religion of the illegitimacy of a cumulative case approach. Since Douglas Geivett's chapter in this volume presents and defends one form of this argument admirably (chap. 14), I will not attempt any summary defense here. I will say, however, that the association of my argument with the cumulative case argument should not be seen as a casting of the shadow of the various problems often thought to plague that approach upon my offering. Rather, the natural and intuitively pleasing appeal of the candidate gods approach should be seen as lending renewed strength and power to the cumulative case argument. In other words, the mere fact (if it is a fact) that mine is a cumulative case argument does not entail or even suggest that my argument is flawed. It more likely demonstrates that the cumulative case argument has even more going for it than many suspected.

However, I believe there is a very important difference in emphasis between the candidate gods approach and traditional expressions of the cumulative case argument, and if I had to venture an opinion concerning whether the former is best understood as a version of the latter, I would have to say no. This key difference can perhaps best be seen by returning to my distinction between logical evaluation and alethic evaluation of arguments.

The cumulative case argument could be construed in the following way:

P1: Natural theology argument 1 requires a being with characteristic A.
P2: Natural theology argument 2 requires a being with characteristic B.
. . .

Pn: Natural theology argument n requires a being with characteristic ϕ.
Pn+1:Theism acknowledges a God with characteristics A, B, . . . , ϕ.
C: Therefore, theism is true.

Call this argument CC. It is quite conceivable that CC receive a favorable logical evaluation. But, as we have seen, any given extended-form natural theology argument (call one such argument NT) will receive a negative logical evaluation. The positive logical evaluation of CC gives no reason to consider NT to be of any help to theism at all. It is perfectly consistent with CC to acknowledge that NT's poor logical evaluation renders it ineffective as a tool of natural theology—a verdict that Hume's stopper is designed to elicit.

The candidate gods approach, on the other hand, gives reason to believe that NT *by itself* is a useful tool for the defense of theism, despite its poor logical evaluation. This is because its alethic evaluation will take into account the kind of reasoning presented in the above sections on "Theism and Other Religions" and "Theism and the Unknown Gods." So while the cumulative case argument approach attempts to avoid the bad logical evaluations of the various arguments by combining them into one large argument that will receive a favorable logical evaluation, the candidate gods approach points out the dialectical limitations of the logical evaluation and looks beyond it to the more critical alethic evaluation. This difference might be construed as a new and better way of thinking about the cumulative case argument, and I would have no real qualms with such a perspective. However, I am inclined to think that it is better to consider it a new way of evaluating natural theology, importantly distinct from the cumulative case.[24]

The second objection I wish to address is that the candidate gods approach abandons the natural theology project all together. The goal of natural theology is to demonstrate the truth of theism by appeal only to the kind of evidence commonly acknowledged among philosophers regardless of religious conviction—the universally recognized and noncontroversial ev-

---

[24]In private correspondence, Michael Sudduth suggests that the candidate gods approach is actually a new, two-tiered form of cumulative case argument. At the first tier, certain natural theology arguments justify the assertion of some disjunctive existence claim, listing the candidate gods. These arguments, in and of themselves, can take us no further than this disjunctive conclusion. However, with the introduction of "facts not in evidence," we are able to move to the second tier and construct further arguments that allow us to conclude that one of the disjuncts (i.e., theism) is in fact the true one. This is a form of the cumulative case argument because the second tier will undoubtedly introduce new information justified by other natural theology arguments. Again, if it turns out that the candidate gods approach is best thought of as a cumulative case argument, I will not be bothered by that. If it turns out to be a *new form* of such argument, so that it actually furthers and bolsters the case for a successful cumulative case, I will be elated. However, I wish at this time to resist Sudduth's suggestion for two important reasons. First, I consider the concept of alethic evaluation to be broader than that of logical evaluation (see n. 15 above), so I resist the urge to think of the candidate gods approach simply as another form of argument. Second (and related), to call the candidate gods approach a cumulative case argument strongly suggests that all of its power is derived from natural theology arguments. However, I do not wish to restrict the alethic evaluation of an extended form natural theology argument to the evidences and conclusions offered by such arguments.

idence bases of empirical data and the truths of reason.[25] By introducing theism as a postulate to be considered prior to the drawing of a conclusion from this neutral evidence base, the approach ceases to be natural theology at all and becomes only so much devotional theology or apologetics at best and thinly veiled question begging at worst.[26]

If the distinguishing characteristic of natural theology is the exclusive appeal to universally accessible and acceptable evidence, then the candidate gods approach is completely above suspicion. The existence of theism as a religious viewpoint and its dialectical history are empirical facts about the world we live in. So are the existence of its competitor gods from other religious traditions, and the comparative histories of those traditions vis-à-vis theism. Addition of the gods without portfolio is an exercise in rational conceptualization, and their logical possibility is a claim open to rational review. The reasons offered to reject the undocumented deities is also grounded in pure reason and open to rational challenge. Finally, while the reasoning narrowing down this list to the theistic God as the best move may be open to rational criticism, it appeals to nothing more than standard patterns of reasoning and displays no nuances that require previous religious commitment to appreciate or accept.

So, despite the appeal to religious concepts in defense of the alethic power of natural theology, the candidate gods approach does not constitute a departure from the philosophical appeal of a publicly accessible evidence base. Consideration of theism as a possible solution does not violate the rules of critical reasoning any more than does consideration of any substantive and controversial hypothesis as the possible answer to an observational conundrum in science. It is the conjecture of such potential explanations and the narrowing of them to a single preferred postulate that is the very heart and soul of inference to the best explanation. (In fact, it seems to me that the candidates approach just *is* the application of abductive reasoning to the findings of natural theology, though I am not at this time prepared to defend that claim.)

This appeal to scientific reasoning in defense of the candidates approach segues to the final objection I want to consider. Any good list of hypothetical explanations for a scientific phenomenon will include what is often called

---

[25]And so it turns out that the term "natural theology" is in fact a misnomer, since the project is best construed as an exercise in philosophy, not theology.
[26]I am grateful to Todd Furman for the original voicing of this objection.

the "null hypothesis"—the possibility that none of the candidate hypotheses is correct and that something hitherto unconceived provides the sought-for explanation. Yet my list of candidate gods contains no such hypothesis.

Without a null hypothesis escape clause, one might object, the disjunctive elimination structure of my argument is deceptive. I argue thus: "Either A or B or C; Not-B; Not-C; therefore A." But if I had included the null hypothesis as I should have, the resulting conclusion would be "Either A or D," with at best no better reason to accept theism than to accept that we simply don't know the answer.

While this objection has significantly more merit than the first two, it is not decisive against my argument. After all, Hume's stopper implies a dialectical concession to the soundness of the (minimal form) argument in focus, insofar as it demonstrates the existence of an entity with a given characteristic. And for several standard arguments, the requirement seems clearly to be for a personal entity. This certainly is the case for the design argument, and most likely for the moral argument and the first cause argument as well.[27] If this is the case, then the null hypothesis is limited to personal solutions, and the list of candidate gods looks much more like an exhausting of viable options. The cautionary note, "It's always possible that you're wrong, that the answer is something you've never even thought of," while certainly appropriate, is no more a barrier to rational acceptance of the sole surviving hypothesis than is the acceptance of any experimentally confirmed hypothesis in science (for which such a cautionary note is also always in order). And, of course, reneging on the stopper's concession renders the entire discussion moot, since it amounts to a rescinding of the stopper objection and pronounces this chapter patently unnecessary—a result I am more than happy to live with.

Conclusion

I began this chapter with a challenging and completely fair question from atheistic philosopher Michael Martin: "Why should we not suppose that these rival hypotheses are more probable than the hypothesis that God exists?" In retrospect it is important to note that Martin himself saw fit to couch the problem before us in the language of scientific method. In essence, he

---

[27]See n. 20 above on the first cause argument. For a famous argument that the existence of morality requires a personal deity, and most likely the God of theism, see book 1 of C. S. Lewis, *Mere Christianity* (published in numerous editions, most recently San Francisco: HarperSanFrancisco, 2001).

is providing us with an outline for the candidate gods approach. His challenge is, "List the competing hypotheses for me, then defend your claim that the God of theism is the preferable hypothesis." Of course, his question is rhetorical; he does not suppose that there is any way to defend such a claim.[28] It has been the burden of this chapter to challenge that supposition. Once it is clearly understood just what the candidates are, the philosophical defense of theism as the best move is a surprisingly straightforward task.[29]

---

[28]A view that he likely shares with Hume (see n. 11 above).

[29]I thank Stephen T. Davis, Dennis Monokroussos and Douglas Groothuis for very helpful comments and reflections on various aspects of this chapter. I also wish to thank John Castelein at Lincoln Christian College and Seminary for penetrating comments on a previous paper, on which the current chapter was based (see note 1). Finally, I express very special gratitude to Todd Furman for extremely useful conversations regarding many of the ideas herein, and to Michael Sudduth, who offered extensive and insightful comments on a previous draft. I only wish I had had time to take account of all of them, Michael!

PART TWO

HUME AND THE ARGUMENTS

6

METAPHYSICAL IMPLICATIONS
OF COSMOLOGICAL ARGUMENTS

Exorcising the Ghost of Hume

Douglas Groothuis

$\mathcal{D}$

Arguments for the existence of God have had a checkered past in the sagas of philosophy and theology. Philosophers have propounded them and denounced them. Theologians have hailed them and cursed them. Although many pronounced the death of theistic arguments subsequent to the criticisms especially of Hume, but also of Kant and twentieth-century analytic philosophers such as Bertrand Russell, natural theology has revived in the past few decades. The theistic arguments are of several different kinds—principally, ontological, cosmological, design, moral and religious experience—and most kinds may come in one or more argument forms—inductive, deductive and abductive. Criticisms of these arguments typically settle into four camps:

1. Theistic arguments are all philosophical failures because their conclusions are not warranted from their premises.

2. God is not the kind of being who should be argued for philosophically (or at least through natural theology). This is impious and devotionally improper for the believer and has no benefit for the unbeliever either.

3. Sufficient warrant for theistic and even Christian belief is available through properly basic beliefs. Believing "in the basic way," as Plantinga puts it, makes one better off than resting in more doubtful rational argu-

ments, although he does not think theistic arguments are colossal failures or without purpose.[1]

4. Even if a particular theistic argument were cogent, the entity concluded from the argument falls so far short of a full-blooded theism (and especially Christian theism), that the rational power of the argument is really beside the point or at least not as theologically weighty as is often supposed. For instance, a first cause of the universe is, it is claimed, a far cry from "the God of Abraham, Isaac and Jacob" or "the Father of our Lord Jesus Christ." This is what James Sennett has dubbed "Hume's stopper."[2]

Criticism 2 has been advanced by the likes of Søren Kierkegaard and Blaise Pascal. I take it to be unwarranted, but I will not address that here.[3] Neither will I pay much attention to criticisms 1 and 3, except to say that a variety of theistic arguments have been defended in analytically rigorous forms, which deserve respect philosophically.[4] Within the past few decades, these arguments have become, in William James's terms, "live options" in much of the philosophical community. The present credibility of the cosmological argument is all I need in order to discuss profitably these arguments' potential metaphysical implications.

I will center my analysis on criticism 4 with respect to two versions of the cosmological argument (CA). The conclusion of such arguments is that there exists a being radically different from the contingent cosmos that is the ontological support for the existence of the cosmos. I will call this being a causally necessary being (CNB). CAs either claim to have demonstrated that the CNB created the universe ex nihilo, or that both the universe and the CNB have always existed, with the former metaphysically dependent on the latter ad infinitum. (By "universe" or "cosmos" I mean the class of all contingent beings—physical and nonphysical.) This distinction between the two kinds of CAs will play a role in our discussion of some of the following points.

---

[1]See Alvin Plantinga, *Warranted Christian Belief* (New York: Oxford University Press, 2000), pp. 268-80.

[2]See James F. Sennett, "Hume's Stopper and the Natural Theology Project," chapter 5 in this volume.

[3]On Pascal's rejection of natural theology, see Douglas Groothuis, "Proofs, Pride, and Incarnation: Is Natural Theology Theologically Taboo?" *Journal of the Evangelical Theological Society* 38 (1995): 67-77; "Pascal's Biblical Omission Argument Against Natural Theology," *Asbury Theological Journal* 52 (1997): 17-26; and "Do Theistic Proofs Prove the Wrong God?" *Christian Scholar's Review* 29 (1999): 247-60.

[4]See, for instance, Robert C. Koons, "A New Look at the Cosmological Argument," *American Philosophical Quarterly* 34 (1997): 193-211.

My central claim is that even some of the most ardent defenders of the CA are often too pessimistic or timid about the kind of being the argument rationally supports. In so doing, they come under the influence of Hume's ghost. Even though various CAs have been revived in recent years, "Hume's stopper"—articulated in his *Dialogues Concerning Natural Religion*—still restrains many philosophers from drawing robust metaphysical implications from their CAs (even though Hume spent more time targeting design arguments than CAs). Some defenders of some versions of the CA often demur at saying that the argument establishes (1) a singular being, (2) a personal being, (3) an omnipotent being or (4) a being who still exists and always will exist. I will address each one in turn, paying more careful attention to points 3 and 4, since less work has been done on them than on points 1 and 2. I will also briefly address some of the logical relationships that emerge between CAs and other kinds of theistic arguments.

DIVINE SINGULARITY AND THE COSMOLOGICAL ARGUMENT

Dallas Willard—who argues for the existence of a nonphysical, originating cause outside of the physical universe—claims that his argument allows for the existence of either an "uncaused being or *beings*."[5] Willard is content, however, that his argument overthrows naturalism and thereby gives us an "ontologically haunted" physical universe that opens conceptual space for theism, as well as for the two other stages of his theistic argument.[6] He here echoes Hume's argument that there may be more than one deity responsible for the universe. Hume was principally addressing the design argument, but the point still stands.[7]

What of Willard's claim that his CA allows for more than one "uncaused being"? Without going into the details of his version, there appear to be two mutually reinforcing responses available to deflate this polytheistic possibility. First, on theoretical grounds, simplicity is typically preferred over complexity with respect to explanation, unless complexity is otherwise warranted. To invoke Ockham's razor, we should not multiply explanatory entities unnecessarily. Therefore, the conclusion that there is one CNB is to

---

[5]Dallas Willard, "The Three-Stage Argument for the Existence of God," in *Contemporary Perspectives on Religious Epistemology*, ed. R. Douglas Geivett and Brandan Sweetman (New York: Oxford University Press, 1992), p. 207; emphasis added. Willard fails to argue why there may be more than one uncaused being; he simply asserts it.

[6]Willard, "Three-Stage Argument," pp. 207-8.

[7]See David Hume, *Dialogues Concerning Natural Religion*, part 5 (see chap. 1 n. 9 and chap. 3 n. 4 for two of the many editions available).

be preferred to the idea that there are more than one, unless there is some overriding reason to posit multiple entities.[8]

The rejection of multiple creators can also find assistance in a successful design argument. Swinburne argues that Hume's objection that there may be many designers instead of one designer seems to break on the rocks of the regularity and unity of the universe, which is more simply and better explained on the basis of one designer, not many finite designers. The latter would be far less likely to cooperate to the degree required to produce the kind of universe we observe.[9] In any event, Willard's ready capitulation to the possibility of polytheism seems entirely unwarranted.[10]

THE CREATION: EVENT CAUSATION OR PERSONAL CAUSATION?

Willard and others also express doubts as to whether or not this self-existent, antecedently existing being is personal.[11] (Willard argues for ex nihilo creation, not merely that the CNB eternally supports the contingent cosmos.) The CNB, for Willard, is immaterial and originating, but may not be personal (given the resources of a CA standing alone). But what is the alternative to a personal being? That would be an *im*personal being, a being that lacks (at least) conscious agency. I take it that agency requires (at minimum) will, understanding and the power to bring about one's will. Again, I do not share Willard's restrictions for the following reasons.

Before the existence of the universe only the CNB existed; then the contingent universe existed as the result of the nature and action of the CNB. How could this be explained if not by the action of an agent, a being who consciously and willfully brings about actions? The most likely other candidate would be an abstract object or platonic form or universal, since these are taken to be immaterial and to exist by necessity. However one parses

---

[8]Some might worry that this argument brings into question the Christian doctrine of the Trinity, which is more complex than a strict unitarian view of monotheism. A quick response is that trinitarianism posits one God in three persons, not three necessary beings. Moreover, the idea of the Trinity does much philosophical work in Christian apologetics, such as providing an ontological grounding for the worth and reality of personal relationships. For some helpful thinking on the coherence of the Trinity philosophically, see Thomas D. Senor, "The Incarnation and the Trinity," in *Reason for the Hope Within,* ed. Michael J. Murray (Grand Rapids: Eerdmans, 1999), pp. 252-60.

[9]See Richard Swinburne, *The Existence of God,* rev. ed. (New York: Oxford University Press, 1991), pp. 141-42.

[10]Richard Swinburne argues against the possibility of multiple *omnipotent* creators in *The Existence of God,* p. 156. This section has only addressed the possibility of several finite creators.

[11]I here invoke Alvin Plantinga's shorthand phrase: the theistic God may be *more* than personal—in the human sense—but not less than personal.

the ontology (or questions the existence) of such abstract objects, they lack causal powers. The number seven, taken platonically, causes nothing. Neither do propositions (platonically conceived) produce states of affairs outside of themselves. These entities may be instantiated in beliefs, utterances and sentences, but they do not originate anything. Therefore, they seem to make poor candidates for causal support of the entire universe (whatever other relationship they may or may not have with the physical and nonphysical world).[12]

But one may say there is another ontological category besides conscious agency or abstract objects that fits the description of a CNB. If the universe were brought forth by an impersonal CNB, the notion of divine agency or creation would be denied. If the universe exists due to the fact of an impersonal CNB, that being's existence would be the cause of the cosmos in the sense that the wind (impersonally and automatically) causes the tree branches to shake when the proper conditions obtain. This sense of causation lacks agency. It is mechanical or automatic, not personal.

If the creation ex nihilo is not the result of conscious agency, it must be the result of an impersonal process or mechanism of some sort. The best category to account for this is event causation (the wind moving the branches), since the categories of personal or impersonal causation exhaust the possibilities. But it seems that the proper explanation for the origination of the universe is something more like personal causation involving an agent rather than event causation. Our examples of event causation always involve antecedent and contingent causal conditions, whereas ex nihilo creation does not. Instances of personal agency always grant the person some vital and determinative role in the actions it brings about.[13] Since creation ex nihilo is the absolute beginning of a causal chain (and not one event in a line of causes and effects), and given our understanding of personal agents as unique initiators in some sense, viewing the CNB as a personal agent better comports with our experience of finite beings bringing about states of affairs through their personal understanding, will and power.

In light of all this, if one is going to grant the existence of an immaterial

---

[12]See William Lane Craig, "Design and the Cosmological Argument," in *Mere Creation*, ed. William Dembski (Downers Grove, Ill: InterVarsity Press, 1998), pp. 335-37.
[13]I don't think we need to solve the compatiblist/libertarian debate with respect to human agency to grant my point, although some would disagree and claim that one must opt for libertarianism. See J. P. Moreland, "The Explanatory Relevance of Libertarian Agency as a Model of Theistic Design," in *Mere Creation*, ed. William Dembski (Downers Grove, Ill: InterVarsity Press, 1998), pp. 265-88.

and causally necessary being outside of the contingent cosmos, it seems overly scrupulous to hesitate to ascribe (at least) conscious agency to this being in order to best explain the act of creation ex nihilo.[14] Although arguments for divine personality usually emerge in design arguments (since they speak of specific patterns of cosmic design and the Mind supposedly behind them), in moral arguments (since they speak of a law-giver behind our moral sense), and in religious experience arguments (if they claim a personal being is sometimes veridically experienced), the ascription of personal agency and agent causation is appropriate for CAs as well on the sheer basis of agency as the best explanation for ex nihilo creation.[15] (Yet even if my— or every—argument for personal agency fails on the basis of creation ex nihilo [alone], claims for divine personality can be advanced through these other theistic arguments.)

Omnipotence and the Cosmological Argument

Omnipotence: Power to act. Several contemporary Christian philosophers seem haunted by Hume's claim that the universe could never supply evidence for an omnipotent being, since we can only infer from the finite effect the power (and knowledge) requisite for that effect, which would always be finite.[16] We need to distinguish two basic forms of the CA in order to determine whether or not the argument can deliver an omnipotent being. Charles Taliaferro rightly claims that CAs concern both the *horizontal* and *vertical* principles of explanation concerning contingent existence. The horizontal aspects trace the existence of something back in history to its temporal origin. The vertical dimension concerns the constellation of factors that keep something in existence in the present, such as the proper environment, the functioning of the entities' constituent parts, and more.[17]

The vertical form of the CA can be traced back to Aristotle and Aquinas, and has been presented more recently by Richard Taylor.[18] This argument,

---

[14]Moreover, as Swinburne has argued, personal explanation has a philosophically legitimate place in cosmology over and above the functioning of scientific laws. See *The Existence of God*, pp. 20-21, 32-42, 45-48, 57-64, 293-97.

[15]For a developed argument for "the personhood of the first cause," see David Braine, *The Reality of Time and the Existence of God: The Project of Proving God's Existence* (Oxford: Clarendon, 1988), pp. 266-96. I have not relied on Braine's arguments in this section, however.

[16]Hume, *Dialogues,* part 5.

[17]Charles Taliaferro, *Contemporary Philosophy of Religion* (Malden, Mass.: Blackwell, 1998), p. 354.

[18]Richard Taylor, *Metaphysics,* 4th ed. (Englewood Cliffs, N.J.: Prentice-Hall, 1992), pp. 99-116.

broadly stated, claims that the universe as a whole is contingent or ontologically dependent on something outside of itself that is not itself contingent but self-existent. The existence of this contingent universe implies or is best explained by a noncontingent or causally necessary being.[19] However, this CNB may be coeternal with the universe. In this construal, "creation" does not mean absolute origination out of nothing, but ontological priority and primacy. That is, without this being there could be no contingent universe. However, this version of the CA does not claim that the contingent universe has its temporal origin in this being's act of creation. This argument does not directly support the doctrine of absolute origination or creation ex nihilo. Aquinas, for instance, thought that temporal ex nihilo creation could be rationally believed by faith through revelation, but that it could not be established by reason alone apart from that divine disclosure.

But would this CNB be omnipotent? It does not seem that the vertical CA can establish such a conclusion easily. The claim is that the universe eternally coexists with and depends upon a CNB. In this case, the CNB's possession of causal necessity can only entail that the CNB is the cause (understood as support) of all contingent existence; it does not demonstrate that the CNB's power extends beyond what that being has eternally caused. The possession of unique causal necessity demands that no other entity be noncontingent, but it does not seem to demand that this singular noncontingent being be omnipotent, since that concept entails the ability to create ex nihilo. The power a CNB possesses could conceivably be less than maximal even though it is the only being possessing self-existence. Hence, a CNB who eternally coexists with a universe that the CNB "creates" has not demonstrated the power to create the universe ex nihilo. All that this kind of CA would *prove* would be the CNB's power to sustain eternally the universe (everything outside of the CNB itself). But this doesn't mean that the CNB

---

[19]Causally necessary should be distinguished from logically necessary. The latter means that it is logically impossible for God not to exist. The former means that the universe cannot exist apart from God, who exists *a se* or noncontingently. This kind of self-existence does not necessarily imply the kind of logical necessity implied by an ontological argument, but seems compatible with it, nevertheless. So, when I refer to a causally necessary being, I am not ruling out the possibility that God is a logically necessary being as well. (In fact, I think God does exist according to the mode of logical necessity.) But it seems that a casually necessary being is all a successful CA can deliver rationally. Hume attacked the notion of a necessary being in the *Dialogues* in part 9. However, Hume did not make the important distinction between a *causally* necessary being and a *logically* necessary being. For a critique of his views of necessity, see Keith Yandell, "David Hume on Meaning, Verification and Natural Theology," chapter 4 in this volume.

so proven *must* lack the (counterfactual) power to create ex nihilo (call that power "exnihilation"). It could be that God simply failed to exercise this power for some reason not issuing from metaphysical weakness.[20] If this CNB exists, it would necessarily have the greatest amount of power in existence, but it would not necessarily possess maximal power, since it has not demonstrated such power by creating ex nihilo. We might, though, coherently and plausibly imagine a possible world in which this same being would create ex nihilo. In other words, while exnihilation is *consistent* with the CNB of the vertical argument, it is not *entailed* or even *strongly supported* by it.

In discussing what he calls the "generic CA" (GCA), Stephen T. Davis claims that this argument, "even if it is an entirely successful theistic proof, does not necessarily prove the existence of the God of theism—unique, all-powerful, all-knowing, loving, etc." However, he does grant that if such an argument works, "it certainly does prove the existence of some sort of divine reality or necessary being [NB]." This NB is one that "(1) is everlasting; there is no moment when it does not exist; and (2) depends for its existence on no other being. In some strong sense of the word 'cannot,' a NB cannot not exist."[21] Davis seems to focus his attention on the vertical version of the CA, as opposed to the horizontal form of the argument, which would establish the CNB as the absolute originator of the universe ex nihilo. However, in connection with the GCA he claims that "we do not know that the universe—physical reality—is everlasting. Indeed, all indications are that it began at the big bang some 6.5 billion years ago (or whenever it occurred)."[22] So, Davis seems to say that even if we can establish that the universe was created ex nihilo by a NB, this does not mean the God of the GCA is "all-powerful." Similarly, William C. Davis claims that "the skeptic can admit that a personal cause of the universe is required without conceding that the God of standard theism exists. The finitely powerful deistic god might be thought sufficient for the narrow task of initiating the sequence of causes."[23]

---

[20]I grant, however, that if both the universe and the CNB have *always* existed, it seems difficult to conceptualize how the CNB could have "decided" not to create ex nihilo.
[21]Stephen T. Davis, "The Cosmological Argument and the Epistemic Status of Belief in God," *Philosophia Christi*, n.s. 1 (1999): 6.
[22]Ibid., p. 13.
[23]William C. Davis, "Theistic Arguments," in *Reason for the Hope Within*, ed. Michael J. Murray (Grand Rapids: Eerdmans, 1999), p. 25. I take Davis to be referring to absolute origination (since he speaks of "*initiating* a series of causes" as opposed to "*supporting* a series of causes"), but this is not entirely clear from the context.

I question this position on the basis of what creation ex nihilo implies about the act of creation and thus the nature of the Actor. One can plausibly argue that if a being possesses causal necessity and self-existence (aseity), and has wrought creation ex nihilo, that being would very likely be unlimited in power. This directly follows from two considerations. First, it seems difficult to imagine a greater expenditure of power than the act of absolute origination or initiation, that of creating the entire universe out of nothing by one's unique action without external assistance. Thus, a fortiori, an exnihilating being's power would admit of no limits, outside those of logic itself (which are not limits in a restrictive sense but are rather invariant conditions for intelligibility and actuality). Crudely put, if a weight lifter can bench press three hundred pounds, all things being equal, he can bench press one hundred pounds. So also, if a CNB creates the universe in all its glory ex nihilo (and is personal, as I argued above), and since exnihiliation is the unique and incomparable exertion of power, there seems to be no reason to believe this being could not perform miracles,[24] bring about its desired ends in history or re-create the universe in the future—some of the more salient requirements of omnipotence.

One might argue against this by claiming that the exnihiliation of our universe does not warrant ascribing omnipotence, since we can imagine another created universe that would require a greater exertion of power than this universe requires. While one can debate whether the CNB could have created—or was under any kind of moral obligation to create—a *better* universe, the notion of a universe requiring the exertion of more divine *power* seems problematic. One can conceive of different configurations for the universe, but this does not imply that a CNB would have expended more *power* in creating such. What aspects of a hypothetical universe would make it metaphysically tougher to create than this one? This seems difficult to answer. Considerations of size or weight or complexity don't seem to apply to such concerns, given the vast configuration of the actual universe. William Davis to the contrary, this act of "initiating the sequence of causes" is hardly "narrow" with respect to divine exnihilating power. In fact, it is difficult if not impossible to imagine a broader scope of power than the creation of the sui generis universe ex nihilo. And, as I will mention below, if the CNB con-

---

[24]I am here assuming that the arguments claming that miracles are logically impossible fail. Even Hume's objections to miracles did not assert that they were metaphysically impossible for a Creator to perform. The epistemological question of recognizing or being justified in believing that a particular miracle occurred is beside the point here.

tinues to uphold or support the existence of the universe, the "narrowness" of its power is further questioned.

A second response to this argument against grounding omnipotence in ex nihilo creation might be given. Let us assume for the sake of argument (and despite the argument just given above) that it is coherent to think that there is a universe "harder" to create than the one the CNB created. Even so, in light of the CNB's exnihilating power and the shape of the actual universe, we could well imagine a possible world in which the CNB has the capacity to create a world requiring more power (if there is such a world) if the CNB had chosen to do so. This idea flows from the notion that exnihilation itself is an unrivaled exercise of power; therefore, if the CNB can exnihilate our world, why not a "harder" one?[25]

From a different perspective, if recent fine-tuning (or strong anthropic) design arguments are correct, the existence of human and other forms of life demonstrates the way the universe could not have been very much different in its laws and processes from how it in fact is.[26] Therefore, one can argue that the exertion of divine exnihiliating *power* was consonant with the divine *knowledge* and *wisdom* in creating conditions hospitable for life. But pursuing this would take us too far into the design arguments and the related problem of evil (although design arguments come up again in a slightly different context below). However, the essential idea indicates that a CNB's exertion of exnihiliating power might be calibrated to the production and continuation of life, including human life. In that case, a greater expenditure of power (if it could occur) might be at odds with the CNB's other concerns about the flourishing of human life.

A second consideration is that such an exnihilating being would be *uniquely* causally necessary and self-existent (or noncontingent), since it alone precedes the existence of the contingent universe and thus is unlimited by any external factors (although this being might freely place certain restrictions upon itself). Such a noncontingent being would be incapable of losing its noncontingent status since, by definition, it depends on nothing

---

[25]Exnihilation seems to be a greater expenditure of power than upholding the universe eternally; if so, one would be more warranted in giving the benefit of the doubt that a exnihilating being could create a "harder universe" than in believing that a CNB that eternally upholds the universe "could have" created it ex nihilo.

[26]See Robin Collins, "A Scientific Argument for the Existence of God: The Fine-Tuning Design Argument," in *Reason for the Hope Within*, ed. Michael J. Murray (Grand Rapids: Eerdmans, 1999), pp. 47-75; "Hume, Fine-Tuning, and the 'Who Designed God?' Objection," chapter 9 in this volume; Swinburne, *The Existence of God*, pp. 300-322.

outside itself for its existence. Nothing, then, could threaten its ontology. (I return to this in the "Divine Persistence" section below.) And if this incorrigibly noncontingent being has created ex nihilo, there seems to be nothing logically possible it could not accomplish at any point even after creation, since an exnihilating and self-existent being could suffer no diminution of the already maximal power it has indicated by the act of universe-making.

It should be granted, though, that in one sense omnipotence—which is a difficult concept to define in the first place—cannot be absolutely demonstrated or exemplified by any action, since one might at least imagine another action requiring more power, which the agent lacks. However, I think William Lane Craig's comments are on mark: "A being with the power to create the entire universe out of nothing not only meets the biblical requirements for being almighty, but the consensus of church theologians has also been that ex nihilo creation is a power belonging to God alone."[27] Claiming that this being is omnipotent as well seems rationally justified, although it may be too much to claim that omnipotence is logically *entailed* by ex nihilo creation. Nevertheless, it seems to be the best explanation for the facts at hand. (This would be no small victory for Christian apologetics. Someone who is convinced through natural theology that it is likely that God is omnipotent is in a good epistemic position to investigate the specifically biblical claims concerning God's omnipotence where one may find further evidence from Scripture itself to support that claim.)

But this argument for the omnipotence of a self-existent and causally necessary being would likely only apply to CAs that claim that the CNB not only causes the existence of the contingent universe by upholding it, but also created the universe from nothing. In other words, this kind of CA goes beyond arguing from the present existence of a contingent universe to the existence of a CNB who has always existed along with the universe. Neither Taylor nor Aquinas, for instance, argues for the temporal origin of the universe, but others using such strategies such as (but not limited to) the *kalam* CA have done so.[28]

Moreover, if any being exercises exnihilating power, then that being must be self-existent, because the act of bringing the universe into existence from

[27]William Lane Craig, "Closing Remarks," in *Five Views of Apologetics*, ed. Steven Cowan (Grand Rapids: Zondervan, 2000), p. 323.
[28]For a recent formulation of the *kalam* CA, see William Lane Craig, "The Kalam Cosmological Argument," in *Philosophy of Religion: A Reader and Guide*, ed. William Lane Craig (New Brunswick, N.J.: Rutgers University Press, 2002), pp. 92-113. Craig has been strenuously presenting and defending this argument for more than twenty-five years in various forums.

nothing eliminates the possibility of the exnihilating agent being dependent on anything extrinsic to itself, precisely because there was nothing in existence prior to creation on which that being depended. Therefore, the concept of exnihilation analytically contains the concept of self-existence; but the concept of self-existence does not analytically contain the concept of exnihilation, although the concept of self-existence allows for the possibility that the self-existent being could also create ex nihilo.

To sum up, a cosmologically established deity may be self-existent and lack the power to create ex nihilo, if all that the CA establishes is eternal "creation" understood as ontological support. Nevertheless, the deity argued for from an ex nihilo CA may both be self-existent and possess exnihilating power. In this case, the being would be unlimited in power.

Omniscience: Power to know. Stephen Davis's doubts that the GCA can establish an "all-knowing being" would be assuaged if omnipotence is strongly implied by ex nihilo creation, since an all-powerful being would seem to be an all-knowing being as well (since knowing is a kind of power)—assuming that a good case can be made that the CNB is personal (see above). Persons are knowers. If the Creator knows how to bring the universe into existence out of nothing, it is not a great leap of logic to claim this being knows much more besides (perhaps everything).

But CAs may receive a metaphysical assist from any successful design argument on this point as well. If the universe reveals the existence of a Mind behind it, this Mind certainly would have the knowledge and wisdom required to design the cosmos and to keep it from devolving into chaos. While design arguments in themselves cannot specify the degree of knowledge the designing mind possesses, that knowledge would be considerable (at least fantastically greater than any intelligence we encounter in the empirical world) given the extent and intricacies of the universe. But if the designing mind is the same being as the being who brought the universe into existence out of nothing,[29] it seems a rational explanation to grant this designing and exnihilating being the property of omniscience. One might also ask, What other act of cosmological creation and design could give better evidence for omniscience?[30] Given these considerations, it seems that knowing is a power

---

[29]The singularity of God was briefly argued for above, so there is no need to separate the God who designs and the God who creates, Hume to the contrary.

[30]One can provide some evidence for God's omniscience from the fulfillment of prophecy as recorded in the Bible (special revelation), but this takes us outside of what natural theology can accomplish.

that an omnipotent CNB would possess to the maximal degree, since this power would appear to be no less metaphysically strenuous than creating our kind of universe from nothing by divine and personal fiat.[31] As argued above with respect to the cosmological argument for omnipotence, this seems to be the best explanation for the facts at hand, but falls short of an entailment.

DIVINE PERSISTENCE AND THE COSMOLOGICAL ARGUMENT

Dallas Willard also maintains that his CA

> doesn't show that the uncaused being or beings which lie at the foundation of the world-causal series still exist—though certainly, we would like to know of any reason, beyond the mere empty logical possibility which might be offered, for them ceasing to exist. (Admittedly, their not being dependent and contingent in the sense of physical states and events does not immediately imply inability to dissipate themselves in some fashion.)[32]

Having briefly addressed the singularity concern earlier, we will assess the anxiety that the CNB might cease to exist. Willard is again, it seems, haunted by the ghost of Hume, who remarked that the originator of our world, being finite, might have died by now.[33] Willard is concerned about the "logical possibility" that the being might somehow "dissipate" itself. Contingent beings may destroy themselves by suicide or other (less dramatic) means. That is, through their own agency they may cause themselves to cease to exist as physical, living beings.[34] But could a noncontingent, self-existent being accomplish such a thing? This would mean exercising agency over its own properties such that all of these properties cease to exist. This would, it may be argued, make its constituting properties contingent, since they may cease to exist. Yet if they ceased to exist, they would not be causally necessary, metaphysically independent and self-existent properties.[35] A contingent being, on the other hand, may un-

---

[31]I leave aside the question of whether omniscience entails the knowledge of counterfactuals, the future actions of libertarian agents, etc. Whatever maximal knowledge is, a CNB would, I claim, possess that degree of knowledge. Biblical theists will parse this out in light of the biblical claims made on behalf of God's knowledge. However, I favor the classic view of omniscience wherein God possesses certain knowledge of the truth values of all propositions, past, present and future.

[32]Willard, "Three-Stage Argument," p. 207.

[33]Hume, *Dialogues*, section 5.

[34]This does not mean that a human being can cause himself to cease to exist as a spiritual being. The religions asserting the existence and immortality of the soul deny this.

[35]Stephen Davis concurs: "In some strong sense of the word 'cannot,' a NB [necessary being]

dercut the conditions necessary to its own survival (by depriving itself of oxygen or nourishment, for instance), but a noncontingent being is, as Willard puts it, "self-subsistent."[36]

One might argue that if a noncontingent being lacks the power to dissipate itself, it cannot be omnipotent, since omnipotence entails the power to do anything. Surely, a fortiori, if a mere finite, contingent being can destroy itself, how much more should an infinitely powerful being be capable of committing a deicide of some sort? If such is possible, it might be actual. Therefore, the CA does not guarantee a presently existing being. The agent who pushed the first domino in a long line of them (leading up to the present) may have expired after some period of time. Or it may expire at some point in the future. The universe may be holding its breath, so to speak, awaiting the potential suicide of such a deity.

However, this objection misunderstands the concept of omnipotence. Omnipotence does not entail the actualization of logically impossible conditions, such as square circles, objects that are smaller than they are, parts that are larger than the whole and so on. According to my analysis, the concept of a CNB *logically* precludes that this being would be capable of dissipating itself, because this would entail that the causally necessary becomes contingent (and nonexistent). The fact that humans can dissipate themselves fails to render them ontologically superior to a noncontingent being. This is because self-dissipation is no virtue (morally or metaphysically); it is not a power to be valued or a power greater than exnihilation or impeccable, incorrigible self-existence. It is a power only in a very negative or degenerative sense—the power to destroy oneself. It can find no place in the nature of a CNB.

But there is another reason why the CA need not fear the (nonmetaphorical) "death of God." Even if one thinks that it is logically possible for the CNB to "dissipate itself" (or somehow to pop out of existence for some other reason), if the universe *continues* to exist as a contingent entity, then it *continues* to require the existence of a noncontingent source of its existence. This would rule out the idea that the CNB may have already ex-

---

cannot not exist." He also says that contingent beings, "unlike NBs, can fail to exist." See Davis, "Cosmological Argument," p. 6 n. 5. Davis seems to be saying that if a NB exists, it cannot fail to exist. In the context of his paper on CAs, he grounds the NB's incorrigibility on factors intrinsic to CAs, not ontological arguments, which argue that God's existence is logically necessary. So, I take it that what Davis means by a NB, is what I mean by a CNB.
[36]Willard, "Three-Stage Argument," p. 207.

pired. We might imagine the agent who pushed the first domino as ceasing to exist while the dominoes continue to fall (despite my criticisms above), but this is only part of the story of the CA. The *vertical* dimension of the CA concerns the ensemble of factors that conserve something in existence. As Aquinas put it at the conclusion of his second argument for God's existence: "Nothing can remain in being when the divine activity ceases."[37] More positively, the claim is that no contingent state of affairs can continue to exist without the divine activity of conserving or preserving its existence.[38]

The absolute origination or ex nihilo CA claims that the CNB is the temporal first cause of all that exists outside the CNB. However, a doubly powerful CA can and should also insist that the existence of a contingent universe requires the existence of the CNB at the present moment in order for the contingent cosmos to *remain* in existence. One way of conceptualizing this is to say that if the CNB willed the universe not to exist, the CNB would remain a noncontingent, extant being. However, if (*per impossibile*, as I have argued) the CNB were to cease to exist, the universe would cease to exist as well, since it *perpetually* depends on the existence of the CNB. The existence of the CNB and the universe are, in this sense, metaphysically asymmetrical. Since the contingent cosmos continues to exist, we know that the CNB continues to exist. Therefore, the CNB's creation of the universe is different from an artist's creation of an artifact, which can exist apart from the artist after it has been created.

Although the absolute origination or horizontal CA has some stronger metaphysical implications than the vertical version (as argued above), the vertical version of the CA does move from the present contingency of the universe to the present existence of a CNB at this moment. Without the assistance of the absolute origination CA, the vertical argument alone entails the present contingency of the universe on a CNB as an eternally occurring state of affairs. But one could combine the horizontal argument with the vertical argument to reach the conclusion that the CNB both sustains and originated the world. Therefore, the two strands of argument—horizontal and vertical—are not incompatible, so long as the absolute origination CA does not undercut the argument that the universe continues to need the CNB as

---

[37]*Summa contra gentiles* 3.65; cited in Taliaferro, *Contemporary Philosophy of Religion*, p. 354.
[38]For an analysis and defense of this thesis, see Frank McCann, "Divine Conservation," in *Guide to the Philosophy of Religion*, ed. Phillip L. Quinn and Charles Taliaferro (New York: Blackwell, 1997), pp. 306-12.

its present ontological support (or for its conservation).[39]

Conclusion: Some Rich Metaphysical Implications

I have argued that a successful CA strongly suggests some rich metaphysical implications, far richer than Hume allowed and richer than those still haunted by his ghost will yet allow. A CNB would be singular, personal, omnipotent and incorrigibly existent (not subject to dissipation or diminution). (This conclusion also receives intellectual support from other theistic arguments.) These divine attributes by no means encompass the full panoply of attributes of the God of Christian theism (and they imply nothing directly about the incarnation), but they are necessary for Christian theism and not insignificant metaphysically or existentially in their own right.[40] Since the CA is only one of several theistic arguments, other divine attributes could be established through other arguments. If a general, but metaphysically robust, theism can be rendered cogent by these arguments, one would have intellectual justification, in addition, to consider the Bible as a possible source of further information—special revelation—about the character and actions of God.[41] One might also be more inclined to seek religious experiences which could contribute to the overall case for a specifically Christian theism, assuming that the CNB is capable of granting such experiences, which seems likely given this being's personal and powerful nature.[42]

---

[39]See also Swinburne's discussion of the impossibility of divine suicide in *The Existence of God*, pp. 96-97.

[40]On some of the existential and spiritual entailments of successful natural theology, see Douglas Groothuis, "Are Theistic Arguments Religiously Useless? A Pascalian Objection Examined," *Trinity Journal*, n.s. 15 (1994): 147-61.

[41]Richard Swinburne uses this argumentative structure in *Revelation* (New York: Oxford University Press, 1992).

[42]My thanks go to James Sennett, Timothy McGrew, Rebecca Merrill Groothuis, Stanley Obitts and David Werther for their helpful comments on earlier versions of this chapter. Any defects remaining should be credited to me, not them.

7

HUME AND THE *KALAM* COSMOLOGICAL ARGUMENT

Garrett J. DeWeese and
Joshua Rasmussen

𝕯

The *kalam* cosmological argument is a member of a family of "cosmological arguments," all of which share a similar structure. In this essay we distinguish the *kalam* from other members of the family and present the argument itself. We then respond to two significant Humean-style objections to the argument, one stemming from Hume's views on causation and the other from what James Sennett has called "Hume's stopper,"[1] the contention that even if successful, the argument cannot conclude that anything like the Christian God exists. We conclude that a version of the *kalam* argument can be offered that is impervious to such objections.

COSMOLOGICAL ARGUMENTS

Cosmological arguments share a similar structure. Beginning with a premise that something of a certain type exists, the argument proceeds via some key principle to the conclusion that something of a very different type exists, a type so different that it must be God. That is,

A. Something with a certain property ϕ exits.
B. The explanation, reason or cause of the existence of ϕ things cannot be another ϕ thing.
C. Therefore, there exists something with property θ, which is the explanation, reason or cause of ϕ things.

---

[1] See chapter 5 of the present volume.

D. Property θ is such that it can only be exemplified by a divine being.

E. Therefore, God exists.

Members of the cosmological argument family differ with respect to the property φ in step A, with respect to the principle invoked in step B and with respect to the property or set of properties θ of steps C and D, which lead to the desired conclusion.

The cosmological argument dates at least to Plato.[2] In its history three versions have emerged as prominent: The first claims the impossibility of an essentially ordered infinite regression. In this version, property φ involves motion, contingency or causality, and concludes that property θ is that of being the prime mover, necessary being[3] or first cause. The arguments of Plato,[4] Aristotle,[5] Thomas Aquinas[6] and John Duns Scotus[7] are examples of this version.

The second version claims that property φ is that of requiring an explanation or reason for the existence of a thing, and property θ is that of being the self-explaining sufficient reason. This version is associated with Benedict Spinoza,[8] Gottfried Wilhelm Leibniz,[9] and Samuel Clarke.[10]

The third version is the *kalam* cosmological argument (KCA), the subject of this chapter. The key claim of KCA is that φ is the universe's having a

[2]For a history of the cosmological argument, see William Lane Craig, *The Cosmological Argument from Plato to Leibniz* (New York: Harper and Row, 1980; reprint, Eugene, Ore.: Wipf and Stock, 2001).

[3]Species of this type of cosmological argument can be subdivided by the sort of necessary being involved. The necessary being may be broadly logically necessary (exists in all possible worlds), causally necessary (exists as the first eternal cause in every world in which it exists) or factually necessary (exists as the first eternal cause in the actual world).

[4]Plato *Laws* 10.884-899d.

[5]Aristotle gives his argument in several places; for example, *Physics* 8.1-6.250b5-260a15.

[6]Although he offers the argument in several places, the best known is found in the first three of Thomas's famous Five Ways; St. Thomas Aquinas *Summa theologiae* 1a, 2-11.

[7]Scotus's modal argument is probably best seen as an example of this version. John Duns Scotus *Opus oxoniense* 1.2.1 in *Philosophical Writings*, trans. Allan Wolter (Indianapolis: Hackett, 1987), pp. 35-52.

[8]Benedict de Spinoza *Ethic* 1.16-17; Scholium, in *Central Readings in the History of Modern Philosophy*, ed. Robert Cummins and David Owen (Belmont, Calif.: Wadsworth, 1992), pp. 46-48.

[9]G. W. Leibniz, *Theodicy: Essays on the Goodness of God, the Freedom of Man, and the Origin of Evil*, trans. E. M. Huggard (London: Routledge & Kegan Paul, 1951), p. 127. Leibniz further defends his argument in several key places in his correspondence with Clarke.

[10]Samuel Clarke, *A Demonstration of the Being and Attributes of God*, reprinted in *Sixteen Sermons on the Being and Attributes of God, the Obligations of Natural Religion, and the Truth and Certainty of the Christian Revelation*, vol. 2 of *The Works of Samuel Clarke* (New York: Garland, 1978).

temporal beginning, but since an infinite temporal series is impossible, θ is the property of not having had a temporal beginning, i.e., of being eternal. KCA seems to have been discovered by medieval Arabic philosophers; indeed, the name *kalam* is an Arabic word from the root for "talk, discussion," which came to be used for one school of medieval Islamic philosophy.[11] KCA is found in the writings of the Islamic philosophers al-Kindi, al-Farabi, Avicenna (ibn Sina), al-Ghazali and Averroës (ibn Rushd),[12] as well as the Jewish philosophers Saadia and Maimonides.[13] Contemporary defenders include William Lane Craig[14] and J. P. Moreland.[15]

The three versions can likewise be distinguished by the basic principle that is centrally employed in premise B. Version 1 arguments invoke a principle of causality (PC), version 2 arguments invoke a principle of sufficient reason (PSR), and version 3 *(kalam)* arguments invoke a principle of determination (PD).[16] Roughly, and subject to qualifications that we will suggest below, the principles may be stated as follows:

PC: Every contingent thing has a cause.

PSR: Every true proposition that entails the existence of some contingent object has a sufficient reason why it is true.

PD: If two qualitatively identical states of affairs are complementary (that is, mutually exclusive: if one obtains, the other cannot at the same time), the obtaining of one rather than the other is due to the will of a free agent.

We shall largely ignore the contingency (Thomistic) and the sufficient rea-

---

[11]William Lane Craig, *The Kalam Cosmological Argument* (New York: Macmillan, 1979; reprint, Eugene, Ore.: Wipf and Stock, 2000), p. 4. Craig notes that the Islamic theologians refer to the early Christian theologian John Philoponus (d. 580?), as a precursor of the *kalam* style of argument against an eternal universe (pp. 8-9).

[12]See Craig, *Cosmological Argument,* chap. 3, for references. For al-Ghazali's argument, see *The Incoherence of the Philosophers,* First Discussion, First Proof, trans. Michael E. Marmura (Provo, Utah: Brigham Young University Press, 2000), pp. 12-30.

[13]See Craig, *Cosmological Argument,* chap. 4, for references.

[14]Craig, *Kalam Cosmological Argument;* and William Lane Craig and Quentin Smith, *Theism, Atheism and Big Bang Cosmology* (New York: Oxford University Press, 1995). No one in recent time has done more to analyze, present and defend the cosmological argument—especially its *kalam* form—than Craig, and our debt to his work is readily acknowledged.

[15]J. P. Moreland, *Scaling the Secular City: A Defense of Christianity* (Grand Rapids: Baker, 1987), pp. 18-42. See also his "A Response to a Platonistic and a Set-Theoretic Objection to the *Kalam* Cosmological Argument," *Religious Studies* 39 (2003): 373-90

[16]See the discussion in Craig, *Cosmological Argument,* pp. 282-87. The relation between these three principles is not straightforward, and the degree to which they are independent will determine the degree to which the different versions of KCA are genuinely independent arguments.

son (Leibnizian) versions of the cosmological argument and will concentrate
on the KCA.

The *Kalam* Cosmological Argument Stated

A vast literature has accumulated on the KCA, and it is not our present purpose to survey all the turns and twists of the debate concerning the argument or to defend the argument in great detail against general objections.
Our more restricted purpose is to consider and respond to objections offered in the spirit of Hume. Still, we must first lay out the argument and indicate the lines of support for its premises.

The KCA may be roughly stated as follows:

1. The universe began to exist.

2. Whatever begins to exist has a cause of its existence.

3. Therefore the universe has a cause of its existence.

4. The (ultimate) cause of the universe must itself be uncaused.

5. God is the uncaused cause of the existence of the universe.

Premise 1 corresponds to step A of the general form, so *beginning to exist*
is the relevant property ascribed to the universe. But there is more below
the surface than it first appears. Although contemporary defenders of
premise 1 typically point to scientific evidence in its favor, the strength of
these a posteriori arguments for the premise that the universe began to exist
is not certain.

The first line of empirical support for (1) is big bang cosmology. The
outline of the big bang theory is generally well known, and we do not
need to go into any detail here. From the observed red shift of distant gal-
axies, the expansion of the universe may be inferred and the current rate
of expansion calculated. If the universe is expanding, it follows that once
the universe was much smaller than it is now. From the mathematics of
general relativity, it has been shown that the limit is not simply a very small
dense region of space-time, but a singularity—an infinitely dense, dimen-
sionless point. Simply reversing the sign on the value of the coefficient of
expansion—analogous to playing the videotape of the big bang in reverse—it is possible to calculate the time that has elapsed since the initial
singularity.[17] This represents the "beginning of the universe," and offers
empirical confirmation for (1).

---

[17]Even if there was an inflationary epoch in the history of the universe, it was very short-lived
and the age of the universe can be determined with impressive accuracy. The results from

In the last thirty years, however, some dissatisfaction with the big bang model has become evident among cosmologists, and a number of alternative theories have been put on the table. Perhaps the best-known variation is the inflationary universe, proposed by Alan Guth, Andrei Linde and others.[18] Inflationary scenarios are consistent with a big bang and so with a beginning of the universe. Other models, however, are not. The Hartle-Hawking hypothesis,[19] and more recently string theory and M-theory ("brane theory"),[20] spring largely from attempts by theoretical cosmologists to unify general relativity and quantum gravity. These models are empirically equivalent to big bang models, but have certain theoretical advantages over either standard or inflationary big bang models. The important point, though, is that on these alternate models there is no big bang, no absolute beginning for the universe. With the proliferation of such models, the claim that empirical support for (1) is forthcoming from cosmology appears to be weakened.[21]

A second line of empirical support for (1) comes from thermodynamics. According to the second law of thermodynamics, entropy in a closed system

the first year of operation of the Wilkinson Microwave Anisotropy Probe (WMAP), published in early 2003, place the age of the universe at 13.7 ± 0.2 billion years. See C. L. Bennet et al., "'Best' Cosmological Parameters: Table 3," available online at <http://lambda.gsfc.nasa.gov/product/map/pub_papers/firstyear/basic/wmap_params_table.pdf>.

[18]See Alan Guth, *The Inflationary Universe* (Reading, Mass.: Addison-Wesley, 1997).

[19]J. Hartle and S. W. Hawking, "Wave Function of the Universe," *Physical Review D* 28 (1983): 2960-75; Stephen W. Hawking, *A Brief History of Time* (New York: Bantam, 1988), pp. 140-41. See also the discussion in the following papers: William Lane Craig, "'What Place, Then, for a Creator?' Hawking on God and Creation," and Quentin Smith, "The Wave Function of a Godless Universe," both in *Theism, Atheism, and Big Bang Cosmology*, pp. 279-300 and 301-37; William Lane Craig, "Hartle-Hawking Cosmology and Atheism"; Quentin Smith, "Quantum Cosmology's Implication of Atheism"; and Robert J. Delete and Reed A. Guy, "Hartle-Hawking Cosmology and Unconditional Probabilities," all in *Analysis* 57 (1997): 291-95; 295-304; and 304-15.

[20]Paul J. Steinhardt and Neil Turok, "A Cyclic Model of the Universe," *Science* 269 (2002): 1436-39; Gerald B. Cleaver, "String Cosmology: God's Blueprint for the Universe," paper presented at the 2003 Annual Meeting of the American Scientific Affiliation, Lakewood, Colo., available online at <http://www3.baylor.edu/~Gerald_Cleaver/presentations/Page_1x.html>.

[21]James Brian Pitts, "Does the Big Bang Strongly Support Creation *Ex Nihilo*?" paper presented at the 2003 Annual Meeting of the American Scientific Affiliation. See also Robert C. Russell, "T=0: Is it Theologically Significant?" in W. Mark Richardson and Wesley J. Wildman, *Religion and Science: History, Method, Dialogue* (New York: Routledge, 1996), pp. 201-24. We note, however, the argument of Arvind Borde, Alan H. Guth and Alexander Vilenkin, "Inflationary Spacetimes are Incomplete in Past Directions," *Physical Review Letters* 90, 151301 (2003), that neither inflationary models nor "brane" models are past-complete, meaning that these models entail a finite past with a boundary. Our thanks to Luke Van Horn for calling this article to our attention.

tends toward a maximum. Assuming, consistent with all cosmological models, that the universe is finite in size, then if the universe were infinitely old (i.e., had no beginning), entropy would be at a maximum. But clearly that is not the case, so it follows that the universe had a beginning a finite time in the past.

As with the first line of empirical support for (1), this line of support is not as strong as once thought. The work of Boltzmann and Gibbs succeeded in giving thermodynamics a statistical interpretation at the microscopic level, resulting in a probabilistic formulation of the second law.[22] According to the probabilistic formulation, there is always a nonzero, noninfinitesimal probability that, during any given interval, a particular closed system will experience a reverse in entropy.[23] Consequently, the empirical support for (1) offered by the nonmaximum value of entropy in the present universe may be challenged.

The challenges we have mentioned to possible support for (1) from big bang cosmology and the second law of thermodynamics are controversial, and some *kalam* arguers continue to appeal to these scientific claims for empirical support.[24]

Be that as it may, fortunately for the *kalam* arguer, there are stronger lines of support for (1) than empirical observations. Indeed, Craig offers two philosophical arguments in support of (1), either of which, if successful, would prove the logical impossibility that the universe is infinitely old.[25] The first philosophical argument relies on the impossibility that an actual infinite exists, and the second on the impossibility of forming an infinite collection by successive addition. The first may be stated this way:

6. An actual infinite collection cannot exist.

7. An infinite temporal regression of events (or moments) is an actual infinite collection.

8. Therefore an actual temporal regression of events cannot exist.

---

[22]Lawrence Sklar, *Physics and Chance: Philosophical Issues in the Foundations of Statistical Mechanics* (Cambridge: Cambridge University Press, 1993), offers a thorough discussion of the issues.

[23]Hans Reichenbach, *The Direction of Time,* ed. Maria Reichenbach (Berkeley: University of California Press, 1954), pp. 117-43.

[24]As evidenced in two recently published debates: Stan W. Wallace, ed., *Does God Exist? The Craig-Flew Debate* (Aldershot, U.K.: Ashgate, 2003), pp. 19-20, 160-61; William Lane Craig and Walter Sinnot-Armstrong, *God? A Debate Between a Christian and an Atheist* (New York: Oxford University Press, 2004), pp. 2-9.

[25]Craig, *Kalam Cosmological Argument,* pp. 65-110.

From (8), of course, it follows that the universe had a beginning. The support for (6) comes from the logical paradoxes generated when one assumes that an actual infinite collection *can* exist ("Hilbert's Hotel" or "Craig's Library" are standard examples).[26] These paradoxes show that, while the mathematical concept of infinity is well defined and fairly well understood,[27] the existence of an actual collection of concrete objects is impossible. The *kalam* arguer can maintain that temporal moments are concrete entities on either an A- or B-theory of time,[28] so the actual existence of an infinite collection of universals, numbers or propositions (to which a Platonist is committed) will not undercut the support offered for (6) by the paradoxes.[29]

A critic of this argument might note that the series of past events (or moments) is unlike a putative infinite collection, each member of which is actually present at the same time. Consequently, the critic will claim that the absurdities that result from assuming the existence of an actual infinite are irrelevant to (1), since the members of a temporal series (on the A-theory of time) do not exist all at once.

Be that as it may, the second argument says that even if the first argument in support of (1) is wrong—if, that is, an actual infinite collection can exist—the temporal series of events or moments cannot be an infinite collection.

---

[26]"Hilbert's Hotel" comes from the great German mathematician David Hilbert (1862-1943). This paradox imagines a hotel with an infinite number of rooms, all of which are full. Then a tour bus arrives with an infinite number of tourists. Surprisingly, this is no problem for the desk clerk, who simply moves the guest in room #1 to room #2, the one in #2 to #4, and so on, each guest in the already-full hotel being moved from room #n to room #2n. In this way an infinite number of rooms (all the odd-numbered rooms) is opened, and the infinite number of new arrivals is accommodated! But clearly this is absurd, so the premise which generated the absurdity must be rejected, namely, the assumption that there could exist an actual infinite collection (of rooms, in this case). For more details on this and other paradoxes, see, for example, J. P. Moreland and William Lane Craig, *Philosophical Foundations for a Christian Worldview* (Downers Grove, Ill.: InterVarsity Press, 2003), pp. 471-76; Craig, *Kalam Cosmological Argument*, pp 65-102.

[27]For example, in Cantorian transfinite mathematics and the treatment of infinity in Zermelo-Fraenkel set theory.

[28]There are two theories regarding the nature of time. The A-theory ("dynamic" or "tensed" time) holds that time is ordered by the determinations of *past, present* and *future*, while the B-theory ("static" or "tenseless" time) holds that time is ordered by the relations of *earlier than, simultaneous with* and *later than*. A-theorists believe that there is a genuine ontological difference between past and present on one hand, and future on the other, and that temporal becoming is real. B-theorists deny this. They believe that there is no such thing as temporal becoming, and that past, present and future are on an ontological par. For more, see Garrett J. DeWeese, *God and the Nature of Time* (Aldershot, U.K.: Ashgate, 2004).

[29]Ibid., pp. 65-99. See also Moreland, "A Response to a Platonistic and a Set-Theoretic Objection."

9. The temporal series of events (or moments) is a collection formed by successive addition.

10. A collection formed by successive addition cannot be an actual infinite collection.

11. Therefore the temporal series of events cannot be an actual infinite collection.

Craig explains the intuitions behind (9): "The collection of all past events . . . is a collection that is instantiated sequentially or *successively* in time, one event following upon the heels of another."[30] Premise 10 follows directly from the concept of *denumerable infinity* (symbolized $\aleph_0$).[31] For every element one adds to a series, one can always add one more, because $\aleph_0$ has no immediate predecessor.

For this second argument, it is irrelevant whether time is relational or substantial—whether we are assuming the A-theory of time or the B-theory of time. Of course, as with any philosophical argument, objections can be raised against it.[32] Nevertheless, the second argument does seem to be strong, so for present purposes we propose to accept (1), and proceed on the assumption that the universe began to exist.

It is interesting that Hume himself, it seems, would agree with the second argument. In his *Enquiry* he says, "An infinite number of real parts of time, passing in succession, and exhausted one after another, appears so evident a contradiction, that no man, one should think, whose judgment is not corrupted, instead of being improved, by the sciences, would ever be able to admit it."[33]

THE PRINCIPLE OF CAUSALITY AND A FIRST HUMEAN OBJECTION

As we noted, Craig claims that the crucial principle in KCA is the principle of determination, but before getting to that step KCA must invoke a principle of causality (PC). Premise 2 of KCA is the claim that whatever begins to exist has

---

[30]Craig, *Kalam Cosmological Argument,* p. 103.
[31]Denumerable infinity is the cardinal number of the set of natural numbers. In other words, it is the cardinality or total number of any infinite collection that can be *counted*—that can be mapped with a one-to-one correlation onto the set of natural numbers.
[32]See for example the exchanges between Graham Oppy and David Oderberg in *Philosophia Christi,* n.s. 3 (2001): 181-96; and 4 (2002): 303-60.
[33]David Hume, *An Enquiry Concerning Human Understanding,* in *The English Philosophers from Bacon to Mill,* ed. Edwin A. Burtt, The Modern Library (New York: Random House, 1939), 12.2, p. 684.

a cause for its existence. Of course, David Hume is notorious for claiming to be skeptical about causation. He argues that "causation" is a name we apply by habit to events that are contiguous in space and successive in time, and no necessary connection between cause and effect can ever be discovered empirically.[34] This leads Hume to argue that "the general maxim in philosophy, that *whatever begins to exist, must have a cause of existence*," is false.[35]

Clearly if Hume is correct, then (2) is false as well, and not only the KCA but any version of the cosmological argument that employs PC is unsound. Why does Hume believe PC is false? Because his empiricism leads him to reject the notion of causation as a necessary relation. He argues,

> It [the mind] must invent or imagine some event, which it ascribes to the object as its effect; and it is plain that this invention must be entirely arbitrary. The mind can never possibly find the effect in the supposed cause, by the most accurate scrutiny and imagination. For the effect is totally different from the cause, and consequently can never be discovered in it. . . . In vain, therefore, should we pretend to determine any single event, or infer any cause or effect, without the assistance of observation and experience.[36]

It is important to understand that Hume's argument, in spite of appearances, is best understood as an epistemological argument. Hume himself wrote,

> But allow me to tell you that I never asserted so absurd a Proposition as *that anything might arise without a cause:* I only maintain'd, that our Certainty of the Falsehood of that Proposition proceeded neither from Intuition nor Demonstration; but from another Source.[37]

There are several responses open to the *kalam* arguer. First, we might offer a perspicuous account of causation that overcomes Hume's empirical skepticism. We believe such an account is on offer in the work of David Armstrong and Michael Tooley, among others.[38] However, the Armstrong-

---

[34]David Hume, *A Treatise of Human Nature*, 2nd ed., ed. L. A. Selby-Bigge, rev. P. H. Nidditch (Oxford: Clarendon, 1978), 1.3.2, pp. 75-78.

[35]Ibid., 1.3.3, pp. 78-82.

[36]Hume, *Enquiry*, 4.1, pp. 600-601.

[37]In a letter to John Stewart, February 1754, in *The Letters of David Hume*, ed. J. Y. T. Greig (Oxford: Clarendon, 1932), 1:187. The *Treatise* was published in 1739/40.

[38]David M. Armstrong, *What Is a Law of Nature?* (Cambridge: Cambridge University Press, 1983); Michael Tooley, "The Nature of Causation: A Singularist Account," *Canadian Journal of Philosophy*, suppl. 16 (1990): 271-322; *Causation: A Realist Approach* (Oxford: Clarendon, 1987; reprint, 2001).

Tooley analysis of causation depends upon certain metaphysical principles that are not uncontroversial. So we will take another route, which involves us in an examination of various statements of PC, which in turn will lead us to an analysis of various forms of the principle of sufficient reason (PSR). In the end, we believe we can offer an argument that will withstand a Humean critique but remains neutral on certain controversial metaphysical matters.

Causal and explanatory principles. Two broad classes of principles emerge from the history of the cosmological argument: first, there is the class involving efficient *causation,* and second, there is the class involving *explanation,* members of which invoke forms of PSR. Efficient causation can be broadly construed as a kind of relation between things or personal agents, where "things" can refer to states of affairs or events.[39] Causation itself is what "brings about" a change of some sort. We do not need to enter the controversy over what exactly this relation involves and how we are to identify when causal relations obtain; this general definition of causation will suffice for the purpose of evaluating the major principles of efficient causation.

These major principles involving efficient causation that have historically been employed in the cosmological argument are as follows:

PC1: Whatever *changes* has a cause.

PC2: Whatever exists, *but could possibly have not existed,* has a cause of its existence.

PC3: Whatever *begins to exist* has a cause of its existence.

We will consider these individually below.

The second major category of principles, inspired largely by Leibniz, involves a principle of *explanation* (or PSR). In general terms, explanation is a relation between *facts* (or alternatively, propositions), where fact A *explains* fact B just in case fact A answers *why* fact B obtains. Leibniz's PSR was the claim that *every* fact has a sufficient explanation, although many of the explanations may not be known to or knowable by us.[40] Modern defenders of neo-Leibnizian cosmological arguments have proposed weaker forms of Leibniz's principle.

PSR may be stated in terms of facts or, equivalently, in terms of propositions. The following three versions of PSR are representative:

---

[39]The reference here may be to either types or tokens of states of affairs and events. A token is a specific, unique instance, while a type is a general descriptive class, whose members are tokens. *My waving my hand at a good friend walking by my house at 8:50 in the morning on June 17, 2004,* is an event token of the event type *My waving my hand.*

[40]Craig, *Cosmological Argument,* p. 260.

PSR1:   Every true proposition has a sufficient reason why it is true.

PSR2:   Every true proposition that entails that some concrete object exists has a sufficient reason why it is true.

PSR3:   There is a sufficient reason why some contingent concrete objects exist rather than none at all.

We will evaluate various PSRs in the following section; for the remainder of this section, we return our attention to the different versions of PC.

Analysis of causal principles. Causal principles may be supported in at least three ways. First, we might claim empirical support: we know the principle by inductive generalization from observed instances of caused facts. Second, we might claim that causation is an indispensable presupposition of all empirical inquiries: If we do not assume the causal principle, we cannot know anything on the basis of observation or induction. Third, we might claim that rational intuition provides the support: We know the principle naturally and directly, without need for any further reason or evidence.

In evaluating the proposed causal principles, we will consider how each particular causal principle is supported, as well as ask whether or not the principle can play a successful role in KCA. A principle will be counted as playing a successful role if a plausible argument can be constructed utilizing the principle, which concludes with a first cause that has at least one property that can only be exemplified by a divine being.

Consider

PC1:   Whatever *changes* has a cause.

The credibility of this principle depends in part on what one means by "change." Roughly, an entity E undergoes change if it has (or lacks) property P at time t_1 and lacks (has) P at t_2, where $t_1 < t_2$.[41] On the A-theory of time, it is possible that E has certain properties at t_1 which E lacks at t_2. If at t_2 E has different properties than E had at t_1, then E has undergone change. On the B-theory of time, the analysis is different. E is an object extended in both the three spatial dimensions (represented by x, y and z) and the one temporal dimension (represented by t). Thus E can have a property P at its four-dimensional extension (x, y, z, t_1) and lack P at (x, y, z, t_2). On the B-theory, this is no more mysterious than claiming that an object can have different properties at different points of its spatial extension. For example, a fire-

---

[41]The properties must be monadic (i.e., nonrelational) so as to exclude nongenuine, so-called "Cambridge" changes. For example, when you travel a mile to the west of Cambridge, Cambridge has changed in that it now has the property of being a mile further east of you than it was before. But this is not a genuine change in the city of Cambridge.

poker might be hot at one end and cold at another, that is, E at (x_1, y_1, z_1, t_1) has different properties than E at (x_2, y_2, z_2, t_1), exhibiting a "change" in its spatial extension. Similarly, the same end of the poker can be hot at one time (x_1, y_1, z_1, t_1) and cold at another time (x_1, y_1, z_1, t_2), thus exhibiting a change in its temporal extension. Change, on the B-theory, is not something that "comes to pass," but merely a matter of change in locations in the space-time continuum.[42]

If the B-theory of time is correct, then it is doubtful that PC1 is true. Causation on the B-theory reduces to a relation that supervenes on the entire history of the universe, or to a statement of certain regularities that obtain. However, if change is understood in terms of the A-theory, in which temporal becoming is real, then there may be good reason to think that change requires a cause. Aristotle offered the following argument that all motion has a cause:[43]

12. Motion is the actualization of a potential.

13. No potential can actualize anything.

14. Therefore, a potential can only be actualized by something already actual.

Clearly, this argument could be generalized to apply not just to motion but to change in general. Hence, given the A-theory of time, there is at least one argument for thinking that PC1 is true.

However, William Rowe suggests that there may be some things that change and yet are not caused to change. Accordingly, it is just a brute fact that these things are changing. Rowe would complain that Aristotle's argument is irrelevant since it does not follow from (14) that no potential can be actual without ever having been actualized. He asks, "Why should we believe that it is never a brute fact that something is changing?"[44] Rowe recognizes that one possible answer would involve resorting to some form of PSR, according to which there cannot be any brute, unexplained facts.[45] If this

---

[42]The literature on four-dimensionalism versus three-dimensionalism is growing. On the side of a 4-D ontology, see Theodore Sider, *Four Dimensionalism: An Ontology of Persistence and Time* (Oxford: Clarendon, 2001); or Hud Hudson, *A Materialist Metaphysics of the Human Person* (Ithaca, N.Y.: Cornell University Press, 2001). On the side of a 3-D ontology, see Trenton Merricks, *Objects and Persons* (Oxford: Clarendon, 2001); Peter van Inwagen, "Four-Dimensional Objects," *Noûs* 24 (1990): 245-55.

[43]Adapted from Craig, *Cosmological Argument*, p. 25.

[44]William L. Rowe, *The Cosmological Argument* (Princeton: Princeton University Press, 1975; reprint, New York: Fordham University, 1998), p. 17.

were true, and if the only form of explanation for change were causal, then PSR would be a reason to think PC1 is true. However, it is doubtful that such a strong version of PSR is true, for reasons to be discussed below.

Despite Rowe's skepticism, one might attempt a probabilistic case for PC1 based on induction from our experiences of change in the world. Bruce Reichenbach argues, rightly in our view, that we are often directly acquainted with change being caused.[46] For example, one can be directly aware that the air movement is causing a page of the open book on the desk to move. Since we've never come across change without a cause, and since we've often been aware of change with a cause, we might conclude that whatever changes probably has a cause for its change. A Humean could object that induction is based on PSR and so is no more warranted than PSR. Although we shall not investigate whether induction must be grounded in PSR, it is worth noting that many thinkers have held to a principle of induction without thinking that PSR is true (which is evident, for example, by the number of scientists who uphold inductive reasoning while believing that the existence of the big bang singularity has no explanation). Thus, it may turn out that a principle of induction is defensible even if PSR is false.

Nevertheless, we doubt that PC1 would be very helpful to the cosmological argument even if adequately defended. For at best, it only gets us to the conclusion that something self-changing (according to Plato) or unchanging (according to Aristotle) exists. But why not think that being self-changing or unchanging can be a property of certain kinds of physical things? Plato argues that for something to change itself, it would have to be a soul.[47] However, we see no reason why this must be the case. Suppose that fundamental particles have within them a principle of change—some changeless property that explains why the other properties of the particles change as they do. Unless there is some reason to doubt that the basic particles could have within them such a principle of change, it is reasonable to conclude that P1 is of little value to the cosmological argument since it fails to yield a conclusion in which something with a property of deity exists.

Now we turn our attention to

PC2:   Whatever exists, but could possibly have not existed, has a cause of its existence.

[45]Ibid., p. 33.
[46]Bruce Reichenbach, *The Cosmological Argument: A Reassessment* (Springfield, Ill.: Charles C. Thomas, 1972), p. 44.
[47]Plato *Laws* 10.884-899d; for discussion, see Craig, *Cosmological Argument*, pp. 1-49.

PC2 is the version of the principle of causation that is relevant to the Thomistic (contingency) form of the cosmological argument. PC2 can be formulated in different ways depending on what is meant by "could possibly have not existed." The notion of possibility here could be taken to mean whatever is not logically necessary, whatever is not causally necessary or whatever is not factual necessary. As Rowe explains the difference, x is *factually necessary* just in case x is the first uncaused cause of all other beings; x is *causally necessary* just in case it is logically necessary that, *if* x exists, it is the first uncaused cause of all other beings; and x is logically necessary just in case the nonexistence of x is logically impossible.[48] The three corresponding causal principles would be

PC2a: Whatever exists and is not logically necessary has a cause of its existence.

PC2b: Whatever exists and is not causally necessary has a cause of its existence.

PC2c: Whatever exists and is not factually necessary has a cause of its existence.

Since PC2a entails PC2b, and PC2b entails PC2c, whatever reasons support the stronger principle (i.e., PC2a) are also reasons that support the weaker principle. One reason to think that PC2a is true is that only a cause can explain why something that is not logically necessary exists at all. But either this reason relies on rational intuitions, which are not universally shared by philosophers who have thought about the issue, or it invokes some form of PSR, and so is only as strong as the relevant PSR.

A second reason to affirm PC2a springs from Thomistic metaphysics, according to which essences exist and are distinct from a thing's existence (unless that thing is a necessary being). Accordingly, there must be a cause that continually conjoins an essence with an act of being if that essence is to be instantiated or exemplified.[49]

One might also offer empirical arguments for PC2a. However, as we already noted, inductive generalizations based on empirical observations will carry little force for a Humean. A probabilistic justification for inductive generalization from the objects of ordinary experience seems weak when applied to objects at the edge of the universe (or, equivalently, in the earliest

[48]Rowe, *Cosmological Argument*, pp. 169-70.

[49]William Lane Craig, "Natural Theology: Introduction," in *Philosophy of Religion: A Reader and Guide,* ed. William Lane Craig (New Brunswick, N.J.: Rutgers University Press, 2002), p. 70.

epochs of the universe's existence), and downright doubtful on a standard interpretation of quantum physics. Given these problems and the severely limited appeal of a Thomistic metaphysical explanation in contemporary philosophy, it seems that our reasons for thinking PC2a is true are reduced to the first one above, and thus to some form of PSR.

Perhaps the best argument for PC2b (and therefore PC2c) is based on Maimonides's argument, following the *Mutakallamim,*[50] that whatever exists and has the potential for nonexistence has at some time in the past come into existence.[51] If Maimonides is right in his claim, then anything that is not causally necessary has a beginning.

Nevertheless, we are not too excited about PC2c or PC2b, since the conclusion that a causally or factually necessary being exists is a weak conclusion, and (apart from a cumulative case for theism) the objector to the KCA can still argue that there is no reason to think that the universe itself is not causally or factually necessary, or (as Bertrand Russell argued in his famous debate with Fr. Frederick Copleston) that the universe is just a brute, unexplained fact. Thus, PC2 fares no better than PC1, since both similarly fail to indicate why the physical universe itself requires a cause apart from invoking a form of PSR.

So we turn our attention to

PC3:   Whatever *begins to exist* has a cause of its existence.

PC3 is simply premise 2 of KCA (as we have stated it). Two reasons have been offered to hold that PC3 is true: First, PC3 is self-evidently true, a shared metaphysical intuition, and second, no one has ever observed something beginning to exist without a cause. Wes Morriston raises several objections to the claim that PC3 is self-evident.[52] Among other objections, Morriston thinks the meaning of "begins to exist" is sufficiently obscure that it is not clear that PC3 is supported by a widely shared metaphysical intuition. If what is meant by "*x* begins to exist" is simply that "*x* exists at a time *t,* and there is no time prior to *t* in which *x* exists," then Craig, who defends PC3, must admit that God began to exist, since God, according to Craig, exists timelessly apart from the beginning of physical time at the moment of cre-

[50]I.e., teachers of the *Mutakallimun,* a school of Islamic philosophical theology.
[51]Moses Maimonides, *The Guide for the Perplexed* 3.4.1, chap. 74 in *Basic Issues in Medieval Philosophy,* ed. Richard N. Bosley and Martin M. Tweedale (Peterborough, Ont.: Broadview, 1997), p. 181.
[52]Wes Morriston, "Must the Beginning of the Universe Have a Personal Cause? A Critical Examination of the *Kalam* Cosmological Argument," *Faith and Philosophy* 17 (2000): 149-69.

ation. Therefore, the very first moment of time (t_0) is such that God exists at t_0 and at no time prior to t_0 (since there *is* no time prior to t_0). Craig's most recent formulation of "begins to exist" avoids this problem by adding several distinct clauses to the analysis. He asserts that "*x* comes into being at *t*" is to be analyzed as:

> *x* exists at *t*; *t* is either the first time at which *x* exists or is separated from any time $t^* < t$ at which *x* existed by a non-degenerate, temporal interval; and *x*'s existing at *t* is a tensed fact.[53]

Morriston finds such a formulation far too complicated for us to have clear intuitions about, so if that is the meaning of "begins to exist" in PC3, then PC3 cannot claim support from rational intuition.[54] Further, Morriston thinks PC3 is not self-evident because many intelligent philosophers have understood PC3 and yet do not find it to be true.

The *kalam* arguer might simply claim different intuitions from Morriston's, but he might also claim that PC3 may be supported inductively (Hume's skepticism notwithstanding). Since we've never observed anything pop into existence uncaused, it is reasonable to assume that it is just false that things can come into existence uncaused. Morriston's rejoinder is that we've only failed to observe things come into existence when there was a prior time in which those things did not exist. Thus, we are not warranted in concluding that the first event has a cause since there was no prior time in which it did not exist.[55]

In response, the *kalam* arguer might maintain that there is an important distinction to be made here with respect to the use of the term *time*. Granted, there was no *physical* time prior to the creation of the universe, but it does not follow that there was no *metaphysical* (or divine) time. We do not have the space here to explore the distinction, but if it is sustainable, then Morriston's argument loses much of its force.[56]

Unfortunately, PC3 (premise 2 of KCA) is tied to the need to show that the physical world began to exist. Some critics have noted that the scientific and philosophical arguments used to establish a *finite past,* even if those arguments are successful, simply do not establish that the universe *began to exist.*

---

[53]William Lane Craig, "Must the Beginning of the Universe Have a Personal Cause? A Rejoinder," *Faith and Philosophy* 19 (2002): 99.

[54]Morriston, "Must the Beginning of the Universe Have a Personal Cause?" pp. 154-55.

[55]Ibid., pp. 162-63.

[56]See DeWeese, *God and the Nature of Time,* pp. 9-11, 263-71; Alan G. Padgett, *God, Eternity and the Nature of Time* (New York: St. Martin's, 1992), pp. 122-46.

For it may be possible for something to have existed for a finite amount of time and yet not have *begun* to exist.[57] Craig himself thinks God has existed for a finite amount of time and yet is without a beginning, since "apart from" the temporal universe God exists atemporally.[58] Indeed, Quentin Smith takes advantage of this possibility in his proposal that the first state of the universe was a timeless state from which the first temporal state emerged.[59]

Craig argues in response both that (1) physical (impersonal) causes must be sufficient for their effects, and (2) a timeless physical cause cannot be sufficient for a temporal effect, so that a timeless physical state cannot be the first state of the universe. Both (1) and (2), however, are controversial theses, and we consider minimal reliance on controversial metaphysical commitments to be a desideratum for a successful KCA. Thus we take seriously the gap between demonstrating that the universe has a *finite past* and showing that the universe *began to exist*.

Nevertheless, we believe that the gap may be bridged by relying on a certain PSR (to be discussed in the next section). For now, it suffices to note that PC3 is at least applicable to the first event, E_1, since E_1 *began to exist*, although it is uncertain (at this point in the dialectic) that PC3 is applicable to the universe as a whole. So unless it can be shown that all cosmological models that posit a finite *beginningless* time are flawed or incoherent, the relevance of PC3 to the *kalam* argument must await support from a successful PSR.

THE PRINCIPLE OF SUFFICIENT REASON

The principle of sufficient reason (PSR) is perhaps most closely associated with Leibniz: "*That [principle] of sufficient reason,* in virtue of which we hold that no fact can be real or existent, no statement true, unless there be a sufficient reason why it is so and not otherwise, although most often these reasons cannot be known to us."[60] The principle has been widely debated in recent literature,[61] and no clear consensus has emerged. Many philosophers

---

[57]Such is the case with the Hartle-Hawking hypothesis, for example, and apparently with M-theory as well.

[58]William Lane Craig, *Time and Eternity* (Wheaton, Ill.: Crossway, 2001), pp. 217-37.

[59]Quentin Smith, "Time was Created by a Timeless Point: An Atheist Explanation of Spacetime," in *God and Time: Essays on the Divine Nature,* ed. Gregory E. Ganssle and David M. Woodruff (New York: Oxford University Press, 2002), p. 95-128.

[60]G. W. Leibniz, "The Monadology," 32 [1714], in G. W. Leibniz, *Philosophical Essays,* ed. Roger Ariew and Daniel Garber (Indianapolis: Hackett, 1989), p. 217.

[61]We here cite only a fraction of the literature which bears directly on cosmological arguments:

take it as a "fundamental presupposition of reason" which "all men, whether they ever reflect on it or not, seem more or less to presuppose."[62] Others argue that the only form of PSR that is clearly true is so weak that it cannot help a cosmological argument.[63]

We understand PSR as an explanatory principle. As Richard Taylor puts it, PSR expresses the belief that "there is some explanation for the existence of anything whatever, some reason why it should exist rather than not."[64] More precisely, if p is an explanation of q, then two conditions are met: (i) p explains why q is true; and (ii) p entails q in the sense of relevance logic. Quentin Smith elaborates:

> Note that (ii) is a stronger condition than the condition that "q strictly implies p," since the proposition that Alice is awake on November 4, 1994, strictly implies that triangles have three sides, but there is no relation of relevant entailment. (Each necessary truth is strictly implied by each contingent truth, but it is not the case that each necessary truth is relevantly entailed by each contingent truth.) Furthermore, condition (ii) about relevant entailment is not enough by itself to give a metaphysically interesting definition of sufficient reason, since condition (ii) by itself gives us many trivial cases of sufficient reasons. For example, the proposition that Alice is attentive most of the day on November 4, 1994, relevantly entails that Alice is awake on November 4, 1994, but the first proposition is a sufficient reason for the second only in a trivial and uninteresting sense. Condition (i) about explanation is not met by this pair of propositions, since Alice's attentiveness does not explain why she is awake but is merely the mode in which she is awake. An example where conditions (i) and (ii) are both met is that the proposition *all bodies in the solar system at a distance from the sun are gravitationally attracted to the sun, and the earth is in the solar system* entails *the earth is gravitationally attracted to the sun.* The first proposition explains and relevantly entails the second proposition and thus is a

Quentin Smith, "A Defense of a Principle of Sufficient Reason," *Metaphilosophy* 26, nos. 1 & 2 (1995): 97-106; Richard M. Gale and Alexander R. Pruss, "A New Cosmological Argument," *Religious Studies* 35 (1999): 461-76; Rowe, *Cosmological Argument,* pp. 60-114; Alexander R. Pruss, "The Hume-Edwards Principle and the Cosmological Argument," *International Journal for Philosophy of Religion* 43 (1998): 149-65; Joseph K. Campbell, "Hume's Refutation of the Cosmological Argument," *International Journal for Philosophy of Religion* 40 (1996): 159-73.
[62]Rowe, *Cosmological Argument,* p. 262, attributes this view to Richard Taylor.
[63]For example, Kevin Davey and Rob Clifton, "Insufficient Reason in the 'New Cosmological Argument,'" *Religious Studies* 37 (2001): 485-90.
[64]Richard Taylor, *Metaphysics,* 3rd ed. (Englewood Cliffs, N.J.: Prentice Hall, 1983), p. 91. Taylor gives no argument for the principle, merely an illustration designed, it seems, to elicit the intuition that the principle is true.

"sufficient reason" for it in a metaphysically interesting sense.[65]

Our evaluation of various versions of PSR will test the principle in terms of its explanatory sufficiency (conditions i and ii above), and in terms of whether or not it will do the necessary work in KCA.

We begin with

PSR1: Every true proposition has a sufficient reason why it is true.

(PSR1 is equivalent to the more familiar formulation in terms of facts: *Every fact has an explanation.*) There is an interesting argument for the falsehood of PSR1.[66] Let C be the maximal conjunctive proposition[67] that corresponds to the actual world W. C thus includes every proposition p or its negation, and every conjunct of C is true. Since W is not logically necessary, C is a contingently true proposition. Now, assume there is a proposition q that is the sufficient reason for W. That is, q explains why W obtains, and q relevantly entails (and so explains) C (and each of its conjuncts). So q is the sufficient reason why every true proposition is true.

The argument proceeds as follows: Either q is contingently true, or necessarily true. If q is contingently true, then (by hypothesis) q is a conjunct of C. If q is a conjunct of C and q explains C, then q explains itself. But contingently true propositions cannot explain themselves; hence, q cannot explain C, contradicting the assumption that q is the sufficient reason for C. On the other hand, if q is necessarily true, then if q entails C, then C is also necessarily true, contradicting the assumption that C is contingently true. Therefore there can be no proposition q that is the sufficient reason why every true proposition is true. Therefore PSR1 is false, and necessarily so. While there have been attempts to salvage PSR1,[68] we shall agree that it is necessarily false.

---

[65]Quentin Smith, "Defense of a Principle of Sufficient Reason," p. 98. Our exposition of PSR1-3 follows Smith's argument. Smith formulates his versions of PSR in terms of reasons why a proposition about the existence of some contingent concrete object is true, whereas the PSR is often stated in terms of reasons for facts which obtain. But the "true proposition" version and the "fact" version are equivalent, so what we say here in terms of a "true proposition" version will apply *mutatis mutandis* to "facts" versions.

[66]This argument is offered in different forms in Rowe, *Cosmological Argument,* p. 106, and Smith, "Defense of a Principle of Sufficient Reason," p. 99. Readers are referred to these works for details of the argument.

[67]A conjunctive proposition is a proposition that is the conjunction of two or more propositions. For example, the proposition, *God exists and some flowers are blue* is a conjunctive proposition built out of the proposition *God exists* and the proposition *Some flowers are blue*. A conjunctive proposition is true if and only if each of its conjuncts is true. The maximal conjunctive proposition C would be the conjunction of each and every true proposition about the actual world.

[68]Richard Gale and Alexander Pruss offer a response to this refutation of PSR1, but in our opin-

We now turn our attention to

PSR2:   Every true proposition that entails that some concrete object exists
has a sufficient reason why it is true.

(PSR2 is equivalent to *Every fact about the existence of things has an explanation*.)[69] The immediate objection to PSR2 comes from quantum mechanics (QM). On a standard interpretation of QM, a virtual particle can come into existence without a cause in a quantum mechanical vacuum. If there is no sufficient reason why a virtual particle comes into existence, then there can be no sufficient reason why it exists. So if the standard interpretation of QM is correct, then PSR2 is false.

It may, of course, be the case that the standard interpretation of QM is false, and there are causes for what appear to be indeterminate quantum events. The deterministic interpretation of QM by David Bohm, for example, is empirically equivalent to the standard interpretation.[70] However, the fact is that the standard interpretation, with its implied acausalities, remains the majority view among particle physicists and philosophers of science alike, so we will not seek to defend PSR2 on the basis of a minority interpretation of QM.[71] The same argument would invalidate a version of PSR phrased in terms of a proposition entailing that a contingent concrete object begins to exist.

This brings us to PSR3:

PSR3:   There is a sufficient reason why some contingent concrete objects
exist rather than none at all.

PSR3, in claiming merely that there is a sufficient reason why some contingent objects exist *rather than none at all,* is compatible with ontological or causal indeterminism. As Smith explains it, "there may be a sufficient reason why there are particles rather than no particles at all. But that does not imply there is a sufficient reason for the existence of each particle."[72]

---

ion, the success of their response is unclear. Gale and Pruss, "A New Cosmological Argument," pp. 461-68. Pruss addresses this in depth in a forthcoming book, which was unavailable to us at the time of this writing.

[69]Rowe, *Cosmological Argument,* p. 113.

[70]See David Bohm, *Quantum Theory* (New York: Prentice-Hall, 1951; reprint, New York: Dover, 1989); and *Wholeness and the Implicate Order* (reissued, New York: Routledge, 2002).

[71]Philosopher of science Michael Friedman has suggested in personal conversation that there is resurgent interest among physicists in some form of global hidden variable theory. William Lane Craig notes as well a growing discontent with indeterministic interpretations of QM and a renewed interest in deterministic formulations of the theory. William Lane Craig, "Design and the Cosmological Argument," in *Mere Creation,* ed. William A. Dembski (Downers Grove, Ill.: InterVarsity Press, 1998), p. 341.

[72]Smith, "Defense of a Principle of Sufficient Reason," p. 104.

Although PSR3 seems to be prima facie plausible, not every philosopher who has considered PSR3 has thought it to be true. For example, William Rowe thinks that PSR3, if it is true, can be used to prove that something very much like God exists. But Rowe, an atheist, argues that no one knows that PSR3 is true since it is neither self-evident and nor is it a required presumption for scientific inquiry.[73] Although Rowe's dismissal of PSR3 is open to challenge, we believe that PSR3 can be grounded in a much weaker, modalized version of PSR:

PSR3′: Possibly there is a sufficient reason why some contingent concrete objects exist rather than none at all.

While the proof is complicated, it can be shown that PSR3′ entails PSR3, which is a favorable result given that PSR3 does not depend upon whether or not ontological or causal indeterminism is true.[74]

Recall that we left undecided the status of

PC3: Whatever *begins to exist* has a cause of its existence.

We are now in a position to see that PC3 is both true and relevant to the *kalam* argument. PSR3 clearly entails that PC3 is true, since, if the beginning of contingent concrete things had no cause, then there would be no explanation for why there are contingent concrete things rather than none at all. The defeater to the *relevance* of premise 2 of KCA under consideration above was the possibility of a finite beginningless universe. But whether the initial state of the universe is a singularity (as in the Hartle-Hawking hypothesis) or a timeless physical state (as in Smith's argument), that state cannot explain why there are contingent concrete things rather than none at all,

[73]Rowe, *Cosmological Argument*, p. 268.
[74]Graham Oppy has argued that a very strong PSR can be deduced from a similar PSR (Graham Oppy, "On 'A New Cosmological Argument,'" *Religious Studies* 36 [2000]: 346-48); and Pruss has devised an independent proof of the same deduction (in Richard M. Gale and Alexander R. Pruss, "A Response to Oppy, and to Davey and Clifton," *Religious Studies* 38 [2002]: 90). Our proof parallels that of Pruss:
  Let *p* be the proposition that some contingent concrete objects exist rather than none at all.
  1. There is a possible world W in which *q* is true and *q* explains *p*. [from PSR3′]
  2. *p* is contingently true and there is no explanation of *p*. [assumption for indirect proof]
  3. There is a possible world W in which (*p* and "there is no explanation of *p*") is true, and in which *q* is true and *q* explains (*p* and "there is no explanation of *p*"). [from (1) and (2)]
  4. In W, *q* explains *p*. [from (3) and the distributivity of explanation over conjunction]
  5. Therefore, in W, *p* both has and does not have an explanation.
  6. It is not the case that *p* is contingently true and there is no explanation of *p*. [from (12)-(19) by indirect proof]
  7. Therefore, it is not the case that, for any proposition *p*, *p* is contingently true and there is no explanation of *p*. [from (6)]

since the state is itself contingent. Thus, given the arguments above for finite time together with the argument for PSR3′, we conclude that premise 2 of the KCA—*Whatever begins to exist has a cause of its existence*—is both true and relevant to the *kalam* argument. So (3) follows: The universe had a cause of its existence.

Recall that premise 4 of KCA claimed that *The (ultimate) cause of the universe must itself be uncaused*. The arguments we have offered for (2), and for different versions of PC and PSR, have the consequence of supporting (4) on pain of a vicious regression. But the move from (4) to (5), the uncaused cause of the universe must be God, remains before us. Or in terms of the general form of the cosmological argument, we need to show that being the uncaused cause is the property θ that can only be exemplified by God.

From the Uncaused Cause to God, and "Hume's Stopper"

Is there a way to unpack the notion of an uncaused cause so that the entity so understood must be divine? That is, can we defeat "Hume's stopper"? Recall that "Hume's stopper" is Hume's contention that even if theistic arguments are successful in demonstrating the existence of some entity of great power, intelligence or goodness, we simply lack the grounds to assert that that entity is God as understood by classical theists.

Well, isn't being an uncaused cause sufficient? Doesn't the divine attribute of aseity entail that a divine being with aseity is the uncaused cause of anything else that exists? Unfortunately, the answer is murky, depending as it does on the position one takes on other notions such as divine simplicity, immutability and the relation of God to abstract objects. So we will not follow what appears to be a direct path from being the uncaused cause of the universe to being God.[75]

Gale and Pruss argued that the uncaused first cause must be a necessary being who is very intelligent and powerful.[76] Jerome Gellman has extended Gale and Pruss's argument to show that this being is essentially omnipotent.[77] This gets us closer to the God of classical theism, to be sure.

---

[75]See, for example, Christopher Hughes, *On a Complex Theory of a Simple God: An Investigation in Aquinas' Philosophical Theology* (Ithaca, N.Y.: Cornell University Press, 1989), p. 50.
[76]Gale and Pruss, "A New Cosmological Argument," pp. 464-69.
[77]Jerome Gellman, "Prospects for a Sound Stage 3 of Cosmological Arguments," *Religious Studies* 36 (2000): 195-201. See also Douglas Groothuis, "Metaphysical Implications of Cosmological Arguments," chapter 6 of the present volume.

Our approach here will be to rely on the third principle used in cosmological arguments, the principle of determination, to show that the uncaused first cause must be a divine person. Above, we gave the following characterization of PD:

PD: If two qualitatively identical states of affairs are complementary, the obtaining of one rather than the other is due to the will of a free agent.

To understand this principle and the role it plays in defeating "Hume's stopper," we shall turn to one of the early proponents of KCA, the Islamic philosopher and theologian as al-Ghazali (1058-1111). Called "the greatest figure in the history of the Islamic reaction to Neo-Platonism,"[78] Ghazali's work was a sustained attack on the *falasifa* school of Islamic philosophy associated with the contingency version of the cosmological argument. As a theologian as well as a philosopher, Ghazali felt the contingency version, with its admission of an eternal universe, was heretical. Consequently he spends nearly a quarter of his best-known work, *The Incoherence of the Philosophers,* in defending the *kalam* claim that the universe had a beginning in time. After demonstrating the temporality of the world, Ghazali (and the other *mutakallamim*) invoked PD to prove that the existence of the world requires a "determinant," which is God. The Arabic word generally translated "determinant" has received much discussion, but it clearly cannot mean simply "efficient cause." Rather, in seeking a "determinant" of the existence of the universe, the *mutakallamim* were asking for a "selecting agent."[79]

Ghazali considers an objection to the claim that the universe began to exist. The objector reasons,

> Before the world's existence, the willer existed, the will existed, and its relation to what is willed existed. No willer came in to existence anew, no will came into existence anew, and no relation that did not exist came to exist for the will anew. For all this is change. How, then, did the object of the will come into existence anew, and what prevented its coming into existence anew earlier?[80]

> The sum total of this is that the necessitating [cause would] exist with all its conditions fulfilled, there remaining no expected thing; and yet, with [all] this,

---

[78]Majid Fakhry, *A History of Islamic Philosophy* (New York: Columbia University Press, 1970), p. 244, cited in Craig, *Kalam Cosmological Argument,* p. 42.
[79]Craig, *Kalam Cosmological Argument,* pp. 14-15.
[80]Al-Ghazali *Incoherence of the Philosophers* 1.1.16, p. 15.

the necessitated [effect] would have been delayed. . . . And this is in itself impossible.[81]

The objection relies on the intuition that there must be some feature of the thing chosen which determines the will of the agent choosing. If there is no difference between options, then the agent has no basis for a choice and so will not choose. Hence, the universe could not have come into existence at some time, since in principle there would be no feature of one time which would cause God to choose to create at that time rather than another. Therefore either creation is eternal, or—*per impossible*—there is no creation.

Ghazali's response is to claim that one function of the will is precisely to determine—to choose—between two indiscernible things.

> The world came to existence whence it did, having the description with which it came to exist, and in the place in which it came to exist, through will, will being an attribute whose function is to differentiate a thing from its similar. . . . For to be similar is to be indiscernible.[82]

Ghazali says that if the name "will" does not correspond to the attribute of being able to choose between indiscernibles, then give it another name, but the attribute itself cannot be denied. In support of his claim that the will has the power to choose between indiscernibles, Ghazali gives an example of a man gazing at two qualitatively identical dates (we may assume that the dates are equally distant from his dominant hand, that he can only take one, etc.). Ghazali says simply that the man inevitably will take one of the indiscernible dates.[83]

Ghazali's discussion foreshadows the extensive contemporary discussion of Buridan's unfortunate ass, caught forever between two indiscernible, equidistant bales of hay. Although sorely tempted, we shall not trace the medieval discussion of the problem in all its fascinating detail.[84] In recent times, the problem has been cast in terms of "picking and choosing."[85] The upshot

---

[81]Ibid., 1.1.21, p. 17.

[82]Ibid., 1.1.41 and 43, p. 22.

[83]Ibid., 1.1,46, p. 23.

[84]Our thanks to Joshua Blander for calling our attention to the wealth of material available, especially the modally sophisticated treatment by Duns Scotus found in *Ordinatio* 1.2.1.1-2, in *Basic Issues in Medieval Philosophy*, ed. Richard N. Bosley and Martin M. Tweedale (Peterborough, Ont.: Broadview, 1997), pp. 63-65.

[85]A historical survey of the discussion is found in Nicholas Rescher, "Choice Without Preference: A Study of the History and of the Logic of the Problem of 'Buridan's Ass,'" *Kant Studien* 51 (1959): 142-75. A clear presentation of the options is in Edna Ullmann-Margalit and Sidney Morgenbesser, "Picking and Choosing," *Social Research* 44 (1977): 757-85.

is this: Some hold, with Ghazali's opponent, that in the absence of some (relevant) distinction between two objects (complementary states of affairs), there is no reason why one rather than the other should be selected, and so *neither will be selected* (no date will be eaten; the ass will starve). Others respond, with Ghazali, that this is plainly false—the will of an agent simply has the power to select one, *even if the alternatives are qualitatively indiscernible.* Let us say that "selecting" is neutral between having or not having reasons for a selection, "choosing" implies selecting where an objective or subjective difference provides a reason for the selection, and "picking" implies selecting where no objective or subjective difference supplies a reason for a selection. Ghazali, then, is a "picker" and his opponent a "chooser."

The "chooser" accepts something like the following "choosing principle":

CP: For any action A and any time *t,* an agent performs A at *t* only if the agent has sufficient reason to perform A at *t.*

Perhaps the motivation behind the "chooser's" insistence on a reason is the strong intuition that in nature there must always be some distinction between two states of affairs that explains why one rather than its complement obtains. That is, there is an intuition that, given two complementary states of affairs S and ~S, and some physical (nonagent) cause C, there must be some real (macroscopic or microscopic) property which S has and ~S lacks that explains why C brought about S rather than ~S. The exception to this intuition is, of course, the realm of quantum mechanics.[86]

It seems that there is an inclination to apply this intuition to agents as well. Some philosophers who do so are motivated by physicalism as a philosophy of mind, according to which mental states are reducible to or supervene upon physical brain states, which in turn are subject to the laws of physics and chemistry. Others have a compatibilist view of freedom, according to which free will is compatible with some form of determinism. But both these views are controversial, and in any case, we are considering a putative act of God, who is uniformly regarded as both nonphysical and free with respect to the creation of the world.

Why should we believe CP applies to God's act of creation? In particular, why assume that God's decision to create is not a case of "picking"? Nicholas Wolterstorff asks,

---

[86]Of the two-dozen or so physical scientists informally surveyed at the 2003 Annual Meeting of the American Scientific Affiliation, *every one* shared this intuition about nonquantum phenomena.

Why *must* there be such a reason? When I reflect on my getting out of bed in the morning, I find that after lying awake for awhile I just, at a certain moment, decide to get up. I don't have a reason for deciding to get up precisely when I do; I just do at a certain moment decide to get up. . . . Why does it have to be different for God?[87]

Let us assume then, at least provisionally, that some form of PD is correct.

We have already established premises 2 and 3 of KCA, that the universe had a beginning and so was caused to exist. Consider the state that obtained "before" the beginning of the universe.[88] God's choice would seem to be between not creating, in which case the resulting state of affairs N is the existence of nothing other than God, and creating, in which case the resulting state of affairs C is some universe. Clearly N and C are complementary. If PD is to apply here, N and C must be qualitatively identical, and clearly they are not (any existing universe is qualitatively different from N). But it does not seem that N and C are strictly incommensurable, so even though God might be free with respect to N or C, it does not follow that there is not some property of N or C that is the reason or explanation of God's choosing N or C. So it doesn't seem in this case that PD will apply.

But we submit that the situation outlined is not the state "before" creation. For God's decision was not simply to create or not to create; rather, it was whether to actualize W_1 or W_2 or W_3 or . . . Each W_n is a possible world that differs from every other, and philosophers are generally agreed that there is an infinite number of possible worlds. Further, N is a possible world, namely, that world with no beings, and there is precisely one such possible world. Peter van Inwagen has argued persuasively that for any two possible worlds, the prior probability of their being actual is equal.[89] If there is an infinite number of possible worlds, then the probability of any one of them, N included, is zero. However, since one possible world must be actual, and

---

[87]Nicholas Wolterstorff, "Unqualified Divine Temporality," in *God and Time: Four Views*, ed. Gregory E. Ganssle (Downers Grove, Ill.: InterVarsity Press, 2001), p. 238.

[88]The "scare quotes" here are to alert the reader to the fact that if there is no metaphysical time, then time itself (physical time) began at the moment the universe began. In this case, "before" must have a logical and not a temporal sense. See Craig, *Time and Eternity*, pp. 233-35. If, however, the universe together with physical time began at some point in metaphysical or divine time, then "before" refers to an earlier point in *that* temporal series. See DeWeese, *God and the Nature of Time*, pp. 263-71. Our argument here is indifferent between these two views.

[89]Peter van Inwagen, "Why Is There Anything at All?" in *Proceedings of the Aristotelian Society* (1996), reprinted in Peter van Inwagen, *Ontology, Identity and Modality: Essays in Metaphysics* (Cambridge: Cambridge University Press, 2001), pp. 61-71.

since it is impossible for it to become actual on its own, given that its prior probability is zero, the only way it could become actual is through the determination of some agent. And if that is correct, then PD does apply.

CONCLUSION

We have shown that the standard formulation of KCA is able to survive Humean style objections to its causal principle, provided we defend a version of the principle of sufficient reason. We have also seen that the incorporation of the principle of determination guarantees that the first cause of the temporal universe must be a free agent. Couple that with the Gale-Pruss-Gellman argument that the first cause must be essentially omnipotent, and we have what we originally asked for. Property ϕ, the property of the first cause which only a divine being can exemplify, is the property of *being essentially an omnipotent free agent.*[90]

Now, a first cause that is essentially an omnipotent free agent is not yet the Christian God, a God of holiness and love, mercy and justice. But such a first cause is far more than Hume's doddering, superannuated deity or a committee of demigods. With this conclusion, we have answered "Hume's stopper" and have seen that the KCA is indeed a viable piece of natural theology, especially when combined with other theistic arguments in a cumulative case argument.

---

[90]Compare Swinburne's argument that all divine attributes can be derived from one essential attribute, that of possessing "pure limitless intentional power." Richard Swinburne, *The Christian God* (Oxford: Clarendon, 1994), pp. 150-58.

8

GIVING THE DEVIL HIS DUE

Teleological Arguments After Hume

James D. Madden

🏵

Among David Hume's many confrontations with natural theology his criticisms of the argument from design, or the teleological argument, may well be the most influential. Even today when one encounters the difficulties of using the arrangement of the natural world as evidence for the existence of God, one finds that it is Hume's original objections to such an enterprise that pose the greatest challenge. Suffice it to say that Hume, rivaled only by Darwin, has done the most to undermine *in principle* our confidence in arguments from design among all figures in the Western intellectual tradition.[1]

Despite Hume's powerful critique, there may be grounds for guarded optimism on the part of the theist. However, such optimism must not be purchased at the price of ignoring the original force of Hume's objections. To do so would be intellectually dishonest and would rob the theist's position

---

[1]Darwin likely has had a greater direct influence on Western culture in general than has Hume, and Darwinism may be the more frequent reason cited for one's rejection of a particular teleological argument. Nevertheless, the Darwinian case against the soundness of the teleological argument does not give us reason in principle to reject the possibility of constructing a sound version of such an argument. Darwin simply gives us a way of explaining the supposed evidence of design without appealing to a designer. If one could produce evidence that cannot be so explained, the Darwinian objection would not have much force. Hume's objections call the entire enterprise of giving a teleological argument for God's existence into question. Hume does not merely offer an alternative explanation of the phenomena appealed to by the proponent of a teleological argument, but instead argues that no such proof of God's existence is plausible. For Hume's anticipation of the Darwinian notion of evolution via unguided adaptation, see David O'Connor, *Hume on Religion* (New York: Routledge, 2001), chap. 7, esp. pp. 130-31.

of its real value. Therefore, this chapter contains both a discussion of the claims of some historically significant teleological arguments and a presentation of criticisms that originate with Hume and remain salient today. With those discussions in place we may then turn our attention to whether a plausible response to Humean objections can be made in light of recent work in the philosophy of religion.

We begin with a discussion of the classical expression of the teleological argument found in the writings of William Paley and St. Thomas Aquinas. Hume subjected this argument to a criticism that to this day calls classical teleological arguments into question. Although the fate of the classical teleological argument has not been sealed, I take Hume's criticism as an occasion to examine a modern version of the teleological argument that is constructed to sidestep the problems of the classical attempts at an argument from design. Nevertheless, we will see that the modern teleological argument is itself subject to a further Humean objection. We then turn to a consideration of contemporary work on the problem of evil and ultimately to principles taken from G. W. Leibniz to find a plausible strategy for defending the modern teleological argument against its Humean critics.

CLASSICAL TELEOLOGICAL ARGUMENTS

Among what are known as teleological arguments we find many different and varied attempts to prove the existence of a designer of the universe.[2] Not only do they vary both in the evidence they cite and the strength of their proposed conclusions, but their proponents argue from disparate philosophical presuppositions. For example, proponents of classical versions of the argument can be found in Aquinas and later Thomists, as well as in William Paley and the nineteenth-century natural theologians, who argue from a decidedly non-Aristotelian perspective. We can also point to examples of contemporary scientifically informed writers who claim that teleological arguments for the existence of a designer need to be taken seriously. In this section we will discuss the teleological argument in its classical form.

The teleological argument most familiar to philosophers in the Anglo-

---

[2]For the purposes of this chapter I treat neither arguments from consciousness nor fine-tuning arguments as teleological arguments. My task is to assess the legacy of Hume's classic criticism of teleological arguments, and these traditional Humean concerns are not directed specifically toward the key issues in the fine-tuning and consciousness arguments. For a treatment of the fine-tuning argument see Robin Collins's chapter 9 of this volume. For a treatment of the argument from consciousness, see J. P. Moreland's chapter 13 of this volume.

American tradition is offered by William Paley in his 1803 treatise *Natural Theology.*[3] Paley imagines finding a functioning watch while strolling along a heath. Unlike many objects one might encounter during an afternoon's stroll (Paley's example is a stone), the watch seems to be resistant to an explanation in terms of mere chance or coincidence. Paley argues that we need a special explanation in the case of the watch, but not in the case of a stone, because "when we come to inspect the watch, we perceive (what we could not discover in the stone) that its several parts are framed and put together for a purpose."[4] In other words, the watch, unlike the stone, has working parts that are intricately arranged so as to serve an obvious purpose. (I will hereafter refer to such collections of purposively arranged working parts as "teleological systems.") Paley's point is that when one encounters a teleological system it is only reasonable to conclude that one has encountered a genuine artifact and not the product of mere chance.

Paley next asks us to consider the structures we commonly encounter in nature, and he has in mind here the complex working parts of organisms and the law-governed phenomena observed by the astronomer. These phenomena, for Paley, are evidence of an intelligent designer of the universe to "a degree that exceeds all computation." He arrives at this conclusion by way of a supposed analogy between artifacts and natural phenomena: since the teleological structuring of the watch leads any reasonable person to infer the existence of a craftsman who has designed and assembled it, likewise the seemingly purposive arrangement of nature should lead us to infer the existence of nature's designer. As Paley puts it, our tendency to affirm the existence of a designer of the found watch is an expression of our acceptance of the principle that "there cannot be design without a designer; contrivance without a contriver; order without choice; arrangement, without anything capable of arranging; subserviency and relation to a purpose, without that which could intend a purpose." Therefore, the evidence of intricate teleological systems we find in nature strongly supports "the presence of intelligence and mind." In short, since all teleological systems that we have encountered in the past—watches,

---

[3]For a more detailed introduction to Paley's argument, its strengths and weaknesses, see Stephen Davis, *God, Reason and Theistic Proofs* (Grand Rapids: Eerdmans, 1997), chap. 6.
[4]William Paley, "The Evidence of Design," in *Natural Theology* (London: Faulder, 1805). All quotations from Paley are taken from William Rowe and William Wainwright, eds., *Philosophy of Religion: Selected Readings,* 3rd ed. (Fort Worth: Harcourt Brace, 1998), pp. 155-62.

mills, etc.—have been the product of design, the weight of human experience should lead us to conclude that natural teleological systems are likewise the products of intelligent design. The intelligent designer of nature's teleological systems is, for Paley, the God of orthodox theism, that is the unique omnipotent, omniscient and perfectly good person who is worshiped in the great Western religions.

Well before Paley, St. Thomas Aquinas offered a teleological argument that does not rely on an analogy between artifacts and natural structures. In the last of his famous Five Ways, Aquinas offers the following argument:

> The fifth way is taken from the governance of the world. We see that things which lack knowledge, such as natural bodies, act for an end and this is evident from their acting always, or nearly always, in the same way, so as to obtain the best result. Hence it is plain that they achieve their end, not fortuitously, but designedly. Now whatever lacks knowledge cannot move towards an end, unless it be directed by some being endowed with knowledge and intelligence; as the arrow is directed by the archer. Therefore some intelligent being exists by whom all natural things are directed to their end; and this being is God. (*ST* 1.2.3)

Some contemporary commentators take this argument as an earlier version of Paley's project.[5] But Aquinas is up to something quite different. His point is not that the structured complexity of natural systems is analogous to teleological systems built by human contrivance. Rather, Aquinas has in mind the Aristotelian principle that a teleological element must operate in all instances of change in the natural world. For the Aristotelian there must be a goal or final cause that determines or guides every natural change; without this purpose for action, the Aristotelian argues, there would be no causality at all. In changes that involve intelligent beings exercising their rational capacity, the final cause is not very difficult to account for—the agent simply acts according to an intention. In the case of "things which lack knowledge" the final cause is more difficult to explain. Aquinas believes that nonrational beings have a natural disposition to their end but, given the fact that the behaviors of such beings for the most part aim toward their good, he concludes that this inclination is not the result of mere chance. Thus,

---

[5]Anthony Kenny at times seems to take a similar line in his interpretation of the fifth way. See *The Five Ways: St. Thomas Aquinas' Proofs for God's Existence* (London: Routledge & Kegan Paul, 1969), pp. 97-98. For a good discussion of why it is best not to read the fifth way in such a manner, see John F. Wipple, *The Metaphysical Thought of Thomas Aquinas* (Washington, D.C.: Catholic University of America Press, 2000), pp. 480-85.

Aquinas concludes, there must be some intelligence that ultimately directs natural beings to their ends by endowing them with proper dispositions, and that being is the God of orthodox theism.[6]

Paley and Aquinas both argue that the existence of the God of orthodox theism is supported strongly by the premises they cite, so we may fairly represent both of their arguments with the same schema, what we will call the "classical teleological argument" (CTA):

1. Certain natural phenomena clearly have feature F (e.g., teleological ordering or intrinsic finality).

2. It is highly improbable that F be caused by something other than the God of orthodox theism.[7]

3. Therefore, it is highly probable that the God of orthodox theism exists.

Although Paley's and Aquinas's arguments can both be placed under the rubric of CTA, there are important differences between their approaches. The feature that Aquinas cites in the first premise (the ubiquity of Aristotelian final causality in nature) is quite different from what Paley has in mind (teleological systems in nature). Moreover, the arguments that each thinker appeals to in defense of the second premise are quite distinct; Paley refers us to the analogy between mechanical artifacts and teleological systems in nature, whereas Aquinas would point out the metaphysical problems that arise for the Aristotelian when one tries to use either chance or efficient causality alone to explain the occurrence of regularities in nature. Nevertheless, both Paley and Aquinas do attempt to establish the existence of the God of orthodox theism by using an argument of the form presented in CTA.

HUME'S OBJECTION TO CTA

David Hume is likely the most influential critic of natural theology in the

---

[6]There is great debate regarding whether Aquinas believes that any one of his Five Ways is individually sufficient to establish the existence of the God of orthodox theism. Many thinkers argue that Aquinas sees the Five Ways as working in conjunction to produce a cumulative case for the existence of God. For a discussion of all sides of this debate see Wipple, *Metaphysical Thought of Aquinas*, pp. 497-501. Since Aquinas explicitly mentions the existence of God as the conclusion of his argument, I will assume for the purposes of this chapter that he believed the fifth way to be sufficient to prove orthodox theism.

[7]It is unclear whether Aquinas intends his teleological argument to be deductive or inductive. Since teleological proofs are generally considered as specimens of inductive reasoning, I will assume for the sake of argument that Aquinas would be satisfied by this premise, which is stated probabilistically.

Western philosophical tradition.[8] Hume's attacks on arguments for God's existence in his *Dialogues Concerning Natural Religion,* his *Enquiry Concerning Human Understanding* and his *Natural History of Religion* have served as the precedents for much of the case for unbelief made during the subsequent centuries (the "Humean legacy" on which this volume is focused). Indeed, Hume's influence can still be seen among many contemporary philosophers of religion. J. J. C. Smart, Michael Martin, J. L. Mackie and a number of other prominent nontheists all employ criticisms whose historical origin can be found in Humean insights.[9]

The teleological argument is certainly not spared Hume's critical attack; indeed the greatest share of Hume's attention to natural theology in the *Dialogues* and the *Enquiry* is given to it. Typical of his doctrines regarding other theistic arguments, Hume's criticism of the teleological argument is held in high esteem by many contemporaries. Bernard Williams, for instance, tells us that Hume's attack on the teleological argument is so compelling that "after it there did not need to be another."[10] Hume makes trouble for the proponent of the teleological argument on a number of fronts, but for the moment I will deal with one of his criticisms that seems to have enjoyed the greatest polemical staying power.

In his discussion of the teleological argument in the *Enquiry,* Hume provides us with the following principle: "[W]hen we infer any particular cause from an effect, we must proportion the one to the other, and can never be allowed to ascribe to the cause any qualities but what are exactly sufficient to produce the effect."[11] In other words, when we argue from a purported effect to a postulation of its cause, we must tailor our hypothesis strictly to

---

[8]There is some debate among Hume scholars regarding whether Hume himself was an unbeliever. Although the standard view is certainly that Hume's voice in the *Dialogues* is that of the atheist Philo, a minority of scholars, most notably Nicholas Capaldi, have argued that there is reason to believe that Cleanthes, a somewhat mitigated believer, may actually speak for Hume. See Nicholas Capaldi, "Hume's Philosophy of Religion: God Without Ethics," *International Journal of Philosophy of Religion* 1 (1970): 233-40. For a recent argument (though somewhat attenuated) for the primacy of Philo as the voice of Hume, see O'Connor, *Hume on Religion,* pp. 214-16.

[9]See J. L. Mackie, *The Miracle of Theism* (New York: Oxford University Press, 1982); John Haldane and J. J. C. Smart, *Atheism and Theism* (Malden, Mass.: Blackwell, 1996); and Michael Martin, *Atheism: A Philosophical Justification* (Philadelphia: Temple University Press, 1992).

[10]B. A. O. Williams, "Hume on Religion," in *David Hume: A Symposium,* ed. D. F. Pears (New York: St. Martin's, 1963), p. 85. Williams also claims that, in the wake of Hume's attack, "little seems to be left of the Argument from Design, or indeed of the Christian conception of God" (p. 87).

[11]David Hume, *Enquiry Concerning Human Understanding,* sec. 11.

the properties of the effect for which we hope to account; we may assume that a purported cause has only those powers that are strictly necessary to bring about the phenomena to be explained. Any discrepancy between the powers of the cause and the properties of the effect is unwarranted by the relevant evidence. Hume's criticism here is really a straightforward application of the commonsense principle known to philosophers as Ockham's razor, that is, all things being equal, we should posit only those entities that are strictly necessary to explain the phenomena being investigated.

This Humean criticism presents a particular difficulty for the proponent of CTA because it is unclear that the evidence cited requires a single, omnipotent, omniscient and perfectly good being to act as its cause. It is logically possible that some combination of lesser designers, or even a single being lacking perfect competence, have acted to produce the range of phenomena considered by Paley and Aquinas.[12] Since Hume's point is that the evidence provided by the proponent of CTA is insufficient to justify the theistic hypothesis, let's call this criticism the "insufficient evidence objection" (IEO).

It is not only agnostics and atheists who have voiced this Humean objection. No less a theist than Alvin Plantinga raises the difficulty IEO poses for the proponents of teleological arguments as follows:

In believing that God exists, the theist believes a proposition logically equivalent to a conjunction. Among the conjuncts we should find at least the following:

    a. The universe is designed.
    b. The universe is designed by exactly one person.
    c. The universe was created ex nihilo.
    d. The universe was created by the person who designed it.
    e. The creator of the universe is omniscient, omnipotent and perfectly good.
    f. The creator of the universe is an eternal spirit, without body, and in no way dependent upon physical objects.

Now, we can put the objection as follows. Perhaps the teleological argument gives us a smidgen of evidence for (a), but it does nothing for (b) through (f).[13]

---

[12]Hume's point here is basically to cite the fallacy Todd Furman calls "jumping the gun" in chapter 3 of this volume.

[13]Alvin Plantinga, *God, Freedom and Evil* (Grand Rapids: Eerdmans, 1974), pp. 83-84.

In other words, even if we admit that there is sufficient evidence to support a design hypothesis (Plantinga's [a]), such evidence is not sufficient to underwrite belief in the existence of a being that fits the description of the deity that is the center of orthodox theism (Plantinga's [b] through [f]). At most we may conclude that such a being is sufficiently powerful to produce the complex teleological systems we encounter in this world. We have no reason to think that it has the power to produce a universe significantly different from the actual world, much less that the designer is omnipotent. We can, so the argument goes, make similar arguments for the other powers ascribed to the God of orthodox theism. The Humean point is that there are a great many equally plausible hypotheses that may explain the evidence of design, none of which require the positing of a perfect being. The evidence, strictly speaking, does not require the positing of such a being, so the theist must produce an independent reason for the supposition of God's existence beyond the evidence cited in classical teleological arguments. This result robs the teleological argument of its force; as Hume puts it in section 11 of the *Enquiry,* IEO shows that the proponent of the classical teleological arguments relies on "the assistance of exaggeration and flattery to supply the defects of argument and reasoning."

Many theists have averred a response to IEO, usually by appealing to the virtues of theoretical simplicity and elegance that, it is supposed, the theistic hypothesis enjoys. That is to say, even though the existence of a unique, all-powerful, all-knowing and perfectly good designer is not strictly implied by the evidence for design, the theistic hypothesis is simpler and more elegant than any other explanatory hypothesis available. Thus, we are within our rights to believe that the evidence of CTA supports the theistic hypothesis. Such a defense of CTA is certainly not without force.[14] Nevertheless, the claim that the theistic hypothesis is the simplest and most elegant explanation of the order of nature is controversial.

Even if we grant the greater simplicity of theism, it is unclear whether or not it is, on the whole, the most elegant alternative. That is to say, it is an open question whether or not theism solves as many problems as it raises. There is a long history of trying to make some sense of the notion of omnipotence, and the relation between an infinitely knowledgeable creator

---

[14]For a recent attempt at such a defense of CTA see Richard Swinburne, "Cosmological and Teleological Arguments," in *The Rationality of Theism,* ed. Adolfo García de la Sienra (Amsterdam: Rodopi, 2000), p. 112.

and the free actions of some of his creatures is certainly not easily explained. Moreover, the problem of reconciling the occurrence of horrendous evil with the God of orthodox theism continues to occupy the attention of theists. One might easily charge that the theistic hypothesis complicates as much as it simplifies. Of course these problems might be solvable, but it is incumbent on anyone who appeals to the theistic hypothesis to provide a way to quell these worries, and we must not beg any questions. Intellectual honesty requires us to admit that at this stage of philosophical progress these questions have not received final answers, although many of us are sanguine about particular avenues for their eventual resolution.[15]

For this reason I take it that, even if we grant the greater simplicity of theism, it is an open question whether God is the most elegant explanation of the relevant data. This is not to say that the case for CTA is a dead issue. However, given this serious problem, we do well to consider other versions of the teleological argument that may be insulated against IEO.

THE MODERN TELEOLOGICAL ARGUMENT

A modern version of the teleological argument has recently been developed by members of the contemporary intelligent design movement, including William Dembski, Michael Denton, Stephen Meyer and others.[16] I will use Michael Behe as an example. Behe is a biochemist who doubts whether Darwinian principles alone are sufficient to explain the complexity of life at its most fundamental levels. In his controversial book, *Darwin's Black Box,* Behe cites the problem of explaining the formation of the flagellum of a bacterium as one of a number of cases that call the viability of Darwinian explanation into question.[17] This biological propulsion system has hundreds of working parts, none of which serves any known purpose integral to the organism's survival distinct from its function within the flagellum—a characteristic Behe labels "irreducible complexity." Yet each of these parts is nec-

---

[15]Also pertinent when considering the limits of any teleological argument is the employment of a cumulative case argument strategy. This approach will be discussed in several places in this chapter. See also R. Douglas Geivett's treatment of the cumulative case argument in chapter 14 of this volume.

[16]See William Dembski, *Intelligent Design* (Downers Grove, Ill.: InterVarsity Press, 1999), and Michael Denton, *Darwinism: A Theory in Crisis* (Bethesda, Md.: Adler and Adler, 1986). For a good summary of the views of the intelligent design movement in general, see Michael Behe et al., *Science and Evidence for Design in the Universe* (San Francisco: Ignatius, 2000).

[17]Michael Behe, *Darwin's Black Box: The Biochemical Challenge to Evolution* (New York: Free Press, 1996), chap. 3.

essary to the operation of the flagellum. If Behe is correct, then none of the parts of the flagellum would have been preserved by natural selection. Therefore, so the argument goes, this particular system resists explanation in terms of a standard Darwinian model. If a Darwinian explanation is unavailable, then we must conclude either that the flagellum is the product of intelligent design or that this complex system came together all at once through the operation of pure chance alone, possibly by mutation.[18] The likelihood of all of the parts of the flagellum coming together by chance are so astronomically slim as to be functionally zero; nobody may reasonably argue that the hundreds of integral parts of the flagellum came together by pure chance. Thus, given that neither natural selection nor mere chance is a plausible explanation in this case, Behe concludes that the best explanation is intelligent design.

There is an important difference between Behe's argument and classical attempts to prove God's existence based on the evidence of teleology in nature. Behe's conclusion is much less ambitious than that of Aquinas and Paley. Behe makes this point clear when he tells us that his "argument is limited to design itself; I strongly emphasize that it is not an argument for the existence of a benevolent God, as Paley's was," and "questions about whether the designer is omnipotent, or even especially competent, do not arise in my argument as they did in Paley's."[19] Behe does not claim that the God of orthodox theism can be derived directly from the evidence he cites in favor of design. All that he claims is that certain facts of biochemistry are sufficient to tip the evidential scale in favor of the design hypothesis. Whether the designer can be shown to be the unique, perfectly good, om-

---

[18]The dilemma between design and pure chance may be a false dichotomy in such cases. Some biologists and philosophers argue that one may appeal to nonselection-based processes, such as coadaptation or genetic drift, in order to account for complexity without resorting to chance or design. For an accessible summary of these views and their critical relevance to Behe's argument, see Michael Ruse, *Can a Darwinian Be a Christian? The Relationship Between Science and Religion* (New York: Cambridge University Press, 2001), pp. 115-22. Since my goal is not to evaluate the scientific status of design arguments, I will leave this issue aside in what follows. For further scientific objections to Behe's position, I also direct the reader to Kenneth R. Miller, *Finding Darwin's God: A Scientist's Search for Common Ground Between God and Evolution* (New York: Cliff Street Books, 1999). Behe's reply to Miller is found in "The Modern Intelligent Design Hypothesis: Breaking Rules," *Philosophia Christi*, n.s. 3 (2001): 165-79. A helpful overview of design arguments in general is Michael Ruse, *Darwin and Design* (Cambridge, Mass.: Harvard University Press, 2003). Chapter 15 contains an assessment of the debate surrounding the intelligent design movement in light of philosophical, theological and scientific considerations.

[19]Behe, "Modern Intelligent Design Hypothesis," pp. 165-66.

nipotent and omniscient being worshiped by the Western religious traditions is a question that Behe is willing to leave to philosophers and theologians.[20] Indeed, Behe is not alone in this interpretation of the implications of the contemporary argument for intelligent design. For example, William Dembski, the foremost figure in the intelligent design movement, explicitly claims that arguments such as Behe's are not works of natural theology.[21]

We may represent the structure of the modern teleological argument (MTA) as follows:

1. Certain natural phenomena clearly have feature F.

2. It is highly improbable that F be caused by something other than an intelligent designer.

3. Therefore, it is highly probable that there exists an intelligent designer of such phenomena.

As noted above, Behe's project is much less ambitious than the classic versions of the teleological argument. He simply argues that a designer or designers, with unknown capacities and moral dispositions, is the best explanation of phenomena observed at the biochemical level. Other teleological arguments with less ambitious pretensions will also likely take this form. Furthermore, it should be clear that the parsimony of the conclusion of MTA insulates it from IEO. Behe does not, nor does any other major member of the intelligent design movement, claim to prove the existence of the God of orthodox theism. Rather, all we are shown is that nature or some systems within nature are products of design. As such the Humean may not assert that the proponent of such an argument has overstepped what can be strictly derived from the empirical evidence.

Although MTA successfully sidesteps IEO, one may wonder what good it does the theist: If the argument does not strongly support the theistic hypothesis, how does it help the cause of belief? The answer is that such an argument may play a role in a *cumulative case* for God's existence. In order to illustrate what is meant by a cumulative case, take the example of a detective investigating the theft of a large sum of money from a bank. Suppose if Smith had perpetrated the crime we would expect (1) he would have been in the vicinity of the bank at the time of the crime, (2) he had recently come into a large sum of money that cannot otherwise be explained, and (3) he

---

[20]Ibid., p. 165.
[21]See Dembski, *Intelligent Design*, pp. 105-9.

had ample motive for taking the money. If our detective can only prove that it is probable that Smith meets any one of these criteria, he has not given us good reason to believe that Smith is guilty; for example, there were probably plenty of people in the vicinity of the bank who did not steal the money. However, if the detective can show that it is probable that Smith meets all three of these descriptions, then there is very good reason to suspect that Smith is indeed the thief. Thus, even though an argument that shows it is highly probable that Smith was in the vicinity of the bank at the time of the robbery is independently insufficient to show that he was likely the thief, the combination of such an argument with other arguments that show he probably meets the other criteria will lead us to be rightfully suspicious of Smith. The combining of separate arguments, each of which is insufficient to prove a particular hypothesis independently, into a single argument for that hypothesis is what is meant here by a cumulative case.

If the God of theism exists, we would expect to find intelligent design in his creation, and the modern teleological argument shows that this expectation has been met. Nevertheless, as we have discussed above, this conclusion alone is not enough to make the theistic God's existence more probable than not. But just as in the case of our suspected thief, if further arguments can show that many of the other expectations we have for a universe created by God have been met, the combination of this evidence may be sufficient to show that we have very good reason to believe that God exists. MTA can assist a cumulative case for God's existence by showing that one of our expectations for what would obtain should God exist has been met. MTA leaves us with more work to do (we still need to determine whether any of our other expectations have been met), but it does provide one very important piece of the puzzle.[22] However, before we may finally settle the issue of MTA, we need to address a further Humean criticism that may rob such an effort even of its role in a cumulative case.

THE COUNTEREVIDENCE OBJECTION

Let us now turn to a second classic Humean criticism, one which we will see raise some trouble for MTA. In the *Dialogues* Philo notes that

---

[22]An example of a cumulative approach to proving God's existence is provided by Richard Swinburne in *The Existence of God*, rev. ed. (New York: Oxford University Press, 1991). Swinburne also provides a less technical version of this case in *Is There a God?* (New York: Oxford University Press, 1996). See Douglas Geivett's contribution in chapter 14 of this volume for an in-depth discussion of the cumulative case argument.

[t]here are many inexplicable difficulties in the works of Nature, which, if we allow a perfect author to be proved a priori, are easily solved, and become only seeming difficulties, from the narrow capacity of man, who cannot trace infinite relations. But according to your method of reasoning, these difficulties become all real; and perhaps will be insisted on, as new instances of likeness to human art and contrivance. At least, you must acknowledge that it is impossible for us to tell, from our limited views, whether this system contains any great faults or deserves any considerable praise, if compared to other possible, and even real systems.[23]

Hume's point here is that nature is full of apparent flaws, which should count as counterevidence to the orthodox theist's hypothesis, and one might say that turnabout is fair play. Hume grants that one can explain away the apparent flaws in nature more easily if one is a proponent of cosmological or ontological arguments. Such theists do not typically cite the arrangement of nature to support their particular views regarding the power and character of the creator, so they gain greater credibility when they shrug off the apparent inconsistency between God's perfection and infelicities in the natural order. According to Hume, the theist who appeals to the arrangement of nature as evidence of God's existence may not make such a move. The proponent of the teleological argument is committed to the view that the arrangement of nature is evidence of the character of its cause. Therefore, the arrangement of nature that a theist may see as evidence for God's existence requires us also to recognize a great deal of evidence that should lead to the opposite conclusion. It is unclear, at least on the face of the matter, which side is better supported by the evidence provided by nature. Thus, MTA undermines itself; if one accepts the strength of the evidence for the theist's conclusion, then one must accept equally strong counterevidence, and any theistic conclusion is thereby compromised. Let's call this criticism the "counterevidence objection" (CO).

CO is also employed by contemporary critics of teleological arguments. David Myers has recently followed such a line and concluded that "there is nothing in the new natural theology, based on the findings of contemporary science, that gives us any new compelling reason to think that, even if there is a cosmic designer, this designer possesses all three attributes of the God of traditional theism."[24] Myers's argument is a good representative of the ba-

---

[23]David Hume, *Dialogues Concerning Natural Religion*, in *David Hume: Writings on Religion*, ed. Anthony Flew (Peru, Ill.: Open Court, 1992), p. 228.
[24]David Myers, "New Design Arguments: Old Millian Objections," *Religious Studies* 36 (2000): 146.

sic Humean approach inspired by CO, so I will flesh it out in some detail. His strategy is to cite evidence that the natural order is not the product of the creative effort of a perfect being, and then claim that the sort of evidence cited by Behe and company does nothing to resolve these doubts.

The counterevidence we are concerned with is said to undermine the omnipotence and omniscience of the creator. Myers claims that omniscience implies knowledge of how best to design things to achieve any particular purpose, and omnipotence implies power to instantiate any such design. On the assumption of the theistic hypothesis, Myers believes that we should "expect a designed structure or system to be such that we cannot imagine how it could be improved."[25] Given this principle, even if we grant that the universe is designed, we may not conclude that the designer is both omnipotent and omniscient if there are ways in which we can envision its having been better designed.

Examples of apparent design flaws in nature are notoriously easy to produce. For instance, the neural wiring of the human eye is such that it creates a natural blind spot, and the structure of the human trachea allows swallowing to interfere with breathing, which gives rise to a considerable risk of choking. One cannot deny that the human eye and trachea would perform better if they lacked these flaws. On the basis of such examples, and they can be multiplied,[26] Myers concludes that, even if we grant that there is complexity at the biochemical level that supports strongly the existence of a supernatural designer, obvious facts of anatomy preclude the conclusion that the designer is both omnipotent and omniscient.

One may be inclined to argue that a perfect creator might have motives unknown to us that are sufficient to justify these apparent design flaws. Myers replies to such an objection that it just seems implausible to claim that any good can come from a blind spot or any of the other defects in nature he cites.[27] Furthermore, I might add that an appeal to ends beyond our ken is a poor strategy for the theist to follow, for it not only asks us to believe in a perfect creator but also to believe that such an artificer has unknown and possibly counterintuitive motivations. This addition to the theistic hypothesis could only weaken the case made by any design argument because the more content we build into a hypothesis, the less con-

---

[25]Ibid., p. 147.
[26]The proponent of CO will also likely point out the weakness of the spine, the narrowness of the birth canal and the presence of the infection-prone appendix.
[27]Myers, "New Design Arguments," p. 151.

firmation it receives by any piece of evidence.[28]

That the *classical* teleological argument is particularly troubled by CO should be clear. The proponent of such an argument is committed to the claim that we can read the existence and character of God directly from the evidence we encounter in nature. However, as a host of skeptical philosophers have pointed out over the millennia, there seems to be as much evidence in nature to speak against a perfectly competent creator as there is evidence that speaks in favor of the theistic hypothesis. Thus, we may take this Humean objection as good reason once again to temper our enthusiasm for CTA.

However, one might be inclined to believe that CO does not really pose a problem for MTA. We have discussed earlier that such an argument is proposed as part of a cumulative case for God's existence. Proponents of MTA merely claim that part of what we expect on the assumption of God's existence does obtain, namely, there is evidence of design in the universe. One then might conclude that CO is not a worry for the proponent of MTA simply because this argument does not claim to give us independent reason to believe the designer is particularly powerful or knowledgeable. Nevertheless, the systems taken as evidence in MTA clearly call for an explanation in terms of intelligent agency. This modest conclusion, one might say, is all that is necessary in order for MTA to make its contribution to a cumulative case for God's existence.

We should not be so quick to assume that there are no troubles posed for MTA by CO. We must keep in mind that MTA is useful to the theist only as part of a cumulative case for the existence of God. The conclusion that such a cumulative case is supposed to support is the notion that God is the creator, designer and sustainer of the universe, and this claim is usually taken to imply that God is intimately involved with the whole of his creation, such that he is responsible for the existence and nature of *everything* in the universe.[29]

---

[28]The problem is discussed in greater detail in the following section, "Defending MTA Against CO."

[29]At this point a theist in the biblical tradition may interject that many of the apparent flaws in design may be accounted for by the Fall. God's original creation was flawless, but the introduction of sin into the universe, which was not by God's design, has caused aspects of creation to go off course. While one may accept this explanation as part of an overall theological understanding of the current state of the universe, it is not a good strategy for the theist when doing natural theology. Appealing to the Fall requires one to pack more information into the theistic hypothesis. This increase in the scope of the hypothesis lowers its overall probability.

The basic claims of theism then provide us with two points relevant to the plausibility of MTA: (1) It is inconsistent with the basic claims of theism that design be a local phenomenon. Since the whole of the universe is supposed to be a product of God's activity, we should expect that all systems in nature would reflect his creative plan. Theism requires a universe that is well designed from head to toe; it is not just this or that natural system that God is supposed to have designed, but the entirety of nature. (2) Therefore, in order for a well-confirmed design hypothesis to be helpful to the theist, the overall structure and arrangement of the systems of nature must be at least *consistent* with the work of a *perfect* designer. Furthermore, even though there is quite a bit of evidence of well-designed systems in nature, if there are equally as many poorly designed systems to found, then the overall probability of the universe's being designed by God has not been shown to be greater.

Thus, if Hume is correct, any positive contribution MTA makes to a cumulative case for God's existence could easily be nullified by a skeptic who points out the all-too-common presence of apparent design flaws. We may grant that systems such as bacterium's flagellum are indeed well crafted enough to support the hypothesis of a perfect designer. On the other hand, we must also admit that something like the human spine, which we all know is quite prone to problems, is not exactly what we would expect of omniscience and omnipotence. Likewise, if one points out the incredible complexity and elegance of the human immune system as evidence of a perfect designer, one must also recognize the evidence against this hypothesis provided by the propensity of the human body to produce cancers. When taken in isolation, the immune system and the flagellum may very well show that it is probable that there is an intelligent designer. As such, the evidence provided by these systems may contribute positively to a cumulative case for God's existence. However, the theistic hypothesis requires that God is responsible for all mechanisms in nature, and therefore the occurrence of frequent spinal injuries and cancer cannot be ignored.

The Humean's point is that this counterevidence to design cancels out the

Thus, appeal to the Fall will make it more difficult for the theist to prove her case. I discuss this strategy in greater detail in the next section of this chapter. For a view divergent from my own that takes the Fall as playing a core role in Christian theism, and therefore does not lower the overall probability of the theistic hypothesis, see Cornelius G. Hunter, *Darwin's God: Evolution and the Problem of Evil* (Grand Rapids: Brazos, 2001). Also helpful on this point is James Sennett, "The Inscrutable Evil Defense Against the Inductive Argument from Evil," *Faith and Philosophy* 10 (1993): 220-29.

evidence provided by flagellum and the immune system. We could expect that the entire universe created by God would be perfectly designed, but, given the prevalence of apparent design flaws, it is at best a 50 percent probability that God has designed nature.[30] That is, MTA shows that it is neither more nor less likely that God is the designer of the universe. If the Humean is correct on this score, it is difficult to see how MTA can be used to raise the overall probability of God's existence, and this particular piece of the puzzle has not been provided. Thus, one should worry whether MTA has anything to offer even a cumulative case for the existence of the God of orthodox theism.[31]

The task then for the MTA proponent is to counter CO by showing that the apparent design flaws we find in nature are actually consistent with the theistic hypothesis. In the following section we will discuss how a strategy taken from the contemporary debate over the problem of evil may be helpful to this end.

Defending MTA Against CO: The Basic Strategy

We have seen above that one should expect the Humean to argue that the supposed imperfections in creation are incompatible with the design of an omnipotent and omniscient creator. Therefore MTA would have no role to play in a cumulative case for God's existence; by drawing evidence for God's existence from nature one is forced to accept equally compelling evidence in favor of the opposite conclusion.

One of the most influential theistic strategies[32] in the debate regarding the problem of evil employed in recent years comes to us in the form of Stephen Wykstra's condition of reasonable epistemic access (CORNEA), which he summarizes as follows:

On the basis of cognized situation s, human H is entitled to claim "It appears

---

[30]I am assuming for the sake of argument that there are (approximately) equally as many apparently well-designed as apparently poorly designed systems in nature.

[31]This objection has no traction if the proponent of MTA does not intend to use his case to help prove God's existence. The occurrence of well-designed systems is perfectly compatible with the occurrence of poorly designed systems. In this way, the MTA could still be a naturalism defeater without contributing significantly to a case for God's existence. For a discussion of how MTA may fulfill this role, see Mark A. Discher and James D. Madden, "What ID Does and Does Not Imply," *Perspectives on Science and Christian Faith* 56, no. 4 (2004): 286-91.

[32]This particular strategy is often referred to as "skeptical theism." For a detailed discussion of the role skeptical theism has played in recent philosophy of religion, see David O'Connor, *God and Inscrutable Evil: In Defense of Theism and Atheism* (New York: Rowman & Littlefield, 1998), chap. 10.

that *p*" only if it is reasonable for *H* to believe that, given her cognitive faculties and the use she has made of them, if *p* were not the case, *s* would likely be different than it is in some way discernable by her.[33]

In other words, if one is going to believe reasonably that some state of affairs obtains on the evidence provided by a particular set of data, she must be able to point out what difference in the evidence we would expect to find if that state of affairs did not obtain. For example, if I were to claim after inspecting a crowded room that Mr. Jones is not in the room, I must be able to say exactly what would be different about the appearance of the room if Mr. Jones were *in* the room. In this case, I would simply need to point out that the appearance of the room would be different in that it would include the appearance of Mr. Jones.

The skeptic in the debate over the problem evil claims that there is no good that could justify certain instances of intense suffering. As such, so the skeptic argues, the evidence of suffering makes it unreasonable to assume the existence of God. However, if we take CORNEA seriously, then it is incumbent on the skeptic to give an account of how the relevant data would be different if there were such a justifying good. Specifically, the skeptic needs to point out how the amount or intensity of suffering in the world would be different were theism true.

The skeptic's task in this case is a difficult undertaking. One may concede both that we would expect all suffering in a world created by God to lead to a greater good and that there is no *known* good, the achievement of which would justify the horrible suffering that occurs with regularity in the current state of the universe. On this much the theist and the skeptic may agree. However, if we admit that there are goods beyond our ken—good states of affairs that human beings in their current state are unable to recognize as being good—then it remains possible that the horrible suffering in the world does indeed serve some end that justifies God's allowing it to happen. We are then unable to say exactly what the relevant difference between our world and a world created by God would be. In other words, if we have reason to believe that there are unknown goods sufficient to justify apparently gratuitous suffering, then it seems the atheist may not reasonably claim

---

[33]Stephen J. Wykstra, "The Humean Obstacle to Evidential Arguments from Suffering: On Avoiding the Evils of 'Appearance,'" *International Journal of Philosophy of Religion* 16 (1984): 85. For a more recent treatment, see Stephen J. Wykstra, "Rowe's Noseeum Arguments from Evil," in *The Evidential Argument from Evil,* ed. Daniel Howard-Snyder (Bloomington: Indiana University Press, 1996), pp. 126-50.

that a certain state of affairs that obtains in the actual world would not obtain in a world created by God because there is no apparent good that comes of it. It is always possible, perhaps even to be expected, that the suffering is justified by a good beyond our ken.[34] Thus, it is unclear exactly what the skeptic expects to be different in a world created by God.[35]

It is not difficult to see how CORNEA can be useful to the proponent of MTA. When pressed with CO, the proponent of MTA should ask his critic to specify how the data provided by the natural order would be different if there were an omniscient and omnipotent designer. The critic's likely response is that, if God existed, we would not expect the prevalence of apparent design flaws. But the proponent of MTA may appeal to CORNEA to point out that the current state of the world is no different from what we might expect on the assumption that God is responsible for the natural order. As long as there are ends of design beyond our ken, it always remains possible that an apparent design flaw is the product of impeccable principles of engineering that are unknown to us. Thus, once again the skeptic is unable to articulate just how creation would be different under the assumption that God exists.

CORNEA provides a promising strategy for the proponent of MTA, but its typical application will not serve that end. By appealing to goods beyond our ken, the theist increases the content of his hypothesis. We are asked not only to believe in an omnipotent, omniscient and perfectly good being that has all the properties associated with the God of orthodox theism, but also we must accept a certain theory of goodness implying that there are goods (for the present, at least) unknowable by the human intellect. Such a claim of unknowability in principle is controversial and lowers the overall probability of the theist's position. The mere fact that the unknowability claim is conjoined with the assertion of God's existence lowers the probability of the entire conjunction. Although there are philosophers, namely, G. E. Moore in *Principia Ethica*, who have held (for independent reasons) that there may be goods of which we have no knowledge, one may worry that appeal to such a theory of goodness is quite ad hoc on the theist's part; there is nothing in the basic theistic hypothesis that requires the existence of good beyond our ken. As a rule of thumb one should attempt to employ a CORNEA

---

[34]For an explication of some reasons why this might be expected, see Sennett, "The Inscrutable Evil Defense."

[35]For a response to skeptical theism from a "friendly atheist," see William Rowe, "The Evidential Argument from Evil: A Second Look," in *The Evidential Argument from Evil*, pp. 262-85.

strategy only by appealing to goods that are both within our grasp and consequences of the minimal claims of orthodox theism.

The task of the proponent of MTA, then, is to articulate principles that are
plausible components of the basic claims of orthodox theism and which
would lead us to expect the occurrence of apparent design flaws. We now
turn to G. W. Leibniz for a presentation of two such goods that can serve us
well in defense of MTA against the Humean attack.

A LEIBNIZIAN APPLICATION OF CORNEA: THE PRINCIPLE OF SIMPLICITY

G. W. Leibniz, a (mainly) seventeenth-century metaphysician, theologian,
political thinker and mathematician, is better known for his cosmological
and ontological arguments, although he does offer a version of CTA. However, we will not need to enter into a discussion of his particular arguments
for God's existence.[36] Rather, Leibniz's more general theological views contain insights into the constraints a perfect creator might operate under, and
these constraints show that apparent design flaws are consistent with a natural order that is the product of divine artifice. Leibniz's thought on divine
creation and his sustained program of theodicy give rise to various vexing
philosophical problems (most famously his claim that the actual world is the
best of all possible worlds), and I cannot defend his views here. Nevertheless, there is at least one doctrine central to Leibniz's project that is certainly
consistent with the basic theistic hypothesis, which we shall address in what
follows.[37]

We should reemphasize at the onset that we need not make any strong
claims in favor of these Leibnizian principles. All that is needed for our purposes is the indication of principles that are both consistent with the theistic

---

[36]For a good introduction to Leibniz's well-known cosmological and ontological arguments, see
David Blumenfeld, "Leibniz's Ontological and Cosmological Arguments," in *The Cambridge
Companion to Leibniz*, ed. Nicholas Jolley (New York: Cambridge University Press, 1995), pp.
353-81.

[37]Leibniz offers a famous argument for a version of idealism in which all of reality is reducible
to immaterial atoms, what he calls *monads*. Moreover, Leibniz accepts a form of essentialism
in which all of the nonrelational properties of any substance are absolutely necessary to it. In
short, much of what Leibniz has to say in his metaphysics is quite controversial. Nevertheless,
the Leibnizian claims we will rely on in this chapter can be separated from Leibniz's more
tendentious metaphysical doctrines. Indeed, the Leibnizian resources we shall draw on in
what follows are all taken from section 5 of his *Discourse on Metaphysics* (see note below),
which may be understood in isolation from his more controversial claims. In short, one need
not accept idealism or essentialism in order to employ a Leibnizian defense of MTA.

hypothesis and sufficient to justify the occurrence of design flaws. Thus, we do not need to claim that Leibniz's principles are necessitated by theism, nor do we need to show that these principles would likely be accepted by most theists. As long as God's pursuit of such principles is possible and these principles are sufficient to justify apparent design flaws, then the Humean will be unable to point out a difference in the relevant data set that must obtain if God exists.

Leibniz's views about the perfection of a world created by God are as famous as they are controversial: "Since all possible things have a claim to existence in God's understanding in proportion to their perfections, the result of all these claims must be the most perfect actual world which is possible."[38] Despite the way his optimism has been infamously satirized by later critics such as Voltaire and Schopenhauer, Leibniz is certainly well aware of the occurrence of apparent flaws in creation that are prima facie inconsistent with ours being the best of all possible worlds. At times when Leibniz addresses these worries he seems to employ something along the lines of CORNEA by appealing to goods beyond our grasp. For example, in one of his most seminal attempts at justifying the order of creation in his *Discourse on Metaphysics,* Leibniz claims that "to understand the reasons in particular which have moved [God] to choose this order of the universe . . . surpasses the power of the finite mind."[39] On the face of the matter, one might believe that Leibniz is apt to appeal to goods beyond our ken—i.e., "the reasons in particular which have moved" God to create—in order to justify the apparently infelicitous arrangement of nature. These remarks then give all the appearance of an application of CORNEA that makes use of an unknown principle to justify God's allowance of apparent design flaws. As such, it would then seem that Leibniz is taking us beyond the requirements of basic theism, and thus offers little help to the proponent of MTA.

We should not be too quick to accept this simple interpretation of Leibniz's theodicy in the *Discourse.* Leibniz goes on to claim in the same section that, although we cannot know all of God's ultimate ends for creation, "some general remarks can be made, however, about the ways of providence in the government of affairs."[40] In other words, no mortal can know all of what motivates God for any single divine act, but we can rationally

---

[38]G. W. Leibniz, *Discourse on Metaphysics,* in *Philosophical Papers and Letters, Second Edition,* ed. and trans. L. E. Loemker (Dordrecht, The Netherlands: Kluwer, 1989), p. 369.
[39]Ibid., p. 305.
[40]Ibid.

discern certain guidelines that a perfect being would follow when creating a world. These principles may in turn, according to Leibniz, reveal why it is that certain apparent infelicities actually are quite consistent with the perfection of the best of all possible worlds.

One such guideline is what I call Leibniz's "principle of efficiency" (PE). Leibniz begins to articulate this principle when he claims that the "simplicity of the ways of God . . . is shown especially in the means which he uses, whereas the variety, opulence, and abundance appears in regard to the ends or results."[41] Leibniz's point here is not that the work of a perfect creator would not exhibit stunning complexity; rather his claim regards the proportion between means and results that is the mark of the competence of a designer. This point can be fleshed out well with an example:

> It can be said, then that he who acts perfectly is like an excellent geometrician who knows how to find the best construction of a problem; or a good architect who makes the most advantageous use of the space and the capital intend for a building, leaving nothing which offended or which lacks the beauty of which it is capable; or a good family head who makes such use of his holding that there is nothing uncultivated and barren; or a skilled machinist who produces his work by the easiest process that can be chosen; or a learned author who includes the greatest number of subjects in the smallest volume.[42]

Leibniz's point is that one sign of true expertise is one's ability to bring about a great number of desired effects with limited resources. Given vast resources, even a mediocre designer may be able to craft a product of great value. However, the most skilled architect is the one who can build something magnificent on a small budget, and the expert engineer is somebody who can produce an intricate and highly effective machine through an efficient process. In short, the ability to produce a grand product through a very small set of resources is evidence of a designer of very high proficiency. PE is not the only mark of sound design, but it is certainly part of what we expect from an artificer of great skill. As such, one mark of a world created by a perfect designer is that a vast number of phenomena are produced with limited resources. We may then conclude that we would expect to find a perfect economy of means and ends in a world designed by a perfect being.

An objection looms here. Certainly it is a mark of great skill when a designer with limited resources is able to craft a highly valuable artifact, but it

[41]Ibid., p. 306.
[42]Ibid., pp. 305-6.

is unclear that God would have limited resources available when creating a universe. The architect has a certain budget for a building project imposed on him, and therefore the range of possibilities for pursing his end is restricted. The wisdom of the architect is then demonstrated if he does not expend any of these resources needlessly; he uses every bit of his capital in the most efficient way available to bring about a building of high value. Since God is omnipotent, all possible plans for design are open to him. No possible plan of design is any more or less difficult for God to execute. There then seems to be no sense in which God must operate on limited resources when designing the universe. As long as God's ultimate ends are met he does not evidence his wisdom by choosing any particular route to his goal, because all such routes are equally easy for him to pursue. There then seems to be no sense in which God can be any more or less efficient. Thus, we might worry that PE is simply not applicable to God.

Leibniz is aware of this concern when he notes that it is "true that nothing costs God anything." Nonetheless, Leibniz goes no to say, "[W]here wisdom is concerned, decrees or hypotheses are comparable to expenditures, in the degree to which they are independent of each other, for reason demands that we avoid multiplying hypotheses or principles, somewhat as the simplest system is always preferred in astronomy."[43] The possibilities for creation are not limited for God; there are infinitely many ways in which his ends could be met. However, God could produce a needlessly complicated universe. God might create a universe that operates according to more natural laws, what Leibniz calls "principles," than are absolutely necessary to bring about the phenomena he wants to establish. These natural principles, according to Leibniz, are God's "means" for bringing about his ends; God fulfills his plan for creation by instantiating a certain set of natural laws that govern creation. If any principles of nature obtain that are not absolutely necessary for God's creative plan, then he is not operating with the highest efficiency. Such a principle would be a needless intellectual "expenditure" on God's part. Thus, God satisfies PE by producing a universe in which there is a perfect ratio between the principles of nature (God's "means") and the phenomena they govern. The degree to which fewer principles subsume a greater number of phenomena is one determining factor in the overall perfection of the universe, and therefore an indication of the perfection of its designer.

---

[43]Ibid., p. 306.

PE enables us to respond to the Humean proponent of CO using a revised CORNEA strategy. As we discussed earlier, the Humean critic cites such familiar phenomena as the faulty human spine and the frequency of cancer in mammals as counterevidence to MTA. PE shows that this supposed counterevidence is consistent with the work of a perfect designer. Leibniz would not deny that God could produce a system of nature that is free of cancer and faulty spinal columns. Nevertheless, it remains possible that elimination of these apparent errors would decrease the overall perfection of the created order by multiplying the number of natural principles. Thus, we need not take the occurrence of apparent design flaws to reflect badly on either the power or wisdom of the creator. It is possible that these infelicities are allowed to occur in the interest of maintaining the best possible proportion between natural principles and the phenomena they govern. One might even say that it is not surprising to see apparent flaws in a world that is guided by a principle of efficiency for, as long as the means available are constrained by considerations of the efficiency of means, the end product may appear less perfect than another world that was governed in an ad hoc manner. (Of course, for Leibniz, this is only an apparent lack of perfection, for the world that is governed by a principle of simplicity really is more perfect.)

If the occurrence of apparent design flaws is consistent with the work of a perfect designer, as PE shows, then CORNEA may be effectively utilized. It is incumbent on the Humean critic to point out exactly how the world would be different from its current state if it were God's work. The claim that it would not contain any particular apparent design flaw is inadequate, since under PE this is at best an open question. Leibniz has shown us that any such appearance is perfectly consistent with the theistic hypothesis. Thus, the evidence cited in MTA supports the theistic hypothesis and the supposed Humean counterevidence is actually consistent with the work of a perfect designer. In short, PE coupled with CORNEA show that Hume's supposed counterevidence is not counterevidence at all.

Unlike appeals to unknown goods, PE will not cost the proponent of MTA anything in terms of the plausibility of the theistic hypothesis. Leibniz does not indulge any special pleading by appealing to principles that remain in principle beyond our grasp. Rather, he points out a readily grasped principle. Indeed, as Leibniz's examples show, we presuppose PE in our everyday evaluation of the expertise of practical designers. Moreover, the fact that PE is consistent with, even suggested by, the theistic hypothesis is readily ap-

parent. We would not expect that God would employ principles that are unnecessary to the creation of a universe that meets his ends.[44] The theist may
then help herself to PE without adding to the weight of her hypothesis.
Therefore, Leibniz gives us good reason to believe that well-designed systems may coexist in nature with apparently flawed systems and still raise the
probability of the existence of an omniscient and omnipotent designer.[45]

CONCLUSION

Although we have seen that Hume's IEO gives us good reason to be cautious about CTA, MTA is immune to this criticism. And although Hume's CO
enjoys some initial promise as an objection to MTA, CORNEA offers hope of
overcoming this difficulty. However, CORNEA in its typical application requires an appeal to goods beyond our ken, which itself may make the theistic hypothesis ad hoc. Leibniz's PE indicates known goods that are sufficient to justify the appearance of design flaws and is entirely consistent with
the basic theistic hypothesis. As such Leibnizian considerations provide us
with a means of defending MTA against Humean concerns about apparent
design flaws in nature.[46]

---

[44]Leibniz would likely prefer a stronger claim here. In his view PE is not merely consistent with
the theistic hypothesis, but is logically implied by God's perfection. However, for our purposes, it is ample that PE only be consistent with theism, and therefore there is no need to
saddle the theist with the claim that theism necessitates it.

[45]One may object that things may not be so simple for the theist on this score. If there is some
reason to believe that the proportion between the laws of nature and the phenomena they
govern in the natural world is less than parsimonious, then the appeal to PE is blocked. However, recent optimism by many physicists regarding the eventual discovery of a single formula
that can ultimately account for all physical phenomena (the fabled "Theory of Everything")
may bode well for PE. Such a formula would show that all natural occurrences are subsumed
under a single natural law, which a Leibnizian would interpret as evidence of the perfect simplicity of God's means.

[46]I owe a great deal of gratitude to Martin Curd and James Sennett for their careful reading and
generous comments on earlier drafts of this chapter. I have done my best to take their criticisms into account, although some of our differences still remain. Gordon Barnes, Mark A.
Discher, Douglas Groothuis and Bryan O'Neal also made helpful recommendations. Thanks
to all. I of course take sole responsibility for the weaknesses and errors contained in this
work.

9

Hume, Fine-Tuning and the "Who Designed God?" Objection

Robin Collins

Elsewhere I have argued that the discoveries in physics and cosmology, along with developments in philosophy, particularly in the logic of inference, have significantly bolstered the traditional teleological argument, or argument from design.[1] Today, I contend, the evidence from physics and cosmology offers us significant, well-formulated reasons for believing in theism. In this chapter I will show how, if properly formulated, the argument from fine-tuning can largely circumvent David Hume's major objections to the teleological argument. I will devote the second half of this chapter to addressing Hume's most important and often-raised objection to the design argument, what could be called the "Who Designed God?" objection. Before considering these objections to the fine-tuning design argument, however, we will need to review the argument briefly.

Review of the Fine-Tuning Argument

The fine-tuning of the laws of nature and the initial conditions of the universe for intelligent life (or conscious observers) has been one of the most widely discussed bodies of cosmological evidence for design, although other aspects of the laws of nature, such as their beauty, elegance and intelligibility also suggest design. The fine-tuning of the cosmos for intelligent life refers to the fact that many of the fundamental parameters of physics and the initial conditions of the universe are balanced on a razor's edge for

[1]For example, see Robin Collins, "The Teleological Argument," in *The Rationality of Theism*, ed. Paul Copan and Paul Moser (New York: Routledge, 2003).

intelligent life to occur. For example, if these parameters were slightly different, life of comparable intelligence to our own would not exist, or would at least be much less likely. The first major claim along these lines was in 1956—that the resonance states of carbon and oxygen had to fall within a narrow range for significant quantities of both carbon and oxygen to be produced in stars. Without enough carbon and oxygen, the existence of carbon-based life would be seriously inhibited.

Many other instances of cosmic fine-tuning have been advanced since then, and much work is continuing. One of the most impressive and widely discussed cases of fine-tuning is that of the "cosmological constant," a term in Einstein's equation of general relativity that governs the rate at which space expands. For the universe to be hospitable to life, this constant must be fine-tuned to at least one part in 10^{53}—that is, one part in one hundred million, billion, billion, billion, billion, billion—of what physicists consider its natural range of values. To get an idea of how precise this is, it would be like throwing a dart at the surface of the earth from the moon and hitting a bull's-eye one trillionth of a trillionth of an inch in diameter—less than the size of an atom!

Elsewhere I have presented the evidence for fine-tuning and developed one version of the argument from the fine-tuning in detail, including addressing various objections to the argument.[2] Here I can only briefly summarize the main features of the argument. I first distinguish between what I call the "atheistic single-universe hypothesis" and the "many-universes hypothesis."[3] According to the former, there is only one universe, and it is ultimately an inexplicable, "brute" fact that the universe exists and is fine-tuned. Many atheists, however, advocate the latter—sometimes also called the "many-worlds hypothesis." According to the most popular version of this hypothesis, there exists some physical process that imaginatively could be thought of as a "universe generator" that produces a very large or infinite

---

[2]A careful presentation of six good cases of fine-tuning is presented in Robin Collins, "The Evidence for Fine-Tuning," in *God and Design: The Teleological Argument and Modern Science*, ed. Neil Manson (New York: Routledge, 2003). An up-to-date rendition of the argument is presented in Robin Collins, "God, Design, and Fine-Tuning," in *God Matters: Readings in the Philosophy of Religion*, ed. Raymond Martin and Christopher Bernard (New York: Longman, 2002), and Collins, "The Teleological Argument" (2003). Further information and updates can be found at <www.fine-tuning.org>.

[3]In this chapter, I take atheism as more than simply the denial of the God of traditional theism, but as also involving the denial of any overall intelligence that could be considered responsible for the existence or apparent design of the universe.

number of universes, with each universe having a randomly selected set of initial conditions and values for the constants of physics. Because this generator produces so many universes, it will eventually—and strictly by chance—produce one that is set just right for intelligent life to occur.

I argue that fine-tuning strongly supports theism over the atheistic single-universe hypothesis and then separately argue that there are reasons to prefer the theistic explanation of fine-tuning over the atheistic version of the many-universes explanation.[4] The argument that the evidence of fine-tuning strongly supports theism over the atheistic single-universe hypothesis is our main concern in this chapter.[5]

Although the fine-tuning argument can be cast in several different forms—such as inference to the best explanation—I believe the most rigorous way of formulating the argument is in terms of what I will call the "prime principle of confirmation" (PPC), a version of the principle that Rudolf Carnap has called the "increase in firmness" principle, and others have simply called the "likelihood principle."[6] The prime principle can be stated as follows: For any two competing hypotheses H_1 and H_2, an observation counts as evidence in favor of H_1 over H_2 if the observation is more probable under H_1 than H_2. Put symbolically, evidence E counts in favor of H_1 over H_2 if $P(E/H_1) > P(E/H_2)$, where "$P(E/H_1)$" and "$P(E/H_2)$" represent the *conditional epistemic probability* of E on H_1 and H_2, respectively. (The notion of *epistemic* probability will be explained below.) Moreover, the degree to which the evidence counts in favor of one hypothesis over another is proportional to the degree to which the observation is more probable under the one hypothesis than the other.[7]

---

[4]It should be noted that theism is not of itself incompatible with the many-universes hypothesis, since, for example, God could have created a life-permitting universe indirectly by creating a physical process that generated multiple universes with different values for the basic parameters of physics.

[5]For an extended treatment of the many-universes hypothesis, see Robin Collins, "The Argument from Design and the Many-Worlds Hypothesis," in *Philosophy of Religion: A Reader and Guide*, ed. William Lane Craig (New Brunswick, N.J.: Rutgers University Press, 2002).

[6]See Rudolf Carnap, *The Logical Foundations of Probability* (Chicago: University of Chicago, 1962). For a basic, but somewhat dated, introduction to confirmation theory and the prime principle of confirmation, see Richard Swinburne, *An Introduction to Confirmation Theory* (London: Methuen, 1973). For literature specifically discussing the likelihood principle, see A. W. F. Edwards, *Likelihood* (Baltimore: Johns Hopkins University, 1992) and Elliot Sober, "Bayesianism—Its Scope and Limits," in *Bayes's Theorem*, ed. Richard Swinburne (Oxford: Oxford University Press, 2002), pp. 21-38.

[7]For those familiar with the probability calculus, a precise statement of the degree to which evidence counts in favor of one hypothesis over another can be given in terms of the odds

To avoid certain potential counterexamples, however, we will restrict the principle to apply only to those cases in which H_1 was not merely constructed to account for E being considered: for example, H_1 has some independent plausibility apart from E, or was at least widely considered viable apart from E.[8] I call this the *restricted prime principle*. The motivation for restricting the principle can be seen by considering the following example. Suppose that I roll a die twenty times and it comes up some apparently random sequence of numbers—say 2, 6, 4, 3, 1, 5, 6, 4, 3, 2, 1, 6, 2, 4, 4, 1, 3, 6, 6, 1. The probability is one in 3.6 x 10^{15}, or about one in a million billion. To explain the die coming up in this sequence, suppose I invented an hypothesis that there is a demon whose favorite number is just the above sequence of numbers, and that this demon had a strong desire for that sequence to turn up when I rolled the die. Now, if this demon hypothesis were true, then the fact that the die came up in this sequence would be expected—that is, it would not be epistemically improbable. Consequently, by the unrestricted prime principle of confirmation, the occurrence of this sequence would strongly confirm the demon hypothesis over the chance hypothesis. But this seems counterintuitive: given a sort of commonsense notion of confirmation, it does not seem that the demon hypothesis is confirmed. Or consider another example. Suppose that Jane Doe wins the lottery. Under the chance hypothesis this is very unlikely—say one in a million—but under the hypothesis that the lottery was rigged in her favor, it is not improbable at all. Thus, contrary to what we might think intuitively, it follows from the unrestricted version of the prime principle that Jane's winning the lottery strongly confirms that it was rigged in her favor.

Now consider a modification of the demon case in which, prior to my rolling the die, a group of occultists claimed to have a religious experience of a demon they called Goodal, who they claimed revealed that her favorite number was the number above and that she strongly desired that number be realized in some continuous sequence of die rolls in the near future. Suppose they wrote this all down in front of many reliable witnesses days before I rolled the die. Certainly, it seems, the sequence of die rolls would count as evidence in favor of their "Goodal" hypothesis over the chance hypothe-

---

form of Bayes's theorem: that is, $P(H_1/E)/P(H_2/E) = [P(H_1)/P(H_2)] \times [P(E/H_1)/P(E/H_2)]$, where $P(x/y)$ represents the conditional epistemic probability of one proposition x on another y. The general version of the PPC stated here, however, does not require the applicability or truth of Bayes's theorem.

[8]Often, the prime principle is stated without this restriction.

sis. Of course, in this circumstance, the Goodal hypothesis was already advocated prior to the rolling of the die, and thus the restricted prime principle implies that the sequence of die rolls confirms the "Goodal" hypothesis. Thus, the restricted version of the principle gives the right results in this case. Similarly, if we already suspected that the lottery was rigged in Jane's favor, we would consider the fact that she won the lottery strong evidence in favor of the rigging hypothesis.[9]

The core of my version of the fine-tuning argument begins by more carefully defining what we mean by fine-tuning. In the literature, "fine-tuning" typically refers to the conjunction of the following two claims: (1) the claim that the range of life-permitting values for the constants of physics is small compared to some properly chosen comparison range R for those values;[10] and (2) the claim that the values of the constants actually fall within the life-permitting range.[11] I will refer to claim 1 as the claim that the constants are fine-tuned, and to claim 2 as the claim that the constants have life-permitting values. Given this distinction, the fine-tuning argument can be stated as follows:

P1: The existence of life-permitting values for the constants of physics is not epistemically improbable under theism.

P2: Because of the fine-tuning, the existence of life-permitting values for the constants is epistemically very improbable under the atheistic single-universe hypothesis.

C: Since both theism and the atheistic single-universe hypothesis were clearly not constructed merely to account for the fine-tuning data, it follows from premises 1 and 2 and the restricted prime principle that the fine-tuning data provide strong evidence in favor of the design hypothesis over the atheistic single-universe hypothesis.

Note several features of this argument. First, the argument does not say

---

[9]The restricted prime principle is not the only way of addressing such counterexamples. A more common way is to argue that the prior probability of the hypothesis in question is so low that the confirmation offered cannot be sufficient to make the hypothesis likely. Although I agree that this latter response is successful, it commits one to the notion of prior probabilities which I prefer to avoid.

[10]The comparison range/region will effectively be that local range/volume in parameter space around the life-permitting region such that we can make determinations as to whether or not a parameter is life-permitting—what I call the epistemically illuminated region. Generally this range/region will be very large, but finite. For more on this, see my website <www.fine-tuning.org>.

[11]For the balance of this chapter, the expression "life-permitting values" should be understood as "intelligent life-permitting values."

that the fine-tuning evidence proves that the universe was designed, or even that it is likely that the universe was designed. Indeed, of itself it does not even show that we are epistemically warranted in believing in theism over the atheistic single-universe hypothesis. In order to justify these sorts of claims, we would have to look at the full range of evidence both for and against the theistic hypothesis, something we are not doing in this chapter. Rather, the argument merely concludes that fine-tuning strongly *supports* theism *over* the atheistic single-universe hypothesis.

In this way, the evidence of the fine-tuning argument is much like fingerprints found on a gun: although they can provide strong evidence that the defendant committed the murder, one could not conclude merely from them alone that the defendant is guilty; one would also have to look at all the other evidence offered. Suppose ten reliable witnesses claimed to see the defendant at a party at the time of the shooting. In this case, the fingerprints would still count as significant evidence of guilt, but this evidence would be counterbalanced by the testimony of the witnesses. Similarly the evidence of fine-tuning strongly supports theism over the atheistic single-universe hypothesis, though it does not itself show that theism is the most plausible explanation of the world, all things considered.

The second feature of the argument we should note is that the type of probability is *epistemic*. Roughly, the conditional epistemic probability of a proposition R on another proposition S can be defined as the degree to which S *of itself* should rationally lead us to expect that R is true. It is important to stress here that, under the atheistic single-universe hypothesis, there is no *statistical* probability that a universe will exist that has life-permitting values for its constants. A statistical probability could only exist relative to some model in which the universe was produced by some physical process that churned out life-permitting universes with a certain relative frequency. The whole point of the atheistic single-universe hypothesis, however, is that there is no such universe generator. Rather, the universe exists as a brute, inexplicable fact. Thus, the probabilities in this case should not be understood as statistical probabilities, but rather as measures of rational degrees of support of one proposition or another.[12] The claim essentially boils down

---

[12]This is an error made by Keith Parsons when he objects that fine-tuning could not be probable or improbable under the atheistic single-universe hypothesis: "If the universe is the ultimate brute fact, it is neither likely nor unlikely, probable or improbable; it simply is." Keith Parsons, "Is there a Case for Christian Theism?" in *Does God Exist? A Debate Between Theists and Atheists,* ed. J. P. Moreland and Kai Nielsen (New York: Prometheus, 1993), p. 182.

to the claim that, because the life-permitting range of a parameter of physics is very small compared to a properly chosen comparison range R, the atheistic single-universe hypothesis, of itself, should strongly lead us to expect that a parameter of physics would not fall into the (intelligent-)life-permitting range. Furthermore, the expectations here are not expectations relative to our total background information—which already includes the information that the values are life-permitting. Rather it is relative to a reduced set of background information in which the fact that a particular parameter has life-permitting values is "subtracted-out."[13]

The third feature of the argument we should note is that, given the truth of the prime principle of confirmation, the conclusion of the argument follows from the premises. Specifically, if the premises of the argument are true, then we are guaranteed that the conclusion is true, that is, the argument is what philosophers call *valid*.

One major argument in support of P1 is that, since God is an all-good being and it is good for intelligent, conscious, embodied beings to exist, it is not surprising or improbable that God would create a world that could support embodied intelligent life. Thus, given fine-tuning, the existence of life-permitting cosmic conditions is not improbable under theism, as P1 asserts.

One might object that, because of the existence of evil, we do not know that the existence of embodied, conscious, intelligent beings is a good thing as the argument seems to assume. To address this objection, let E represent the claim that embodied, conscious beings exist and let E' represent the claim that embodied conscious beings exist in the universe *and* that their embodied existence is a positive good (that is, something that increases the overall value of reality). Then, it follows from the above argument that claim E' is not highly improbable under theism. But, E' entails E and if one claim R entails another claim S, then the probability of S is greater than or equal to that of R. Hence, if E' is not highly improbable under theism, then it follows that E isn't either.

In defense of P2 an appeal is often made to some sort of an analogy, such as the improbability of a randomly tossed dart hitting a very small bull's-eye. It is helpful, however, to have a more principled justification of this claim. To do so, we must appeal to some principle that allows us to move from the

---

[13]This is one way of addressing the standard problem of "old evidence," of which this version of the fine-tuning argument is an instance. The issue of how to subtract the evidence in question unambiguously is beyond the scope of this chapter. See Collins, "How to Rigorously Define Fine-Tuning," *Philosophia Christi*, forthcoming.

fact that the life-permitting range of the parameters of physics is very small to the claim that it is improbable that the parameters of physics would fall into the life-permitting range under the atheistic single-universe hypothesis. I do this by appealing to a version of the probabilistic *principle of indifference,* what I will call the *restricted principle of indifference.* Applied to the case at hand, this principle could be roughly stated as follows: *When we have no reason to prefer any one value of a parameter over another, we should assign equal probabilities to equal ranges of the parameter,* **given that the parameter in question directly corresponds to some physical magnitude** *(or occurs in the simplest way of writing the fundamental theories in the relevant domain).*[14]

Specifically, if the comparison range (that is, the range allowed by the relevant background theories) of such a parameter is R and the life-permitting range is r, then the epistemic probability is r/R (r divided by R). Suppose, for instance, that the comparison range, R, of values for the strength of gravity runs from zero to the strength of the strong nuclear force, that is, 0 to $10^{40}G_0$ (where G_0 represents the current value for the strength of gravity). I have argued elsewhere that the life-permitting range r for the strength of gravity is at most 0 to $10^9 G_0$, and probably closer to 0 to $10^3 G_0$.[15] Now, *of itself* (specifically, apart from the knowledge that we exist), the atheistic single-universe hypothesis gives us *no* reason to think that the strength of gravity would fall into the life-permitting range instead of any other part of the comparison range. Thus, assuming the strength of gravity constitutes a real physical magnitude or occurs in the simplest way of writing the relevant theories, the restricted principle of indifference would state that equal ranges of this force should be given equal probabilities, and hence the probability of the strength of gravity falling into the life-permitting range would be at most r/R = $10^9/10^{40}$ = $1/10^{31}$—an astronomically unlikely probability.[16]

---

[14]As an example of what it means to directly correspond to some physical magnitude, consider the mass of an object. A physical parameter m that designates the mass directly corresponds to a physical quantity, whereas a physical parameter u that designates that mass squared (u = m^2) does not directly correspond to a physical quantity but to an artificial variable. When conflicting parameters arise—e.g., two equally simple ways of writing a theory with different sets of parameters functionally related to each other—then one should take the probability as being given by the range of probability values formed by applying the restricted principle to each parameter separately. A full statement and defense of this principle may be found at my website <www.fine-tuning.org>.

[15]Collins, "The Evidence for Fine-Tuning."

[16]A full-scale, rigorous justification of the restricted principle of indifference, and of P2, is be-

HUME'S OBJECTIONS ANSWERED

Objections to analogy. The first of Hume's objections is with the argument for design from analogy, which is the way the argument was typically formulated in Hume's day, before careful work was done on the logic of inference. This version of the argument rests on the principle that similar effects have similar causes.[17] It is then argued that the universe is similar in the relevant respects to a human contrivance, such as a work of art or a watch, and thus has a similar cause. Thus, since human contrivances are products of intelligent design, if the universe is analogous to a human contrivance in the relevant respects, then by the above principle we should infer that the universe is a product of a similar cause, namely, an intelligent agent.

This version of the argument faces at least two major types of objections, which Hume elaborated. The first derives from the principle that the more similar the effect, the more similar the cause. Thus, the more the universe seems to be like a human artifact, the more we should claim that the cause of the world is like a human being, just much more powerful (e.g., an alien with a brain and a body who created the universe in a lab). But this is not what the argument from design is supposed to show.

The second objection is that the analogy between human artifacts and the features of the universe that supposedly exhibit design are tenuous. The fact that the values of the constants of physics are in an extremely narrow life-permitting range, for instance, might be enough to suggest design, but in many ways it is disanalogous to the "fine-tuning" characteristic of a human artifact. No actual human artifact has fundamental physical constants that are adjusted just right; rather, it has certain material parts that are configured in the way needed to achieve some end. One must therefore interpret the falling of the parameters of physics within some narrow range as relevantly similar to the material parts of an artifact being in some narrow range of po-

---

yond the scope of this chapter. A sketch of how such a justification would proceed is presented in the appendix of Collins, "The Fine-Tuning Design Argument," and to a lesser extent in Collins, "God, Design, and Fine-Tuning." In those papers I explain how certain well-known objections to the principle of indifference, such as the Bertrand Paradoxes, can be circumvented. I hope to present a full-scale justification of the principle in a book, currently in progress and tentatively titled *The Well-Tempered Universe: God, Fine-Tuning, and the Laws of Nature.* The important point in the present text is that, by providing a principled justification of P2, the fine-tuning argument can get beyond merely being an argument from analogy. See also <www.fine-tuning.org>.

[17]David Hume, *Dialogues Concerning Natural Religion and the Posthumous Essays,* ed. Richard Popkin (Indianapolis: Hackett, 1980), pp. 15. Hereafter references will be given in the text with DNR and page numbers.

sitions. Although such a subjective interpretation might be enough to suggest design, it clearly does not provide a sufficient basis for a rigorous development of the fine-tuning argument. In any case, whatever the merits of this analogical version of the fine-tuning argument, it is not the argument I have developed. My version of the fine-tuning argument is not an argument from analogy at all and is therefore not subject to either of these Humean objections.

The alternative explanation objection. Another objection that Hume raised to the design argument was that one cannot infer the God of theism from fine-tuning, since there are many alternative explanations (DNR 35-38). For example, perhaps our world is the result of a committee of gods, or some finite deity (or, again, a powerful alien who has discovered how to create universes in a lab). Of course, a theist might respond that hypothesizing such beings simply pushes the design problem up one level, to who or what designed the minds of these gods or alien intelligences. To this, an atheist can respond that the same problem confronts the theistic hypothesis. If we invoke God as an explanation of the fine-tuning, haven't we just pushed the issue of design up one level to who or what designed God? As mentioned in the introduction, this is probably the most common objection to the design argument, whether the fine-tuning version or some other version. We will address this objection extensively in the latter part of this chapter. There we will see that the God hypothesis avoids this objection, whereas the many gods and finite god hypotheses do not.

For now we can simply observe that, as I have formulated the argument, it circumvents this issue. It merely says that the evidence of fine-tuning strongly confirms theism over the atheistic single-universe hypothesis. That is, if theism and the atheistic single-universe hypothesis are the main contenders, then the evidence of fine-tuning should significantly raise confidence in theism and lower confidence in the truth of the atheistic single-universe hypothesis in comparison with what such confidences would otherwise be. Although this does not establish everything we might want, it does establish something of great significance (provided my version of the fine-tuning argument is sound).[18] Of course, other explanations—such as the many-gods hypothesis—are also confirmed over the atheistic single-universe

---

[18]For example, I argue in "The Fine-Tuning Design Argument" that the fine-tuning offers a stronger and more solid argument for theism (versus the atheistic single-universe hypothesis) than the probabilistic version of the argument from evil offers against theism.

hypothesis. So, at the end of the day, if one is interested in which hypothesis to believe, one would have to provide other reasons for preferring the theistic explanation—arguments such as the cosmological argument, the moral argument, the argument from religious experience, or considerations based on simplicity, as Richard Swinburne does.[19] But this is a task beyond the scope of the design argument.[20]

Of itself, the *primary focus* of the fine-tuning design argument is to provide us good reason for preferring theism over the atheistic single-universe hypothesis, which is historically the leading contender to theism among Western intellectuals. Other considerations can then be offered for preferring theism to other leading contenders, particularly what I call the many-universes generator hypothesis (see above) and the appeal to a grand unified theory (which speculates that the values of the constants of physics are a consequence of the ultimate laws and physical principles underlying the universe) to explain fine-tuning. For example, one of the major objections that can be offered to both the many-universe generator hypothesis and the appeal to a grand unified theory is that they simply move the design problem up one level. To the many-universes generator hypothesis, one can argue that the physical process that produces the many-universes must have just the right laws and processes to produce life-sustaining universes.[21] And, with regard to a grand-unified-theory explanation, one would have to have just the right ("well-designed") set of laws to yield life-permitting values for the constants. As astrophysicists Bernard Carr and Martin Rees note, "Even if all apparently anthropic coincidences could be explained [in terms of some grand unified theory], it would still be remarkable that the relationships dictated by physical theory happened also to be those propitious for life."[22] Given that these hypotheses transfer the design problem up one level, we can then use a variation of the kind of reasoning used above in the case of the atheistic single-universe hypothesis to show that the evidence of fine-tuning confirms theism over the atheistic versions of these hypotheses.

---

[19]Richard Swinburne, *The Existence of God* (Oxford: Clarendon, 1979), pp. 102-6.

[20]For an additional reason, based on the "Who Designed God?" objection, for rejecting these alternative hypotheses, see the end of this chapter.

[21]Collins, "God, Design, and Fine-Tuning" and "The Argument from Design and the Many-Worlds Hypothesis." In the latter article, I also critique what I call the metaphysical many-universes hypothesis, according to which all possible universes exist out of some sort of metaphysical necessity.

[22]B. J. Carr and M. J. Rees, "The Anthropic Cosmological Principle and the Structure of the Physical World," *Nature* 278 (1979): 612.

The problem of evil objection. Another objection to the fine-tuning argument raised by Hume is that since there is so much evil in the world, the teleological argument only allows one to infer to a morally apathetic creator (DNR 66-68). To understand Hume's objection, let's briefly reconstruct his argument. One way of understanding Hume is that he looks at two collections of data: the existence of evil and the appearance of design. He then argues that the theistic God is not necessarily the best explanation for these two collections taken together. Rather, a designer who is morally neutral (or incompetent) is at least as good an explanation, if not better.

One problem with Hume's line of argument is that, if we are going to add other things we know about the world to the data of design, then to avoid arbitrariness we should add everything else we know about the world. This would include features such as religious experiences, our sense of morality and the like. But once these features are added, it is no longer clear that a morally neutral designer is as good a hypothesis as the theistic God. For example, both religious experiences and our sense of morality point to a non-apathetic deity, one who is at least good. And once one ascribes goodness to the designer, it seems less arbitrary to ascribe perfect goodness. Again, one could also argue with Swinburne that the theistic hypothesis is simpler than these other hypotheses and thus constitutes a better explanation.[23]

Another way of reading Hume here is simply as saying that, taken alone, the data of apparent design cannot allow one to infer to an all good deity. One response is simply to grant Hume's claim, and then point out that the design argument as I have developed it does not try to infer to an all good deity. Rather, as elaborated above, our version of the fine-tuning argument only shows that the existence of life-permitting values for the constants of physics strongly confirms theism over the atheistic single-universe hypothesis. This would be true even if a morally apathetic deity, or even an evil deity, would offer at least as good an explanation of the existence of a life-permitting universe. From this point of view, whether at the end of the day we should infer to the all good deity of theism will rest on considerations of all the evidence both for and against theism.

However, a more interesting line of response is to call into question the claim that a morally apathetic or evil deity is not significantly confirmed by the fine-tuning argument. To see this, note that, in the argument above, our main reason for claiming that the existence of a life-permitting universe is

---

[23]Swinburne, *The Existence of God*, pp. 102-6.

not improbable under theism appealed to God's goodness, since God's goodness gives God a reason to create such a universe. Thus, one could argue, at the very least, that a morally apathetic being would have less reason to bring about a universe with conscious life in it than one who is perfectly good, and therefore everything else being equal the design argument gives preference to a perfectly good being over a morally apathetic being.

THE "WHO DESIGNED GOD?" OBJECTION

Perhaps the most common objection that atheists raise to the argument from design is that postulating the existence of God does not solve the problem of design, but just transfers it up one level. This objection was hinted at by Hume:

> For aught we can know *a priori,* matter may contain the source or spring of order originally within itself, as well as mind does; and there is no more difficulty conceiving that the several elements, from an internal unknown cause, may fall into the most exquisite arrangement, than to conceive that their ideas, in the great universal mind, from a like unknown cause, fall into that arrangement. (DNR 17-18)

This same sort of objection has been repeated in various forms by a host of atheist philosophers and thinkers, such as by J. L. Mackie, George Smith, J. J. C. Smart, Richard Dawkins and Colin McGinn.[24] Here are a few representative quotations showing the different forms this argument takes:

> The argument for design, therefore, can be sustained only with the help of a supposedly *a priori* double-barreled principle, that mental order (at least in a god) is self-explanatory, but that all material order not only is not self-explanatory, but is positively improbable and in need of further explanation.[25]

> If the universe is wonderfully designed, surely God is even more wonderfully designed. He must, therefore, have had a designer even more wonderful than He is. If *God* did not require a designer, then there is no reason why such a relatively less wonderful thing as the universe needed one.[26]

> If we want to postulate a deity capable of engineering all the organized complexity in the world . . . that deity must already have been vastly complex in

---

[24]Colin McGinn, *The Mysterious Flame: Conscious Minds in a Material World* (New York: Basic Books, 1999), p. 86. Other references are given below.

[25]J. L. Mackie, *The Miracle of Theism* (Oxford: Clarendon, 1982), p. 144.

[26]George Smith, "Atheism: The Case Against God," in *An Anthology of Atheism and Rationalism,* ed. Gordon Stein (Amherst, N.Y.: Prometheus, 1980), p. 56.

the first place. . . . If we are going to allow ourselves the luxury of postulating organized complexity without offering an explanation, we might as well make a job of it and simply postulate the existence of life as we know it![27]

If we postulate God in addition to the created universe we increase the complexity of our hypothesis. We have all the complexity of the universe itself, and we have in addition the at least equal complexity of God. (The designer of an artifact must be at least as complex as the designed artifact.) . . . *If the theist can show the atheist that postulating God actually reduces the complexity of one's total world view, then the atheist should be a theist.*[28]

The above quotations show that the claim that *if the universe needs a designer, so does God,* is a standard atheist objection to design arguments for theism. Therefore, if the fine-tuning argument is really going to be convincing, we must directly address this objection. Many of the responses I give, however, will apply to any version of the design argument.

The first response to the above atheist objection is to point out that neither Hume, Mackie, Smith, Dawkins, Smart nor McGinn offer any argument for the central premise of their objection, namely, that the designer of an artifact must be at least as complex as the designed artifact. Moreover, their claim is certainly not self-evident. But I do believe that their claim has some initial intuitive plausibility. For example, in the world we experience, organized complexity seems only to be produced by systems that already possess it, such as the human brain/mind, a factory or an organism's biological parent. However, this intuitive plausibility may not be much help. Atheists will not wish to infer a general principle from these cases, since this would force them into denying the adequacy of evolution based on unguided chance plus natural selection to account for the organized complexity of life, and instead would force them into hypothesizing some cause of this complexity that was itself as complex as life. As one of the leading atheist evolutionary biologists Richard Dawkins states, the explanatory force of Darwin's theory is that it can purportedly explain the generation of organized complexity where there was none before.[29]

A second response is to point out that, at most, this objection only works against a version of the design argument that claims that all organized com-

[27]Richard Dawkins, *The Blind Watchmaker* (New York: Norton, 1986), p. 316.
[28]J. J. C. Smart, "Laws of Nature and Cosmic Coincidence," *The Philosophical Quarterly* 35 (1985): 275-76; emphasis mine.
[29]Dawkins, *Blind Watchmaker,* p. 316.

plexity needs an explanation, and that God is the best explanation of the organized complexity found in the world. The version of the argument I presented against the atheistic single-universe hypothesis, however, only required that the fine-tuning be more epistemically probable under theism than under the atheistic-single-universe hypothesis. But this requirement is still met even if God exhibits tremendous internal complexity, far exceeding that of the universe. Thus, even if we grant the atheist assumption that the designer of an artifact must be as complex as the artifact, the fine-tuning would still give us strong reasons to prefer theism over the atheistic single-universe hypothesis.

To illustrate, suppose we discovered a complex domed structure on Mars with all the right configurations of metal and other substances to maintain an oxygen/nitrogen/carbon dioxide atmosphere that could support life. By the restricted prime principle of confirmation, the existence of such a "biosphere" would still give us strong reasons for believing that intelligent, extraterrestrial life had once been on Mars, even though that alien life would most likely have to be much more complex than the biosphere itself. After all, we would reason, such a structure would be enormously unlikely to occur by chance—say by some series of volcanic eruptions—but not unlikely to occur if Mars was once inhabited by some alien race. And this would be true even if we had no account (such as the theory of evolution) of how complex, intelligent life could come into being. Of course, this inference works because the extraterrestrial hypothesis is not completely ad hoc: it already was considered by many to have some viability apart from the evidence in question. Or, for those who want to employ the idea, the prior epistemic probability of the extraterrestrial hypothesis does not seem nearly as low as the probability of the structure coming into existence by chance. Hence, given the existence of the biosphere, it follows from Bayes's theorem[30] that the extraterrestrial hypothesis is more likely than the chance hypothesis.

In reply, the atheist could claim that the existence of a God with the necessary sort of internal complexity is more improbable than the existence of a life-permitting universe. If this were the case, then even though the fine-tuning would still significantly support theism over the atheistic single-universe hypothesis, it could never raise theism's probability enough to make it more probable than atheism, since theism would have been so im-

---

[30]See note 7 above.

probable to begin with.[31] To illustrate, suppose a group of New Age cultists tried to explain the existence of the Martian biosphere by claiming that it was built by Martian robots who, the cultists asserted, simply spontaneously formed on Mars from various volcanic eruptions. Although the existence of the biosphere would raise the probability of the robot hypothesis, it never could of itself make this hypothesis more likely than the hypothesis that the biosphere itself spontaneously formed by chance. Why? Because the spontaneous formation of these robots is at least as improbable as the spontaneous formation of the biosphere.

I see no reason for thinking that the existence of the God of classical theism would be extremely epistemically improbable apart from the evidence of fine-tuning or other "design-like" features of the universe.[32] First, we have plausible, independent reasons for believing in God—for example, religious experience and the cosmological argument. Thus, God's existence is *not* extremely improbable on our background information, as this atheist reply requires. Second, even if God must exhibit great internal order, that in itself does not necessarily make God's existence a priori improbable, since we have no good reason to think that the existence of order is a priori improbable. Indeed, atheists themselves often claim that the existence of an orderly physical world is not a priori unlikely.[33] In contrast to order in and of itself, the reason the order exhibited by the fine-tuning seems extremely improbable is that (1) there seems to be a vast range of other theoretically possible values for the constants of physics, the initial conditions of the universe and even the laws of physics themselves; and (2) the values needed for life seem to be tiny in proportion to all the theoretically possible values. But no such line of reasoning can be applied to the case of God's mind. For example, we have no basis for thinking that there is a vast number of possible types of order that a supermind such as God's could exhibit, of which the relevant order in

---

[31]If we adopt the Bayesian form of the prime principle of confirmation in note 7, one can easily show this; otherwise, one can show this by looking at other relevantly similar cases of confirmation.

[32]I am here assuming that certain classic objections to theism, such as the problem of evil, the paradoxes of divine omnipotence, etc., can be adequately answered.

[33]Bertrand Russell argued along these lines in his well-known essay "Why I Am Not a Christian," in Bertrand Russell, *Why I Am Not a Christian: And Other Essays on Religion and Related Subjects* (New York: Touchstone Books, 1967). Michael Tooley's and David Armstrong's metaphysical theories of natural laws also imply that it is likely that nature would turn out orderly. Michael Tooley, *Causation: A Realist Approach* (Oxford: Oxford University Press, 1988) and David Armstrong, *What Is a Law of Nature?* (Cambridge: Cambridge University Press, 1983).

God's mind constitutes a tiny proportion.[34]

Moreover, theists have traditionally considered it plausible, independent from the argument from design, to hold that God necessarily exists, and hence that the existence of God, along with any mental order in God, is self-explanatory. Of course, if the theist says that God necessarily exists, the atheist can claim the same thing about the universe itself. This reply, however, is weak in the case of fine-tuning. First, the claim that God exists necessarily is not ad hoc, since theists have traditionally believed this for reasons independent of the design argument. But typically atheists have not claimed this about the universe, and thus their reply is at least to some extent ad hoc. Second, and more important, it seems highly implausible to most people to think that the laws, constants and initial conditions of the universe *must* have been fine-tuned to just those range of values that would allow for life to occur, even though there seems to be an enormous range of other possible values they could have had. If there is some principle of necessity requiring that the constants and initial conditions of the universe fall within some range of values, it seems extraordinarily surprising that this principle would be one which required that the values be just those needed for intelligent life to exist. So the atheist's reply along these lines just seems to transfer the improbability or surprise up one level.[35]

The only exception to this is if the principle has some sort of intuitive viability in and of itself. One possibility is the Neo-Platonic principle promoted by philosopher John Leslie: of necessity, what ought to exist does exist.[36] Since a reality in which a universe with conscious observers exists is better

---

[34]By the "relevant order" in God's mind, I mean the order that God's mind must display in order to create a well-designed universe. There could be a certain kind of contingent order in God's mind that is a result of God's free choice that itself is not relevant to God's ability to create a well-designed universe. If there were many other types of mental order that God's mind could have in which God would *not* have the ability to create such a universe, then the theistic hypothesis would simply move the design problem up one level to why God's mind has just the right order needed to produce a well-designed universe, instead of one of the other vast array of other possible mental orderings.

[35]As explained above, the type of probability here is what philosophers call "epistemic probability," which is a measure of the rational degree of belief we should have in a proposition. Since our rational degree of belief in a necessary truth can be less than 100% (even though its metaphysical probability is 100%), we can sensibly speak of it being improbable for a given law of nature to exist necessarily. For example, we can speak of an unproved mathematical hypotheses (such as Goldbach's conjecture that every even number greater than 2 is the sum of two odd primes) as being probably true or probably false given our current evidence, even though all mathematical hypotheses are either necessarily true or necessarily false.

[36]John Leslie, *Universes* (New York: Routledge, 1989), chap. 8.

than a reality without such a universe, Leslie argues that it follows from this principle that a life-permitting universe would exist. Leslie points out, however, that his Neo-Platonic principle is compatible with theism, and might even entail theism, since God is a being of supreme value, and consequently, a reality with God would be better than a reality without God. Thus, even if we adopt Leslie's hypothesis, this would not necessarily provide an alternative to the theistic explanation of the fine-tuning of the universe.[37]

Finally, although I believe the above theistic responses to the "Who Designed God" objection are strong, an atheist could reply that they rest partly on ignorance of what the order in God might be like. If we only understood the complex order that God's existence requires, they could contend, we would see how improbable it is. Although I consider this reply weak, I nonetheless address it in the next section by developing an independently plausible model that explicitly shows how postulating the existence of a mind like God's radically reduces the total amount of unexplained complexity in the world.

THE MODEL

My model begins by noting that a mind has the ability to "search" through the realm of possibilities and then *select* that possibility that appears best to meet its goal. When engineers develop a car, for instance, they consider many different configurations of elements, not only for the car as a whole but for various parts of the car, and then select one of them. An engineer working on the carburetor might mentally consider a whole series of carburetor configurations and eventually select the one that she judges to function the best given the other constraints on the car.

Of course, since God is omniscient, this process of examining various possibilities and then selecting one of them cannot be thought of as occurring in some temporal sequence, such as God's first looking at one possibility, then a moment later considering another and so on. Rather, all possibilities would be present to the divine mind in a single instant. Depending on God's relation to time, this "selecting" among the various possibilities could

---

[37]It should be noted, however, that Leslie has more recently argued for a pantheistic conception of God based on this principle and other considerations. See John Leslie, *Infinite Minds: A Philosophical Cosmology* (Oxford: Clarendon, 2001). For a critique of this book (and Leslie's response), see Robin Collins, "Theism or Pantheism? A Review Essay on John Leslie's *Infinite Minds*," and John Leslie, "Pantheism and Platonic Creation: A Reply to Robin Collins," both in *Philosophia Christi*, n.s. 5 (2003): 563-74; 575-80.

then be thought of as occurring timelessly or from "all eternity" or even temporally following God's considering the possibilities. Whatever view one holds regarding God's relation to time, the process of considering the possibilities and selecting among them could arguably be considered in some sense *logically* analogous to the way human minds make selections. For example, God's willing one possibility over another could be thought of as logically dependent on the act of God's considering the various possibilities and thus *logically* posterior to it, even though it is not temporally posterior to it.

Clearly, this model of the mind producing order is very similar to the Darwinian picture of the origin of biological complexity, the main difference being that selection is occurring intentionally instead of through the impersonal mechanism of natural selection. Indeed, all three major explanations of the origin of organized complexity—intelligent design, the many-universes hypothesis and Darwinian evolution—explain the existence of organized complexity by some sort of selection mechanism. In the case of intelligent design, this selection mechanism is the purposes of the designing agent (for example, the desires flowing out of God's goodness). In the case of the many-universes hypothesis, a sort of self-selection occurs, since the only universes that intelligent beings find themselves in are fine-tuned. And in the case of Darwinian evolution, it is natural selection. So, if atheists claim that Darwinian evolution can produce organized complexity from where it was lacking, as almost all of them do, then they should admit the same thing for the mind, given that the above model is correct.

But, one might object, don't those complex *possible* design plans that an engineer considers already have to exist somewhere? So, applied to God, aren't we back to hypothesizing a preexisting complex order (consisting of possible design plans in God's mind) that is as much in need of explanation as the organized complexity of the universe?

The first reply to this objection is that this same problem arises for Darwinians: their evolutionary model seems to presuppose a realm of preexisting *possible* organism configurations through which the organism travels (for example, Dawkins's "biomorph" space).[38] The second response begins by noting that, since God is in the business of creating whole worlds, the "possible design plans" that God would be considering are nothing less than what philosophers call "possible worlds," and the existence of possible

---

[38]Dawkins, *Blind Watchmaker*, chap. 4.

worlds is thought to be self-explanatory. Possible worlds can be thought of as a complete representation, including every detail, of a possible way things could be. These descriptions can be thought of as something like complete novels that not only describe a possible way the world could be, but fill in every single detail and are logically consistent. Of course, unlike real novels, these representations are not representations in any human language; rather, a possible world can be defined as a maximal set of propositions or states of affairs. These would exist even if there were not any human beings. Now, one might wonder why someone would think that possible worlds really exist. The reasons are many and varied, and almost all independent of the argument from design. All that I will say here is that the reasons are powerful enough to have convinced a large percentage of philosophers, both atheists and theists, that possible worlds exist.[39] Moreover, almost all philosophers—both atheists and theists—who believe in possible worlds hold that they exist *necessarily:* that is, it is absolutely impossible for a possible world not to exist.[40]

What exists necessarily, however, is self-explanatory, for the only time we need to explain why something is a certain way is when it is possible for it to be another way. Hence, since it is impossible for possible worlds not to exist, their existence is self-explanatory, even if in some sense they contain complex internal structure.

To intuitively understand why anything that necessarily exists is self-explanatory, consider the following two analogies. Suppose I were in the weight room bench-pressing one hundred pounds and someone asked me why I'm only lifting one hundred pounds instead of, say, three hundred pounds. I would most likely reply that I *cannot* lift more than one hundred pounds and I would consider this fact an adequate explanation of why I was

---

[39]Indeed, one major reason some philosophers deny the existence of possible worlds is that they cannot see where they could exist. Theists, going all the way back to St. Augustine, have often claimed that they exist as conceptualizations in the mind of God, though considerable metaphysical work is necessary to work this proposal out in detail. See, for example, Christopher Menzel and Thomas V. Morris, "Absolute Creation," *American Philosophical Quarterly* 23 (1986): 353-62; Christopher Menzel, "Theism, Platonism, and the Metaphysics of Mathematics," *Faith and Philosophy* 4 (1987): 365-82; and Brian Leftow, *God and Necessity* (Oxford: Oxford University Press, forthcoming) for some recent work on this issue.

[40]Many standard metaphysics textbooks have discussions of the case for and against the existence of possible worlds and other abstract objects. Good places to start are Michael Jubien, *Contemporary Metaphysics: An Introduction* (Malden, Mass.: Blackwell, 1997); Michael Loux, *Metaphysics: A Contemporary Introduction* (New York: Routledge, 2002); and Michael Loux, ed., *The Possible and the Actual: Readings in the Metaphysics of Modality* (Ithaca, N.Y.: Cornell University Press, 1979).

not lifting three hundred pounds. That is, given that there are only two alternatives (lifting one hundred pounds or lifting three hundred pounds), we would consider the fact that one alternative (lifting three hundred pounds) is *impossible* to be an adequate explanation of why the other alternative (lifting one hundred pounds) occurred. Or consider another illustration. Suppose someone asked you why there are no objects in the world that are both perfect cubes and perfect spheres. You would not answer by claiming, for instance, that the factory designed to produce these objects went bankrupt. Rather, you would say that the reason there are no such objects is that it is *impossible* for there to exist an object that is a perfect cube and a perfect sphere at the same time. The fact that the existence of these objects is *impossible* explains why they do not exist. Thus by analogy, in the case of something that necessarily exists, such as a possible world, the fact that the alternative of nonexistence is impossible explains why the other alternative, that of existence, is the case.

In sum, then, given this model, one can respond to the "Who designed God?" objection as follows: *God's mind selects among possible worlds, and even though these possible worlds can be thought of as highly structured, we have independent reasons, accepted both by theists and nontheists, to believe that they exist and that their existence is self-explanatory.* Consequently, God does not exhibit a complex order that is as much in need of explanation as that of the universe. Insofar as there is preexisting complex order, it exists as part of the structure of possible worlds, and the existence of these are considered by theists and atheists alike not to be in need of explanation. Although I haven't proved the key premise of this response, namely, that these possible worlds exist, many philosophers hold that they exist for reasons entirely independent of theism. Thus, what I have shown so far is that the theist has a plausible response to the "Who designed God?" objection, and a plausible account of the ultimate origin of order and complexity.[41]

Some further objections. But, the skeptic might object at this point: just as the human mind needs a highly organized brain to function, doesn't God's mind need to contain some other type of order that accounts for God's ability to grasp possible worlds and then bring those possible worlds into being? So, even under this account, don't we have to postulate that God

---

[41]Although many theistic philosophers think that these possible worlds, and other abstract objects, are thoughts or conceptualizations in the mind of God, the same arguments for thinking that abstract objects exist out of metaphysical necessity, and hence are self-explanatory, still apply.

exhibits internal, unexplained complexity at least as great as the universe? I
see no reason to think this. First, consider the human analogy. If we gave
some human being enough time, it seems possible that she could create artifacts the sum of whose complexity eventually surpassed the human brain
itself. At the very least, there is no obvious argument that this is not the case.
Thus, contrary to Smart, the complexity of designed artifacts, taken together,
could surpass that of the designer. Thus, even if God's mind requires an incredible amount of complexity, its complexity could be far less than that of
the universe. It is still possible to think, therefore, that hypothesizing God
reduces the total amount of unexplained order.

Second, and more importantly, we have metaphysical reasons for thinking that minds do not, by their inherent nature, require high levels of internal complexity, and this is true even though all the minds we are familiar
with require the organized complexity of the brain to operate. To begin
with, there are significant philosophical reasons based on considerations of
the unity of consciousness for thinking that consciousness (or the soul) is
simple and without internal complexity, as Plato, Descartes and mind/body
dualists have traditionally thought. Perhaps the strongest argument for this
thesis is that we normally experience our own conscious self as a single, unified center that is aware of the world and can act in the world. For example,
I am currently simultaneously aware of the hum of the air conditioner, the
sound of my hands typing and the letters on my computer screen. I cannot
explain this experience by supposing that my self has three parts and that
one part is experiencing the hum, the other my typing, and the other is seeing letters on the computer screen, for then there would be three separate
experiencers, one corresponding to each part. But there seems to be only
one experiencer—I—that perceives all three things. Thus, it seems that I
must suppose there is one unified experiencer that cannot be reduced to a
bunch of parts. (Compare this to a red and green striped ball: although we
say that the ball, as a single entity, is striped, this can be explicated in terms
of various parts of the ball being colored either red or green.)[42]

Now that we have argued it is plausible to think that the conscious, think-

---

[42]For further discussion of this argument, see William Hasker, "Emergentism," *Religious Studies*
18 (1982): 473-88; Philip Quinn, "Tiny Selves: Chisholm on the Simplicity of the Soul," in *The
Philosophy of Rodrick Chisholm*, ed. Lewis Edwin Hahn, Library of Living Philosophers 25
(Chicago: Open Court, 1997); and Stuart Goetz, "Substance Dualism," in *In Search of the Soul:
Four Views of the Mind-Body Problem*, ed. Joel Green and Stuart Palmer (Downers Grove, Ill.:
InterVarsity Press, 2005).

ing self is inherently simple, we need to argue that hypothesizing that it has the ability to grasp possible worlds and bring them into existence does not introduce further complexity or contingency. First, as George Bealer argues, the ability to grasp abstract objects, of which possible worlds are one species, seems to be an essential, even defining, feature of the mind and consciousness.[43] So hypothesizing that a mind has this ability does not add any complexity to it since it is already part of its essential nature. Moreover, the other feature of God's mind that my model needs—the ability to actualize possible worlds—also does not seem to require a well-designed internal structure. Indeed, if one thinks that the "I"—that thing behind the scenes that is conscious, that does the thinking and the like—is simple, as we have been suggesting, then it follows that a person's power to perform what philosophers call *basic* actions must be simple and thus without any further structure. One could think of a person's power to act as analogous to the most fundamental causal powers of the basic constituents of matter; these powers must be simple for otherwise they could be further analyzed and hence they would not be fundamental. Therefore, based on the above considerations, it is plausible to think that minds do not necessarily require great internal complexity.

But an atheist might further object at this point that my explanation merely transfers the problem of design up one level. After all, I must assume that God has the desire to create a world with intelligent, embodied beings. But why would God have any more desire to create this sort of world than any of the other possible worlds that exist? So isn't God's having this desire as improbable as the fine-tuning itself? The answer to this objection is to appeal to God's goodness. If God is good, then it is not extremely improbable that God would create a world with intelligent beings because the existence of such beings is good. Moreover, assuming that a being who had the power and knowledge to design the universe would be good is in and of itself quite plausible. For, as Swinburne has argued, if one assumes a moral order to reality, then it seems likely that any sufficiently intelligent and powerful being would come to grasp that order, and upon grasping it act in accordance with it.[44] The reason is that, because God is omnipotent, God would not be subject to the sort of internal or external forces that distort our judgment and impel us to do things against our most deeply held values. The only motive

---

[43]George Bealer, *Quality and Concept* (Oxford: Clarendon, 1982).
[44]Swinburne, *The Existence of God*, pp. 97-102.

for God's actions, Swinburne argues, would be God's perception of ethical and other kinds of value.[45]

CONCLUSION

I end by suggesting two merits my model has over and above answering atheists such as Mackie and Dawkins. First, if my line of argument is correct, then design arguments can be put on even surer philosophical footing, since the basic principle invoked above—that we should infer to those hypotheses that reduce the total amount of unexplained organized complexity—is widely held by philosophers, both theists and atheists. Second, this line of argument provides an important reason for preferring theism over some of the other major alternative hypotheses, such as the many-universe generator hypothesis or the many-gods hypothesis, as an explanation of the fine-tuning of the universe. Further, as I have argued elsewhere,[46] we have good reasons to believe that the many-universes generator must itself have significant organized complexity of a kind that requires fine-tuning to produce life-sustaining universes. Thus, since we have solid metaphysical reasons for thinking God does not have significant unexplained organized complexity, the atheist's own principle provides strong additional reasons for preferring theism over the atheistic version of the many-universes generator hypothesis. Of course, the atheist could simply hypothesize that the universe generator either lacks complex internal order or that its complex internal order necessarily exists. But such a hypothesis is surely ad hoc apart from some metaphysical account of how this could be the case. Similarly, the many-gods hypothesis seems to involve a higher level of unexplained organized complexity than the theistic hypothesis, since there would have to be some account of how the many gods interrelate with each other. If one responded that these interrelations exist of necessity, then one is likely to simply be advocating something like the much discussed social concept of the Trinity (with perhaps more than three persons) and thus not really advocating a nontheistic view. The finite-god hypothesis also seems to involve an increase in organized complexity since some account would have to be given for why such a god had whatever specific finite limits on power, knowledge, etc., it had instead of some other set of limits. These are potentially fruitful

---

[45]The reasoning here is independent of whether one thinks that the moral order exists in or outside God.

[46]E.g., Collins, "The Argument from Design and the Many-Worlds Hypothesis."

lines of argument that I cannot explore here.

I conclude by recalling the words of noted atheist philosopher J. J. C. Smart, quoted earlier in this chapter: "If the theist can show the atheist that postulating God actually reduces the complexity of one's total world view, then the atheist should be a theist." I hope that atheists who read this chapter take such Smart advice.

10

HUME AND THE MORAL ARGUMENT

Paul Copan

𝔇

David Hume's *Treatise of Human Nature* purports to be a "compleat system of the sciences, built on a foundation almost entirely new, and the only one upon which they can stand with scrutiny."[1] Hume's ambitious attempt, despite its many flaws, has exerted a powerful influence in the history of philosophy. So striking is Hume's project that Thomas Reid observed that, prior to the *Treatise*, it was assumed that sensation cannot exist without a mind or sentient being: "For till that time, no man, as far as I know, ever thought either of calling in question that principle, or of giving a reason for his belief of it."[2]

Undaunted by historical precedent, Hume set forth his case so forcefully that he would awaken Immanuel Kant from his "dogmatic slumber." In more recent days, philosophers such as J. L. Mackie,[3] Antony Flew[4] and Michael

---

[1] *A Treatise of Human Nature,* ed. L. A. Selby-Bigge (Oxford: Clarendon, 1740; reprint, 1888), p. xx. Hereafter references will be given in the text with THN and page number(s).

[2] Thomas Reid, *An Inquiry into the Human Mind: On the Principles of Common Sense,* 4th ed., ed. Derek R. Brookes (Edinburgh: University of Edinburgh, 1997), 2.6.28-30, p. 32. Regarding Hume's denial of the self, for instance, Reid sarcastically remarks that "it is certainly a most amazing discovery, that thought and ideas may be without any thinking being." Presumably then, the *Treatise* had no author after all! It is only a set of ideas which came together, and "arranged themselves by certain associations and attractions" (2.6.13-14, p. 35).

[3] See J. L. Mackie, *Hume's Moral Theory* (London: Routledge & Kegan Paul, 1980) and *The Miracle of Theism* (Oxford: Clarendon, 1982). In the latter work, Mackie explicitly endorses a post-Humean skepticism regarding any moral argument in favor of a "subjectivistic or sentimentalist account of morality": "We can find satisfactory biological, sociological, and psychological explanations of moral thinking which account for the phenomena of the moral sense and conscience in natural terms" (p. 118).

[4] Antony Flew, *Hume's Philosophy of Belief* (London: Routledge & Kegan Paul, 1961).

Martin[5] bear the imprint of Hume's thought. Philosophy of science,[6] philosophy of religion, epistemology, philosophy of mind and my topic, morality, cannot ignore Hume's impact.

A theistic response to Hume's work on morality demands much more than the brief chapter I am writing. In this case, brevity demands modesty, but we can explore some key ideas in Hume's moral thought—along with some of his epistemological and metaphysical assumptions—and note where they fall short. Moreover, we can adduce good reasons for thinking that objective moral values do exist, that humans have intrinsic dignity and worth, and that these serve as pointers to the existence of a good God, in whose likeness human beings have been made.

First, I shall sketch out Hume's position on morality. Second, I shall expose some of its faulty skeptical assumptions and conclusions.[7] Third, I shall show that a theistic (and specifically Reidian) understanding of morality—with its self-evident first principles—is a far more plausible approach to ethics and that objective moral values are best explained by the existence of a good, personal, supernatural Being as the ground of objective morality and human worth or value. The moral argument does not purport to show that the ultimate standard of goodness is necessarily all-powerful and all-wise,

---

[5]Michael Martin, *Atheism: A Philosophical Justification* (Philadelphia: Temple University Press, 1990).

[6]For example, take the problem—or "the old riddle"—of induction. Barry Stroud summarizes it: "Hume claims that, for any particular thing any human being believes about what he has not yet experienced, the person has no more reason to believe it than he has to believe its contradictory." Barry Stroud, *Hume* (London: Routledge & Kegan Paul, 1977), p. 14.

[7]Although Hume has commonly been labeled an atheist, some have observed that Hume's position is not actually atheistic but more accurately deistic. For example, see H. O. Mounce's essay "Reason and Theology" in his book *Hume's Naturalism* (London: Routledge, 1999), pp. 99-130. John Earman asserts that Hume was "a theist, albeit of a vague and weak-kneed sort." John Earman, *Hume's Abject Failure* (New York: Oxford University Press, 2000), p. 4. For instance, Hume (assuming Philo expresses his position) writes, "That the cause or causes of order in the universe probably bear some remote analogy to human intelligence." *Dialogues Concerning Natural Religion* (New York: Hafner, 1948), p. 94. David O'Connor considers Hume's minimalist religious belief to be deistic as opposed to theistic. *Hume on Religion* (London: Routledge, 2001), p. 15. Hume elsewhere wrote, "The whole frame of nature bespeaks an intelligent author; and no intelligent inquirer can, after serious reflection, suspend his belief a moment with regard to the primary principles of genuine theism and Religion." *Natural History of Religion,* in *The Philosophical Works of David Hume,* ed. T. H. Green and T. H. Grose, 4 vols. (London: n.p., 1874-1875; ed. reprint, Aalen: Scientia Verlag, 1964), 4:309. Beyond this vague conception, one could not be more specific. Such a position does not affect the thrust of my chapter, since Hume clearly approaches ethics naturalistically and as a moral sense theorist. Thus tying a moral realism to God's existence undercuts Hume's position.

but it is sufficient to render us morally accountable to a personal Being in whose image we have been made.

HUME'S POSITION ON MORALITY

For our purposes, Hume's view of morality can be summarized by the following six points.

First, *Hume is a moral sense theorist.*[8] In the tradition of Lord Shaftesbury and Francis Hutcheson, moral sense theory presented an alternative to *moral rationalism* on the one hand, and the radical *egoism* of Thomas Hobbes on the other. Moral rationalism proposed that reason is able to judge a situation or action as good and to direct the desires accordingly. The passions or sentiments are thus a "slave" of reason. And against Hobbes's egoism, moral sense theorists noted a general benevolent, other-directed tendency among human beings. In his *Enquiry Concerning the Principles of Morals,* Hume speaks of "what surely, without the greatest absurdity cannot be disputed"—namely, "that there is some benevolence, however small, infused into our bosom; some spark of friendship for humankind; some particle of the dove kneaded into our frame, along with elements of the wolf and serpent."[9] This would appear to make Hobbes's egoism untenable.

Moreover, because human nature is universal and fixed (found "in all nations and ages"), it could be studied in a very scientific manner—so much so that human actions and reactions can be predicted with remarkable accuracy (THN 2.1.3, pp. 280-81). "[I]n judging of the actions of men we must proceed upon the same maxims as when we reason concerning external objects" (THN 3.2.1, p. 403). Our sense of obligation or *oughtness* is rooted in human nature; we have been hard-wired, say, to show natural affection for our children, and without this hard-wiring, "no one cou'd lie under any such obligation" (THN 3.2.5, p. 519).

Hume's "scientific" study of human nature is essentially a causal theory of moral perception.[10] Hume describes his view of morality in this way: "virtue is distinguished by the pleasure, and vice by the pain, that any action, sentiment or character gives us by the mere view and contemplation" (THN

---

[8]These comments are based on James Baillie, *Hume on Morality* (London: Routledge, 2000), pp. 15-18.

[9]David Hume, *Enquiry Concerning the Principles of Morals,* ed. Tom L. Beauchamp (Oxford: Clarendon, 1998), 9.1, p. 74.

[10]David Fate Norton, "Hume and the Foundations of Morality," in *The Cambridge Companion to Hume,* ed. David Fate Norton (Cambridge: Cambridge University Press, 1993), p. 164.

3.1.2, p. 472). Pain or pleasure, arising from viewing an action or quality, "constitutes its vice or virtue, and gives rise to our approbation or blame" (THN 3.5, p. 614).

Second, *reason cannot move us to action but is the slave of the passions:* According to Hume, the passions are impressions, not the less "vivid" ideas which are formed from—and are copies of—impressions. All ideas—whether simple or complex—originate from impressions. Because passions or desires are ultimately impressions that motivate human action, they cannot be true or false: "[R]eason and the passions are not the sorts of mental entities that can oppose one another."[11] Hume declares, "Reason is, and ought only to be the slave of the passions, and can never pretend to any other office than to serve and obey them" (THN 2.3.3, p. 415). Reason by itself cannot produce action, nor can it give rise to volition or prevent volition (THN 2.3.3, pp. 414-15). Reason may provide information on how to satisfy certain ends, but is powerless to motivate behavior; it does not give rise to our inclinations. Reason *alone* cannot move us to action, nor is it the source of our desires in a particular interest. David Hume claimed that morality is "more properly felt than judg'd of" (THN 3.1.2, p. 470). Indeed, the origin of morality is found *within*. One can never find vice "till you turn your reflexion into your own breast, and find a sentiment of disapprobation, which arises in you, towards this action" (THN 3.1.2, pp. 468-69). Thus Hume's view is that morality is not discovered by reason alone.[12]

Third, *moral judgments are not demonstrable, nor do they reflect objective reality.* For Hume, morality is rooted in the rousing of sentiment, not discerning a fact or relation. So he asks: How can we condemn incest among humans but not the same sorts of actions by animals?[13]

Also, in Hume's view, morality is essentially a human product and is thor-

---

[11]Terence Penelhum, *David Hume: An Introduction to His Philosophical System* (West Lafayette, Ind.: Purdue University Press, 1991), p. 143. Cp. *Treatise* 2.3.3, p. 416.

[12]As presented by Jonathan Harrison in *Hume's Moral Epistemology* (Oxford: Clarendon, 1976), pp. 5-15.

[13]THN 3.1.1, p. 467. Although we cannot treat the question of intrinsic human superiority to the beasts, see James B. Reichmann, *Evolution, Animal "Rights," and the Environment* (Washington, D.C.: Catholic University of America, 2000). For instance, Reichmann argues that a human being brings about events as an uncaused cause; nothing *causes* it to react to its physical or intellectual environment the way it does. Nonhuman animals are *caused causes* in that their thinking and actions are "a spontaneous response to the automatic internal calculus determined by its own nature" (p. 159). See also David S. Oderberg's essay on "Animal Rights," in *Applied Ethics* (Cambridge: Blackwell, 2000).

oughly embedded in a naturalistic worldview.[14] Moral intuitions do not refer
to anything beyond themselves. They just *are*—like any other physical or
psychological state. Hume declares: "When I am angry, I am actually possessed with the passion, and in that emotion have no more a reference to
any other object than when I am thirsty, or sick, or more than five foot high"
(THN 2.3.2, p. 415).

Moreover, following Locke's primary-secondary distinction of qualities,[15]
Hume treats vice and virtue as "secondary" properties or qualities that are
found not in objects themselves, but in perceptions of the mind. Comparing
morals to physics, Hume writes, "Vice and virtue, therefore, may be compared
to sounds, colors, heat and cold, which according to modern philosophy, are
not qualities in objects, but perceptions of the mind" (THN 3.1.1, p. 469).

Thus, according to Terence Penelhum, Hume's ethic cannot properly be
called moral realism but rather *intersubjectivism,* in which one (under normal circumstances) feels and expresses the same sorts of sentiments others
do.[16] Penelhum further describes Hume as broadly *utilitarian* (what is virtuous is useful). Hume maintains that justice, honor and fidelity are "artificial" virtues (i.e., useful to oneself or to others) in contrast to "natural" virtues such as cheerfulness, modesty, dignity or affability (which are
agreeable in themselves).[17] Hume is also an *emotivist.* That is, moral judgments merely express human sentiments.[18] Thus, even though Hume states
that what promotes happiness among our fellow humans "is good" and
"what tends to their misery is evil, without any farther regard or consideration,"[19] good and evil do not refer to anything outside human sentiments.
J. Baird Callicott writes,

> [O]bjective qualities . . . are, in Hume's terms, neither "matters of fact" nor "real
> relations" *among objects.* We find them rather "in our own breast"; they are

---

[14]Penelhum, *David Hume,* p. 136.

[15]For Locke (in his *Essay Concerning Human Understanding* [1717]), *primary* qualities are utterly inseparable from bodies and really exist in them (e.g., solidity, extension, figure and motion or mobility). *Secondary* qualities, on the other hand, are simply power to produce various sensations in *us* (e.g., color, odor, sound, warmth and smell).

[16]Penelhum, *David Hume,* p. 151. Cp. Nicholas Capaldi, *Hume's Place in Moral Philosophy*
(New York: Peter Lang, 1989), p. 151.

[17]For a discussion on these distinctions, see S. L. Vodraska, "Hume's Moral *Enquiry:* An Analysis
of Its Catalogue," in *David Hume: Critical Assessments,* ed. Stanley Tweyman, vol. 4: *Ethics,
Passions, Sympathy, "Is" and "Ought"* (London: Routledge, 1995), pp. 12-40.

[18]Penelhum, *David Hume,* p. 137. Hume writes, "The very *feeling* constitutes our praise or admiration" (THN 3.1.2, p. 471).

[19]Hume, *Enquiry Concerning the Principles of Morals,* 5.2, pp. 37-38.

feelings of approbation or disapprobation, warm approval or repugnance, which spontaneously arise in us upon the contemplation of some action or object.[20]

Fourth, *through detached contemplation, what humans generally approve is "virtuous" and what they disapprove is "vicious."* Hume emphasizes that we feel pleasure at the contemplation of a virtuous character. True, we do love persons whose characters may be seriously deficient (e.g., an alcoholic relative), but Hume stresses how stepping back, surveying, and contemplating a character "in general"—setting personal interests aside— "causes such a feeling or sentiment as denominates it morally good or evil" (THN 3.1.2, p. 472).

Fifth, *obligation* (ought) *can never be logically derived from observation* (is), *and, despite Hume's purported universal "science of human nature," radical ethical egoism cannot be avoided as an implication of Hume's sentimentalist theory.* For Hume, there is a great chasm between nature and moral obligation: nature does not in itself contain moral entailments. Moral oughtness does not demonstratively follow from an empirical statement, or even a host of them. This principle, which has come to be known as "Hume's law" (or the "naturalistic fallacy") states that it is impossible to derive *ought* from *is.* Any attempt at such a derivation is a surreptitious smuggling in of an illegitimate conclusion.

Hume's attempt to avoid a Hobbesian egoism fails here. If a person follows her own sentiments, she cannot, by Hume's own logic, be accused of moral wrongdoing—even if her actions fly in the face of culture's conventions and expectations. After all, there is no logical reason to "prefer the destruction of the world to the scratching of my finger." What compelling reason could be given not to choose "my total ruin, to prevent the least uneasiness of an *Indian* or person wholly unknown to me"? (THN 2.3.3, p. 416). Hume assumed, with most of his contemporary philosophers, that there was a common, fixed human nature; that there was a universal, descriptive ethic based upon "general causal laws of human moral psychology."[21] But what prevents individual human beings from preferring their own ruin? The theory of ethical egoism, of course, suffers from many a problem: it is unable to universalize itself as a

---

[20]J. Baird Callicott, "Hume's *Is/Ought* Dichotomy and the Relation of Ecology to Leopold's Land Ethic," in *In Defense of the Land Ethic: Essays in Environmental Philosophy* (Albany: State University of New York, 1989), p. 120; emphasis in the original.

[21]Arthur F. Holmes, *Fact, Value, and God* (Grand Rapids: Eerdmans, 1997), p. 113.

principle; it leads others to doubt constantly the advice of the egoist; it arbitrarily limits *all* ethical considerations to an isolated individual's concerns; and so on. Thus egoism should be rejected.

Sixth, *Hume's epistemology and moral theory are deeply intertwined.*[22] Reason, for Hume, is not an independent faculty, "in possession of the throne, prescribing laws, and imposing maxims with an absolute sway and authority" (THN .4.1, p. 186). Reason is embedded in the passions, desires, habits and sentiments of mind,[23] and it is, as we have seen, a slave of the passions. By this Hume does not mean that reason is wholly impotent, but simply limited.[24] Reason does not move us to act; the passions do. Reason may be involved in resisting evil, but our passions—"the general appetite to good and the aversion to evil"—serve as the basis for action (THN 2.3.3, p. 417).

As with reason, morality and virtue are rooted in the same cause-and-effect "science of man." Both are rooted in the perceptions, which are divided into *impressions* and the less-vivid *ideas*. Indeed, all mental events are simply "successive perceptions" that "constitute the mind" (THN 1.4.6, p. 256).

As we shall discuss below, we rightly hold certain rational and moral beliefs that arise out of our experience with a prima facie plausibility or likelihood (noninferred or underived or properly basic beliefs). In the absence of any defeaters for them, there is no reason to deny such beliefs, which include moral intuitions (e.g., we ought to be kind, unselfish, truthful; we ought not rape, murder, torture for fun). They appear obvious to us. Yet Hume's science of human nature disqualifies rational or moral beliefs that we can justifiably call "knowledge"—which may simply be highly plausible or likely and does not need to rise to the level of Cartesian certainty. For Hume, human morality is strictly rooted in nature, and any divinely implanted "moral sense" is out of the question; morality cannot be separated from psychology but indeed is reduced to it. Given Hume's gap between *is* and *ought*, moral realism is eliminated from his system; any argument for God's existence based upon objective morality or intrinsic human dignity is discounted by Hume.

---

[22]This is contra K. B. Price, "Does Hume's Theory of Knowledge Determine His Ethical Theory?" in *David Hume: Critical Assessments*, ed. Stanley Tweyman, vol. 4: *Ethics, Passions, Sympathy, "Is" and "Ought"* (London: Routledge, 1995), pp. 3-11.

[23]Paul Stanistreet, *Hume's Skepticism and the Science of Human Nature* (Hants, U.K.: Ashgate, 2002), p. 214.

[24]Penelhum, *David Hume*, p. 144.

A RESPONSE TO HUME'S MORAL THEORY

Though he has been accused of overstatement, Reid does have a point when he asserts that Hume's approach "overturns all philosophy, all religion and virtue, and all common sense."[25] Indeed, it is inadequate to account sufficiently for the following features of our experience: certain basic moral intuitions; moral obligations; the trustworthiness of our capacities to perceive, to reason and to form moral beliefs; our conviction—expressed or implicit—about human dignity or worth and about moral responsibility and punishment; the important correlation or "fit" between philosophical moral theory and its application. These are the sorts of features a theistic moral realism is better able to ground and ones we could readily expect given theism.

First, *Hume's empiricistic methodology itself appears to be incoherent.* Reid writes, "I am persuaded, that the unjust *live by faith* as well as the *just*."[26] And Hume is no exception. Well known are Hume's contemptuous remarks regarding any volume of "divinity or school metaphysics," which should be consigned to the flames since "it can contain nothing but sophistry and illusion."[27] His epistemology is dogmatically empiri*cistic*—not simply empiri*cal:* "'tis still certain we cannot go beyond experience" (THN p. xxi). But Hume's own starting points and assumptions themselves are questionable and thus hardly philosophically axiomatic. Hume's empiricism eliminates from the outset the possibility of knowing that substances (as opposed to bundles of properties), the human ego/self or objective moral values exist. Thus, Hume himself *goes beyond* what experience (i.e., the empirical) can show by asserting we cannot go beyond it. Just as Kant's declaration that we cannot know things in themselves *(noumena)* is knowledge of something in itself, so Hume's declaration that we can only know what is empirical cannot itself be empirically discerned. This is a philosophical assumption, not a scientific discovery.

Thus, Hume's nascent logical positivism falls prey to the same kinds of criticisms launched against the Vienna Circle and its verificationist principle: *Hume's own empiricistic approach cannot be empirically shown to be the only justifiable basis for knowledge.*[28] For example, that divine revela-

---

[25]Reid, "Dedication," in *Inquiry into the Human Mind*, p. 5.

[26]Ibid., p. 4; emphasis in the original.

[27]Hume, *An Enquiry Concerning Human Understanding*, ed. L. A. Selby-Bigge (reprint, Oxford: Clarendon, 1951), 7.3, p. 165.

[28]For a recent response to attempted *post-mortem* defenses of the verificationist principle, see

tion is dismissed from consideration before the philosophical fight begins is arbitrary, even arrogant. Thus, in Hume's own attempt to formulate a quasi-Newtonian science of human nature,[29] he makes dogmatic statements that go well beyond scientific study. Precisely because science is not the domain for recognizing whether a self (an "I") exists, Hume's claim that we cannot know whether it exists is a question-begging enterprise. Hume's very methodology assumes the existence of a knowing self—that it is more than just a bundle of properties. Moreover, Hume's system, by mere fiat, restricts explanations for human actions to deterministic causation, prohibiting teleological explanations (and even dismissing them as nothing more than the mere imposition of human minds upon naturalistic processes). However, it is not the domain of science to exclude the possibility of knowing essences, cause and effect, objective moral values, and libertarian free will. Hume's "compleat" scientific systematization of human nature is laden with philosophical assumptions, many of which are dubious.

Hume's famous "fork"—distinguishing between "relations of ideas" (e.g., "three times five is half of thirty") and "matters of fact" (whose negation is conceivable)—presents problems of self-referential incoherence. As with the logical positivists who came after him, Hume's own assertion that only what is analytically true (relations of ideas) or empirically true (matters of fact) is meaningful (or true) is itself not true by definition or in any other way necessarily true, nor is this the result of empirical discovery.[30] Hume's fork is either false or meaningless, or cannot be justifiably believed. It is self-referentially incoherent, and thus we are justified in rejecting it.

Thus, Hume goes well beyond the purview of the "science" he claims to espouse. His inchoate verificationism cannot escape the charge of incoherence since Hume is making a philosophical assertion *about* the empirical, not simply furnishing the results *of* empirical observation.

Second, *Hume's skeptical methodology, which bears upon his moral theory, is an epistemic tar baby; Hume must first bracket or deny skepticism in order to generate his skeptical conclusions.* Penelhum claims that Hume's view of our beliefs, in which instincts invest our perceptions with meanings

---

William P. Alston, "Religious Language and Verificationism," in *The Rationality of Theism*, ed. Paul Copan and Paul K. Moser (London: Routledge, 2003), pp. 17-34.

[29]Terence Penelhum, "Hume's Moral Psychology," in *The Cambridge Companion to Hume*, ed. David Fate Norton (Cambridge: Cambridge University Press, 1993), p. 122.

[30]See Douglas Groothuis, "Questioning Hume's Theory of Meaning," *Kenesis* 18 (1992): 27-38.

that are useful and adaptive, "is essentially a Darwinian view."[31] Following this claim to its logical conclusion leads to an ultimate skepticism about our beliefs. Even Charles Darwin wondered how his cognitive faculties could be trusted:

> With me the horrid doubt always arises whether the convictions of man's mind, which has been developed from the mind of the lower animals, are of any value or at all trustworthy. Would any one trust in the convictions of a monkey's mind, if there are any convictions in such a mind?[32]

Yet like Darwin, Hume *un*skeptically presumes that his cognitive faculties are trustworthy as he works toward his skeptical conclusions. He assumes his capacities of ratiocination are reliable and not in doubt.[33] As Reid would argue, our capacity to reason properly is a *first principle;* to deny it as a first principle is to utilize it. As we shall see, first principles also exist in the moral realm.

Because Hume is purportedly following a strictly empirical methodology, he sees reason as the mere capacity to analyze and neutrally describe. He rejects a priori that reasoning has a teleological orientation (in which reason must function toward a certain end—say, in proceeding syllogistically from sound premises to a correct conclusion). Yet, ironically, the refusal to accept a teleological account of reason results in an epistemic trap. Says John Rist, "If we refuse to move to a more teleological account of reason, we are left in the hole where Hume has dumped us."[34] We can merely describe how we *do* think, not assert how we *ought* to think or that we have arrived at *true* conclusions. The fundamental problem with such a view is that we can no

---

[31]Penelhum, "Hume's Moral Psychology," p. 124. Also, James Reichmann observes that Darwin's underlying epistemology is "decidedly Humean." *Evolution, Animal "Rights,"and the Environment,* p. 160.

[32]Letter to William Graham Down, July 3, 1881, in *The Life and Letters of Charles Darwin Including an Autobiographical Chapter,* ed. Francis Darwin (London: John Murray, Abermarle Street, 1887), 1:315-16.

[33]Plantinga calls this "the scandal of skepticism": "[I]f I *argue* to skepticism, then of course I rely on the very cognitive faculties whose unreliability is the conclusion of my skeptical argument." Alvin Plantinga, *Warranted Christian Belief* (New York: Oxford University Press, 2000), p. 219 n. For further elaboration, see Alvin Plantinga's *Warrant and Proper Function* (New York: Oxford University Press, 1993), pp. 216-37. For additional refinements of Plantinga's evolutionary argument against naturalism see "Reply to Beilby's Cohorts," in *Naturalism Defeated?* ed. James Beilby (Ithaca, N.Y.: Cornell University Press, 2002), pp. 204-75 (esp. pp. 269-71 on Hume); Victor Reppert, *C. S. Lewis's Dangerous Idea* (Downers Grove, Ill.: InterVarsity Press, 2003).

[34]John Rist, *Real Ethics: Rethinking the Foundations of Morality* (Cambridge: Cambridge University Press, 2001), p. 144.

longer claim to have knowledge, since *truth* is an essential component of knowledge.[35]

Without a teleological account, there is no place for discerning moral truth either. Penelhum summarizes: "While Hume's analysis of the nature of moral judgments does indeed allow for rational dispute about them, it is not clear that it can provide for moral truth and falsity, as opposed to moral co-incidence or dissonance within one social unit."[36] Hume's method is *descriptive* of how humans happen to form moral judgments (enabling us to discern only whether one set of moral beliefs coincides or clashes with another) rather than *prescriptive* (how humans ought to think morally). Thus Hume omits the teleological and intentional components of moral knowledge requisite for discrimination between true moral judgments and false ones.

Hume's strictly sentimentalist (and thus reductionistic) account of morality negates the possibility of making *objective moral claims*. Moreover, given that Hume's methodology leads to skeptical conclusions about beliefs in general (despite his confidence in his own belief-forming processes), the same pertains to his beliefs about morality as well. If Hume is correct, then it is by sheer accident that he is correct, since anyone's beliefs just are what they are.

Third, *Hume is guilty of an unnecessary and unwarranted reductionism, in which morality is shrunk down to simple feeling or instinct.* While no one denies that feelings and desires usually accompany moral judgment, we must question whether moral judgments can be reduced to them. Reid argues that what Hume described as "the pleasing sentiment of approbation"[37] involves not feeling alone, but both a judgment of what is right (or wrong) and a feeling.[38] So the order of explanation is paramount here: are the sentiments the source of our motivations (as Hume argues), or are they simply a manifestation of our recognizing certain rational requirements in our motives?[39] While certain pleasant feelings, say, may accompany a virtuous judgment, it is a non sequitur to say the judgment is reducible to those feelings.

---

[35]See Dallas Willard's essay "Knowledge and Naturalism," in *Naturalism: A Critical Analysis*, ed. J. P. Moreland and William Lane Craig (London: Routledge, 2000), pp. 24-48.

[36]Penelhum, *David Hume*, p. 153.

[37]David Hume, "Appendix I: Concerning Moral Sentiment," in *An Enquiry Concerning the Principles of Morals*, ed., Charles W. Hendel Jr. (New York: Charles Scribner's Sons, 1927), p. 241; cited without original italics.

[38]Keith Lehrer, *Thomas Reid* (London: Routledge, 1989), p. 242.

[39]Thomas Nagel, *The Last Word* (New York: Oxford University Press, 1997), p. 108.

From the vantage point of everyday human experience, Hume jumps too far in his conclusions about the relationship of reason and passions. Hume's claim that it is "not contrary to reason to prefer the destruction of the whole world to the scratching of my finger" (THN 2.3.3) brings us to "one of Hume's worst arguments," according to Penelhum.[40] Hume wrongly assumes that desires cannot be reasonable or unreasonable. I may be enraged at a supposed injury, and this rage may be reasonable if I believe someone has deeply wronged me. Even if I happen to realize I am wrong and my rage dissolves, it would not have been unreasonable while I felt anger.[41] Thus, while sentiments or feelings are associated with moral judgments, this is hardly the same as making sentiments the basis for moral judgments. *An act can be moral regardless of feelings associated with it.* The object of a moral judgment is distinct from the feelings of the one making the judgment.

Fourth, *one could argue that the sentiments shared by morally sensitive human beings actually reflect an objective moral order.* As noted earlier, we can simply shift the vantage point by asserting that feelings of approbation accompanying virtuous action reflect a transcendent moral order and that we have been designed by a Creator to function properly when aligning ourselves with that moral order.

Think of Feuerbach's attempt to explain away theistic realism with his theory of human projection of the divine—humans creating God in their image to get through the harsh realities of life. But it may actually be that our longing for the transcendent has actually been placed in us by God himself, that God has set eternity in our hearts (Eccles 3:11),[42] and that our hearts are restless until they find rest in him.[43] Loving and trusting in God are part of what it means to be functioning properly.

Likewise, when we are functioning according to the divine design plan, then these common human sentiments that well up "in our breast" serve as pointers beyond themselves to a transcendent moral order. Rather than psychologizing (away) moral intuitions, we can actually turn Hume's reduction-

---

[40]Penelhum, *David Hume,* p. 143.

[41]Ibid., pp. 143-44.

[42]In Ecclesiastes, Qohelet (the "Teacher") appears to have a cynical, pessimistic view of God—one which needs correcting at the very end of the book (12:13-14). In 3:11, Qohelet (incorrectly) suggests that God has given humans the drive to know matters of purpose and destiny but without ever satisfying this longing. See Tremper Longman III's excellent commentary, *The Book of Ecclesiastes,* New International Commentary on the Old Testament (Grand Rapids: Eerdmans, 1998).

[43]Augustine *Confessions* 1.1.

ism on its head. We can posit the normative function of moral intuitions as reflecting an objective moral order. In fact, Hume's own commitment to the stability of human nature "in all nations and ages" reinforces this point.

Fifth, *Hume's epistemology is counterintuitive and practically unlivable, which serves to undermine Hume's position.* Hume frankly admitted that he was "confounded" by questions about identity and existence and life after death, producing a "philosophical melancholy and delirium." But "relaxing this bent of mind" or undertaking some avocation such as backgammon or dining with friends, Hume claims, would cure this affliction of philosophitis and thus "obliterate all these chimeras" (THN 1.4.7, p. 269).

When one's philosophy is fundamentally unlivable and flies in the face of commonsense or everyday experience, an adjustment in philosophy is needed—not just a game of backgammon. For example, Hume admits that there is no logical reason to "prefer the destruction of the world to the scratching of my finger," but why would *any* human actually prefer this?[44] Such a statement is, to echo Nicholas Rescher's judgment, "clearly strange stuff."[45] Reid rightly remarks:

> If there are certain principles, as I think there are, which the constitution of our nature leads us to believe, and which we are under a necessity to take for granted in the common concerns of life, without being able to give a reason for them; these are what we call the principles of common sense; and what is manifestly contrary to them, is what we call absurd.[46]

Hume's empiricism leads to reductionism, which means that Hume cannot practice what he preaches. Hume certainly *acts* as though the external world exists, that it is not five minutes old, that other minds exist, that his rational faculties are reliable, and he admits that the philosopher must live as the "vulgar" do if he is to get through life. But in making such a claim, he sides with the theist, who can trust such faculties precisely because human beings are made in the image of a rational and truthful God.[47] Because Hume's praxis is constantly at odds with his philosophy, perhaps we should

---

[44]Hume makes another statement (cited earlier) that is, in Penelhum's words, "so clearly false" that Hume, not surprisingly, does not repeat it or offer a substitute for it in the *Enquiry* (Penelhum, *David Hume*, p. 144): "When I am angry, I am actually possessed with the passion, and in that emotion have no more a reference to any other object, than when I am thirsty, or sick, or more than five foot high" (THN 2.3.2, p. 416).

[45]Nicholas Rescher, *Objectivity: The Obligations of Impersonal Reason* (Notre Dame, Ind.: University of Notre Dame Press, 1997), p. 177.

[46]Reid, *Inquiry into the Human Mind*, 2.6.9-13, p. 33.

[47]See Plantinga's discussion in *Warranted Christian Belief*, pp. 222-27.

look elsewhere for a better match between theory and practice.

We could go further. If Hume is correct that we act benevolently or mercifully according to a moral impulse or instinct rather than reason, one wonders how Hume could criticize the one who lives according to the Darwinist mantras of "survival of the fittest" or "nature, red in tooth and claw."[48] Even if we recognize that humans tend to act benevolently toward others in society, why *ought* we be compelled to act that way if we can get away with not doing so? In other words, if there is no objective moral order, there is no reason why those "in the know"—who see the Noble Lie for what it is—*ought* to be benevolent rather than take advantage of the "vulgar" herd of fools and suckers.[49]

Thankfully, we have no need of Hume's hypothesis. A more plausible one is at hand. Because we are God's image-bearers who are designed to function properly and thrive when we live morally and rationally, we can reject the ineluctable counterintuitive dissonance into which Hume's position leads us.

OBJECTIVE MORAL VALUES AND THE EXISTENCE OF GOD

Why think theism presents the most plausible hypothesis to account for human moral experience? First, *objective moral values are properly basic and undeniable; those who reject them are failing to function properly.* There are some beliefs that (a) we are justified in holding (we are doing our epistemic duty with respect to these beliefs) and (b) are not based on or inferred from other beliefs (e.g., via sense experience or memory beliefs, such as my having had breakfast this morning).[50] To reject such basic beliefs would do serious damage to our noetic structure.[51] Such beliefs are properly basic.

Thomas Reid argued that some moral beliefs are included among the properly basic. We intuitively—noninferentially, prephilosophically—recog-

---

[48]Alfred Lord Tennyson, *In Memoriam A. H. H.* 56.15.

[49]Rist, *Real Ethics,* p. 160.

[50]This is consistent with the soft/modest (particularistic) foundationalism of Reformed Epistemology—as opposed to a hard (methodological) Cartesian one, which, if followed, would lead to the rejection of many beliefs that are very plausibly true, though not self-evident, evident to the senses, or incorrigible. See David K. Clark's discussion, "Faith and Foundationalism," in *The Rationality of Theism,* ed. Paul Copan and Paul K. Moser (London: Routledge, 2003), pp. 35-54.

[51]Alvin Plantinga, "Reason and Belief in God," in *Faith and Rationality,* ed. Alvin Plantinga and Nicholas Wolterstorff (Notre Dame, Ind.: University of Notre Dame Press, 1983), p. 60.

nize the existence of some basic moral values and first principles of morality that arise naturally out of our own experience (e.g., treating others as we would want to be treated). To reject these beliefs would do serious damage to our belief structure and how we come to form moral beliefs. While such beliefs are not infallible or indefeasible, we justifiably believe them in the absence of any overriding considerations or undercutting defeaters. They are innocent until proved guilty (Reid's credulity principle).

Philosopher Martin Heidegger said of Hitler, "He alone is the German reality of today, and of the future, and of its law." But when the Germans were defeated in World War II, the French confiscated Heidegger's property because of his Nazi sympathies. In response, he wrote an indignant letter to the commander of the French forces: "What justice there is in treating me in this unheard of way is inconceivable to me."[52] To Heidegger's mind, there was not a "German morality" and a different "French morality." Despite being mesmerized by Hitler, he was assuming some universal standard of justice that even the French could understand.

As C. S. Lewis has documented in *The Abolition of Man*,[53] the same sorts of moral standards—don't murder, don't take another's property, don't defraud, etc.—continually surface across civilizations and cultures and throughout history. We need not look far to find commonalities. Such moral principles are *discovered,* not *invented.* Even if gray areas exist in the moral realm, we can still get the basics right. In making moral judgments, we must begin with the clear and move to the unclear, not vice versa. Just because moral uncertainty or ambiguity exists, this doesn't eclipse the morally obvious. As Dr. Samuel Johnson put it, "The fact that there is such a thing as twilight does not mean that we cannot distinguish between day and night."

Atheist philosopher Kai Nielsen comments on the vileness of child abuse and wife-beating:

> It is more reasonable to believe such elemental things to be evil than to believe any skeptical theory that tells us we cannot know or reasonably believe any of these things to be evil. . . . I firmly believe that this is bedrock and right and that anyone who does not believe it cannot have probed deeply enough into the grounds of his moral beliefs.[54]

---

[52]"Mit welchem Rechtsgrund ich mit einem solchen unerhörten Vorgehen betroffen werde, ist mir unerfindlich." Cited in Hugo Ott, *Martin Heidegger: Unterwegs zu seiner Biographie* (Frankfurt: Campus Verlag, 1988), p. 296.
[53]*The Abolition of Man* (San Francisco: Harper, 2001), appendix.
[54]Kai Nielsen, *Ethics Without God*, rev. ed. (Buffalo, N.Y.: Prometheus, 1990), pp. 10-11.

Likewise, Nicholas Rescher notes, "If [members of a particular tribe] think that it is acceptable to engage in practices like the sacrifice of first-born children, then their grasp on the conception of morality is somewhere between inadequate and nonexistent."[55]

Contrary to Hume's assertions, factual knowledge does not always depend upon causal inferences or beliefs arising from constant conjunction. Reid is correct to assert that some beliefs are simply basic, spontaneous and natural—*first principles* from which we begin reasoning or inferring. To deny the basicality of these first principles, which are *"the common sense of mankind,"* is "what we call *absurd.*"[56] It flies in the face of how we have been constituted by the Almighty. Indeed, the strength of these principles is that they make good sense, "which is often found in those who are not acute in reasoning."[57] To deviate from such common sense by metaphysical arguments is "metaphysical lunacy."[58] Thus, as J. L. Mackie notes, Reid "abandons the attempt to introduce moral features by demonstration" since the first principles of moral reasoning are self-evident.[59]

As with sense perception, so also with moral awareness. Those without these self-evident, basic moral sensitivities are like the colorblind. As with reliable perception of color patches, to have a decently operating conscience is normal for rightly functioning human beings (cf. Rom 2:14-15; Amos 1 and 2). Basic moral principles (e.g., the mandate to treat others as we wish to be treated)[60] are universally self-evident to those mature in char-

---

[55]Nicholas Rescher, *Moral Absolutes: An Essay on the Nature and Rationale of Morality*, Studies in Moral Philosophy 2 (New York: Peter Lang, 1989), p. 43.

[56]Reid, *Inquiry into the Human Mind*, p. 215, emphasis in the original.

[57]Ibid.

[58]Ibid., p. 216; Reid's emphasis.

[59]Mackie, *Hume's Moral Theory*, p. 139. See also Paul Stanistreet's *Hume's Skepticism and the Science of Human Nature*, esp. chap. 6. Stanistreet observes that Reid believed that "the whole basis of Hume's philosophy was the theory of ideas" (p. 183). Reid rejected these ideas or mental representations or images. They are "not *objects* of perception, but *acts* or *operations* of the mind through which we *directly* perceive external objects"; so Reid proposed replacing the theory of ideas with his philosophy of common sense (p. 184). So while we cannot rationally prove that, say, the universe exists, it is self-evident and prephilosophical.

[60]Reid offers this rudimentary principle: "Every man knows certainly, that what he approves in other men he ought to do in like circumstances, and that he ought not to do what he condemns in other men." Dugald Stewart, ed., *Works of Thomas Reid*, 3 vols. (New York: Bangs and Mason, 1822), 2:381. "If the rules of virtue were left to be discovered by demonstrative reasoning, or by reasoning of any kind, sad would be the condition of the far greater part of men, who have not the means of cultivating the power of reasoning. As virtue is the business of all men, the first principles of it are written in their hearts, in characters so legible, that no man can pretend ignorance of them, or of his obligation to practise them." Ibid.

acter and possessing a properly functioning mind. By virtue of our very constitution (which Hume admits is universal), we recognize moral duties apart from social contracts, human conventions or social usefulness.[61]

The way out of the Humean swamp is theism, in which we have been divinely designed to function when we align ourselves with God's purposes in this moral universe. As Reid puts it,

> The sceptic asks me, Why do you believe the existence of the external object which you perceive? This belief, sir, is none of my manufacture; it came from the mint of Nature; it bears her image and superscription; and, if it is not right, the fault is not mine. I ever took it upon trust, and without suspicion.[62]

As with science, morality begins with certain first principles. First principles are self-evident to the person who has not hardened his conscience. Reid said that the law of God is written in our hearts (conscience), and to reject its fundamental inclinations is to act unnaturally.[63] The reason the atheist can recognize the same moral truths as the theist is that "the faculty [is] given him by God." Both are made in the same divine image. If God had not bestowed this faculty upon man, "he would not be a moral and accountable being."[64]

Moreover, if a person does not recognize his moral obligations, Reid remarks, "I know not what reasoning, either probable or demonstrative, I could use to convince him of any moral duty."[65] Such a person does not need improved reasoning powers (he may be a self-deceived or hardhearted sophist), as these basic principles are readily accessible to all morally sensitive human beings. Rather, such a person needs psychological and spiritual help.

As we discussed earlier, the *credulity principle* (we should reasonably believe what is apparent or obvious to us unless there are overriding reasons to the contrary) is appropriate with regard to our *sense* perceptions, our *reasoning* faculty and our *moral* intuitions. They are innocent until proved guilty. Furthermore, if a trustworthy God has created our noetic structure,

---

[61]Lehrer, *Thomas Reid,* pp. 245-46.
[62]Keith Lehrer and Ronald E. Beanblossom, eds., *Thomas Reid's Inquiry and Essays* (Indianapolis: Bobbs-Merrill, 1975), pp. 84-85.
[63]Thomas Reid, "Of the First Principles of Morals," Essay 3 in *Essays on the Active Powers of the Human Mind,* intro. Baruch A. Brody (Cambridge, Mass.: MIT Press, 1969), pp. 364-67.
[64]Thomas Reid, "Whether Morality Be Demonstrable," Essay 7 in *Essays on the Intellectual Powers of Man,* in *Works of Thomas Reid,* 2:381.
[65]Ibid., 2:380.

then we have all the more reason for generally trusting these faculties or capacities rather than constantly doubting their reliability (even though, here and there, we may get things wrong). Indeed, we have been designed to trust our faculties, and constantly failing to trust them is a sign of cognitive malfunction.[66] This pertains to the moral realm as well as the perceptual and analytical. Calling into question the properly basic belief in human dignity and objective moral values will lead to the kinds of Humean inconsistencies produced by an empiricistic philosophy that meshes poorly with practical living.

While Hume could theoretically be correct in his inconsistency (and while theism could be both consistent and false), this Humean dissonance disallows a consistent or "compleat" science of human nature. The practical must be cordoned off from the philosophical. But perhaps a richer, more consistent and comprehensive science of human nature (which we can expect) under theism points us to what is the more adequate worldview. Perhaps the human longing for an "eco-niche"—a good fit between mind and reality, between theory and practice—is an indication of a true science of human nature, whereas discord is not.[67] Under theism, we have the benefit of rightly expecting consistency between worldview and everyday living. So long as Hume's "science" neglects to factor in the "concord" element, to that degree it remains "incompleat."

Second, *the is-ought gap stems from an arbitrary (and reductionistic) limitation to merely scientistic ones; all objective axiological categories are eliminated ab initio—not to mention many important metaphysical ones.* Philosopher John Searle admits to having a common intuition: we know "we could have done something else" and that human freedom is "just a fact of experience."[68] However, because of his "bottom-up" view of the world (like Hume), he rejects libertarian freedom since we would have to postulate a self that could potentially interfere with "the causal order of nature."[69] Similarly, despite the commonsense intuitions we have about human rights and moral obligations, Hume's bottom-up approach would never admit them into his worldview. But, in keeping with the principle of credulity, we

---

[66]Plantinga, *Warranted Christian Belief,* p. 185.

[67]Huston Smith, "The Religious Significance of Postmodernism: A Rejoinder," *Faith and Philosophy* 12 (1995): 415.

[68]John Searle, *Minds, Brains, and Science* (reprint, Cambridge, Mass.: Harvard University Press, 1986), pp. 87-88.

[69]Ibid., p. 92.

should accept such commonsense intuitions and work out how objective moral values (or human freedom) harmonize with nature—something for which theism has ample room. The burden of proof is upon the one who would deny these.

A rigid empiricism has no room for axiological considerations. Hume's causal, mechanistic view of human action implies that moral praise or blame cannot be applied on the ground that someone has chosen a course of action that she need not have chosen. Because of his pursuit of a predictable science of human behavior, Hume must—and indeed does—deny that praise and blame are relevant categories.[70] But Hume's science cannot account for moral praiseworthiness or blameworthiness, nor can it offer any objective, nonutilitarian basis for punishing rapists or murderers.[71] As with the substantial self, human freedom or essences, the existence of value and the dignity of human beings cannot be discerned by the constricting empirical method alone. Hume needs to open his metaphysical tent more widely to better account for fundamental features of human existence. If (a) objective moral values, moral obligations, human dignity and freedom are properly basic, and if (b) a Humean account of morality eliminates these as features of the world, then we must look elsewhere for an alternative worldview that can better accommodate them.

Third, *a theistic explanation for objective moral values and human dignity is superior to a naturalistic one.* Ironically, we live in a time when many claim everything is *relative,* yet they believe they have *rights.* But if morality is just the product of naturalistic evolution or cultural development, fiat or personal choice, then rights in any objective sense do not exist. As we saw, Hume's naturalism does not inspire confidence in our belief-forming mechanisms, whether moral or epistemic. Indeed, naturalism has the potential to undermine our conviction that rationality and objective moral values exist. If our beliefs are merely survival-enhancing byproducts of Darwinistic evolution, why think that we actually *have* dignity, rights and obligations, or even that we are thinking rationally? For instance, an

---

[70]Penelhum, "Hume's Moral Psychology," p. 132.

[71]See Gordon Graham, *Evil and Christian Ethics* (Cambridge: Cambridge University Press, 2001), pp. 135-36. According to Graham, Hume's reductionistic view of morality renders Jeffrey Dahmer or Charles Manson to be mere statistical aberrations. There is nothing "wrong" with multiple murderers or serial killers. They are only highly individualistic or perhaps "malfunctioning"—not "evil."

animal may be extremely skittish, incorrectly believing danger to be at every turn and in every tree. While this skittishness may enhance survival (better safe than sorry), the animal is incorrect a good percentage of the time. A theistic worldview, on the other hand, does assure us that we can know moral (and epistemic) truths, even if they do not necessarily contribute one whit to our survival.

Against Hume, we have seen that moral values are basic and that we generally take for granted that human persons truly have value in and of themselves—regardless of what their culture or the high priests of scientism say. But if this is so, then what is the *basis* for this value? Did this intrinsic value come from impersonal, nonconscious, unguided, valueless processes over time? Unlike Hume, some naturalists claim that objective moral values *do* exist but that they emerge naturalistically—that moral properties supervene upon nonmoral ones (say, when the brain and nervous system arrive at a certain level of complexity through the evolutionary process).[72]

Unfortunately for the naturalistic moral realist, the contextual fit is not a good one.[73] Objective values are out of place. The more natural context for moral values and human dignity is the theistic one: We have been made by a personal, self-aware, purposeful, good God to resemble him in certain important ways. Naturalism is hard-pressed to account for what most of us take for granted: that personal, self-aware, valuable, morally responsible persons exist. There are at least three reasons for thinking that theism presents a better fit for objective moral values than does naturalism.

Reason #1: There is a more natural fit between God's existence and objective moral values or human dignity than between valueless processes that produce such value and dignity. There is a smooth transition between a good, supremely valuable God and objective moral values or human dignity. This is not so with naturalism, in which we move from valueless processes to valuable beings, from *is* to *ought*. Given the naturalistic context,

---

[72]For example, David O. Brink, *Moral Realism and the Foundations of Ethics* (New York: Cambridge University Press, 1989); Michael Martin, *Atheism, Morality, and Meaning* (Amherst, N.Y.: Prometheus, 2002). I respond in more detail to naturalistic moral realism in my essay "The Moral Argument," in *The Rationality of Theism*, ed. Paul Copan and Paul K. Moser (London: Routledge, 2003), pp. 149-74.

[73]I do not here address Eastern monism (e.g., of the Advaita Vedanta school of Hinduism), which claims that no ultimate distinction between good and evil exists—an outlook that serves to support relativism.

moral values and human dignity could hardly be predicted as emerging from
the materialistic, unguided processes that preceded them. Because of this
natural-fit criterion, we have good reason to affirm theism's superiority over
naturalism as an explanation of morality.

*Reason #2: The theistic grounding for objective moral values and human
dignity is a more basic and less ad hoc explanation than is a purported naturalistic grounding.* Some naturalistic moral realists will argue that moral
values and human dignity exist and that we must take them as basic. Full
stop. But what if one theory goes beyond the full stop to a more basic level
of explanation or offers a metaphysical framework to account for objective
moral values and human dignity unavailable in competing theories? When
moving from the overarching theory (theism vs. naturalism) to the entity in
question (objective moral values, human dignity), a merely ad hoc explanation will be inferior to the more basic, less-contrived one. Naturalistic moral
realism becomes increasingly ad hoc by virtue of its embracing the massive
additional assumption that a valueless context can somehow produce valuable personal beings.

Theism requires no such additional, background-defying assumptions
and is thus more basic. Human persons derive naturally from a valuable divine personal Being. No context-defying measures are necessary for such an
outcome.[74] Just as consciousness makes better sense in a world in which a
supremely self-aware Being exists,[75] so objective moral values make better
sense in a world in which a supremely good Being exists. Just as the attempt
to explain the emergence of consciousness naturalistically is plagued with
gaps and conundrums,[76] so is the attempt to move from valuelessness to
value—a point a good number of nontheists themselves have had to admit.[77]
As Del Ratzsch notes, "When a value is produced by a long, tricky, precari-

---

[74]For an excellent essay on the oddity of moral obligation given naturalism, see George I.
Mavrodes, "Religion and the Queerness of Morality," in *Rationality, Religious Belief, and
Moral Commitment,* ed. Robert Audi and William Wainwright (Ithaca, N.Y.: Cornell University
Press, 1986), pp. 213-26.

[75]See J. P. Moreland's contribution in chapter 13 of the present volume.

[76]Naturalist philosopher Colin McGinn admits: "How is it possible for conscious states to depend upon brain states? How can technicolour phenomenology arise from soggy grey matter?
. . . How could the aggregation of millions of individually insentient neurons generate subjective awareness? We know that brains are the *de facto* causal basis of consciousness, but we
have, it seems, no understanding of how this can be so. It strikes us as miraculous, eerie, even
faintly comic." *The Problem of Consciousness* (Oxford: Blackwell, 1990), pp. 10-11.

[77]One could list the likes of Bertrand Russell, Jean-Paul Sartre, J. L. Mackie, Richard Dawkins,
Daniel Dennett, Jonathan Glover, Steven Weinberg, Peter Singer, etc.

ous process, when it is generated and preserved by some breathtaking complexity, when it is realized against all odds, then intent—even design—suddenly becomes a live and reasonable question."[78]

Reason #3: The capacity of theism to unify certain phenomena more adeptly than its rivals gives it greater—and thus preferential—explanatory power. When we consider important phenomena and processes in the world (moral, metaphysical, cosmological, astrophysical, biological, chemical, etc.) against the backdrop of theism (God's will, character and activity) and of naturalism (numerous, disparate processes), theism offers a more unified explanation than naturalism. Consider table 10.1.

To claim, as some naturalists do, that naturalism is the simpler explanation just because it invokes fewer entities (i.e., a nontheistic world is more pared down than a theistic one) is not much help here. Spontaneous generation or abiogenesis is quite a simple explanation (no intermediate mechanism between life and nonlife), but it is clearly inadequate. Something more is obviously needed.

Getting back to the question raised at the outset of this section (why theism presents the most plausible account of human moral experience), we can note, fourth, that *the intrinsic connection between God's existence and objective moral values has been noted by even nontheistic thinkers of all stripes, and if objective moral values exist (as appears obvious), this fact would serve as a pointer to God's existence.* Atheists have been made in the image of God and can therefore recognize the same sorts of moral values Christians can. Atheists don't need the Bible to recognize basic objective moral values. They have been created or constituted to be able to recognize them—even if they disbelieve. All humans are hard-wired the same way: they are made to function properly when living morally. This moral awareness is part of God's general self-revelation. We see something of God in the moral order of the universe.

Atheist Michael Martin asks: "why would the nonexistence of God adversely affect the goodness of mercy, compassion, and justice? . . . One could affirm the objective immorality of rape and deny the existence of God with perfect consistency,"[79] that is, that even if God didn't exist, we could

---

[78]Del Ratzsch, *Nature, Design, and Science* (Albany: State University of New York Press, 2001), p. 68. On the very live option of intelligent design, see William A. Dembski, *The Design Revolution* (Downers Grove, Ill.: InterVarsity Press, 2004).

[79]Michael Martin, "Atheism, Christian Theism, and Rape (1997)," available online at <www .infidels.org/library/modern/michael_martin/rape.html>.

Table 10.1

Phenomena We Recognize/Observe/Assume	Theistic Context	Naturalistic Context
(Self-)consciousness exists.	God is **supremely self-aware/conscious**.	The universe was produced by **mindless, nonconscious** processes.
Personal beings exist.	God is a **personal** Being.	The universe was produced by **impersonal** processes.
We believe we make **free personal decisions/choices**.	God is **spirit** and **a free Being**, who can freely choose to act (e.g., to create or not).	We have emerged by **material, deterministic processes and forces** beyond our control.
We trust our senses and rational faculties as generally reliable in producing true beliefs.	A God of **truth and rationality** exists.	Because of our impulse to survive and reproduce, our **beliefs** would only **help us survive, but** a number of these **could be completely false.**
Human beings have **intrinsic value/dignity** and **rights**.	God is the **supremely valuable** Being.	Human beings were produced by **valueless** processes.
Objective **moral** values exist.	God's character is the source of **goodness/moral values**.	The universe was produced by **nonmoral** processes.
First **life** emerged.	God is a **living**, active Being.	Life somehow emerged from **nonliving** matter.
Beauty exists (e.g., not only in landscapes and sunsets but also in "elegant" or "beautiful" scientific theories).	God is **beautiful** (Ps 27:4) and capable of creating beautiful things according to his pleasure.	Beauty in the natural world is **superabundant** and in many cases **superfluous** (often not linked to survival).
The **universe** (all matter, energy, space, time) **began to exist** a finite time ago.	A powerful, personal **Being**, God, **caused the universe to exist**, creating it out of nothing.	The universe popped into existence, uncaused out of nothing (or possibly self-caused). **Being emerged from non-being.**
The universe is **finely tuned for human life** (known as "the Goldilocks effect"—the universe is "just right" for life).	God is a **wise, intelligent Designer**.	All the cosmic constants **just happened to be right**; given enough time and/or many possible worlds, a finely tuned world eventually emerged.
Real evils—both moral and natural—exist/take place in the world.	Genuine evil assumes (a) some **design plan** (of how things *ought* to be but are not) or even (b) a **standard of goodness** (a corruption or absence of goodness, by which we judge something to be evil). (a) God is the **Intelligent Designer** of the universe. (b) **God's good character** provides a moral standard or moral context to discern evil.	Atrocities, pain and suffering **just happen**. This is just **how things** *are*—with no "plan" or standard of goodness to which things *ought* to conform.

still know that objective morality exists. The Christian will cite the same reasons as the atheist about the wrongness of rape: "It violates the victims rights and offends her dignity. It also contributes to the destruction of society." The atheist appears to be vindicated. He can say to the theist: "See? Your reasons didn't even appeal to God's existence. The very reasons you give are the ones I give."

This is too hasty. We must distinguish between knowing and being—and get clear on which is more fundamental. At one level (knowing), Martin's argument appears to make sense. Because human beings have been made in God's image as intrinsically valuable (endowed with rights, dignity, conscience, moral responsibility and the basic capacity to recognize right and wrong), we should not be surprised that an atheist holds similar beliefs about human rights, dignity and obligation. They do not have to believe in God to know right from wrong.

Thus Martin's defense of objective morality only works at this level of knowing.[80] The more fundamental level of being—that is, the actual ground or basis (which makes moral knowledge possible)—is inadequate.[81] One could also add that leaving God out of one's metaphysic will diminish or obliterate certain important virtues: contentment (which springs from God's wisely, sovereignly directing history) rather than worry, gratitude to God instead of murmuring, forgiveness as a reflection of divine grace, trust in God instead of a self-sufficient spirit, and the like. Theism offers us greater moral richness and depth than atheism.[82]

If the naturalist claims that intrinsic dignity somehow emerges when an organism is sufficiently neurologically complex, the problem of accounting for the emergence of value or dignity remains. As Kant argued regarding the actual infinite,[83] so can we regarding human worth: *dignity cannot be formed by successive addition.* Intrinsic value must be given at the outset; otherwise, it doesn't matter how many nonpersonal and nonvaluable components we happen to stack up. From valuelessness, valuelessness comes.

---

[80]For further support of this thesis, see Paul Copan, "The Moral Argument," pp. 149-74.

[81]See Paul Copan, "Is Michael Martin a Moral Realist? *Sic et Non,*" *Philosophia Christi,* n.s. 1 (1999): 45-72; "Atheistic Goodness Revisited: A Personal Reply to Michael Martin," *Philosophia Christi,* n.s. 1 (2000): 91-104. Martin offers an online response that, very strangely, actually brings up charges and issues already addressed in the aforementioned essays. "Copan's Critique of Atheistic Objective Morality" <http://www.infidels.org/library/modern/michael_martin/copan.html>. For a partial response, see Copan, "The Moral Argument."

[82]See Charles Taliaferro, "The Intensity of Theism," *Sophia* 31 (1992): 61-73.

[83]Immanuel Kant, *Critique of Pure Reason,* trans. Norman Kemp Smith (New York: St. Martin's, 1965), A 426 / B 454.

I would argue that a personal Creator, who made human persons in his image, serves as the ontological basis for the existence of objective moral values, moral obligation, human dignity and rights. Without the existence of a personal God, there would be no persons at all; and if no persons existed, then no moral properties would be instantiated in our world. Thus, God is necessary to ground the instantiation of moral properties; his own existence as a personal Being instantiates these properties, and by virtue of our creation in God's image, we human persons are further instantiations of these properties. Moral categories (right/wrong, good/bad, praiseworthy/blameworthy) get to the essence of who we fundamentally are. They apply to us *as persons,* who have been made to reflect the divine image.[84]

The atheistic moral realist claims that the proposition *Murder is wrong* would hold true even if God does not exist. Let me offer the following responses. First, even if we grant that moral facts are just brute givens and necessarily true (just as logical laws are), the huge cosmic coincidence of the correspondence between these moral facts and the eventual evolutionary development of self-reflective moral beings who are obligated to them and recognize them begs for explanation. These moral facts, it appears, were anticipating our emergence.[85] A less ad hoc explanation is that a good God made valuable human beings in his image.

Second, the necessity of moral truths does not diminish their need for grounding in the character of a personal God. God necessarily exists in all possible worlds, and God can be the source of necessary moral truths that stand in asymmetrical relation to God's necessity.[86] So God would still be explanatorily prior to these moral values. We just noted above that moral properties are instantiated through personhood (which is ontologically rooted in God's personhood). It just is not obvious that an independent Platonic realm (or its naturalistic equivalent) containing forms of Justice and Goodness exists.[87] As Douglas Groothuis argues, "God's objective character supplies a different category of external explanation that does not reduce rationality to non-

---

[84]David S. Oderberg, *Moral Theory: A Non-Consequentialist Approach* (Cambridge: Blackwell, 2000), p. 1.

[85]See Copan, "Atheistic Goodness Revisited," and Gregory E. Ganssle, "Necessary Moral Truths," *Philosophia Christi,* n.s. 2, no. 1 (2000): 105-12.

[86]See William Lane Craig's discussion in *Does God Exist? The Craig-Flew Debate,* ed. Stan W. Wallace (Burlington, Vt.: Ashgate, 2003), pp. 168-73.

[87]See Paul Copan and William Lane Craig, *Creation Out of Nothing: A Biblical, Philosophical, and Scientific Exploration* (Grand Rapids: Baker, 2004), pp. 167-95. See also Craig, *Does God Exist?* pp. 170-71.

rational factors or reduce morality to nonmoral factors."[88] Besides, even if this Platonism is true, there is still no good reason to think that valuable, morally responsible human beings should emerge from valueless processes.[89]

So the reason theism makes better sense of human dignity and objective moral values is that morality and personhood are necessarily connected. That is, moral values are rooted in personhood, as persons are intrinsically value-bearing beings. The moral argument points to a personal, good Being to whom we are responsible. Only if God exists can moral properties be realized or instantiated. The naturalistic assumption that objective moral values can exist without God is, as John Rist suggests, an "ethical hangover from a more homogeneous Christian past."[90]

CONCLUSION

David Hume's powerful influence is certainly being felt today in moral theory. But we have reason to question Hume's empiricistic and reductionistic approach to knowledge and ethics, which leads to a vicious circle when it comes to knowledge claims. Human dignity, moral responsibility and moral obligations are properly basic (we assume these constantly in our personal lives and in the public square). Rightly functioning human beings will recognize these bottom-line, intuitive moral principles. If moral values, human dignity and personal responsibility exist, it seems that theism has ample resources to account for these facts (being made in the image of a good, personal God). Without such a personal, good God, there would be no moral values because there would be no persons, in whom value resides.[91]

Of course, a successful moral argument does not reveal that the God of Abraham, Isaac, Jacob and Jesus exists—a full-blown theism. This argument does, however, reveal a supreme personal moral Being (1) who is worthy of worship, (2) who has made us with dignity and worth, (3) to whom we are personally accountable and (4) who may reasonably be called "God."[92]

---

[88]Douglas Groothuis, "Thomas Nagel's 'Last Word' on the Metaphysics of Rationality and Morality," *Philosophia Christi*, n.s. 1 (1999): 119.

[89]Some may wish to interject the Euthyphro dilemma at this point (is something good because God commands it or does God command it because it is good?). I have argued elsewhere that this is a red herring. See Copan, "The Moral Argument."

[90]Rist, *Real Ethics*, p. 2.

[91]On the implications of the meaning of life without God, see Thomas V. Morris, *Making Sense of It All: Pascal and the Meaning of Life* (Grand Rapids: Eerdmans, 1992); J. P. Moreland, "Reflections on Meaning in Life Without God," *Trinity Journal*, n.s. 9 (spring 1988): 3-18.

[92]Thanks to Doug Groothuis, James Sennett and Charles Taliaferro for their helpful comments on an earlier draft of this chapter.

11

DAVID HUME, EXPERIENTIAL EVIDENCE
AND BELIEF IN GOD

Keith Yandell

✌

D avid Hume offers an account of what constitutes human experience on which experience of God is not even a possibility. He adds an account of what we can know on which, even should such experience occur, it could not be evidence that God exists. He also thinks we can blamelessly believe things we cannot have evidence for, though belief in God is not among these things. In this chapter we consider his views on what constitutes human experience, what we can know, and what we can believe without doing violence to our natures. Here, these views are explained, examined and assessed.

HUME'S ACCOUNT OF WHAT CONSTITUTES HUMAN EXPERIENCE

Hume offers a doctrine of human experience. On that doctrine, neither experience of trees nor experience of God is possible. Yet Hume believes that there are trees and does not believe that there is a God. He offers an account of human experience on which no experiential knowledge of God or experiential evidence for the existence of God is available to anyone. While the topic of *nonexperiential knowledge of God* is beyond the scope of this chapter—it raises too many complex issues to be dealt with here—we will consider his claim regarding *experiential evidence for the existence of God*. As we will understand these ideas here, *direct* experiential evidence for God's existence would be a matter of experiencing God; *indirect* experiential evidence for God's existence would be a matter of experiencing something other than God, which represents God to us, and on the basis of which we could legitimately claim to (close enough) experience God.

Some relevant Humean data. I suspect that no report of "the data" regarding what Hume held is uncontroversial; by now Hume's writings have become what Luther said the pope made the Bible, namely, a wax nose twisted into whatever shape an interpreter pleases.[1] But since I want to discuss Hume's views, I must do my own interpreting while denying that an interpretation must twist and doing as little twisting as I can.

Notoriously, Hume begins *A Treatise of Human Nature*—his most detailed philosophical work—by telling us that "All the perceptions of the human mind resolve themselves into two distinct kinds, which I will call impressions and ideas" (THN 1).[2] While, as the discussion progresses, it is not clear whether the impression/idea distinction is of degree or kind, and perhaps not really clear what the degree/kind distinction amounts to here, Hume has lots of things to say about perceptions.

The nature of experience as constituted by perceptions. Among the things that Hume says regarding perceptions are these. Perceptions are

- the only kind of things that we can conceive the existence of (THN 67-68; 218);

- "internal and perishing existences, [which] appear as such" (THN 194);

- the only existences of which we are certain (THN 212);

- "immediately present to us by consciousness, [so that they] command our strongest assent, and . . . [are] the first foundation of all of our conclusions" (THN 212);

- the only things we are ever aware of (THN 1, 67);

- mind-dependent (THN 193, 210);

- things that exist with no need of anything else to support their existence[3] (THN 233, 252);

---

[1]I've defended the general sort of interpretation of Hume presented here in some detail in *Hume's "Inexplicable Mystery": His Views on Religion* (Philadelphia: Temple University Press, 1990). In particular, readers are referred to the discussion there of Hume's *Natural History of Religion* (which is only briefly touched here) and his *Dialogues Concerning Natural Religion* (the relevance of which to our topics is best seen in the light of the *Treatise of Human Nature* and the *Natural History*).

[2]*A Treatise of Human Nature* (1739, 1740; reprint, Oxford: Clarendon, 1978; 2nd ed. with analytical index by L. A. Selby-Bigge, with text revised and notes by P. H. Nidditch). References are to this edition, cited as THN followed by the page number.

[3]This is relevant to his rejection of the core premise of the cosmological argument. See, for his rejection of this premise, Keith Yandell, "David Hume on Meaning, Verification and Natural Theology," chapter 4 in this volume.

- effects (THN xvii, 13, 269);
- *individual* in the sense of being *fully determinate* (THN 18, 19);
- nonrepresentational or nonintentional (THN 189);
- internal and perishing (THN 194);
- once gone, always gone (THN 85); and
- successive (THN 204, 220).

Since, in Hume's view, perceptions *constitute* our experience, his view as to what we can learn from experience is massively affected by his account of what perceptions are. As we will explain, there is no room whatever for even the possibility that God be perceived or that God be represented by any perception. So, of course, if one starts with a Humean account of experience, experiential evidence for God's existence or an experiential awareness of God is simply out of the question.

Some things Hume says about perceptions do not fit well with other things he says about them. He claims, we noted, that each perception is ontologically mind-dependent but also ontologically independent, and to save Hume from inconsistency here presumably one must claim that a single and independent perception is a one-perception mind. Even so, on his doctrine each of the members of a two-membered collection of perceptions (a two-perception mind) has two features: each perception depends for its existence on being a member of the collection of which it is a member and each perception exists independent of anything other than itself, which requires that each of the two perceptions is ontologically independent of everything else and also exists dependent on something else. This, obviously, is inconsistent.

Another inconsistency in Hume's doctrine is more important for our purposes. Hume says that impressions, which are the basic perceptions (the perceptions that are not derived from other perceptions) are not intentional or representational. They are not *of* anything; they do not represent there being anything. Consider a headache or a sense of dizziness; these experiences are nonintentional, not (even apparently) *of* anything; they do not represent anything. They are not experiences of mind-independent items, nor do they seem to be so. Ideas (derivative perceptions), however, Hume says are copies of impressions, yet they are said to be intentional (at least apparently) *of* something, representational. A mere copy of a nonintentional item cannot be an intentional item. Yet Hume says this is so: every idea is merely a copy of an impression, and impressions are nonintentional, non-representational, not *of* anything; yet ideas are intentional.

Another way of putting the point here is by reference to what philosophers typically call *qualia* (singular *quale*). A migraine headache is a quale[4]—a mental state with (in this instance) a painful content that does not seem to be, and is not, an experience of some mind-independent item. Generalized anxiety or euphoria are not matters of feeling anxious or euphoric *at anything;* they are just mental states with an anxious feeling content or with a euphoric feeling content. They are qualia. So is dizziness, an itch, a burning sensation, or a vague sense of unease that is directed at nothing. Impressions, according to Humean doctrine, are qualia. In contrast, actually seeing a tree or merely seeming to see a tree that is not there (e.g., hallucinating a tree) are perceptual experiences, but they are not qualia. They are matters of at least seeming to experience some item such that, if that item exists at all, it exists independent of its being perceived. On Hume's account, impressions are, and ideas are not, qualia. Impressions of sensation—the components of sensory experience—are not intentional. Impressions of reflection—the components of introspective experience—are not intentional. Ideas—the components of thought about experience—are intentional. Yet the latter supposedly are mere copies of the former. A rationale for the *ideas are mere copies of impressions* doctrine is to construct the mind out of perceptions rather than construing the mind as the recipient of perceptions. Yet on Hume's own account of the mind, it is a *creative* copy machine, and simply composed of originals and copies.

While Hume holds, as we have noted, that perceptions are the only existent things of which we are certain, they do not represent *there being objects* to us. On this, Hume insists:

> That our senses offer not their impressions as the images of something *distinct,* or *independent,* and *external,* is evident; because they convey to us nothing but a single perception, and never give us the least intimation of any thing beyond. A single perception can never produce the idea of a double existence, but by some inference either of the reason or imagination. (THN 189)

Impressions are nonintentional, and are thus no sound basis for an inference to items that are not impressions that cause them or resemble them in some manner. "When the mind looks farther than what appears to it, its con-

---

[4]More accurately, no doubt, a collection of qualia, but here is not the place to get into the question of identity conditions for qualia.

clusions can never be put to the account of the senses; and it certainly looks
farther, when from a single perception it infers a double existence, and supposes the relations of resemblance and causation betwixt them" (THN 189).

But Hume, however inconsistently, thinks of ideas as intentional: "Whatever ideas are adequate representations of objects, the relations, contradictions and agreements of the ideas are applicable to the objects; and this we
may in general observe to be the foundation of all human knowledge" (THN
29). This opens a line of reasoning that is unwelcome to a Humean.

Intentional indirect realism and intentional direct realism. A *realist*
regarding some category of things holds that there really are such things;
talk about them is not really disguised talk about something else; experience
of them is actually an encounter with them, not some sort of illusion or hal-
lucination, or merely an experience of something else. Botanists are realists
about trees. Theists are realists about God.

An *indirect realist* about trees holds that we are aware of something other
than trees from which we properly infer the existence of trees. The "something other" are perceptual experiences that represent trees—pictures of
trees or perceptual states that we have that represent *there being trees,* and
so on. While we don't typically perform such an inference, we would reason
properly were we to infer from *I am having a perception that pictures a tree*
and *If I am having a perception that pictures a tree, then (probably) there is
a tree there* to *There is a tree there.* (*Imagining* a tree is not having a *perception* that pictures a tree; it isn't *perceiving* at all.)

Hume is no indirect realist. Insofar as perceptual experience is a matter
of having qualia, indirect realism cannot get started; qualia are nonrepresen-
tative. But if we have perceptions that are intentional or representational,
things are different. An indirect realist claims that our perceptions typically
are not matters of having qualia; to perceive is to have images of things that
exist independent of the mind. Roughly, perceptions are typically mental
pictures that represent to us the existence of objects, and they typically are
caused by the objects that they represent. To perceive a tree is to have a
mental picture that represents *there being a tree* where the tree itself is the
cause of the picture. The indirect realist grants that there are cases in which
perceptions represent things as being other than as they are—illusions, hal-
lucinations and the like. But these, the indirect realist claims, typically can
be detected by reference to other perceptions; we discover that not all of
our pictures can be accurate, and we have developed tests for coming to
reasonable conclusions about which ones are not to be trusted.

Hume is explicitly aware of indirect realism as a possible view. About it, he comments:

> Even after we distinguish our perceptions from our objects, 'twill appear pres-
> ently, that we are still incapable of reasoning from the existence of one to that
> of the other; so that upon the whole our reason neither does, nor is it possible
> it even should, upon any supposition, give us an assurance of the continued
> and distinct existence of body. That opinion must be entirely owing to the
> *imagination*. (THN 193)

But on a view that our perceptions are composed of Humean ideas rather than of Humean impressions, indirect realism has a conceptual foothold that it lacks on the view that our perceptions are composed of Humean impressions or qualia.

Direct realism claims that to have a perceptual experience simply is to be aware of an item that exists independent of one's experience of it. In perception one is aware of (say) a tree—not of an image, picture or representation of a tree, but of the very bark-bearing item itself. One sometimes seems to be aware of an item that isn't there, and there are ways of coming to a reasonable conclusion about when that happens. Hume thinks that direct realism can't be right. He holds that our knowledge of our own perceptions is necessarily free from error—that it is, in the language of later philosophers, incorrigible or infallible. He writes:

> [E]very impression . . . is originally on the same footing . . . they appear, all of
> them, in their true colors as impressions or perceptions. And, indeed, if we
> consider the matter aright, 'tis scarce possible it should be otherwise, nor is it
> conceivable that our senses should be more capable of deceiving us in the sit-
> uations or relations, than in the nature of our impressions. For since all actions
> and sensations of the mind are known to us by consciousness, they must nec-
> essarily appear in every particular what they are, and be what they appear.
> Every thing that enters the mind being in *reality* a perception, 'tis impossible
> any thing should to *feeling* appear different. This were to suppose, that even
> where we are most intimately conscious, we might be mistaken. (THN 190)

Even if we grant Hume this last claim, his view does not follow. Most philosophers (and most nonphilosophers) would claim that when we perceive, it at least seems to us that we are perceiving *things*—items that exist independent of our perceptions. What I seem to see just now is a bookcase, not a picture of a bookcase—let alone a quale of some sort.

There is an argument in Hume's quotation. It is this: we cannot be mistaken about what we are immediately or directly conscious of; we can be mistaken about whether there is a mind-independent item that we perceive; so we cannot be immediately or directly conscious of a mind-independent item. The direct realist can grant a claim very like the one that Hume makes. Suppose I seem to see a tree. Either there is one there or not. If there is, then I am directly aware of a tree. If there isn't, then I am not. In both cases, it seems to me that I see a tree, and this is something that I cannot be wrong about. I cannot be mistaken about *it seeming to me that there is a tree,* but I can be mistaken about *there actually being a tree.* The sense in which I cannot be mistaken in my "most intimate" conscious perception is captured by noting that I can't be mistaken about how things perceptually seem to me. It does not follow that I cannot be mistaken about whether there is an actual tree that I am perceptually aware of, or whether what is happening instead is that I am having a picture—a representation—of a tree when none is there. So the direct realist has a reply to this argument by Hume, and an indirect realist has an analogous reply. (I will not here get into the further question as to whether perceptual consciousness really is, in some relevant sense, incorrigible or infallible.)

Sensory and introspective experience and religious theistic experience. It is high time to ask what all this has to do with theistic religious experience—with experiences that at least seem to their subjects to be experiences of God. Hume thinks that there aren't any such experiences. The reason for this is straightforward. If all of our experience is composed of qualia, then we can't even seem to experience a mind-independent item, whether the item in question is a tree or God. Qualia are mental states with certain conscious contents. Crossculturally and over a good deal of time persons have reported having had experiences of God.[5] A typical treatment of appeals to religious experience by critics supposes that these experiences

---

[5]Some sense of what this amounts to can be gleaned from Timothy Beardsworth, *A Sense of Presence* (Oxford: Religious Experience Study Unit, 1977) and Alistair Hardy, *The Spiritual Nature of Man* (Oxford: Clarendon, 1979). Caroline Franks Davis, *The Evidential Force of Religious Experience* (Oxford: Clarendon, 1989) offers a good discussion of relevant social science issues, but assumes that somehow all religious experience is somehow of the same sort of thing, an assumption that seems to me gratuitous and false. William P. Alston, *Perceiving God* (Ithaca, N.Y.: Cornell University Press, 1991) is widely discussed; its practice-oriented epistemology seems to me in the end incurably relativistic. Nonetheless, both Davis and Alston rightly challenge epistemological dicta that arbitrarily rule out appeal to religious experience as evidence. Nelson Pike, *Mystic Union* (Ithaca, N.Y.: Cornell University Press, 1992) is a superb treatment of the phenomenology of religious experience, admirable in both the distinctions and points it does make and the frequent errors that it avoids.

are qualia. This, of course, is what Hume's claim (that impressions are the paradigmatic constituents of experiences) entails if one applies it to religious experience. But in fact, these experiences are not qualia. If I may coin a slogan that should be writ large at the outset of every discussion concerning whether or not apparent experience of God is evidence for the existence of God, *Experience of God is not a godly experience;* it is not an experience with a godlike flavor.[6] Typically, those who have such experiences are humbled, if not overwhelmed, by the sense of a Presence that seems to exist quite independent of themselves and their experiences.

Experiences that seem to their subjects to be experiences of God are intentional, to be understood and described either in intentional indirect (representationalist) realist or intentional direct realistic terms. This claim is central to any formulation of the argument from religious experience. This provides the background for two lines of argument, one by an intentional representationalist realist and one by an intentional direct realist.

Both arguers can and should admit that it is logically possible for an intentional experience to represent or appear to be of an object that does not in fact exist. It is also logically possible that, for every such experience whatever that has ever occurred or will ever occur, there is no corresponding object. That is the nature of any sort of intentional experience—any (and all) intentional experience may be such that its putative objects do not exist.[7] My computer seems to be in front of me. But it is logically possible that I am merely subject to a systematic barrage of computer-perceptions that occur in the complete absence of any actual computer. The arguments to be considered are fully compatible with that possibility, though of course they do not require that the possibility be realized.

As an indirect realist (an intentional representationalist) concerning experience of God, one will hold that, in experiences where the subject at least seems to experience God, the subject has an experience that represents to the subject *there being God* and, if the subject then believes that she has had an experience of God, she does so properly.

If Abe seems to see a cat, and the indirect realist is right, then Abe is hav-

---

[6]There is some excuse for the critic's treatment of such experience in the practice among theists of not distinguishing in kind between experiences whose accurate phenomenological description is something like, say, feeling more comfortable or no longer anxious and experiences whose accurate phenomenological description is something like, say, encountering a being to whom only worship is an appropriate response.

[7]Setting aside the question as to whether or not *God exists* is a necessary truth.

ing a cat image—a picture that represents there being a cat in front of him. If things are as they are represented, an Abe-independent feline object is in Abe's neighborhood. If Abe at least *seems* to see a cat, then let us say that, if the indirect realist account is right, Abe has a *cat-representation*. Then the indirect realist can offer the following argument;

1.   Abe has a cat-representation.

2.   Cat-representations are evidence that a cat is present.

So:

3.   There is evidence that a cat is present.

Premise 2 is the sort of claim that is, if true, necessarily true. If it is true, it can't be that cat-representations just *happen to be* evidence of the presence of cats. The evidence, of course, is experiential.

Similarly, one can argue relative to theistic religious experiences as follows. Suppose:

1:*   Abe has a God-representation (an experience in which Abe at least seems to experience God, understood along indirect realist lines).

2:*   God-representations are evidence that God exists.

So:

3:*   There is evidence that God exists.

Like premise 2 above, premise 2* is the sort of claim that is, if true, necessarily true. If it is true, it can't be that God-representations just *happen to be* evidence of the existence of God. The evidence, of course, is experiential.

Consider things instead from the direct intentional realist perspective. If Abe at least *seems* to perceive a cat, then Abe has an intentional experience in which he at least apparently is actually aware of a cat; he at least apparently actually, so to speak, has an encounter of the feline kind. Call such experiences *cat-encounters*. Then the direct intentional realist can offer the following argument:

1A: Abe experientially seems to have a cat-encounter.

2A: Apparent cat-encounters are evidence that a cat is present.

So:

3A: There is evidence that a cat is present.

Like its predecessors, premise 2A is the sort of claim that is, if true, necessarily true. If it is true, it can't be that apparent cat-encounters just *happen to be* evidence of the presence of cats. The evidence, of course, is experiential.

An intentional direct realist concerning theistic religious experiences can offer the following sort of argument:

1A*: Abe experientially seems to have a God-encounter.

2A*: Apparent God-encounters are evidence that God exists.

So:

3A*: There is evidence that God exists.

Once again premise 2A* is the sort of claim that is, if true, necessarily true. If it is true, it can't be that apparent God-encounters just *happen to be* evidence for the existence of God. The evidence, of course, is experiential.[8]

A cautious[9] cat lover who is philosophically inclined can offer this argument:

1B: Abe has a cat-representation or Abe experientially seems to have a cat-encounter.

2B: Cat-representations are evidence that a cat is present and apparent cat-encounters are evidence that a cat is present.

So:

3B: There is evidence that a cat is present.

Given that Abe nonculpably has nothing to say against his pro-cat experiences, if he believes that there is a cat present then he believes in accor-

---

[8]A reviewer suggested that the varieties of premise 2 are not necessary truths, and that their being necessarily true is not necessary for the arguments. He points out that just because (say) at least apparent cat-encounters are evidence in the actual world that there are cats, it does not follow that they would be such evidence in all worlds. Of course, I didn't claim that this did follow. My own view is that 2A* is a necessary truth, and that a world in which at least apparent encounters with cats never were encounters with actual cats would still be a world in which such apparent encounters with cats would be evidence for the existence of cats, and that such a possible world would be defective relative to the fact that what we had evidence for regarding the presence of cats turned out always to be evidence for a falsehood. That a claim is false is no reason whatever that we cannot have evidence for it. I don't think there is anything more clearly true than 2A* from which it follows, so I don't offer an attempted proof of it. What can be said on its behalf is mainly the price of rejecting it, which I take to be exorbitantly high. But what is relevant here is that what I'm engaged in is showing that Hume didn't show that arguments for theism from religious experience were doomed to failure from the outset. What I'm pointing out, then, is that none of the various arguments from religious experience noted here (which can't all be good arguments—taken together, their premises form an inconsistent set) are ruled out by Humean considerations. I stick by my claim that each of the varieties of premise 2 is, if true, then (informally) necessarily so.

[9]Actually, the caution here is more apparent than real. The cautious arguer does not have to decide between intentional representationalism and intentional realism, but she does have to embrace the view that both cat-representations and cat-encounters are evidence, whereas neither the intentional representationist nor the intentional realist has to think this. The same applies below to the cautious theist.

dance with the evidence and with reason's approval when he embraces the
view that he has feline company. The next move is obvious. The theist who
wishes to remain neutral regarding indirect and direct realism can argue:

1B*: Abe has a God-representation or Abe experientially seems to have
      a God-encounter.

2B*: God-representations are evidence that God exists and apparent
      God-encounters are evidence that God exists.

So:

3B*: There is evidence that God exists.

Given that Abe nonculpably has nothing to say against his pro-God experiences, if he believes that there is a God then he believes in accordance
with the evidence and with reason's approval when he embraces the view
that he has divine company.

A theist can offer yet another sort of argument from theistic religious experience as follows:

1C: There are God-representations or apparent God-encounters.

2C: The best explanation of the fact that there are God-representations
     or apparent God-encounters is that God exists.

3C: If E is the best explanation of some data we know to exist, then
     those data are evidence that E is true.

So:

4:   There is evidence that God exists.

Part of that evidence—the part that justifies 1C—is experiential.

Each of these arguments requires discussion of at least two matters. First,
each argument contains a premise that asserts that certain sorts of experience
occur. In presenting a full-fledged version of an argument from religious experience, one must provide good reason to think that such experiences have
occurred. It seems to me that this task has been taken far too lightly by those
who have offered such arguments. Second, each of the arguments above
contains a premise that concerns evidence, and one concerns evidence and
best explanation; those premises require explication, discussion and defense. It is not my purpose here to attempt to provide discussions of these
matters beyond arguing that Hume has not shown that arguments of these
sorts cannot succeed. We have discussed the first matter, but not (so far) the
second. (It is worth noting that a person who offers one of these sorts of
arguments need not have had the requisite experience herself. She need

only have good reason to think that someone has had such experience.)

So far as I can see, Hume nowhere offers good reason to think that any of these sorts of arguments must fail. If this is correct, then the least one can say is that an argument from theistic religious experience for the existence of God is still a live option after Hume has done his worst. We have already seen that Hume breaks his own rules regarding perceptual experience being inherently nonintentional, and that his claim that perceptual experience is nonintentional seems plainly false. There are, however, other aspects of his epistemology—his views about the nature of knowledge and true belief, and the conditions under which they can be achieved—that are also relevant to his rejection of the idea that a theist can have any experiential evidence for his theistic beliefs, and these should be taken into account as well. His rejection of any claim like those expressed in the various second premises of our arguments requires examination. To that task, we now turn.[10]

HUME'S CRITERIA FOR WHAT CAN BE KNOWN

It will be helpful to set Hume's views in contrast to a position for which he felt some attraction but which he rejected. That view was presented by Descartes (though he himself ultimately saw problems with it). What is at issue here, for our purposes, is whether one could ever know any of the versions of the second premise in the arguments from religious experience described above.

Foundationalism. Foundationalism, in its classic form, holds that (1) one can noninferentially know only certain sorts of propositions and (2) one can only inferentially know what *strictly follows* from propositions of those sorts. Descartes, I take it, is the paradigm foundationalist. He held—at least I shall here take him to have held—to the following claims:

D1: For any person S and proposition P, S knows that P only if it is logically impossible that S believe that P and P be false.

D2: For any person S and proposition P, S reasonably believes that P only if there is some proposition Q such that S knows that Q and Q entails P.

In the developed epistemology to which these claims are basic, *S's reasonable beliefs* and *S's inferred knowledge* are extensionally equivalent—any

---

[10]Of course the second premise one accepts must be positively defended as well as rebutting Hume's critique thereof. But that is a task for another occasion. Cf. Keith Yandell, *The Epistemology of Religious Experience* (Cambridge: Cambridge University Press, 1993).

238   In Defense of Natural Theology

proposition that belongs to the one class will also belong to the other.

The scope of knowledge construed along the lines of D1 and D2 is limited to logically necessary truths and belief-entailed propositions, where proposition P is belief-entailed relative to person S if and only if *S believes that P entails P is true.* A famous example is *I exist*—if I manage to have that belief, I cannot be mistaken in having it. These, and these alone, are *Cartesian foundational propositions.* Descartes takes *cogito* propositions ("I exist" propositions), including not only such claims as *I exist now* and *I am thinking now,* but also what later philosophers would call "sincere attentive reports" of the immediate contents of one's consciousness (e.g., "I am feeling pain" or "I am angry"), to be belief-entailed. The task of a Cartesian foundationalist is to derive theological and external-world propositions[11] from Cartesian foundational propositions known to be true. Standing on Descartes's shoulders, we can see that the task cannot be accomplished. *That there are physical objects* (that is, mind-independent extended objects), for example, is not itself Cartesian foundational, and no set of propositions containing only propositions that are Cartesian foundational can entail any conclusion that is not Cartesian foundational. (We can reasonably read Descartes as having come to see this.)

One who took his cue from Hume's claim that perceptions are, as we noted, "immediately present to us by consciousness, [so that they] command our strongest assent, and are the first foundation of all of our conclusions" (THN 212), might remember one of Hume's more famous remarks and be led to see Hume as a foundationalist:

> Indeed, if we consider the matter aright, 'tis scarce reasonable it should be otherwise, nor is it conceivable that our senses should be more capable of deceiving us in the situation and relations, than in the nature, of our impressions. For since all actions and sensations of the mind are known to us by consciousness, they must necessarily appear in every particular what they are, and be what they appear. Every thing that enters the mind, being in *reality* a perception, 'tis impossible it should to *feeling* appear any different. This were to suppose, that even where we are most intimately conscious, we might be mistaken. (THN 190)[12]

---

[11]Propositions, that is, concerning objects and minds that exist independent of and distinct from one's own mind.

[12]"It" being that "every impression, external and internal, passions, affections, sensations, pains, and pleasures, are originally on the same footing; and that whatever other differences we may observe among them, they appear, all of them, in their true colors, as impressions or perceptions."

There are, then, in Hume's view, foundational propositions—propositions that concern the existence and observable features of our perceptions. These we can know to be true. But the idea that Hume held that we can justifiably (on the basis of truth-preferring reasons or evidence) infer, say, *There are physical objects* from Cartesian or Humean foundational propositions I take to be simply preposterous, and I shall say no more about it. His view was that such derivation is impossible regarding beliefs that there are mind-independent material objects, causal connections or God, or that one is an enduring mental substance.

Something Like Cartesian Foundationalism. One wishing to come as close to Cartesian foundationalism as possible might reason along these lines. Let person S's experience E be intentional if and only if S's having E is a matter of its experientially seeming to S that there exists some object O such that if O does exist (if things are as they experientially seem to S to be) then O exists independent of S and of being experienced by S. Then our quasi-Cartesian might argue, regarding a typical person S, that:

1D: S frequently has experiences that are intentional.

2D: If S has an experience E that is intentional regarding object O then, unless S is aware of a reason to think that E is faulty, *S's having E* gives S reason to think *There exists object O* is true.

3D: S seldom is aware of reason to think her intentional experiences to be faulty.

So:

4D: S often has experiences that give S evidence that an object exists.

If premise 2D is a necessary truth, it can be Cartesian foundational. Further, premise 2D is a proposition that has this feature: if it is true, it is (informally) necessarily true.[13] Premise 1D, I take it, would count within Cartesianism as foundational provided event-memory reports can so count; otherwise, it could be replaced by a claim that reported that *S's present sensory experience is intentional regarding object O*. Premise 3D will do only if reports regarding the potential faultiness of one's experiences can be belief-entailed (they will not be necessary truths). More plausibly, our quasi-Cartesian can suggest, not 3D, but

3D': S is nonculpably aware of no reason to think her present experience that is intentional regarding object O is faulty, and if S is nonculpa-

---

[13]Strictly, if true it is informally necessarily true. For a light touch on this notion, see Yandell, "David Hume on Meaning."

bly aware of no reason to think it faulty it is reasonable of S to take
that experience to be evidence that O exists, and unreasonable of
S not to so take it.[14]

(Then 2D would have to altered similarly.)

Even if each of 1D through 3D′ is Cartesian foundational, what follows is
not that there are objects, but only that one has evidence that there are. Still,
an argument whose premises met the high Cartesian standards and yielded
even that conclusion would not be unwelcome to physical object realists.
But plainly Hume offers no such argument. Whatever the status of 2D and
3D relative to Hume's philosophy, he denies premise 1D. In the first section
of this chapter, we discussed various deep problems with that denial. But
Hume would also deny 2D.

One can take one's cue from the quasi-Cartesian argument regarding material objects and construct a parallel argument along these lines. Consider
some person S who has had an experience that seemed to her to be an experience of God—an experience whose phenomenological content made
the belief that it was an experience of God sensible (of course one who offered the argument in some detail would have to discuss what such content
might be):

1D*: S had an experience that was intentional and seemed to S to be an
      experience of God.

2D*: If S had an experience E that was intentional and seemed to S to be
      of an item O then, unless S is aware of a reason to think that E is
      faulty, *S's having E* gives S reason to think *There exists item O* is true.

3D*: S is aware of no reason to think her intentional experience that
      seemed to S to be an experience of God to be faulty.

So:

4D*: S had an experience that gives S evidence that God exists.

This argument does not appeal to historical claims about other persons having experiences that at least seem to them to be experiences of God because
of the (rather arbitrary) restrictions that apply to a quasi-Cartesian argument.
But it is more than a Humean could allow; a Humean would deny 2D*. (This
is so even if 2D* and 3D* are altered so as to preclude culpable ignorance.)

Essentially, the reason for this denial is simple and well-known, and we

---

[14]I have discussed how this sort of claim might best be framed in Yandell, *Epistemology of Religious Experience;* see part 4.

can present it briefly. The reason is that Hume is committed to the view that the only statements that can be true or false are (1) statements that are true or false by definition (what he calls "relations of ideas" statements) and (2) statements that are made true or false by perceptions (what he calls "matters of fact" statements). None of the varieties of premise 2 of any of the arguments from the previous section, nor those from this section, is true or false by definition. None of them is made true, or made false, by perceptions. So none of the varieties of premise 2 can be either true or false; so they can't be true.

The reply is simple and devastating. Consider Hume's claim that *Only statements that are true or false by definition, and statements that are made true or false by perceptions, actually are either true or false.* This is not a statement that is true or false by definition nor is it a statement made true or false by perceptions. So, on its own terms, it isn't true or false; so it isn't true. It cannot, then, provide a good reason for rejecting the possibility that one or another variety of premise 2 may be true.

It is worth noting that necessary truths come in two varieties. In the case of one variety, a proposition is a necessary truth if and only if its denial is formally contradictory. Thus *The moon both exists and does not exist,* taken literally, is contradictory, and thus *It is not the case that the moon both exists and does not exist* is a necessary truth of the first sort. But the denial of a necessary truth of the second sort does not produce a formal contradiction. *If Sarah smiles then her smile has shape* is a necessary truth of the second type. More interesting examples are *If a proposition is a necessary truth, then it is necessarily a necessary truth, If X is metaphysically identical to Y then necessarily, X is metaphysically identical to Y,* and *Nothing is both a person and in principle incapable of consciousness.*

The relevant point here is that the varieties of premise 2 are, if true, then necessarily true and of the second sort. So the truths among them fall under the rubric of Cartesian foundational propositions, provided we expand the notion of a recognizably necessary truth to include both sorts of necessary propositions.

Thus far we have considered Humean objections to the very idea of experience of God, and the sorts of propositions that have to be known, or reasonably believed, if we are to rationally take experiences that are at least apparently experiences of God to be evidence that God exists. We have found no reason to think that attempts to find experiential evidence that God exists from such sources is somehow an endeavor that is irrational, inescapably flawed or inevitably doomed to failure. We now turn to two other relevant features of Hume's views—namely, his contention that some beliefs are quite properly accepted without evidence and his view that belief in the existence of God is not among them—that theistic belief is irrational and harmful to our natures as believing beings.

Beliefs It Is Proper to Have Without Evidence

Hume is not your standard Enlightenment figure who thinks it wrong ever to believe anything in the absence of sufficient evidence and denies that there is sufficient evidence for Christian, or even robust theistic, belief. He is a complicated skeptic concerning knowledge of what we think of as very ordinary things, who thinks it neither possible nor desirable for us always to constrain our beliefs to the limits of our evidence. He does not even think that doing so would he healthy for us. But he does think that belief in God is unhealthy for us. Here he thinks it both possible and desirable to refrain from believing more than that the cause or causes of order in nature bear some resemblance to the human mind—a vague belief with no practical consequences to speak of, a belief undemanding regarding conduct and empty of hope or real interest.

Of course Hume believes that there are material objects. He tells us, "I am naturally led to regard the world, as something real and durable, and as preserving its existence, even when it is no longer present to my perception" (THN 197). But he offers a famous account of belief in the existence of objects in which the actual existence of objects has no role to play in that belief's production. If explanation of belief in the existence of Bs is given only in terms of there being As, and there being As neither is nor is taken by the explanation to be evidence for the existence of Bs, then acceptance of this explanation does not commit one to there being Bs. Hume's explanation of our belief that there are bodies in no way appeals to their actually being bodies, and it denies that the existence of anything that the explanation appeals to provides any evidence for the existence of bodies. So that explanation does not commit him to there being bodies.

Briefly, he says that when we have a sequence of perceptions that greatly resemble one another, we have a propensity to see them as perceptions of an enduring object, and when we have a sequence of perceptions that follow the same recognized pattern as past perceptions, we have a propensity to see them as perceptions of a series of events involving enduring objects.

In both cases objects are thought to exist distinct from and independent of our perceptual experiences. He views that not as a conscious inference, but as the unfolding of tendencies that constitute our natures—utterly unfounded in evidence but inevitable in fact. In Hume's view, the propensities or tendencies are universal, operating in everyone to produce belief in mind-independent material objects and elicited in everyone by sequences of perceptions of the sorts noted.[15] In Hume's view these beliefs are not justified by evidence or derivable from known foundational propositions. But neither are we blameworthy for having them.

Evidentialism. Again, it will be helpful to consider Hume's views in comparison and contrast to a view that, in its purer forms, he rejected. Evidentialism, in those purer forms, is an account of the conditions a person must meet in order to have a belief that he has reason to think true—a belief justified by evidence. Often evidentialism combines with foundationalism and holds that rational belief is limited to propositions whose denials are recognized as impossible, or propositions evidently true given sensory or introspective observation, or propositions recognizably entailed (or at least rendered probable) by beliefs of the first two sorts. In its impure form, it concerns conditions under which a person may be justified (at least in the weak sense of not irrational) in holding a belief. Hume is not a pure evidentialist, but he does seem to be an impure one.

Evidentialism, as I shall understand it here, is a doctrine regarding the condition that a person S must meet regarding a belief that P so that S's belief that P is reasonable. As opposed to epistemological nihilism, it holds that there *is* some such condition—that it is false that just any belief held by anyone whatever is reasonable simply because they hold it. Further, it offers an account of what that condition is.

As thus far defined, evidentialism could have many versions. The doctrine that a person is reasonable in having a belief if and only if the proposition believed is one that she has seen expressed by an English sentence written in blue ink on old parchment is a version of evidentialism. But as the term itself suggests, the conditions for reasonability in believing are supposed to have something to do with there being evidence for the proposition that is believed, and with the believer having that evidence and believing in the light that the evidence casts.[16]

---

[15]For details, see Yandell, *Hume's "Inexplicable Mystery,"* chap. 2.
[16]Evidentialism, then, is not a version of pragmatism. If you show me your fist, you give me

Relevant versions of evidentialism, then, will hold to some such doctrine as this:

E: Person S is reasonable in believing proposition P only if S has some truth-preferring evidence favoring P.

This rather generic version of (pure) evidentialism does not tell us what evidence is, specify what shall count as evidence, explain whether we should in the end think of belief as a relationship between a person and a proposition, or say what should be thought about cases in which there is evidence voting for, but also evidence voting against, P's truth. It will be useful to have somewhat of a refinement on E, though we will not need to fine-tune E so as to deal with all of these issues.

If S has stronger truth-preferring evidence for P than against, then let us say that S's evidence *prefers P.* Truth-preferring evidence against P might be truth-preferring evidence for not-P or truth-preferring evidence for Q where Q's truth was evidence against P's truth. Consider, then, these versions of evidentialism:

E1:   If S's evidence prefers P, then S is reasonable in believing that P.

E2:   If S belongs to a kind K whose members cannot help but believe that P if they are in circumstance C, and S is in C, then S is reasonable in believing that P if S's evidence does not prefer not-P.

And a slightly more complex version:

E3:   If S belongs to a kind K whose members tend to believe that P if they are in circumstance C, and S is in C, and S's evidence does not prefer not-P, then S is reasonable in believing that P unless belief that P subverts the operation of the propensities by which belief that P arises in members of K who are in C.

While E1 is a version of pure evidentialism, E2 and E3 are impure versions. Each of these claims is relevant to understanding Hume's overall epistemological stance. Note that as one shifts from E1 to E2 and E3, the focus changes from evidence regarding the truth of a proposition in E1 through avoidance of error while behaving typically for one's kind in E2 to avoiding damage to one's kind-defining properties in E3. To anticipate, Hume does

---

truth-preferring evidence that you have a fist. If you explain what your fist will do to me if I do not believe that I am a turtle, you may give me reasons for preferring to believe that I am a turtle rather than continuing to embrace my current nonturtle self-conception, but you do not give me any evidence that this change in the makeup of my beliefs is in the interests of truth. Evidentialism trades only in evidence—only what is belief-preferring by way of being truth-preferring.

not accept E1—pure evidentialism. He accepts the impure evidentialism of E3 where being justified in having a belief is a matter of accepting the belief because it is one's nature to do so in the circumstances that one is in. E2 is a version of impure evidentialism that worries about believing against evidence but does not worry about subverting one's nature. It is E3 that captures the crucial element in Hume's impure evidentialism. We need next to look at Hume's account of belief.

Belief. Hume has, of course, much to say about belief—for example:

[A]n opinion or belief is nothing but an idea, that is different from a fiction, not in the nature, or the order of its parts, but in the manner of its being conceived . . . this feeling I would endeavor to explain by calling it a superior force, or vivacity, or solidity, or firmness, or steadiness. (THN 628-29)

and

[A]s belief does nothing but vary the manner, in which we conceive any object, it can only bestow on our ideas an additional force and vivacity. An opinion or belief may be most accurately defined as a lively idea related to or associated with a present impression. (THN 96)[17]

He also writes:

Whatever ideas are adequate representations of objects, the relations, contradictions and agreements of the ideas are applicable to the objects; and this we may in general observe to be the foundation of all human knowledge. (THN 29)

Ideas, this last passage says, are representations of objects; they can be accurate representations, their relations can be applicable to the relations that hold among objects. This view is central to Hume's account of belief, where he plainly treats ideas as representations. Influenced by his view that minds are only collections of perceptions, he treats beliefs as perceptions of a particular sort. Strictly, if perceptions are qualia, this can only be a matter of such things as sharpness of color or intensity of pain. But he also speaks of the "manner . . . of being conceived," which suggests an attitude taken by the mind toward an idea. But continuing these reflections would lead us into the problems related to Hume's notion of the mind.

---

[17]Cf. "[B]elief consists not in the nature and order of our ideas, but in the manner of their conception, and in their feeling to the mind . . . it is something felt by the mind, which distinguishes the ideas of the judgment from the fictions of the imagination. It gives them more force and influence; makes them appear of greater importance, infixes them in the mind; and renders them the governing principles of all our actions" (THN 629).

To believe, according to Hume, that there is a chair is to have a picture of a chair that is sufficiently "forceful and vivacious." It is to have an idea in a particular manner that he describes as having "solidity, firmness, and being steady." To believe in God would be to have the idea of God in a forceful and vivacious manner, were Hume's account of belief true. Natural beliefs—beliefs produced by propensities that constitute human nature—will then be either forceful and vivacious ideas or ideas forcefully and steadily held. (This line is obviously different from, and incompatible with, the nonintentionalist line discussed in the first section.)

Skepticism. Hume is a complex sort of skeptic. Our purposes here require that we say what kind that is. Let a first-order proposition be a proposition that is not about another proposition. Let a commonsense proposition be one that ascribes an observable property to an observable public object, ascribes an enduring existence to oneself or claims that some event is causally related to another event. Alternatively, let a commonsense proposition be one that a human person will inevitably come to accept, given that she has perceptions of a sort that every human person has. (On Hume's view, the types of propositions captured by one of these descriptions will be the same as those captured by the other.) Distinguish, then, between these varieties of skepticism:

Philosophical skepticism (PS): For any first-order proposition P and person S, S has no better reason to accept P than to accept not-P.

Restricted philosophical skepticism (RS): For any proposition P and person S, S has no better reason to accept P than to accept not-P, unless (1) P is recognizably true by definition or (2) P can be confirmed by S's immediate perceptual experience.

Hume is a restricted philosophical skeptic, and hence not a pure philosophical skeptic.

Consider also this version:

Commonsense skepticism (CS): For any commonsense proposition P and person S, S has no better reason to accept P than to accept not-P.

Hume is a commonsense skeptic. He holds that we lack good reasons for believing commonsense propositions. But in the case of commonsense propositions, he also holds that we believe them anyway because we cannot do otherwise.

Fideism. As a restricted philosophical skeptic, Hume accepts

H: No person has better reason to accept any theistic belief than to believe its contradictory.[18]

But that fact about religious belief does not, on Humean terms, condemn
it. One could accept H and be a fideist believer in God—a theist who held
that theistic belief is not, and cannot be, based on evidence of any sort (either because there isn't any such evidence or because any belief based on
evidence would be incompatible with the element of trust that is an essential
part of theistic faith[19]). A theist who held one of the versions of fideism just
described presumably would hold to some version of

Religious fideism (RF): There is a source K of belief other than reason, theistic belief that is held in a grade-A manner will derive from K, and *deriving from K* is not evidence or reason or ground for *being thought true.*

This, after all, is parallel to what Hume thinks about commonsense beliefs—
he is, if you like, a fideist concerning them.

"Reason" as it appears in PS and CS is used in the "truth-preferring support" sense. Specific values for K in RF are such terms as "a capacity to receive divine revelation, identified as such in its reception" and "a religious

---

[18]By itself, of course H does not have much bite. Many devout religious believers, some sadly
but others with delight, have asserted H as not incompatible with, or even as something at
least very like part of, their religious creed. One who holds any of a variety of epistemological
perspectives regarding religious belief can embrace both some set of religious beliefs and H,
and do so with equanimity. Consider any of a number of positions that claim that at least
some propositions (some among them expressing religious beliefs) are properly accepted
without their recipient having better reason than not to do so. These positions will be variations on the general theme expressed by RT: There is a source K of belief other than reason;
some but not all religious beliefs derive from K; deriving from K is not evidence or reason or
ground for being thought true; but whatever religious beliefs derive from K are true. "Reason"
in RT means something like "the capacity to see necessary truths, and to assess the evidential
status of beliefs." It cannot include "seeing inferential connections" or "understanding a proposition" since the capacities referred to by these expressions need to be included in the concepts of those capacities whose names replace K in RT. So we have "reason" used in RT to
refer to a very limited but important set of capacities in a rather typical fashion in discussions
intended to separate religious belief from products of reason; capacities required for the very
having of a belief and for seeing what is implied (both theoretically and practically) by that
belief are set apart from the capacities dubbed "rational" in order that reason may apparently
be irrelevant to matters religious. There is also "reason" in the sense of "a truth-preferring
support for belief," and supporters of some specific doctrine falling under RT may or may not
want to separate religious belief from "a reason or reasons" in this sense.

[19]This latter suggestion—that belief based on evidence would be incompatible with the element
of trust that is an essential part of theistic faith—seems to me plainly false. Why can't a person
both have evidence that God exists and also trust that God will act toward her in a loving
and merciful manner? A different suggestion is that faith is somehow improper, immature or
second-rate if it is based on evidence—that really proper or mature or first-rate faith has no
basis in evidence whatever. This idea too seems to me dubious.

sentiment that responds believingly to religious propositions," where the manner of reception provides no evidence for what is received. No one who accepts either version of RF that is produced by adding reference to any such capacity or sentiment will be bothered even if H is true. Thus, whether there is bite to H or not depends on what the epistemic proprieties are regarding religious belief; of course philosophers differ on this matter.

Hume is a skeptic regarding statements not true by definition or true concerning the contents of one's immediate momentary consciousness. But in contrast to most skeptics, he does not think it wrong of one to believe beyond one's evidence. Indeed, he thinks such belief inevitable given human nature and blameless so long as it does not include theistic religious belief. (At least, theistic belief is the exception on which Hume focuses.)

Evidentialism again. It will be useful to return again to evidentialism, characterized a bit differently from before. One evidentialist perspective regarding epistemic proprieties goes somewhat as follows. Let a proposition that is *epistemically privileged* with respect to person S be any proposition P such that S sees that not-P is contradictory or S is directly aware of a sensory or introspective state whose obtaining (as S recognizes) renders P true. Then one variety of (pure) evidentialism contends that

E4:   For any person S and proposition P, S properly believes that P if and only if P is privileged relative to S or there is some proposition Q that is privileged relative to S such that S recognizes that Q evidentially supports P and no proposition that is privileged relative to S evidentially supports not-P as well as Q supports P.

If an evidentialist (of the pure variety) also has some notion of epistemic rights and wrongs, presumably she also embraces something like

E*:   For any person S and proposition P, it is wrong of S to believe that P is true if S's doing so is not proper by the standards enunciated in E4.

One who accepts E4 and E*, or something much like them, presumably will reject varieties of religious fideism and think that beliefs that are derived from religious sentiment or alleged special revelation are neither privileged nor endowed with privileged support; both are no more properly believed than their denials and are not properly believed. While Hume holds a moral sense theory, he embraces no corresponding theory regarding religious belief. Further, he holds that there is no evidence or reason or ground for any religious belief. Thus, if he embraced E* and was consistent, he would hold

U: For any person S and proposition P, if P expresses a theistic religious belief and S believes that P, then S's belief that P is improper.
All theistic belief, on this account, is improper. But Hume does not embrace E* or E1 or E4 or any other version of pure evidentialism. Nonetheless,
he embraces U for reasons that are not of a pure evidentialist sort. It turns
out, then, that Hume's own problem with theistic belief[20] does not have to
do with its (alleged) being unfavored by the evidence. Other beliefs that he
takes to be unfavored by evidence do not receive his disapproval. What,
then, does he think is wrong with theistic belief?

WHAT, FOR HUME, IS WRONG WITH THEISTIC BELIEF?

Hume's replacement for E*. While Hume holds U, the claim that all theistic belief is improper, he rejects E*—the claim that what makes it improper
is lack of favorable evidence. This leaves us asking why he holds U; one can
hold E* and H and, without inconsistency, decline U. In his *Natural History
of Religion* Hume holds something along the lines of

HN: Human nature is comprised by a set of propensities that, stimulated
       by experiences that everyone has, yields beliefs that commonsense
       propositions are true.

and

EU: For any person S and proposition P, if S's belief that P is produced
       by S's human-nature-constitutive propensities, then it is false that S
       is unreasonable in believing that P.

Rather than accepting exactly E*, then, Hume holds something like

ER: For any person S and proposition P, it is reasonable of S to believe
       that P is true if S's doing so is proper by the standards enunciated
       in EU.

And in holding ER he is rejecting the inference from *It is not reasonable
of S to believe that P* to *It is unreasonable of S to believe that P*. Position ER
states sufficient conditions for reasonable belief, not necessary conditions.

As I understand the position of the *Natural History* relevant to these matters, Hume's view is that

NB1: No religious beliefs are produced by propensities that are constitutive of human nature.

NB2: Some religious beliefs are produced by propensities that are widely

---

[20]Hume's view will also hold for nontheistic religious beliefs; he just does not deal with such
beliefs.

had and widely activated, and this does not render them either reasonably held or not unreasonably held.

Of beliefs produced by propensities not constitutive of human nature but widely had and widely activated, the best Hume says is that, if (1) they are vague enough so as to have no practical consequences (e.g., no influence on morality) and (2) they are not integrated into a set of beliefs caused by propensities that are constitutive of human nature from which set one then infers further propositions, then one's having them does less harm than otherwise. This very modest epistemic status is the best that theistic belief can hope for within the confines of a Humean epistemology, and no beliefs likely to be of much interest to actual believers will be found among them.

Hume, then, isn't an evidentialist—at least of any standard sort—but what he says about the propriety of holding theistic beliefs rejects them as strongly as does an evidentialist who thinks (as does Hume) that there isn't any truth-preferring evidence or reason on behalf of theistic beliefs.[21] The belief that God created the world of dependent things is ruled out, since it blends with natural beliefs (beliefs produced by human-nature-constituting propensities to yield, for example, the view that our natural environment was made by God and should not be desecrated, or the view that human beings are created in God's image and deserve respect).

Hume on Human Nature. Hume holds that human nature is fragile. His view can be put as follows: The propensities that constitute it are in competition with various emotions and various other propensities (including propensities that produce religious belief) and are in constant danger of being overcome by their competitors in the battle for being the actual belief-producers for each person. To the degree that propensities, emotions or other factors other than human-nature-constituting propensities do produce beliefs in us, our natural belief-producing mechanism fails to operate well. This endangers us, not simply because we may thereby end up with inconsistent or incoherent views, but mainly because our very unity as human beings is threatened. In spite of the fact (noted earlier) that our minds, for Hume, creatively copy impressions rather than merely being composed of perceptions and—as we have more recently remarked—have propensities to produce beliefs, Hume's fundamental notion of the mind views it as a

---

[21]Relevant here are also Hume's comments on the problem of evil and on the alleged inherent bad effects of theistic belief on morality. But these are topics for another occasion.

loosely connected bundle of mental simples (impressions and ideas) each existing on its own and only contingently related to others. Further, the effectiveness of the constitutive propensities or tendencies of the mind to work together to yield the beliefs that are their natural products he views, as we noted, as a precarious and fragile matter.

A widely held theistic view tells us that human beings are created with a tendency to see divine power in natural order, power and beauty, and to find in moral duty a source of obligation beyond themselves to whom they owe obedience and respect. Hume's criterion for a propensity or tendency being constitutive of human nature is that it is effective in everyone and produces similar beliefs in all. If one allows also that a propensity can constitute human nature if it is present in all, but (1) can be inhibited by cultural factors and individual resistance, so that it does not always yield belief, and (2) together with resisting factors may produce different beliefs than those that it would if not resisted, then one can defend the wider theistic account of human nature. But this matter does not cut to the core of the problem with Hume's view here.

The account of human nature that is required by Hume's views concerning the destructiveness of religious belief to human nature is plainly not composed of propositions that themselves, consistently with Hume's own views about what we can have evidence for, can enjoy evidential support. Nor is the account, even if one accepts it, such as to justify the claim that accepting *it* is somehow inevitable for a human being who has the nature the account ascribes to her. So accepting Hume's views regarding theistic belief is, on Hume's own terms, of course to violate the canons of pure evidentialism, which he rejects anyway. What will matter to a Humean is that acceptance of Hume's views concerning theistic belief, and the account of human nature and human propensities on which it rests, will be—on Hume's own view and for Hume's own reasons—as destructive of human nature, construed along Hume's own theory, as he alleges that acceptance of theistic belief itself is. Accepting Hume's account of human nature is not itself produced by any of the propensities that constitute our nature.[22] It is perhaps the ultimate irony that if one takes Hume's own medicine for the alleged illness of theistic belief, one produces in oneself the very illness one intended to avoid.

---

[22]If there is an exception, it is the propensity to seek a system of thought that orders our particular views. But of course if one appeals to that, theism itself is a system of thought.

Conclusion

The idea, then, that Hume showed, implicitly at least, that religious experience cannot be evidence for religious belief is simply radically mistaken. Neither his account of what constitutes experience, nor his restrictions on what certain sorts of propositions relative to certain sorts experiential evidence can support, is defensible. His popular idea that having theistic religious belief is inherently psychologically self-destructive, no matter what it involves in detail, equally shows that the theory on which he bases that idea to be self-destructive in the same manner. Hume's critique of theistic belief, in those portions of it discussed here, is vastly more famous than it is intellectually powerful. The reception of his critique in the circles of the learned sadly illustrates the point that Hume makes in his introduction to the *Treatise:*

> Amidst all this bustle 'tis not reason which carries the prize, but eloquence. . . . The victory is not gained by the men of arms who manage the pike and the sword; but by the trumpeters, drummers, and musicians of the army. (THN xviii)

12

THE ARGUMENT FROM
REASON AND HUME'S LEGACY

Victor Reppert

☞

C. S. Lewis left an enormous legacy, including literary scholarship, children's stories, science fiction novels, other fictional writings, autobiography, essays on various Christian subjects and, of course, Christian apologetics. Lewis offered rational arguments in support of his theistic beliefs, and it is evident from his autobiographical *Surprised by Joy* that such arguments played a crucial role in his conversions first to theism and then to Christianity. One of his most important arguments in his conversion is one that I have been calling the "argument from reason." (Perhaps it would be more accurate to call it the "argument from rational inference," but since I have used the former name several times in print, it's probably too late now to change it.)[1] This argument purports to show that, if naturalistic atheism is true, then no one would know that atheism is true, or know anything else, at least not by a process of rational inference.

Although Lewis is the argument's best-known proponent, he cannot be regarded as the argument's originator.[2] It seems to appear in Kant, though not as a theistic argument.[3] Arthur Balfour, the former British prime minister, used the argument in his books *The Foundations of Belief* and *Theism and*

---

[1]My most complete discussion of this argument is found in Victor Reppert, *C. S. Lewis's Dangerous Idea* (Downers Grove, Ill.: InterVarsity Press, 2003).

[2]The most developed statement of the argument is found in C. S. Lewis, *Miracles: A Preliminary Study* (New York: Macmillan, 1978), pp. 12-24.

[3]For a discussion of the Kantian foundations of this argument, see H. Allison, "Kant's Refutation of Materialism," *The Monist* 79 (April 1989): 190-209.

Humanism, the latter of which Lewis is known to have admired.[4] The argument from reason is the argument that Anscombe criticized, causing Lewis to revise it for the second edition of *Miracles.*[5] More recently the argument has been used against physical determinism by J. R. Lucas,[6] James Jordan[7] and William Hasker,[8] and has been used as an argument for theism by Richard Purtill[9] and J. P. Moreland.[10] A similar argument has been used to argue for theism as opposed to naturalism by Alvin Plantinga.[11]

Rational inference occurs when a person concludes that a given claim is true in virtue of believing that other claims are true, and seeing the logical relationship between the believed premises and the inferred conclusion. Consider the familiar syllogism:

1. All men are mortal.

2. Socrates is a man.

3. Therefore, Socrates is mortal.

If one really draws this rational inference, then one must, it seems, have the belief that each of the premises is true, and then reach the conclusion because one believes (a) that the premises are true and (b) that the conclusion follows logically from the premises. The activity of drawing rational inference is a key element in mathematics and all the natural sciences.

However, the existence of rational inference as a human activity has a number of implications. In particular:

a. States of mind have a relation to the world we call "intentionality," or "aboutness."

b. Thoughts and beliefs can be either true or false.

c. Human beings can be in the condition of accepting, rejecting or sus-

---

[4]Arthur Balfour, *The Foundations of Belief: Notes Introductory to the Study of Theology,* 8th ed. rev. with new introduction and summary (New York: Longmans, 1918), pp. 279-85.

[5]G. E. M. Anscombe, *Metaphysics and the Philosophy of Mind,* vol. 2 of *The Collected Papers of G. E. M. Anscombe* (Minneapolis: University of Minnesota Press, 1981), pp. 224-31.

[6]J. R. Lucas, *The Freedom of the Will* (Oxford: Oxford University Press, 1970).

[7]James Jordan, "Determinism's Dilemma," *Review of Metaphysics* 23 (1969-70): 48-66.

[8]William Hasker, "The Transcendental Refutation of Determinism," *Southern Journal of Philosophy* 11 (1973): 175-83; *Metaphysics* (Downers Grove, Ill.: InterVarsity Press, 1983); and "Why the Physical Isn't Closed," chap. 3 of *The Emergent Self* (Ithaca, N.Y.: Cornell University Press, 1999), pp. 58-80.

[9]Richard Purtill, *Reason to Believe* (Grand Rapids: Eerdmans, 1974), pp. 44-46.

[10]J. P. Moreland, *Scaling the Secular City* (Grand Rapids: Baker, 1987), pp. 77-105.

[11]Alvin Plantinga, *Warrant and Proper Function* (New York: Oxford University Press, 1993), pp. 216-37. Plantinga acknowledges the similarity between his argument and Lewis's in the book's final footnote.

pending belief about propositions.

d. Logical laws exist.

e. Human beings are capable of apprehending logical laws.

f. The state of accepting the truth of a proposition plays a crucial causal role in the production of other beliefs, and propositional content is relevant to the playing of this causal role.

g. The apprehension of logical laws plays a causal role in the acceptance of the conclusion of the argument as true.

h. The individual who entertains thoughts of the premises is the same one who then draws the conclusion.

i. Our processes of reasoning provide us with a systematically reliable way to understand the world around us.

Only in a universe in which all nine of these conditions obtain can there be the kind of rational inference required for the possibility of mathematics, natural science and philosophical argumentation. But could these elements exist in just any universe whatsoever? Clearly not. A universe containing only a turnip with a little whipped cream on top would not be a universe in which rational inference would be possible. There is no contradiction in suggesting that the universe is nothing but a turnip with whipped cream on top, but to suggest that the turnip, or the whipped cream, could discover this would seem clearly not to be a coherent suggestion.

THE PROBLEM WITH NATURALISTIC WORLDVIEWS

The argument from reason, first and foremost, is an argument for the claim that theism is rationally preferable to philosophical naturalism. A worldview qualifies as naturalistic just in case reason or mind is not a fundamental feature of what is real, but rather is a byproduct of a blind evolutionary process. Naturalists are committed, in my view, to three fundamental doctrines:

- *The basic elements of the universe function blindly, without purpose.* Man is the product, says Bertrand Russell, of forces that had no prevision of the ends they were achieving.[12] Daniel Dennett insists that the upshot of modern science is the conclusion that everything can be explained in terms of cranes (bottom-up explanations) and that skyhooks (top-down, mind-first explanations) must be eschewed.[13]

---

[12]Bertrand Russell, "A Free Man's Worship," in *Mysticism and Logic, and Other Essays* (reprint, London: George Allen & Unwin: 1949), pp. 47-48.

[13]Daniel C. Dennett, *Darwin's Dangerous Idea* (New York: Simon & Schuster, 1995).

827077123

63680771

- *The natural world is a closed system.* There is nothing transcendent to the natural world, capable of interacting with that natural world. Furthermore, the natural world exists independently, and was not created by anything other than itself.

- *Whatever is not definable in the sort of scientific terms used in the science of the fundamental elements of the natural world (usually physics) supervenes on the state of that basic reality.* Given the state of the basic elements, there is only one way the nonbasic elements can possibly be.

However, is the universe I just described a universe that could house rational inference? Lewis thought otherwise. He distinguishes cause and effect relationships from ground and consequent relationships.

> Unless our conclusion is the logical consequence from a ground, it will be worthless and could only be true by a fluke. Unless it is the effect of a cause, it cannot occur at all. It looks, therefore, as if, for any train of thought to have any value, these two systems of connection must apply to the same series of mental acts.[14]

Since these two systems of connections are "wholly distinct," Lewis concludes,

> Even if grounds do exist, what exactly do they have to do with the actual occurrence of belief as a psychological event? If it is an event, it must be caused. It must in fact be one link in a causal chain going back to the beginning and forward to the end of time. How could such a trifle as a lack of logical grounds prevent the belief's occurrence and how could the existence of grounds promote it?[15]

Lewis concludes that the only face-saving solution to this problem is to say that one thought can cause another not by being a ground for it, but by *being seen to be* a ground for it. But how (if all causes are blind and mechanistic) can the fact that A is grounds for B have anything to do with the fact that thought of B follows thought of A? Richard Dawkins maintains that everything in nature, including human beings, is the product of the blind operations of random variation and natural selection.[16] But the argument from reason maintains that if the watchmaker (the evolutionary process) was

---

[14]Lewis, *Miracles,* p. 16.
[15]Ibid., pp. 16-17.
[16]Richard Dawkins, *The Blind Watchmaker: Why the Evidence of Evolution Reveals a Universe Without Design* (reprint, New York: W. W. Norton, 1996).

really, truly and completely blind, then Dawkins would never discover that this is so, or discover that anything else is so.

Recall the simple argument concerning the mortality of Socrates above. If rational inference is to be possible, it must be the case that one can be caused to believe that (3) is true in virtue of entertaining and accepting (1), entertaining and accepting (2), and having those two states cause the thinker to reach a state of accepting (3). Hence the existence of mental causation seems necessary for the possibility of rational inference. But there seems to be more involved even than the mere existence of mental causation. One mental event must cause another mental event *in virtue of* the propositional content of those events. If the thought "All men are mortal" is brain state A, and "Socrates is a man" is brain state B, and "Socrates is mortal" is brain state C, and brain states A and B cause brain state C, it might still be the case that the propositional content of these brain states is irrelevant to the way in which they succeed one another in the brain.

Consider the following example. Suppose the baseball used in Luis Gonzalez's series-winning hit in the 2001 World Series is thrown and breaks a window. We might say that a Luis Gonzalez baseball was used to shatter the window, but it would not follow from this at all that the window broke in virtue of its having been hit by Gonzo. What determined whether or not the window shattered upon impact is a function of the velocity of the baseball and the strength of the glass, and its use in the series-winning hit would be simply irrelevant to the present causal transaction.

Similarly, in the case of rational inference, it is not enough for one thought to cause another thought. In order for there to be rational inference, the propositional content of the initial thought must play a crucial role in the production of the inferred thought.

The argument can be put as follows:

4. Some thoughts cause other thoughts in virtue of their propositional content.
5. If some thoughts cause other thoughts in virtue of propositional content, then reason is a fundamental feature of the universe.
6. If reason is a fundamental feature of the universe, then naturalism is false.
7. Therefore, naturalism is false.

Objections to Lewis's Argument from Reason

A number of objections have been put forward against this line of argument.

Some of those criticisms deny that the nine presuppositions of reason, (a)-(i) above, are necessary for the possibility of rational inference. Elizabeth Anscombe objected to Lewis's argument on the grounds that reasons-explanations are not causal explanations. As she argues:

> It appears to me that if a man has reasons, and they are good reasons, and they are genuinely his reasons, for thinking something—then his thought is rational, whatever causal statements can be made about him.[17]

Similarly, Keith Parsons argues

> My own (internalist) view is that if I can adduce reasons sufficient for the conclusion Q, then my belief that Q is rational. The causal history of mental states of being aware of Q and the justifying grounds strike me as quite irrelevant. Whether those mental states are caused by other mental states, or caused by physical states, or just pop into existence uncaused, the grounds still justify the claim.[18]

The difficulty for this response is that when we are dealing with beliefs that are supposed to have been not merely rational, but rationally *inferred,* then whether the belief was indeed brought about by a rational inference or in some other way has to be highly significant. Consider the case of Charles Darwin being persuaded to accept natural selection, in part, because of evidence provided by his observations of the Galapagos finches. If Darwin's mental states just popped into existence uncaused, or if indeed those thoughts were not causally produced by the mental states having to do with his reasons for believing in natural selection, then we cannot say that he inferred his beliefs from the evidence. No doubt some beliefs can be justified without having been rationally inferred from other beliefs, but inferred beliefs are central to the scientific, mathematical and philosophical enterprises.

    If you were to meet a person, call him Steve, who can argue with great cogency for every position he holds, you might on that account consider him a very rational person. But suppose it were to turn out that, on all disputed questions, Steve rolls dice to fix his beliefs permanently and uses his reasoning skills only to generate the best available arguments for those randomly selected beliefs. I think that such a discovery would prompt you to withdraw from him the honorific title "rational." While Steve's beliefs are undoubtedly *rationalized,* they are hardly rational. Clearly the question of

---

[17]Anscombe, *Metaphysics and the Philosophy of Mind,* p. 229.
[18]Keith Parsons, "Further Reflections on the Argument from Reason," *Philo* 3 (2000): 101.

whether or not a person is rational cannot be answered in a manner that leaves out entirely any account of how those beliefs are produced and sustained.

Without mental causation in virtue of propositional content, no one could have discovered that the Pythagorean theorem is true, no one could have come to believe (or disbelieve) the theory of evolution based on the evidence, and no one could come to disbelieve in the existence of God because of the argument from evil. It is not enough that such beliefs are produced by reliable belief-producing mechanisms, nor is it enough that someone is able to give the reason sincerely as an explanation for why, say, he believes in evolution. And if the reason causes the belief, it has to be in virtue of the propositional content of the belief in order for it to be genuinely inferred. As Jerry Fodor put it, "If it isn't literally true that my wanting is causally responsible for my reaching, and my itching is causally responsible for my scratching, and my believing is causally responsible for my saying . . . if none of that is literally true, then practically everything I believe about anything is false and it's the end of the world."[19] It is certainly the end of the scientific enterprise as we know it. And that is a devastating conclusion for the philosophical naturalist.

Other replies to the argument from reason maintain that human reasoning is what common sense says that it is, but at the same time hold that reason thus understood can be housed within a naturalistic universe. Naturalists often advert to the existence of computers to resolve this difficulty and to demonstrate the compatibility of mechanism and purpose. And it is undeniable that computers are physical systems operating under physical laws. But in the case of computers, the compatibility is the result of mental states in the background that deliberately create this compatibility. Thus, the chess computer Deep Blue defeated the world champion Garry Kasparov in their 1997 chess match. But Deep Blue's ability to defeat Kasparov was not the exclusive result of physical causation, unless the people on the programming team (such as Grandmaster Joel Benjamin) are entirely the result of physical causation. And that, precisely, is the point at issue between naturalists on the one hand and advocates of the argument from reason on the other. As William Hasker points out,

Computers function as they do because they have been constructed by human

---

[19]Jerry A. Fodor, *A Theory of Content and Other Essays* (Cambridge, Mass.: MIT Press/Bradford Book, 1990), p. 156.

beings endowed with rational insight. A computer, in other words, is merely an extension of the rationality of its designers and users; it is no more an independent source of rational thought than a television set is an independent source of news and entertainment.[20]

The argument from reason says that reason cannot emerge from a closed, mechanistic system. The computer is, narrowly speaking, a mechanistic system, and it does follow rational rules. But it is not a *closed* system, and the framework of meaning according to which it operates is provided by its programmers and users. To presume that these programmers and users are themselves physical systems and part of a closed physical universe would be to beg the question against the argument from reason, which attempts to show the opposite.

It isn't just that humans made the computer, they also provide the framework of meaning in which the activity of the computer can be regarded as "reasoning." The intentionality found in the computer is derived intentionality, not orignal intentionality.

Consider the following. Imagine a possible world just like ours, except that in that world chess is never invented. Along with my fellow card-carrying members of the Guild of Chess-Playing Philosophers, I call this world *I* for Impoverished. In *I*, a pair of computers, connected to one another, miraculously appears in the Gobi desert and goes through all the physical states which in our world occurred in a chess game between Fritz and Shredder in the World Computer Championship. The question is, did these computers play chess? Since chess was never invented in *I*, since no terms in the world refer to *rook, bishop, exchange sac, en passant* or *Dragon variation,* I suggest that these computers did not play a chess game.

Another response that is frequently given to the argument from reason is the claim that evolution would select for rationality as opposed to irrationality. Therefore, we should not be surprised if our reasoning capabilities are good at getting us the truth. If they were not very good, our ancestors would have died without passing on their genes, and we wouldn't be here. However, Hasker reminds us of what the real commitments of naturalism are:

> Certain complex assemblages of organic chemicals develop a kind of dynamic stability in their interactions with the environment, together with a capacity for self-replications, which leads us to say that they are alive. A variety of random

---

[20]William Hasker, *Metaphysics* (Downers Grove, Ill.: InterVarsity Press, 1983), p. 49.

physical forces leads to variations in the self-replicating assemblages, and some of the assemblages are more successful than others in maintaining and reproducing themselves. Over time, some of these assemblages become more complex than the earliest forms by several orders of magnitude, and their behaviors and interactions with the surrounding environment also become more complex. Nevertheless, the entire process is governed by, and explicable in terms of, the ordinary laws of physics and chemistry. Put differently, it is never necessary to go outside of the physical configurations and physical laws in order to predict the future behavior of these assemblages; this is the "closure of the physical."[21]

The problem is this: If the physical realm is causally closed, then it looks on the face of things as if it will go on its merry way regardless of what mental states exist, and if this is the case, then mental states simply do not matter with respect to what events are caused in the physical world.

The Darwinian argument, if it works at all, would show how, if there were mental states, and if those mental states could be causally effective in virtue of their content, then sound strategies would prevail over unsound strategies. However, this response can be effective only if intentionality, truth, mental causation in virtue of content, and the logical efficacy of logical laws are all possible in a physicalist world. And that is what the argument challenges.

But let us assume that, contrary to my previous argument, there can be mental causation in virtue of content in a naturalistic world. Even granting this assumption, it seems to me that, although some confluence between our epistemic interests and our Darwinian interests can be thought to obtain (i.e., false beliefs about man-eating tigers are likely to get one eaten before one passes on one's genes), nonetheless our epistemic and Darwinian interests are in other respects at cross-purposes with one another. The Darwinian argument assumes that a generally applicable faculty for knowing the truth about the world would be of survival value and therefore be selected for by natural selection, even though its applicability goes far beyond what might be useful for survival in the particular environment.

But I think that such a claim is by no means obviously correct. Clearly some creatures are able to survive and procreate without any beliefs whatsoever. What is required for survival is *effective response to* the environment, not *accurate knowledge of* that environment. So perhaps evolution could se-

---

[21]William Hasker, *The Emergent Self* (Ithaca, N.Y.: Cornell University Press, 1999), p. 77.

lect for something that wasn't so accurate in depicting the environment but provided a more efficient way of getting the biologically correct response to the environment. If the chief enemy of a creature is a foot-long snake, perhaps some inner programming to attack (or run away from) everything a foot long would be more effective from the point of view of survival than the complicated ability to distinguish reptiles from mammals or amphibians. The more complex our knowledge abilities are, the larger a brain will be required to house these faculties. As a result, creatures with large brains will have a longer period of immaturity and vulnerability, and more things can go wrong before their genes can be passed along. It is far from clear that a general ability to learn what is true will be helpful from an evolutionary standpoint. Rather, there are good prima facie reasons to accept Alvin Plantinga's assessment that if naturalism is true, then the probability that our faculties will be reliable is low at worst and inscrutable at best.[22] This contrasts unfavorably with the situation given theism. If we are the creation of a good God interested in our epistemic well-being, then we should expect to have epistemic faculties that are reliable.[23]

Two objections against this argument seem to me to be the most Humean in nature, and so I will devote more attention to them than to the others I have mentioned. Suppose we successfully show that rational inference really is profoundly mysterious from a naturalistic point of view. Does this constitute a reason to enact a change in worldviews and accept theism as opposed to naturalism? Two Humean lines of objection—the inadequacy objection and Hume's stopper—attempt to show that, even if the phenomenon of rational inference is deeply mysterious from a naturalistic point of view, it is not rational to remedy that mysteriousness by accepting theism instead of naturalism.

The inadequacy objection, to use Theodore Drange's term,[24] maintains that whatever difficulties there may be in accounting for the phenomena of rational inference in naturalistic terms, appealing to the existence of God or any other supernatural beings provides only a pseudo-explanation for these phenomena. In Hume's *Dialogues Concerning Natural Religion* Philo responds to Cleanthes' design argument as follows:

---

[22]Plantinga, *Warrant and Proper Function*, pp. 216-37.
[23]The above line of argument was suggested to me by Dennis Monokroussos.
[24]Theodore M. Drange and Douglas Wilson, "The Drange-Wilson Debate," "First Rebuttal," available online at <http://www.infidels.org/library/modern/theodore_drange/drange-wilson/drange2.html>.

How, therefore, shall we satisfy ourselves concerning the cause of that Being whom you suppose the Author of Nature, or, according to your system of Anthropomorphism, the ideal world, into which you trace the material? Have we not the same reason to trace that ideal world into another ideal world, or new intelligent principle? But if we stop, and go no further; why go so far? Why not stop at the material world? How can we satisfy ourselves without going on *ad infinitum?* And, after all, what satisfaction is there in that infinite progression? Let us remember the story of the Indian philosopher and his elephant. It was never more applicable than to the present subject. If the material world rests upon a similar ideal world, this ideal world must rest upon some other; and so on, without end. It were better, therefore, never to look beyond the present material world. By supposing it to contain the principle of its order within itself, we really assert it to be God; and the sooner we arrive at that Divine Being, so much the better. When you go one step beyond the mundane system, you only excite an inquisitive humour which it is impossible ever to satisfy.[25]

In other words, if we explain human reason in terms of the reason of God, then the reason of God will have to be explained, and we will have failed to provide any explanation at all. The only way that human reason can be genuinely explained would be if that reason could be explained in terms of something that is without reason, something like, say, the blind evolutionary process.

In the context of the argument from reason, Keith Parsons put the objection this way:

[C]reationist "explanations" do not explain. When we appeal to the inscrutable acts and incomprehensible powers of an occult being to account for mysterious phenomena, we only deepen the mystery. Like Nagel, . . . I regard such "explanations" as mere markers for our ignorance, placeholders for explanations we hope to someday get.[26]

For example, some scientific creationists point out difficulties with evolutionary theory, but when there are difficulties put forward for their own theory (for example, the difficulty of seeing how, from the point of view of flood geology, creatures from all over the earth could be brought to Noah's ark, fitted into it, and then distributed back to the far corners of the earth),

---

[25]David Hume, "Dialogues Concerning Natural Religion, Part IV," in *The Philosophy of David Hume,* ed. V. C. Chappell (New York: Random House, 1963), pp. 534-35.
[26]Keith M. Parsons, "Defending Objectivity," *Philo* 2 (1999): 84.

they think it a sufficient answer to say that the ways of God are mysterious. Creationist arguments of that type seem to be setting up a "heads I win, tails you lose" situation, and critics have rightly pointed out that using an all-purpose escape clause for explanatory difficulties makes for very bad science.

Nevertheless, "supernatural" explanations are primarily intentional, teleological or personal explanations that cannot in principle be reduced to impersonal mechanistic explanations. To say that such explanations are always placeholders for mechanistic explanations seems to me to be a mistake. If we want to know why I attend church on Sunday morning, a detailed neurophysiological analysis will probably not be as helpful as knowing that I am a practicing Christian who believes in corporate worship. If, as I believe, God is a rational, personal being, then that makes it more likely that rational beings will arise in the world God creates, because persons by nature are interested in communicating with other persons. So the probability that rational beings should emerge given the existence of God looks to me to be pretty good; the emergence of rational beings in a naturalistic universe seems very unlikely if not impossible.

While we do not know any strict laws governing God's conduct, we certainly have beliefs about God that would render one action on God's part more likely than another. For example, I believe that if God were to raise someone from the dead from the twentieth century, Mother Teresa would be a more likely candidate than Adolf Hitler. If such a resurrection were to occur, I would not be at a loss to explain why Mother Teresa was chosen and Hitler was not.

The inadequacy objection gratuitously assumes that matter is what is clearly understandable, and that "mind" is something mysterious, the very existence of which has to be explained in terms of unmysterious matter. But is this an accurate picture? According to Galen Strawson,

> This is the assumption that we have a pretty good understanding of the nature of matter—of matter and space—of the physical in general. It is only relative to this assumption that the existence of consciousness in a material world seems mystifying. For what exactly is puzzling about consciousness, once we put the assumption aside? Suppose you have an experience of redness, or pain, and consider it to be just as such. There doesn't seem to be any room for anything that could be called failure to understand what it is.[27]

---

[27]Galen Strawson, "Little Gray Cells," *New York Times Book Review*, July 11, 1999, p. 13; quoted in Charles Taliaferro, "Emergentism and Consciousness: Going Beyond Property Dualism," in *Soul, Body and Survival: Essays on the Metaphysics of Human Persons*, ed. Kevin Corcoran (Ithaca, N.Y.: Cornell University Press, 2001), p. 68.

On the other hand, matter is described by modern physics in the most mystifying terms imaginable. The philosopher of science Bas van Fraassen writes, "Do concepts of the soul . . . baffle you? They pale beside the unimaginable otherness of closed space-times, event horizons, EPR correlations, and bootstrap models."[28]

Parsons says, "When I am told that consciousness and reasoning are due to the inscrutable and miraculous operations of occult powers wielded by an undetectable entity that exists nowhere in the physical universe, I am not enlightened."[29] I will not comment on whether or not this description of mind/body dualism or theism is an apt one, though I actually consider it to be misleading. Nonetheless, I would simply point out that to be enlightened is to discover the truth, and if this is the truth, then it is enlightening, even though it may be epistemically frustrating to someone like Parsons. Second, the "obscurantism" that I am advocating may be necessary to preserve science itself, while (if I am right) a mechanistic analysis of the mind undermines the scientific enterprise itself. Parsons's own theory makes Einstein's theory of relativity and Darwin's theory of evolution the result of blind physical causes. In the last analysis, whose theory is more obscurantist?

Therefore, I maintain that the inadequacy objection gratuitously assumes that the only real explanations are mechanistic explanations, and that this is evidently false. It is supposed to be part of God's nature to be rational. If we explain one thing in terms of something else, and that something else in terms of something else again, the chain of explanation will have to terminate somewhere; and the theist explains the existence of rationality in the universe by appealing to the inherent rationality of God. It cannot be the case that the materialist can actually argue that one ought never to explain anything in terms of something having such and such a nature. One cannot go on giving reductive explanations forever. If, as I have argued, we have good reason to suppose that reason cannot be built up out of nonintentional and nonteleological building blocks, then in order to preserve reason and the logical foundations of science, we have good reason to accept a nonmaterialist understanding of the universe. If the foregoing argument is correct, then explaining reason in terms of unreason explains reason *away,* and undercuts the very reason in which the explanation is supposed to be based.

---

[28]Paul Churchland and Clifford Hooker, *Images of Science: Essays on Realism and Empiricism, With a Reply from Bas C. Van Fraassen* (Chicago: University of Chicago Press, 1985), p. 285. Quoted in Taliaferro, "Emergentism and Consciousness," p. 69.

[29]Keith M. Parsons, "Need Reasons Be Causes?" *Philosophia Christi,* n.s. 5 (2003): 74-75.

A second Humean objection to the argument from reason is what James Sennett calls "Hume's stopper."[30] Hume's stopper is the claim that natural theology arguments, even if sound, show a good deal less than claimed. For example, the *kalam* cosmological argument may successfully demonstrate that there is a first cause of the universe distinct from the universe itself. William Lane Craig has maintained that the argument also successfully shows that the cause of the universe is personal.[31] But the God of theism isn't just a personal first cause, but also an omnipotent, omniscient and perfectly good being.

In the context of the argument from reason, Hume's stopper can be used to argue that, even if some kind of reason is fundamental to the universe, it need not be the reason of a personal God, much less the God of theism. The argument from reason does not contribute at all to natural theology, according to the stopper, because the phenomenon it seeks to explain can equally well be explained on other worldviews, such as absolute idealism or some forms of pantheism.

However, this involves an incorrect assumption concerning what natural theology can reasonably be expected to do. If we accept classical foundationalist assumptions concerning the role of natural theology, then perhaps Hume's stopper works. But these assumptions have been rejected, and with good reason, by contemporary philosophy of religion. The classical foundationalist assumptions are the following:

- Theistic arguments exist to shoulder a burden of proof that properly lies with the theist. The theist is making an existence claim; therefore, he must prove that God exists in order to avoid a charge of irrationality.

- Proofs of God's existence must be successful, not merely from the point of view of the arguer or even the listener, but to the satisfaction of all reasonable persons. Thus a proper inquiry into the question of the existence of God must be presuppositionless; one must begin inquiry from a neutral perspective and demonstrate God's existence from that perspective.

- Proofs of God's existence are not cumulative. They must prove that God exists on their own, apart from any other arguments. Otherwise they are abject failures.

---

[30]James F. Sennett, "Hume's Stopper and the Natural Theology Project," chapter 5 of the present volume. See also James Sennett, "Stopping Hume's Stopper: A Rejection of a Traditional Attack on Natural Theology," *The Stone-Campbell Journal* 5 (2002): 207-16.

[31]William Lane Craig, "The Craig-Jesseph Debate—Does God Exist? Dr. Craig's Opening Arguments" Leadership University, available online at <http://www.leaderu.com/offices/billcraig/docs/jesseph-craig2.html>.

This model of evaluating natural theology is taught in many undergraduate philosophy classes, invariably resulting in the conclusion that natural theology is a manifest and demonstrable failure. Under this model Hume's stopper looks like it is capable of stopping the argument from reason. If that were the case, the argument would have to shoulder the whole weight of showing that theism is true and that all other metaphysical views are false. If it is given that kind of a burden, then I will admit that the argument cannot carry it. In fact, I would not even consider it an absolute refutation of naturalism. It may succeed in showing that reason is deeply mysterious from the point of view of naturalism, but if all else fails (and I think all else does fail), the naturalist can make a "mystery maneuver." That is, she can "bite the bullet" and say that, even though reason is mysterious given naturalism, there simply must be a reconciliation of reason with naturalism (since naturalism is true), even though she has no idea what it is. (This would parallel the way many theists handle the problem of evil.)

But does this make the argument from reason a failure? I maintain that it does no such thing. While it may not be able to shoulder the burden that the stopper places on it, it can still play a significant role in getting a reasonable person to jump ship from atheism to theism.

First we must ask, does theism really bear such a burden of proof? More to the point, can the burden of proof be assigned in an objective manner? Does the absence of "proof" in the required sense mean that the theist is open to irrationality charges? Alvin Plantinga has argued that belief in God can be "properly basic," that is, perfectly rational to believe even in the absence of philosophical proof.[32]

Second, is it reasonable to demand that theistic arguments be assessed from a neutral perspective? Do we have to do this with other beliefs? Descartes thought he could provide a foundation for all his beliefs by doubting everything and accepting only what he could be absolutely sure of. But whatever Descartes's other merits as a philosopher, it is the overwhelming consensus in present-day philosophy that this ambitious project of his failed. Empiricists thought that Descartes started in the wrong place, and tried to build the majestic mansion of knowledge on the foundation of experience rather than reason, but Hume himself discovered a number of common-

---

[32]Alvin Plantinga, "Reason and Belief in God," in *Faith and Rationality: Reason and Belief in God,* ed. Alvin Plantinga and Nicholas Wolterstorff (Notre Dame, Ind.: University of Notre Dame Press, 1983), pp. 16-93.

sense beliefs that could not be given a foundation built up from what is given in experience. In particular, on the basis of Humean empiricism, the following beliefs cannot be proved:

- The existence of a mind-independent physical world.
- The existence of the "self."
- The existence of causal necessity.
- The principle that the future will resemble the past.
- Ordinary beliefs concerning what is right and wrong, such as "It is wrong to inflict pain on little children for your own amusement."

With respect to at least the last three of these beliefs, Hume appeals to our passional nature to justify continuing to believe these things. Concerning cause and effect and induction, Hume said that we should continue to accept these things because they are natural and practical. Our moral convictions are based not on rational proof but on human sentiment. "Proofs" for all five of these claims are "stopped" in Hume's own thought, yet he does not consider this to be a reason for jettisoning or even doubting the beliefs in question.

EPISTEMICALLY CONTEXTUAL BEINGS

What the history of modern epistemology teaches us, I believe, is that attempts to generate rational justification from a neutral perspective simply do not work. We are epistemically contextual beings, and to require us to set that context aside and consider the question of God from a neutral perspective is not reasonable. If we apply classical foundationalism not merely to the existence of God but to other beliefs (like the five above), we will find ourselves skeptics about the self, the external world, cause and effect, induction, and our most fundamental moral convictions. So I suggest that we replace the classical foundationalist model with a different model, one in which we don't try to build our belief system from the ground up, but rather accept the belief systems that we have and modify them as needed by evidence and argument.

What this means is that for some people natural theology will not be a necessity. I see no irrationality in someone believing in God because it is natural to believe in God, and because they see no good reason to reject belief in God. However, some people do go from unbelief to belief, and some people go from belief to unbelief, and sometimes this takes place in response to arguments. Nothing in my understanding of rational arguments prevents such development from occurring in rational people. Autobiographical accounts of the intellectual migrations, however, suggest that these belief changes occur from a wide range of considerations as opposed to some single argument.

Certainly this seems to have been the case with C. S. Lewis, as can be seen in his autobiography *Surprised by Joy*. Lewis began his career at Oxford as an atheist committed to some form of naturalism, but was persuaded by his friend Owen Barfield that his position was inconsistent. The arguments Barfield used included a version of the argument from reason.

> [H]e convinced me that the positions we had hitherto held left no room for any satisfactory theory of knowledge. We had been, in the technical sense of the term, "realists"; that is, we accepted as rock-bottom reality the universe revealed by the senses. But at the same time we continued to make for certain phenomena claims that really went with a theistic or idealistic view. We maintained that abstract thought (if obedient to logical rules) gave indisputable truth, that our moral judgment was "valid" and our aesthetic experience not merely pleasing but "valuable." The view was, I think, common at the time; it runs through Bridges' *Testament of Beauty* and Lord Russell's "Worship of a Free Man." Barfield convinced me that it was inconsistent. If thought were merely a subjective event, these claims for it would have to be abandoned. If one kept (as rock-bottom reality) the universe of the senses, aided by instruments co-ordinated as to form "science" then one would have to go much further, and accept a Behavioristic view of logic, ethics and aesthetics. But such a view was, and is unbelievable to me.[33]

However, this conviction did not lead Lewis to accept theism immediately. Instead he accepted the doctrine, widely held at that time, of absolute idealism. Rather than believing in God, Lewis came to believe in an impersonal absolute mind. So we might say that Hume's stopper stopped Lewis; it was somewhat comforting to Lewis (who seems to have suffered from what Thomas Nagel subsequently called "the fear of religion") to accept the view that, although reason is fundamental to the universe, it is not the reason of a personal, theistic God.

Nevertheless a variety of other considerations led Lewis to become a theist, and then finally a Christian. Two major considerations in favor of theism as opposed to absolute idealism arose when Lewis attempted to make ide-

---

[33]C. S. Lewis, *Surprised by Joy* (San Diego: Harcourt Brace, 1955), p. 208.

alism clear enough for tutoring purposes and when Lewis came to believe that the idealist philosophy was to be applied to his own conduct. He concluded that idealism differed from theism in being less clear than theism, and that when you tried to make it clear enough to teach or to live by, it became indistinguishable from theism. Hence the argument from reason served to help convince Lewis that theism was true, along with some other considerations relevant to absolute idealism.[34]

William Hasker discusses the situation in which a philosopher might find himself who finds that naturalism cannot adequately account for rational inference but who nonetheless is not sure that theism is the only, or the best, way to account for rational inference within one's worldview.

> But now I want to suggest that this third stage can indeed be viewed as a Best Explanation argument: having established the conditions required for the existence and intelligibility of rational inference, one goes on to consider which non-naturalistic worldview provides the best explanation for the obtaining of these conditions. This, roughly speaking, seems to be the stage Thomas Nagel has reached in his own philosophical explorations. Theists will press the claim that it is theism that best fills this role, no doubt developing the point along the lines suggested by Reppert. For the non-theist, however, a difficulty arises, one of which Nagel is keenly aware: It is hard to find worldviews other than theism that satisfy the requirements for rational inference and that have even minimal credibility in our current intellectual environment. It would nevertheless be unwise to assume that this situation will continue indefinitely: the ingenuity of philosophers (and others) in finding alternatives to theism is remarkable. No one should ever promise the natural theologian an easy life![35]

No, the life of a natural theologian is not an easy one. However, in dealing with real-life dialogue about worldviews, the argument from reason is hardly stopped by Hume's stopper. It was one of the considerations that led C. S. Lewis to abandon naturalism, and it helped open the door to his subsequent acceptance of theism. Hume's stopper is an important reminder of the limitations of philosophical argument. Recognition of those limits, however, does not stop natural theology; it merely bids us recalibrate its scope and limits. Within the framework of a proper understanding of the scope and limits of natural theology, the argument from reason, along with other arguments in natural theology, can still do the job assigned to it.

---

[34]Ibid., pp. 212-29.
[35]William Hasker, "What About a Sensible Naturalism?" *Philosophia Christi*, n.s. 5 (2003): 53-62.

13

HUME AND THE ARGUMENT
FROM CONSCIOUSNESS

J. P. Moreland

Consciousness is among the most mystifying features of the cosmos. Geoffrey Madell opines that "the emergence of consciousness, then is a mystery, and one to which materialism signally fails to provide an answer."[1] Naturalist Colin McGinn claims that its arrival borders on sheer magic because there seems to be no naturalistic explanation for it: "How can mere matter originate consciousness? How did evolution convert the water of biological tissue into the wine of consciousness? Consciousness seems like a radical novelty in the universe, not prefigured by the after-effects of the Big Bang; so how did it contrive to spring into being from what preceded it?"[2] Finally, naturalist William Lyons argues that "[physicalism] seem[s] to be in tune with the scientific materialism of the twentieth century because it [is] a harmonic of the general theme that all there is in the universe is matter and energy and motion and that humans are a product of the evolution of species just as much as buffaloes and beavers are. Evolution is a seamless garment with no holes wherein souls might be inserted from above."[3]

[1]Geoffrey Madell, *Mind and Materialism* (Edinburgh: Edinburgh University Press, 1988), p. 141.
[2]Colin McGinn, *The Mysterious Flame* (New York: Basic Books, 1999), pp. 13-14. See G. K. Chesterton's claim that the regular correlation between diverse entities in the world is magic that requires a Magician to explain it. *Orthodoxy* (John Lane Company, 1908; reprint, San Francisco: Ignatius Press, 1950), chap. 5.
[3]William Lyons, Introduction to *Modern Philosophy of Mind*, ed. William Lyons (London: Everyman, 1995), p. lv. In context, Lyons's remark is specifically about the identity thesis, but he clearly intends it to cover physicalism in general. Similarly, while he explicitly mentions an entity in the category of individual—the soul—the context of his remark makes clear that he includes mental properties and events among the entities out of step with scientific materialism.

Lyons's reference to souls being "inserted from above" appears to be a veiled reference to the explanatory power of theism for consciousness. Some argue that, while finite mental entities may be inexplicable on a naturalist worldview, they may be explained by theism, thereby furnishing evidence for God's existence. In this chapter, I shall defend this argument from consciousness (AC) by describing two relevant issues in scientific theory acceptance, presenting a summary of AC, characterizing naturalism and showing why mental entities are recalcitrant facts for naturalists and evaluating four explanations of consciousness that serve as rivals for AC.

Before we proceed, a few words are in order about AC and Hume and Hume's legacy. Three areas of Hume's thought are relevant to AC: natural theology, philosophy of mind and causation. Regarding natural theology, while Hume was surely skeptical of the "theistic rationalists" of his day, there is genuine debate about exactly where he stood regarding the value of arguments for God's existence, especially the design argument. The same sort of debate rages about the precise details of Hume's philosophy of mind. Surely, he was no substance dualist, but whether he was some sort of entity dualist or a precursor to Russell's neutral monism is in question. Given these ambiguities, it is unclear just exactly how AC relates to Hume's thought. Regarding causation, things are a bit clearer. It is well known that Hume removed "necessitation" from causality (or at least from the *idea* of causality), and his views about regular correlation and spatial/temporal contiguity are most closely related to John Searle's position (see below).

In developing AC, I will not respond to Hume directly, but my critique of Searle may fairly be taken to be a response to a Humean view of the explanatory requirements for the emergence of consciousness and its lawlike correlations with (ordinary) physical states. When it comes to the so-called Humean legacy things are clearer. That legacy takes it to be the case that naturalism has won the day and natural theology is a failed project. It should be clear that if AC is a good argument, it provides grounds for rejecting both of these claims.

PRELIMINARY POINTS

Two preliminaries are important. First, for two reasons I shall assume that theism and naturalism are the only worldviews relevant to the chapter. These are, indeed, the only live options for many who debate this topic, so I shall limit my arguments to this audience. Furthermore, other worldviews (e.g., Buddhism) are far from univocal in their commitment to the actual re-

ality of consciousness or of the cosmos itself, so dialogue with their advocates may require spadework before AC may be fruitfully discussed, and I
cannot do that work here. Second, I shall assume a commonsense understanding of mental states such as sensations, thoughts, beliefs, desires, voli-
tions and the selves that have them. So understood, mental states are in no
sense physical since they possess *five* features not owned by physical states:

1. There is a raw qualitative feel or a "what it is like" to have a mental
   state such as a pain.

2. At least many mental states have intentionality—*ofness* or *aboutness*—
   directed towards an object.

3. They are inner, private and immediate to the subject having them.

4. They require a subjective ontology—namely, mental states are necessarily owned by the first person sentient subjects who have them.

5. They fail to have crucial features (e.g., spatial extension, location) that
   characterize physical states and, in general, cannot be described using
   physical language.

Space considerations prevent me from arguing for these claims, but this
is not necessary for present purposes, since many (but not all) critics of AC
assume with its advocates a dualist construal of consciousness.[4]

ISSUES IN SCIENTIFIC THEORY ACCEPTANCE

Three issues in the adjudication of scientific rivals. While theism and
naturalism are broad worldviews and not scientific theories, three issues that
inform the adjudication between rival scientific theories are relevant to AC.
The first issue involves deciding whether it is appropriate to take some phenomenon as *basic* such that only a description and not an explanation for it
is required, or whether that phenomenon should be understood as something to be explained in terms of *more basic* phenomena. For example, attempts to explain uniform inertial motion are disallowed in Newtonian mechanics because such motion is basic on this view, but an Aristotelian had
to explain how or why a particular body exhibited uniform inertial motion.
Thus, what is basic to one theory may be derivative in another.

---

[4]For defenses of dualism see William Hasker, *The Emergent Self* (Ithaca, N.Y.: Cornell University
Press, 1999); J. P. Moreland and Scott Rae, *Body & Soul: Human Nature and the Crisis in Ethics*
(Downers Grove, Ill.: InterVarsity Press, 2000); Richard Swinburne, *The Evolution of the Soul*,
rev. ed. (Oxford: Clarendon, 1997); Charles Taliaferro, *Consciousness and the Mind of God*
(Cambridge: Cambridge University Press, 1994).

Issue two is the *naturalness* of a postulated entity in light of the overall theory of which it is a part. The types of entities postulated, along with the sorts of properties they possess and the relations they enter should be at home with other entities in the theory. Some entity (particular thing, process, property or relation) *e* is natural for a theory T just in case either *e* is a central, core entity of T or *e* bears a relevant similarity to central, core entities in *e*'s category within T. If *e* is in a category such as substance, force, property, event, relation or cause, *e* should bear a relevant similarity to other entities of T in that category.

This is a formal definition and the material content given to it will depend on the theory in question. Moreover, given rival theories R and S, the postulation of *e* in R is ad hoc and question begging against advocates of S if *e* bears a relevant similarity to the appropriate entities in S, and in this sense is "at home" in S, but fails to bear this relevant similarity to the appropriate entities in R.[5]

The issue of naturalness is relevant to theory assessment between rivals in that it provides a criterion for advocates of a theory to claim that their rivals have begged the question against them or adjusted their theory in an inappropriate, ad hoc way. And though this need not be the case, naturalness can be related to basicality in this way: naturalness can provide a means of deciding the relative merits of accepting theory R, which depicts phenomenon *e* as basic, versus embracing S, which takes *e* to be explainable in more basic terms. If *e* is natural in S but not in R, it will be difficult for advocates of R to justify the bald assertion that *e* is basic in R and that all proponents of R need to do is describe *e* and correlate it with other phenomena in R as opposed to explaining *e*. Such a claim by advocates of R will be even more problematic if S provides an explanation for *e*.[6]

---

[5]For example, suppose theory S explains phenomena in terms of discrete corpuscles and actions by contact, while R uses continuous waves to explain phenomena. If some phenomenon *x* was best explained in corpuscularian categories, it would be ad hoc and question begging for advocates of R simply to adjust their entities to take on particle properties in the case of *x*. Such properties would not bear a relevant similarity to other entities in R and would be more natural and at home in S.

[6]For example, suppose that R is neo-Darwinism and S is a version of punctuated equilibrium theory. Simply for the sake of illustration, suppose further that R depicts evolutionary transitions from one species to another to involve running through a series of incrementally different transitional forms except for some specific transition *e* which is taken as a basic phenomenon—say, the discrete jump from amphibians to reptiles. S pictures evolutionary transitions in general, including *e*, as evolutionary jumps to be explained in certain ways that constitute S. In this case, given the presence of S, it would be hard for advocates of R to claim that their treatment of *e* is adequate against S. Phenomenon *e* clearly counts in favor of S over against R.

Issue three involves *epistemic values*. Roughly, an epistemic value is a normative property which, if possessed by a theory, confers some degree of rational justification on that theory. Examples of epistemic values are these: theories should be simple, descriptively accurate, predictively successful, fruitful for guiding new research, capable of solving their internal and external conceptual problems, and should use certain types of explanations or follow certain methodological rules and not others (e.g., "appeal to efficient and not final causes"). Studies in scientific theory assessment have made it clear that two rivals may solve a problem differently depending on the way each theory depicts the phenomenon to be solved.

Moreover, it is possible for two rivals to rank the relative merits of epistemic virtues in different ways or even give the same virtue a different meaning or application. Rivals can differ radically about the nature, application and relative importance of a particular epistemic virtue. Thus, given rivals A and B, in arguing against B, it may be inappropriate for advocates of A to cite its superior comportment with an epistemic value when B's proponents do not weigh that value as heavily as they do a different one they take to be more central to B. For example, given rivals A and B, if A is simpler than B but B is more descriptively accurate than A, then it may be inappropriate—indeed, question begging—for advocates of A to cite A's simplicity as grounds for judging it superior to B.

Necessitation and physical causal explanations in realist constru-als of natural science. Though some demur, at least five reasons have been proffered for the claim that causal explanations in the natural sciences exhibit a kind of causal necessity, that on typical realist construals of natural science, physical causal explanations must show—usually by citing a mechanism—why an effect must follow given the relevant causal conditions:

1. Causal necessitation unpacks the deepest, core realist notion of causation, namely, causal production according to which a cause "brings about" or "produces" its effect.

2. Causal necessitation fits the paradigm cases of causal explanation (e.g., macrosolidity/impenetrability in terms of microlattice structures, repulsive forces; mass proportions in chemical reactions in terms of atomic models of atoms/molecules, bonding orbitals, energy stability, charge distribution) central to the core theories (e.g., the atomic theory of matter) that constitute a naturalist worldview and in terms of which it is purported to have explanatory superiority to rival worldviews.

3. Causal necessitation provides a way of distinguishing accidental generalizations from true causal laws.

4. Causal necessitation supports the derivation of counterfactuals (if that
chunk of gold had been placed in aqua regia, then it would have dis-
solved) from causal laws (gold dissolves in aqua regia).

5. Causal necessitation clarifies the direction of causality and rules out the
attempt to explain a cause by its effect.

Three points of clarification are in order about causal necessity and the
reasons for it. First, minimally, the sort of modality involved may be taken
as physical necessity, a form of necessity that runs throughout possible
worlds relevantly physically similar to our actual world (e.g., in having the
same physical particulars, properties, relations and/or laws). Second, strong
conceivability is the test that is used to judge causal necessitation (given the
lattice structures and so forth of two macroobjects impenetrable with respect
to each other, it is strongly inconceivable that one could penetrate the
other).

Finally, principles 3-5 have sometimes been offered as additions to a covering-law form of explanation to provide an adequate natural scientific
causal explanation. Strictly speaking, a covering-law "explanation" is just a
description of what needs to be explained and not an explanation. But by
adding a causal model that underwrites it and that exhibits causal necessitation, the total package provides explanations for both what and why the
phenomena are as they are. For brevity's sake, below I will talk as if a covering-law explanation is, in fact, an explanation, but it should be understood
that when I speak of a covering-law explanation I include in it an underwrit-
ing causal model.

In sum, as Timothy O'Connor points out, emergent properties, especially
mental properties, must be shown to arise by way of causal necessitation
from a micro-physical base if we are to "render emergent phenomena naturalistically explicable."[7] Among his reasons for this claim is the assertion that
if the link between microbase and emergent properties is a contingent one,
then the only explanation for the existence and constancy of the link is a
theistic explanation.[8] To see why O'Connor is correct about this, we turn to
an examination of AC and its naturalistic rivals.

---

[7]Timothy O'Connor, *Persons & Causes* (New York: Oxford University Press, 2000), p. 112.
[8]Ibid. pp. 70-71 n. 8.

THE ARGUMENT FROM CONSCIOUSNESS

AC may be expressed in inductive or deductive form. As an inductive argument, AC may be construed as claiming that, given theism and naturalism as the live options fixed by our background beliefs, theism provides a better explanation of consciousness than naturalism and, thus, receives some confirmation from the existence of consciousness.

AC may also be expressed in deductive form. Here is one deductive version of AC:

1. Genuinely nonphysical mental states exist.

2. There is an explanation for the existence of mental states.

3. Personal explanation is different from natural scientific explanation.

4. The explanation for the existence of mental states is either a personal or natural scientific explanation.

5. The explanation is not a natural scientific one.

6. Therefore, the explanation is a personal one.

7. If the explanation is personal, then it is theistic.

8. Therefore, the explanation is theistic.

Theists such as Robert Adams[9] and Richard Swinburne[10] have advanced a slightly different version of AC which focuses on mental/physical correlations and not merely on the existence of mental states. Either way, AC may be construed as a deductive argument.

Premises 2, 4 and 5 are the ones most likely to come under attack. We are granting (1) for the sake of argument.[11] Premise 3 turns on the fact that personal explanation differs from event causal covering-law explanations employed in natural science. Associated with *event* causation is a covering-law

---

[9]See Robert Adams, "Flavors, Colors, and God," reprinted in *Contemporary Perspectives on Religious Epistemology,* ed. R. Douglas Geivett and Brendan Sweetman (New York: Oxford University Press, 1992), pp. 225-40.

[10]See Richard Swinburne, *The Existence of God* (Oxford: Clarendon, 1979), chap. 9; *The Evolution of the Soul,* pp. 183-96; *Is There a God?* (Oxford: Oxford University Press, 1996), pp. 69-94; "The Origin of Consciousness," in *Cosmic Beginnings and Human Ends,* ed. Clifford N. Matthews and Roy Abraham Varghese (Chicago and La Salle, Ill.: Open Court, 1995), pp. 355-78.

[11]I have already listed five features of mental properties and events that justify the claim that they are not physical properties and events. It is beyond the scope of this chapter to defend the irreducible mental nature of mental properties and events against strict physicalist alternatives. Our focus is the more limited one of comparing AC with rivals that accept (1). For a defense of a dualist construal of consciousness, see the sources in n. 4 above.

model of explanation according to which some event (the *explanandum*) is explained by giving a correct deductive or inductive argument for that event. Such an argument contains two features in its *explanans:* a (universal or statistical) law of nature *and* initial causal conditions.

By contrast, a *personal* explanation (divine or otherwise) of some state of affairs brought about intentionally by a person will employ notions such as the intention of the agent and the relevant power of the agent that was exercised in causing the state of affairs. In general, a personal explanation of some basic result R brought about intentionally by person P where this bringing about of R is a basic action A will cite the intention I of P that R occur and the basic power B that P exercised to bring about R. P, I and B provide a personal explanation of R: agent P brought about R by exercising B in order to realize I as an irreducibly teleological goal.

To illustrate, suppose we are trying to explain why Wesson simply moved his finger, R. We could explain this by saying that Wesson, P, performed an act of endeavoring to move his finger, A, in that he exercised his ability to move (or will to move) his finger, B, intending to move the finger, I. If Wesson's moving his finger was an expression of an intent to move a finger to fire a gun to kill Smith, then we can explain the nonbasic results (the firing of the gun and the killing of Smith) by saying that Wesson, P, performed an act of killing Smith, I_3, by endeavoring to move his finger, A, intentionally, I_1, by exercising his power to do so, B, intending thereby to fire the gun, I_2, in order to kill Smith. An explanation of the results of a nonbasic action (like going to the store to get bread) will include a description of an action plan. A personal explanation does not consist in offering a mechanism, but rather, in correctly citing the relevant person, his intentions, the basic power exercised and, in some cases, offering a description of the relevant action plan.[12]

Advocates of AC employ the difference between these two modes of explanation to justify premise 2. Briefly, the argument is that given a defense of premises 4 and 5, there is no natural scientific explanation of mental entities. Thus, the phenomena cited in premise 1 may not be taken as sui generis facts that can be explained naturalistically. Moreover, the appearance of mental entities and their regular correlation with physical entities are puzzling phenomena that cry out for explanation. Since personal explanation is something people use all the time, this distinctive form of explanation is

---

[12]For a more detailed defense of this premise, see J. P. Moreland, "Searle's Biological Naturalism and the Argument from Consciousness," *Faith and Philosophy* 15 (1998): 68-91.

available, and its employment regarding the phenomena cited in (1) removes our legitimate puzzlement regarding them.

Premise 7 seems fairly uncontroversial. To be sure, Humean style arguments about the type and number of deities involved could be raised at this point, but these issues would be intramural theistic problems of small comfort to naturalists. That is, if the explanation for finite conscious minds is supernatural, then naturalism is false. Further, direct responses to these Humean style arguments are available. Since many of these responses are taken up elsewhere in this volume, I shall only gesture at a few lines of rebuttal here. Regarding the *number* of deities, the principle of economy would move us in the direction of one rather than a plurality of deities: why posit multiple entities when one entity will suffice? Regarding the *type* of deity, arguments for God's existence are—or should be—generally modest in what they attempt to show (e.g., the design argument is not intended to show that God is *all*-knowing or supremely good or the uncaused cause). Furthermore, bringing the various arguments together furnishes us with a much less pared-down understanding of this God. This is sufficient to render us personally accountable to this Being, and does not in any way conflict with the revealed God of Judeo-Christian theism.

Premise 4 will be examined in conjunction with two alternatives to AC that reject it: Colin McGinn's position and panpsychism.

That leaves (5). At least four reasons have been offered for why there is no natural scientific explanation for the existence of mental states (or their regular correlation with physical states).

1. *The uniformity of nature.* Prior to the emergence of consciousness, the universe contained nothing but aggregates of particles/waves standing in fields of forces relative to each other. The story of the development of the cosmos is told in terms of the rearrangement of microparts into increasingly more complex structures according to natural law. On a naturalist depiction of matter, it is brute mechanical, physical stuff. The emergence of consciousness seems to be a case of getting something from nothing. In general, physico-chemical reactions do not generate consciousness, not even one little bit, but they do in the brain, yet brains seem similar to other parts of organism bodies (e.g., both are collections of cells totally describable in physical terms). How can like causes produce radically different effects? The appearance of mind is utterly unpredictable and inexplicable. This radical discontinuity seems like an inhomogeneous rupture in the natural world. Similarly, physical states have spatial extension and location but mental states seem to

lack spatial features. Space and consciousness sit oddly together. How did spatially arranged matter conspire to produce nonspatial mental states? From a naturalist point of view, this seems utterly inexplicable.

2. *The contingency of the mind/body correlation*. The regular correlation between types of mental states and physical states seems radically contingent. Why do pains instead of itches, thoughts or feelings of love get correlated with specific brain states? Based on strong conceivability, zombie and inverted qualia worlds are possible. No amount of knowledge of the brain state will help to answer this question. Given the requirement of causal necessitation for naturalistic causal explanations, there is *in principle* no naturalistic explanation for either the existence of mental states or their regular correlation with physical states. For the naturalist, the regularity of mind/body correlations must be taken as contingent brute facts. But these facts are inexplicable from a naturalistic standpoint, and they are radically sui generis compared to all other entities in the naturalist ontology. Thus, it begs the question simply to announce that mental states and their regular correlations with certain brain states are natural facts. As naturalist Terence Horgan acknowledges, "[I]n any metaphysical framework that deserves labels like 'materialism,' 'naturalism,' or 'physicalism,' supervenient facts must be explainable rather than being sui generis."[13]

Since on most depictions, the theistic God possesses libertarian freedom, God is free to act or refrain from acting in various ways. Thus, the fact that the existence of consciousness and its precise correlation with matter is contingent fits well with a theistic personal explanation that takes God's creative action to have been a contingent one. God may be a necessary being, but God's choice to create conscious beings and to correlate certain types of mental states with certain types of physical states were contingent choices, and this fits nicely with the phenomena themselves.

3. *Epiphenomenalism and causal closure*. Most naturalists believe that their worldview requires that all entities whatever are either physical or depend on the physical for their existence and behavior. One implication of this belief is commitment to the causal closure of the physical. On this principle, when one is tracing the causal antecedents of any physical event, one will never have to leave the level of the physical. Physical effects have only

---

[13]Terence Horgan, "Nonreductive Materialism and the Explanatory Autonomy of Psychology," in *Naturalism*, ed. Steven J. Wagner and Richard Warner (Notre Dame, Ind.: University of Notre Dame Press, 1993), pp. 313-14.

physical causes. Rejection of the causal closure principle would imply a rejection of the possibility of a complete and comprehensive physical theory of all physical phenomena—something that no naturalist should reject. Thus, if mental phenomena are genuinely nonphysical, then they must be epiphenomena—effects caused by the physical that do not themselves have causal powers.

But epiphenomenalism is false. Mental causation seems undeniable and, thus, for the naturalist the mental can be allowed to have causal powers only if it is in some way or another identified with the physical. The admission of epiphenomenal nonphysical mental entities may be taken as a refutation of naturalism. As naturalist D. M. Armstrong admits, "I suppose that if the principles involved [in analyzing the single all-embracing spatio-temporal system which is reality] were completely different from the current principles of physics, in particular if they involved appeal to mental entities, such as purposes, we might then count the analysis as a falsification of Naturalism."[14]

4. *The inadequacy of evolutionary explanations.* Naturalists are committed to the view that, in principle, evolutionary explanations can be proffered for the appearance of all organisms and their parts. It is not hard to see how an evolutionary account could be given for new and increasingly complex physical structures that constitute different organisms. However, organisms are black boxes as far as evolution is concerned. As long as an organism, when receiving certain inputs, generates the correct behavioral outputs under the demands of fighting, fleeing, reproducing and feeding, the organism will survive. What goes on inside the organism is irrelevant and only becomes significant for the processes of evolution when an output is produced. Strictly speaking, it is the output, not what caused it, that bears on the struggle for reproductive advantage. Moreover, the functions organisms carry out consciously *could just as well have been done unconsciously.* Thus, both the sheer existence of conscious states and the precise mental content that constitutes them is outside the pale of evolutionary explanation. As Howard E. Gruber explains:

> [T]he idea of either a Planful or an Intervening Providence taking part in the day-to-day operations of the universe was, in effect, a competing theory [to Darwin's version of evolution]. If one believed that there was a God who had originally designed the world exactly as it has come to be, the theory of evo-

---

[14]D. M. Armstrong, "Naturalism: Materialism and First Philosophy," *Philosophia* 8 (1978): 262.

lution through natural selection could be seen as superfluous. Likewise, if one believed in a God who intervened from time to time to create some of the organisms, organs, or functions found in the living world, Darwin's theory could be seen as superfluous. Any introduction of intelligent planning or decision-making reduces natural selection from the position of a necessary and universal principle to a mere possibility.[15]

Gruber's concession is a serious one. It amounts to the recognition that *in principle* the evolutionary naturalist account can explain the origin of all organisms and their parts. If some aspect of living things such as their mental lives is in principle incapable of evolutionary explanation, this provides support for a theistic mode of explanation for this aspect of living things and, indeed, weakens the hegemony of evolutionary naturalistic explanation in those cases where the explanandum is in principle within its pale.

We have looked at four reasons why many scholars, including many naturalists, hold that naturalism requires the rejection of consciousness construed along dualist lines. Paul Churchland is representative of those who accept this implication of taking the naturalistic turn. Speaking of the conjunction of naturalism and evolution, Churchland asserts:

> The important point about the standard evolutionary story is that the human species and all of its features are the wholly physical outcome of a purely physical process. . . . If this is the correct account of our origins, then there seems neither need, nor room, to fit any nonphysical substances or properties into our theoretical account of ourselves. We are creatures of matter. And we should learn to live with that fact.[16]

THE NATURALISTIC WORLDVIEW

At this point, it may be wise to look briefly at the nature of naturalism as a worldview to gain further insight into why consciousness is such a problem for naturalists. Naturalism usually includes

1. different aspects of a naturalist epistemic attitude (for example, a rejection of so-called first philosophy along with an acceptance of either weak or strong scientism);[17]

---

[15]Howard E. Gruber, *Darwin on Man: A Psychological Study of Scientific Creativity* (Chicago: University of Chicago Press, 1974), p. 211.
[16]Paul Churchland, *Matter and Consciousness* (Cambridge, Mass.: MIT Press, 1984), p. 21.
[17]The *strong* version of scientism maintains that science provides us with the *sole* basis of knowledge; the *weaker* version claims that science furnishes us with the *most certain* basis of knowledge, even if other disciplines provide more weakly justified beliefs or knowledge.

2. a Grand Story which amounts to an etiological account of how all entities whatsoever have come to be, told in terms of an event causal story described in natural scientific terms with a central role given to the atomic theory of matter and evolutionary biology;

3. a general ontology in which the only entities allowed are those that either (a) bear a relevant similarity to those thought to characterize a completed form of physics or (b) can be explained according to the causal necessitation requirement in terms of the Grand Story and the naturalist epistemic attitude.

For most naturalists, the ordering of these three ingredients is important. Frequently, the naturalist epistemic attitude serves as justification for the naturalist etiology, which, in turn, helps to justify the naturalist's ontological commitment. Moreover, naturalism seems to require a coherence among the postulates of these three different areas of the naturalistic turn. For example, there should be a coherence among third-person scientific ways of knowing; a physical, evolutionary account of how our sensory and cognitive processes came to be; and an ontological analysis of those processes themselves. Any entities that are taken to exist should bear a relevant similarity to entities that characterize our best physical theories; their coming-to-be should be intelligible in light of the naturalist causal story; and they should be knowable by scientific means.

For our purposes, it is important to say a bit more about naturalist ontological commitments. A good place to start is with what Frank Jackson calls the location problem.[18] According to Jackson, given that naturalists are committed to a fairly widely accepted physical story about how things came to be and what they are, the location problem is the task of locating or finding a place for some entity (for example, semantic contents, mind, agency) in that story. As an illustration, Jackson shows how the solidity of macroobjects can be located within a naturalist worldview. If solidity is taken as impenetrability, then given the lattice structure of atoms composing, say, a table and chair, it becomes obvious why they cannot penetrate each other. Given the naturalist microstory, the macroworld could not have been different: the table could not penetrate the chair. Location is necessitation.

There are three constraints for developing a naturalist ontology and locating entities within it:

---

[18]Frank Jackson, *From Metaphysics to Ethics* (Oxford: Clarendon, 1998), pp. 1-5.

a. Entities should conform to the naturalist epistemology.
b. Entities should conform to the naturalist Grand Story.
c. Entities should bear a relevant similarity to those found in chemistry and physics or be shown to depend necessarily on entities in chemistry and physics.

Regarding the naturalist epistemology, all entities should be knowable by and only by third-person scientific means. Regarding the Grand Story, one should be able to show how any entity had to appear in light of the naturalist event causal story according to which the history of the cosmos amounts to a series of events governed by natural law in which microparts come together to form various aggregates with increasingly complex physical structures. The four arguments listed above, in one way or other, claim that consciousness cannot be located in the naturalist ontology under the relevant constraints.

Given theism and naturalism as rivals, theists who employ the argument from consciousness seek to capitalize on the naturalistic failure to come to terms with consciousness by offering a rival explanation for its appearance. That failure is why most prominent naturalists (e.g., John Bishop, Daniel Dennett, D. M. Armstrong, Paul Churchland, David Papineau and Jaegwon Kim) reject premise 1 of AC ("genuinely nonphysical mental states exist") and either eliminate or, in one way or another, identify conscious states with physical ones.[19]

Unfortunately for naturalists, consciousness has stubbornly resisted treatment in physical terms. Consciousness has been recalcitrant for naturalists and (1) is hard to dismiss. Aware of this problem, various alternatives to theism and AC have been provided which accept (1). In the next section, we shall look at the main options.

ALTERNATIVES TO AC

Frank Jackson and the location of mental facts. Frank Jackson begins his attempt to develop a naturalistic account of the mental by contrasting two very different approaches to metaphysics. The first he calls "serious

---

[19]John Bishop, *Natural Agency* (Cambridge: Cambridge University Press 1989); Daniel Dennett, *Elbow Room* (Cambridge, Mass.: MIT Press, 1984); D. M. Armstrong, *Universals and Scientific Realism*, vol. 1: *Nominalism & Realism* (Cambridge: Cambridge University Press, 1978), pp. 126-35; Armstrong, "Naturalism: Materialism," 261-76; Paul Churchland, *Matter and Consciousness;* David Papineau, *Philosophical Naturalism* (Oxford: Blackwell, 1993); Jaegwon Kim, *Mind in a Physical World* (Cambridge, Mass.: MIT Press, 1998); Jaegwon Kim, *Philosophy of Mind* (Boulder, Colo.: Westview, 1996).

metaphysics." Serious metaphysics is not content to draw up large pluralistic lists of sui generis entities. Rather, it is primarily explanatory metaphysics, advocates of which seek to account for all entities in terms of a limited number of basic entities. The second we may call a "shopping list" approach whose primary goal is a careful description and categorical analysis of reality.

Possibly taking his clue from the methodology of physical science and its emphasis on theoretical simplicity, Jackson claims that the scientific naturalist will prefer serious metaphysics. Moreover, given that naturalists are committed to a fairly widely accepted physical story about how things came to be and what they are (the Grand Story), serious metaphysics presents the naturalist with a difficulty called "the location problem": the task of locating or finding a place for some entity (for example, semantic contents, mind, agency) in that story.

For Jackson, the naturalist must either locate a problematic entity in the Grand Story or eliminate the entity. Roughly, an entity is located in the Grand Story just in case it is entailed by it. Otherwise, the entity must be eliminated. Jackson provides three examples of location. First, just as density is a different property from mass and volume, it is not an additional feature of reality over and above mass and volume in at least this sense: an account of things in terms of mass and volume implicitly contains, that is, entails the account in terms of density. Second, Jones's being taller than Smith is not an additional feature of reality over and above Jones's and Smith's heights because the relational fact is entailed, and in this sense located, by the latter.

More important, Jackson focuses on the location of macrosolidity. He acknowledges that, prior to modern science, there was a widely accepted commonsense notion of macrosolidity, namely, being everywhere dense. However, due to modern science, this notion has been replaced with being impenetrable. So understood, macrosolidity may be located in the basic microstory: given a description of two macroobjects in terms of their atomic parts, lattice structures, and sub-atomic forces of repulsion, this description entails that one macroobject is impenetrable with respect to the other.

Jackson believes there are four important sorts of troublesome entities that the naturalist must locate: mental properties/events, facts associated with the first-person indexical, secondary qualities and moral properties. Focusing on mental properties/events, Jackson claims that the naturalist must argue that they globally supervene on the physical. He unpacks this claim with two clarifications. First, he defines a *minimal physical duplicate of our* *world* as "a world that (a) is exactly like our world in every physical respect (instantiated property for instantiated property, law for law, relation for relation), and (b) contains nothing else in the sense of nothing more by way of kinds or particulars than it *must* to satisfy (a)."[20] Second, he advocates what he labels "B*": *Any world which is a minimal physical duplicate of our world is a psychological duplicate of our world.*

Jackson concludes in this way:

> Let ϕ be the story as told in purely physical terms, which is true at the actual world and all the minimal physical duplicates of the actual world, and false elsewhere; ϕ is a hugely complex, purely physical account of our world. Let ψ be any true sentence which is about the psychological nature of our world in the sense that it can only come false [sic] by things being different psychologically from the way they actually are: every world at which ψ is false differs in some psychological way from our world. Intuitively, the idea is that ψ counts as being about the psychological nature of our world because making it false requires supposing a change in the distribution of psychological properties and relations. . . . [E]very world at which ϕ is true is a world at which ψ is true—that is, ϕ entails ψ.[21]

Has Jackson succeeded in providing a naturalistic explanation of mental properties/events that provides a more reasonable alternative to AC? For at least two reasons, the answer is no: (1) Jackson fails convincingly to locate mental properties in the Grand Story; and (2) his employment of serious metaphysics begs the question against advocates of AC.

First, Jackson fails convincingly to locate mental properties in the Grand Story. Jackson selects solidity as a paradigm case of location to which he will assimilate other located entities (e.g., semantic contents). But Jackson does not really locate solidity, and even if he does, solidity and its location are a bad analogy with consciousness and its location such that the successful location of the former does not provide grounds for locating the latter. As Jackson acknowledges, the prescientific notion of solidity is being everywhere dense. But this notion is not located in the basic physical story—there are minimal physical duplicates of our world whose macroobjects do not exemplify being everywhere dense. So what actually happens is that, rather than being *located*, the notion of being everywhere dense is *eliminated* in favor of being impenetrable.

---

[20]Jackson, *From Metaphysics to Ethics*, p. 13.
[21]Ibid., p. 25.

However, even if we grant the location of solidity, this paradigm case, along with the other two (density, being taller than) provide inadequate analogies for justifying the claim that mental properties may be located in accordance with B*. For one thing, solidity is part of the Grand Story—there is both macro- and microsolidity. But, granting that panpsychism is false and assuming—with (1) of AC—that mental properties are sui generis emergent and not structural properties, mental properties are not part of the Grand Story.

Second, it seems pretty clear that it is on the basis of strong conceivability—positive insight into the nature of the relevant properties and relations—that, given mass/volume, given particulars and their heights, and given lattice structure, atomic parts and forces of repulsion, the relevant macroentities are located. Given the microstory, it is simply inconceivable that there could be a possible world where the corresponding macroobjects failed to have a certain density or stand in a certain "taller than" relation or be impenetrable with respect to each other. Once one grasps the microstory, one can just see the modality involved. But, clearly, this is not so with respect to mental properties. It seems pretty obvious to many people that zombie worlds and various inverted qualia worlds are within the range of minimal physical duplicates of the actual world. No description of the actual world's physical particulars, properties, laws or relations entails anything whatsoever about the presence or nature of the mental features of the world in question. The connection between the mental and physical is radically contingent. When physicalists deny this claim, they have to dig in their heels in a question-begging way that is completely unnecessary for the modal claims about Jackson's three paradigm cases.

Third, B* requires a stop clause—"contains nothing else in the sense of nothing more by way of kinds or particulars than it *must* to satisfy (a)"—that is not at all necessary for a formulation of B* that is adequate for facts about macrodensity, solidity and relational facts about height. Jackson himself states a general principle B that he narrows into B* to focus on the supervenience of psychological facts. His B is *Any world which is a minimal physical duplicate of our world is a duplicate* simpliciter *of our world*. Clearly, B does not require a stop clause to be adequate for the location of density, solidity and relational facts. But the location of mental facts does require the stop clause; hence, B*.

But the stop clause is not itself explicit or even implicit in the Grand Story nor is there any strictly scientific argument from the naturalist epistemic attitude for its inclusion in B*. Indeed, it seems that Jackson's employment of it gives unintended testimony to the fact that the physical world alone is not sufficient to locate mental properties, so something more (no mental substances may be allowed) is required. Thus, the stop clause is ad hoc and question begging against advocates of AC, but no such charge could be leveled against B and the location of the three paradigm macrofeatures.

In addition to his failure convincingly to locate mental properties in the Grand Story, Jackson's employment of serious metaphysics is question begging against advocates of AC. To see this, recall that one epistemic value may be crucially relevant for justifying one theory but a different epistemic value may be crucial to its rival. When this happens, it is inappropriate to fault a rival theory A for not measuring up to an epistemic value that is important to rival B but not to A. Given the implicit reductionism and micro-to-macro forms of explanation that express the naturalist epistemic attitude and that constitute the core of the Grand Story, it is easy to see why naturalists must prefer serious metaphysics to a shopping list metaphysics. But on a theistic view it is at least arguably the case that a shopping list approach is preferable. There are two reasons for this.

First, the freedom and creativity at the core of our notion of a person—especially a divine person—provide grounds for preferring a shopping list approach to ontology. There is a positive and negative side to this claim. Positively, if God exists, he may well create a variety of kinds of entities, and he may create various kinds ex nihilo or by actualizing potentialities in precursors that go far beyond what is countenanced in the Grand Story. Given theism, one would expect creative variety in being and there is no bar to holding that various kinds of things are quite discrete. Indeed, early creationist taxonomists such as Carl Linnaeus exemplified a "shopping list" approach to biological taxonomy precisely because, as theists, they employed a top-down typological essentialist perspective that is not at home in a naturalist approach dictated by the Grand Story.

Second, the theist has no need to begin with a basic account and try to locate other entities in terms of a limited number of basic entities. Such an approach is either eliminativist or reductionist (macroentities must be located by being entailed by the Grand Story) as Jackson acknowledges, and this places a premium on explanatory versus descriptive metaphysics, along with theoretical simplicity and serious metaphysics as a crucial component of a naturalist approach to metaphysics. But the theist is free to describe metaphysical data whether he can locate them or not. Thus, in doing ontology, the theist will prefer the value of descriptive accuracy (it is no accident that Husserl was both a theist and a phenomenologist in ontology) to theoretical simplicity understood in accordance with Jackson's characterization of serious metaphysics. So it is question begging for Jackson to employ serious metaphysics as common ground for the adjudication of naturalism vis-à-vis theism and AC.

John Searle's biological naturalism. John Searle has developed a naturalistic account of consciousness which would, if successful, provide justification for rejecting premise 5 of AC ("The explanation is not a natural scientific one").[22] According to Searle, for fifty years philosophy of mind has been dominated by scientific naturalists who have advanced different versions of strict physicalism because it was seen as a crucial implication of taking the naturalistic turn. For these naturalists, if one abandons strict physicalism, one has rejected a scientific naturalist approach to the mind-body problem and opened oneself up to the intrusion of religious concepts and arguments about the mental.

By contrast, Searle's own solution to the mind-body problem is *biological* naturalism: while mental states are exactly what dualists describe them to be, nevertheless, they are merely emergent biological states and processes that causally supervene upon a suitably structured, functioning brain. Brain processes cause mental processes, which are not ontologically reducible to the former. Consciousness is just an ordinary (i.e., physical) feature of the brain and, as such, is merely an ordinary feature of the natural world.

Given that he characterizes consciousness as dualists do, why does Searle claim that there are no deep metaphysical implications that follow from biological naturalism? More specifically, why is it that biological naturalism does not represent a rejection of scientific naturalism which, in turn, opens the door for religious concepts about and explanations for the mental? Searle's answer to this question is developed in three steps.

In step one, he cites several examples of emergence (liquidity, solidity, features of digestion) that he takes to be unproblematic for naturalists and claims that emergent consciousness is analogous to the unproblematic cases.

In step two, he formulates two reasons why consciousness is not a problem for naturalists. First, the emergence of consciousness is not a problem if we stop trying to picture or image consciousness. Second, in standard

---

[22]John Searle, *The Rediscovery of the Mind* (Cambridge, Mass.: MIT Press, 1992).

cases (heat, color), an ontological reduction (e.g., identifying a specific color with a wavelength) is based on a causal reduction (e.g., claiming that a specific color is caused by a wavelength) because our pragmatic interests are in reality, not appearance.

In these cases we can distinguish the *appearance* of heat and color from the *reality,* place the former in consciousness, leave the latter in the objective world, and go on to define the phenomenon itself in terms of its causes. We can do this because our interests are in the reality and not the appearance. The ontological reduction of heat to its causes leaves the appearance of heat the same. Regarding consciousness, we are interested in the appearances, and thus the irreducibility of consciousness is merely due to pragmatic considerations, not to some deep metaphysical problem.

In step three, Searle claims that an adequate scientific explanation of the emergence of consciousness consists in a detailed, law-like set of correlations between mental and physical state tokens. Part of his justification for this is that some explanations in science do not exhibit the type of necessity that explains why certain things must happen (e.g., macroimpenetrability) given that other things have obtained (e.g., microstructure). Searle cites as an example the inverse square law, which is an explanatory account of gravity that does not show why bodies have to have gravitational attraction.

Several things may be said in response to Searle's position. Regarding steps one and two, his cases of emergence (rigidity, fluidity) are not good analogies to consciousness since the former are *easy* to locate in the naturalist epistemology and ontology, but consciousness is *not.* Given a widely accepted physicalist description of atoms, molecules, lattice structure and the like, the rigidity or fluidity of macroobjects follows necessarily. But there is no clear necessary connection between any physical state and any mental state. For example, given a specific brain state normally "associated" with the mental state of being appeared to redly, inverted qualia worlds (worlds with that physical state but radically different mental states "associated" with it), zombie worlds (worlds with that physical state and no mental states at all) and disembodied worlds (worlds with beings possessing mental states with no physical entities at all) are still metaphysically possible. It is easy to locate solidity in a naturalist framework but the same cannot be said for consciousness. This is why there has been turmoil for naturalists in philosophy of mind but not in the philosophy of solidity. Searle's emergent entities follow necessarily given the naturalist Grand Story, but consciousness does not.

Further, the emergence of genuinely new properties in macroobjects that are not part of the microworld (e.g., heat construed as warmth, color construed commonsensically as a quality) presents problems for naturalists in the same way consciousness does and, historically, that is why they were placed in consciousness. Contrary to Searle, they were not so placed because of the pragmatics of our interests. For example, historically, the problem was that if so-called secondary qualities were kept in the mind-independent world, there was no naturalistic explanation for why they emerged on the occasion of a mere rearrangement in microparts exhaustively characterized in terms of primary qualities. Secondary qualities construed along commonsense lines are not among the primary qualities employed to characterize the microworld and, indeed, seem contingently linked to the microworld.

It is this straightforward ontological problem, not the pragmatics of reduction or the attempt to image consciousness, that presents difficulties for naturalism: How do you get secondary qualities or consciousness to come to be merely by rearranging purely physical entities bereft of the emergent features? Given their existence, why are secondary qualities and conscious states regularly correlated with purely physical states similarly bereft?

In fact, the emergence of mental properties is more like the emergence of normative (e.g., moral) properties than the properties of solidity or digestion. Even the atheist J. L. Mackie admitted that the emergence of moral properties provided evidence for a moral argument for God's existence analogous to AC: "Moral properties constitute so odd a cluster of properties and relations that they are most unlikely to have arisen in the ordinary course of events without an all-powerful god to create them."[23] Mackie is right on this point. Given theism, if a naturalist were simply to claim that the emergence of moral properties was a basic naturalistic fact, this would be an ad hoc, question-begging ploy of assuming a point not congruent with a naturalistic worldview. Searle's "explanation" of consciousness is guilty of the same charge.

Regarding step three, "explanations" in science that do not express the sort of necessity we have been discussing are better taken as *descriptions,* not *explanations.* For example, the ideal gas equation is a description of the behavior of gases. An explanation of that behavior is provided by the atomic theory of gas. Curiously, Newton himself took the inverse square law to be

---

[23]J. L. Mackie, *The Miracle of Theism* (Oxford: Clarendon, 1982), p. 115.

a mere description of gravity and not an explanation; so Searle's own example counts against him. Further, given theism and AC, along with our earlier discussion of scientific theory acceptance, it is question begging and ad hoc for Searle to assert that mental entities and mental/physical correlations are basic, since such entities are natural in light of theism but unnatural given philosophical naturalism.

Our current belief that there is no causal necessity to specific mind/brain correlations is not due to our ignorance of how the brain works, but on an understanding of the radical differences between mental and physical entities. As naturalist Jaegwon Kim notes, the correlations are not explanations. They are the very things that need explaining, and, given a proper understanding of the real questions, no naturalistic explanation seems to be forthcoming.

> How could a series of physical events, little particles jostling against one another, electric current rushing to and fro . . . blossom into a conscious experience? . . . Why shouldn't pain and itch be switched around? . . . Why should *any* experience emerge when these neurons fire?[24]

By misconstruing the problem, Searle fails to address the real issue and, weighed against AC, his position is inadequate.

Colin McGinn's agnostic "naturalism." Naturalist Colin McGinn has offered a different solution.[25] Given the radical difference between mind and matter as it is depicted by current or even an ideal future physics, there is no naturalistic solution that stays within the widely accepted naturalist epistemology and ontology. Darwinian explanations fail as well because they cannot account for why consciousness appeared in the first place. What is needed is a radically different kind of solution to the origin of mind, one that must meet two conditions: (1) it must be a naturalistic solution; and (2) it must depict the emergence of consciousness and its regular correlation with matter as necessary and not contingent facts.

McGinn claims that there must be two kinds of unknowable natural properties that solve the problem. There must be some general properties of matter that enter into the production of consciousness when assembled into a brain. Thus, all matter has the potentiality to underlie consciousness. Further, there must be some natural property of the brain he calls

---

[24]Kim, *Philosophy of Mind,* p. 8.
[25]McGinn, *Mysterious Flame.*

C* that unleashes these general properties.

According to McGinn, the temptation to take the origin of consciousness as a mystery, indeed, a mystery that is best explained theistically, is due to our ignorance of these properties. However, given C* and the general properties of matter, the unknowable link between mind and matter is ordinary and commonplace and necessitates the emergence of consciousness. Unfortunately, evolution did not give humans the faculties needed to know these properties and, thus, they are in principle beyond our grasp. We will forever be agnostic about their nature. However, they must be there since there must be some naturalistic explanation of mind as all other solutions have failed.

McGinn offers two further descriptions of these unknowable yet ordinary properties that link matter and mind: (1) they are not sense perceptible, and (2) since matter is spatial and mind nonspatial, they are either in some sense prespatial or are spatial in a way that is itself unknowable to our faculties. In this way, these unknowable properties contain at least the potentiality for both ordinary spatial features of matter and the nonspatial features of consciousness as judged by our usual concept of space.

In sum, the mind-matter link is an unknowable mystery due to our cognitive limitations resulting from our evolution. And since the link is quite ordinary, we should not be puzzled by the origin of mind, and no theistic explanation is required.

Does McGinn's solution succeed? For at least three reasons, it must be judged a failure. First, given McGinn's agnosticism about the properties that link mind and matter, how can he confidently assert some of their features? How does he know they are nonsensory, prespatial or spatial in an unknowable way? How does he know some of these properties underlie all matter? Indeed, what possible justification can he give for their reality? The only one he proffers is that we must provide a naturalistic solution and all ordinary naturalistic ones either deny consciousness or fail to solve the problem. But given the presence of AC, McGinn's claims are simply question begging. Indeed, his agnosticism seems to be a convenient way of hiding behind naturalism and avoiding a theistic explanation. Given that theism enjoys a positive degree of justification prior to the problem of consciousness (see other chapters in this volume), he should avail himself of the explanatory resources of theism.

Second, it is not clear that his solution is a version of naturalism, except in name only. In contrast to other entities in the naturalist ontology,

McGinn's linking properties cannot be known by employment of the naturalist epistemology, nor are they relevantly similar to the rest of the naturalist ontology. Thus, it becomes vacuous to call these properties "naturalistic." McGinn's own speculations strike one as ad hoc in light of the inadequacies of naturalistic explanations. In fact, McGinn's solution is actually closer to an agnostic form of panpsychism (see below) than to naturalism. Given AC, McGinn's solution is an ad hoc readjustment of naturalism.

Third, McGinn does not solve the problem of consciousness; he merely relocates it. Rather than having two radically different entities, he offer us unknowable properties with two radically different aspects, namely, his links contain the potentiality for ordinary spatiality and nonspatiality, for ordinary materiality and mentality. Moreover, these radically different aspects of the linking properties are just as contingently related as they seem to be without a linking intermediary. The contingency comes from the nature of mind and matter as naturalists conceive it. It does not remove the contingency to relocate it as two aspects of an unknowable third intermediary with both.

Panpsychism. Currently, there are few serious advocates of panpsychism, though it has been suggested by Thomas Nagel and David Chalmers.[26] Roughly, panpsychism is the view that all matter has consciousness in it. Since each parcel of matter has its own consciousness, the brain is conscious since it is just a collection of those parcels. Consciousness is pervasive in nature, so its apparent emergence in particular cases is not something that requires special explanation. One can distinguish two forms of panpsychism. According to the strong version, all matter has conscious states in it in the same sense that organisms such as dogs and humans do. According to the weak form, regular matter has consciousness in a degraded, attenuated way in the form of protomental states that, under the right circumstances, yield conscious mental states without themselves being conscious.

The strong form is quite implausible. For one thing, regular matter gives no evidence whatever of possessing consciousness. Further, if all matter has consciousness, why does it emerge in special ways only when certain configurations of matter are present? And if conscious human beings are in some sense merely combinations of little bits of consciousness, how are we

---

[26]Thomas Nagel, *The View from Nowhere* (New York: Oxford University Press, 1986), pp. 49-53; David J. Chalmers, *The Conscious Mind* (New York: Oxford University Press, 1996), pp. 293-301.

to account for the unity of consciousness and why do people have no memory of the conscious careers of the bits of matter prior to their combination to form humans? There is no answer to these questions and few, if any, hold to strong panpsychism.

What about the weak version? Given the current intellectual climate, a personal theistic or a naturalistic explanation would exhaust at least the live—if not the logical—options. It is widely recognized that weak panpsychism has serious problems in its own right, such as explaining: (1) what an incipient or protomental entity is; (2) how the type of unity that appears to characterize the self could emerge from a mere system of parts standing together in various causal and spatio-temporal relations; and (3) why certain physical conditions are regularly correlated with the actualization of consciousness when the connection between consciousness and those conditions seems to be utterly contingent.[27]

Moreover, panpsychism is arguably less reasonable than theism on other grounds. I cannot pursue this point here but other chapters in this volume take up other aspects of the case for theism. In light of that case, theism enjoys positive epistemic justification prior to the issue of consciousness, but the same cannot be said for panpsychism.

Also, panpsychism is merely a label for, and not an explanation of, the phenomena to be explained. As Geoffrey Madell notes, "the sense that the mental and the physical are just inexplicably and gratuitously slapped together is hardly allayed by adopting . . . a pan-psychist . . . view of the mind, for [it does not] have an explanation to offer as to why or how mental properties cohere with physical."[28]

CONCLUSION

Prominent naturalist David Papineau admits that if the naturalist refuses to identify consciousness with strictly physical properties and, instead, admits the reality of consciousness as a range of commonsense mental properties correlated with physical properties, the naturalist is in trouble. "But then we still seem to face the question: *why* does consciousness emerge in just those cases? And to this question physicalists' 'theories of consciousness' seem to provide no answer."[29] Papineau's solution is to deny the reality of conscious-

---

[27]For a critique of panpsychism in the process of defending AC, see Stephen R. L. Clark, *From Athens to Jerusalem* (Oxford: Clarendon, 1984), pp. 121-57.

[28]Madell, *Mind and Materialism*, p. 3.

[29]Papineau, *Philosophical Naturalism*, p. 119.

ness as a genuinely mental phenomenon.[30]

Another prominent naturalist, Jaegwon Kim, has observed that "if a whole system of phenomena that are prima facie not among basic physical phenomena resists physical explanation, and especially if we don't even know where or how to begin, it would be time to reexamine one's physicalist commitments."[31] For Kim, genuinely nonphysical mental entities are the paradigm case of such a system of phenomena. Kim's advice to fellow naturalists is that they must simply admit the irreality of the mental and recognize that naturalism exacts a steep price and cannot be had on the cheap.[32] If feigning anesthesia—denying that consciousness construed along commonsense lines is real—is the price to be paid to retain naturalism, then the price is too high. Fortunately, the theistic argument from consciousness reminds us that it is a price that does not need to be paid.

---

[30]Ibid., pp. 106, 114-18, 120-21, 126.
[31]Kim, *Mind in a Physical World,* p. 96.
[32]Ibid., chap. 4, esp. pp. 118-20.

14

DAVID HUME AND A
CUMULATIVE CASE ARGUMENT

R. Douglas Geivett

☞

Early in his book *On the Existence and Nature of God,* Richard Gale acknowledges that "theism has found . . . a powerful new formulation" during the past few decades. The robustness of this new formulation suggests "a need for a return visit from Hume's Philo."[1] Gale is referring, of course, to the fictitious character who controls the conversation in Hume's *Dialogues Concerning Natural Religion,* and who (owing to his creator's genius) is supposed by many to have demolished the case for theism.[2] Hume makes only a few cameo appearances in Richard Gale's neo-Philonian enterprise. But Hume's spirit is present on nearly every page. In truth, Hume's spirit prevails among philosophers of atheistic and agnostic persuasion, and continues to haunt the ongoing dialogue—between educated believers and nonbelievers—about the possibility of rationally justified belief in God.

I'll argue that David Hume's challenge to natural theology is systematically misguided. This can be seen by considering the resilience of a care-

---

[1]Richard M. Gale, *On the Nature and Existence of God* (Cambridge: Cambridge University Press, 1991), p. 2.
[2]When I say that Philo controls the conversation, I don't mean to deny that Cleanthes is the presumed hero, as Norman Kemp Smith calls him, echoing Dugald Stewart. See Norman Kemp Smith's Introduction, in David Hume, *Dialogues Concerning Natural Religion,* ed. Norman Kemp Smith (Indianapolis: Bobbs-Merrill, 1947), pp. 58-59. Philo, most scholars agree, is Hume's own spokesman. Does Philo actually control the conversation? Yes, his presence dominates; much of what Cleanthes and Demea say in the dialogue rings hollow in comparison with Philo's contribution; Cleanthes speaks in generalities that tend to set things up for Philo; Philo consistently lures his interlocutors along a path of his own design (see Smith, Introduction, pp. 59 and 62. References to Hume's *Dialogues* are cited in the text by DNR and page number).

fully conceived cumulative case for theism. I'll sketch a cumulative case that exhibits the main structural relations between the components of the case. In due course it will emerge that the best case for theism is at the same time a strong case for a particular version of theism, namely, Christian theism.

HUME'S EVIDENTIALISM

Hume's challenge to natural theology is rooted in a basic principle of rationality that he expresses very simply: "A wise man . . . proportions his belief to the evidence."[3] This stipulation is stated in the context of Hume's appraisal of miracles. But it clearly governs his reflections on the rationality of religious belief generally. Hume's requirement is a version of evidentialism. Evidentialism holds that, for any belief to be justified, it must be grounded in adequate evidence. Thus, if belief in God is justified, there must be adequate evidence for the existence of God.

Hume's own version of evidentialism requires *proportionality* of belief to evidence. It is not entirely clear what this is supposed to mean. What is clear is that Hume insists that religious belief is not rational unless it is grounded in adequate evidence. In his writings on religion, he argues that belief in God does not satisfy this requirement.

There are various ways to respond to this sort of claim. Perhaps Hume's requirement is illicit. What if belief in God could be rational even if it is not grounded in adequate evidence? Hume's particular conception of evidence may be skewed. Suppose there is a more satisfactory conception of evidence; maybe the case for theism fares better under some other more plausible conception. It could be that Hume's alleged refutations of specific arguments for the existence of God can be rebutted. Or it could be that there are powerful new arguments that Hume did not address in his critique of theism. Each of these strategies has been adopted, and each may have merit.

My response here pursues a different course. I'll argue that Hume failed to consider an important dimension of evidential support for a general metaphysical hypothesis like theism. I refer to the structural framework into which the totality of evidence may be fitted for the purpose of showing that belief in God is justified. Hume's critique of theism is piecemeal. Like so

---

[3]This stipulation occurs early in section 10, "Of Miracles," in David Hume's *Enquiry Concerning Human Understanding*. In this chapter, all citations of Hume's *Enquiry* are from the 1777 edition edited by L. A. Selby-Bigge and reprinted in a 3rd edition with textual revisions and notes by P. H. Nidditch (Oxford: Clarendon, 1978). "Of Miracles" is on pp. 109-31 of this edition.

many other opponents of theism, he tends to isolate individual evidential components in the case for theism, impose an inordinate evidential burden on each component, and then conclude that each component withers under such searching scrutiny. Many of these individual components, I think, promise to be more viable and quite strong relative to more modest conclusions featured at various stages of a carefully organized cumulative case for theism. In my response to Hume, I'll concentrate on his most important contribution to the philosophy of religion, his *Dialogues Concerning Natural Religion.*

THEISM? OR CHRISTIAN THEISM?

Hume's *Dialogues* are not explicitly concerned with the rational appraisal of *Christian* theism in particular. But the cumulative case to be developed in this chapter is a case for Christian theism. Am I being opportunistic here? Am I using a critique of Hume as a foil for proselytizing on behalf of Christianity? I don't think so. But then what am I up to? Why not show how a cumulative case may be made for God's existence, demonstrate its viability in relation to Hume's criticisms of traditional natural theology, and be done with it? Why bring Christianity into the picture when we're simply assessing Hume's critique of natural theology?

Let's keep in mind that Hume was writing for an audience more familiar with Christian theism than with any other variety of theism. The tradition of "natural religion" that he challenges is none other than the tradition of Christian natural theology. The arguments and positions expounded and opposed by Hume in the *Dialogues* are predominantly those of Hume's Christian contemporaries and their forbears.[4] Clues appear here and there throughout the *Dialogues* that it is the theism of Christians that Hume has taken to task.

But isn't the theism of Christians pretty much the same thing as the theism of Jews and Muslims? Aren't the three great monotheistic religions of the world, Judaism, Christianity and Islam, alike in worshiping the same God? And even if these three traditions differ on the question of special divine revelation—the Hebrew Scriptures of Judaism, the Old and New Testaments of Christianity, and the Qur'an of Islam—aren't all three "Abrahamic faiths," agreeable in their identification of God as "the Father of Abraham, Isaac and Jacob"?

---

[4]Qualification: Hume does not name these figures, nor is he always clearly scrutinizing a specific argument known to have been sponsored by a particular Christian intellectual.

These are interesting questions. A full answer has two parts. First, identity of potentially plural entities is not a function of whether they have certain properties in common but of whether they have all properties in common. So even if three monotheistic traditions agree that God has certain essential attributes, such as omnipotence, omniscience and moral perfection, this does not entail that the monotheism of each of the three refers to the same God. Each of the three traditions might attribute to God some essential property that neither of the other two traditions attributes to God. That would be sufficient for denying identity, and hence for denying that Jews, Christians and Muslims all worship the same God.

Certainly, one and the same experienced entity may be differently conceptualized. Alternative monotheistic traditions may conceptualize God in irreconcilable ways. Judaism, Christianity and Islam are, to a significant degree, defined by their respective conceptions of the Godhead. This is indicated, for example, when Muslim scholars object to Christianity on the grounds that its Trinitarianism entails the denial of monotheism. Is Islam essentially anti-Trinitarian? I think so. Is Christianity essentially Trinitarian? I believe it is. This sort of disparity doesn't hold with respect to Christianity vis-à-vis historic Judaism.

Even nonmonotheistic religions may describe the same object of experience, call it "the Transcendent," in still other ways. They may all be conceptualizing one and the same Reality. But identity conditions for sameness of entity within alternative theologies would not be satisfied. In short, there are two ways to apply the principle of identity in this context, one with respect to the entity as experienced, and the other with respect to the entity as conceptualized within a systematic theology.

Second, the Bible adopts a familiar locution when referring to the particularity of God, in relation to gods others believe in and worship. The locution is used to express particularity by referring to "the God of so-and-so"— of Abraham, Isaac and Jacob, for example. In this way, the fuller content of God's nature, as understood by these prominent figures of the faith, can be picked out in a simple convention of linguistic reference. Following this practice, Christians might say they believe in and worship "the God of Abraham, Isaac, Jacob and Jesus." This locution particularizes the reference to God in at least two ways. First, it identifies Jesus, along with Abraham and Isaac and Jacob, as a primary representative of God to his people. Second, it implies an extension of what can be said about God on the basis of the content of Jesus' own belief and teaching about God.

More to the point of this chapter, however, there is another reason for distinguishing between the theism of Christianity on the one hand and the theisms of Judaism and Islam on the other hand. The evidence concerning the identity and mission of Jesus brings into clearer focus the nature of God. Furthermore—and this is the critical point—it also enriches the case for theism.

If I'm right about this, a Christian theist responding to Hume should make the cumulative case for theism a case for Christian theism and not for some merely generic theism. As I hope to show, "generic theism" is an unstable hypothesis that threatens either to collapse into deism or to flower into something more particular and better confirmed, into a conception of theism enriched by the content of special revelation. For our purposes, the emphasis is on *better confirmed*. A theism without the particularity provided by a revelation is infirm in more than one respect. Its conclusion—that God exists—is truncated and anticlimactic. And its support is weaker than it would be if accompanied by the special evidences of Christianity. All this I hope to make clear in outline form in what follows.

Sketch of a Cumulative Case

Since this is a cumulative case argument with a logical progression that is more or less linear, it will be helpful to sketch the case as a series of steps or stages. This is artificial in three respects. While the progression to be described is logical, it need not be presented in concrete situations of witness and apologetics in such a lifeless series of steps. Also, my enumeration of individual steps is somewhat arbitrary, since each step groups together a number of points, subarguments and other elements. These elements are, however, grouped together for a reason. This grouping reflects a unit of material or a sort of complete component in the total cumulative case. Finally, each step could certainly be developed more fully than is possible here. Each step could probably be developed indefinitely, as our knowledge of the human situation grows, as we learn more about the physical universe, as the implications of the case so far developed become better understood, and so forth. But what can be pieced together on the basis of evidence now available is sufficiently rich and evidentially strong to constitute an adequate case for the truth of Christian theism. This sketch is a kind of tour of highlights in a cumulative case.

My enumeration has eight steps. The following summary describes each step in terms of the evidence that is relevant and how it is related to the immediately adjacent step or steps.

Step one: Cosmological evidence. Scientific and philosophical evidences converge in support of the conclusion that the universe had a beginning.[5] The effort to make intelligible sense of this phenomenon leads to the inference that the universe was caused to exist by a personal being of great power and intelligence. Since the beginning of the universe is an event, as such it has a cause. But the cause of the beginning of the universe could not be some previously occurring event since the beginning of the universe is the first event in the series of events making up the total history of the universe. If the beginning of the universe has a cause, but that cause was not an event, then it must be an agent. And this agent must have sufficient power, intelligence and motive for bringing into existence a universe such as ours.

We should pause to consider why this is a particularly fitting place to begin a cumulative case for theism. The physical universe is the theater of human existence. We live our lives within a physical context that conditions the form our lives can take. The meaning of our existence is tied to our embodiedness and to the connection we have to the physical environment in which we live. This must be a major reason why the worldview of materialism has tempted so many great minds, past and present. In an effort to understand humanity and the human condition, it makes sense to examine the nature of the physical backdrop of the human situation, and especially the evidence of cosmology.

This choice of starting point is also fitting because it takes us back to the beginning of literally everything that has a beginning, and yet it does so without sending us on a detour away from the quest for a plausible cumulative case for theism. While the conclusion so far reached does not yet count as a full-blown theism, as it is stated in the above summary, an agent of sufficient power and intelligence to act effectually with the express purpose of bringing a universe into existence out of nothing is a strong candidate for deity. We may not be able to tell that the power required to create such a universe must be on the scale of omnipotence, nor be able to deter-

---

[5]This claim has been developed and supported by a number of Christian philosophers. For my own elaboration of the argument, see Geivett, *Evil and the Evidence for God* (Philadelphia: Temple University Press, 1993), pp. 99-122; "The *Kalam* Cosmological Argument," in *To Everyone an Answer,* ed. Francis J. Beckwith, William Lane Craig and J. P. Moreland (Downers Grove, Ill.: InterVarsity Press, 2004), pp. 61-76; and "Reflections on the Explanatory Power of Theism," in *Does God Exist? The Craig-Flew Debate,* ed. Stan W. Wallace (Aldershot, U.K.: Ashgate, 2003), pp. 51-52. See also chapter 7 of the present volume, by Garrett J. DeWeese and Joshua Rasmussen.

mine that the intelligence required must rise to the level of omniscience.[6] But the degree of each that is required is well nigh unimaginable. And their coexistence and exercise for the supposed purpose of creating our universe may entail that this agent has other properties, properties that theism ascribes to God.

At any rate, the agent described in the conclusion at step one is a candidate for deity, and, so far as we can tell, has properties compatible with being the God of theism and no properties incompatible with being the God of theism. Admittedly, this is a more modest conclusion than the conclusion normally associated with a cosmological argument for the existence of God. But this is a virtue of a cumulative case for theism. Critics of natural theology often complain that this or that argument does not yield the intended conclusion, namely, that God exists.[7] Instead, they add, the argument permits only a more modest conclusion, such as the one I've drawn here in step one. It is puzzling that some critics who argue in this way do not accept even the weaker conclusion.[8]

Step two: Design evidence. With the conclusion of step one in the background (i.e., the universe owes its existence to an extranatural personal agent of great power and intelligence), we proceed naturally to contemplate what is often called "the evidence of design" in the universe. At step one, the initial evidence is merely that the universe had a beginning, that it has the property of being temporally finite. But a fuller description of salient features of the universe will sooner or later refer to a multitude of complexities manifest at every level of observation, whether with the naked eye or with the aid of the telescope, the microscope or some other device to assist empirical observation. These other properties of the universe redound to the credit of the originator of the universe and bespeak an intelligence and a purpose stretching beyond the limits drawn in step one.

It would be a remarkable stroke of good luck—for us, at least—if the creator, intent on creating a different sort of thing or just experimenting wildly with the possibilities, accidentally caused a physical environment like ours

---

[6]However, see chapter 6 of the current volume, by Douglas Groothuis.

[7]For a rebuttal of this objection, see chapter 5 of the current volume, by James F. Sennett.

[8]Readers might be surprised to hear that two prominent atheists have confided to me that they do accept the more modest conclusion on the grounds I have offered in step one. Respect for confidentiality prevents me from giving their names. But this concession, I believe, confirms the wisdom of the strategy I'm outlining here. Conversion often takes place in stages, and it helps if there are gradual stages for one to convert to along the way toward the climactic one that represents the greatest departure from where one began.

to exist. It is especially remarkable that our universe is so conducive to the physical flourishing of human persons and other living organisms. This is indicated by the fine-tuning of the universe and the earth's biosphere, as well as the complexity-linked-to-function of physical organisms.[9] All this suggests that if that sort of universe was brought into existence by a being of sufficient power and intelligence to do so, it must have been for a reason. Presumably, our creator has a plan and is good at what he does.

Even the most entrenched naturalists allow that the universe has the appearance of design;[10] what they don't allow is that this phenomenon can best be explained in terms of the activity of a divine designer. The reason for this, I believe, is that they are naturalists first. They don't come to their naturalism because they can provide some naturalistic explanation for the wonders of our intergalactic neighborhood. But when they are confronted with the evidence of design, their naturalism forces them to strain the evidence through a reductive filter. Thus, while naturalists often express some admiration for the design argument for the existence of God, in the end they conclude that this argument simply does not justify the conclusion that God exists.

Naturalists firmly believe that design features of the universe can be explained in terms of the laws of nature. Never mind that these laws are themselves in need of explanation since they behave in such an orderly way, are not in place at the origin of the universe, and play no role in determining the initial conditions of the universe. So perhaps the design argument, as a stand-alone argument for the existence of God, can be defended against the reductive efforts of naturalists to explain away the impressive appearance of design.[11]

But our cumulative case argument suggests a different sort of response. Notice how we are led to contemplate the evidence of design, and recall what we already have good reason to believe when we behold the spectacular grandeur of the universe. With apologies to the resolute naturalist, toiling away with his reductive project, we find our universe to be "ontologi-

---

[9]See chapter 9 of the present volume, by Robin Collins.

[10]One thinks, for example, of Richard Dawkins. See his bestselling book, *The Blind Watchmaker* (London: Longman, 1986; London: Penguin, 2000). The *Dialogues* show that Hume also allowed that there is an impressive degree of order in the universe. But Hume was probably not a naturalist.

[11]See Richard Swinburne's approach in his essay "The Argument from Design," reprinted in *Contemporary Perspectives on Religious Epistemology*, ed. R. Douglas Geivett and Brendan Sweetman (New York: Oxford University Press, 1992), pp. 201-11.

cally haunted" by the fact that it was caused to exist by an extranatural agent.[12] This alone gives us every reason we could realistically require for thinking that what looks like design is design. Gone is the motive to demand a naturalistic account of design that isn't design. In its place is a powerful incentive to acknowledge that there is design and to attribute this design to the very agent who brought the universe into existence in the first place.

So far I have only referred to the design we encounter in the physical universe. But the evidence of design goes beyond the data of the physical universe. It includes the data of human consciousness and of human moral experience.[13] Consciousness has a structure. Morality has an order. The psychophysical unity of moral agents involves the interaction of physical and nonphysical states for ends that have moral significance. This also attests to the realization of a purpose-driven design plan that is never utilized as a datum in traditional moral arguments for the existence of God or standard ways of arguing for the existence of God from consciousness. In the cumulative case described in this chapter, there is a progression within step two from one expression of design to another until we reach a structured unity whose design is remarkable in its own right and which cannot be captured by any single traditional argument for the existence of God.

Confronted with this additional evidence of design, naturalists have launched a truly ambitious research program. They are busily pursuing the ultimate physicalist explanation for the phenomena of mind. We can be sure they haven't come to their naturalism on the basis of a plausible naturalistic explanation of these phenomena, since the vision of a complete "science of the mind" has yet to be realized. In fact, some naturalists have lost hope of ever doing so and have embraced what Colin McGinn, himself a naturalist, calls "mysterianism" about the mind.[14]

The manifestations of design referred to in this step cannot be fully described on this occasion. But it should be clear that the evidence of design is extensive and multifaceted. The thing to notice especially is that, at this stage, we have more evidence for the existence of a being of great power

---

[12]The universe was first described as "ontologically haunted" by my teacher and friend Dallas Willard in "The Three-Stage Argument for the Existence of God," in *Contemporary Perspectives on Religious Epistemology,* ed. R. Douglas Geivett and Brendan Sweetman (New York: Oxford University Press, 1992), p. 216.

[13]For one type of argument from consciousness, see chapter 13 of the present volume by J. P. Moreland. On the moral argument, see chapter 10 by Paul Copan.

[14]Colin McGinn, *The Mysterious Flame: Conscious Minds in a Material World* (New York: Basic Books, 1999).

and intelligence, and at the same time have the basis for making additional inferences about this agent. If causing the universe to begin to exist suggests intelligent purpose, how much more so the arrangement of the physical structure of the universe into a fit habitat for humanity and other living organisms? At the very least, the creator seems to have had a reason to arrange for the existence of creatures such as ourselves. We should wonder why.

We now have a working hypothesis, with strong initial support, that there is purpose to human existence that is linked to the creator's own intentions. As it happens, we also have the wherewithal to test this hypothesis against other data to be considered in subsequent steps.

Step three: The human condition. The exploration of design in step two presented us with evidence pertaining to the human situation. Now that it has come to that, it is appropriate to develop a realistic description of the human condition and to get into focus those aspects that are most relevant to the question of God's existence. An honest description, it must be admitted, is a mixed bag of positive and negative aspects. At this stage, we pay special attention to the negative aspects of the human situation, since these, in combination with the results of steps one and two, lead us directly to step four.

A full description of the human condition will refer to such things as moral failure and moral confusion, undeserved physical and mental suffering, mortality, uncertainty about an afterlife, the quest for personal meaning, alienation (from self, others and our creator), dashed hopes and dreams, and so forth. These features of human experience must be set alongside the impressive dimensions of human life that indicate an incredibly intricate design plan. This can't be done without feeling a certain tension, genuine perplexity about what this design plan might be if the world of human experience is such a mixed bag of goods and evils. The whole point of step three is to get this tension into focus, so that at step four we are prepared to ask a question of pivotal significance in the cumulative case for theism.

Step four: The need for revelation. What exactly does the creator have in mind? Is the downside of human existence an indication that the conclusion developed in steps one and two is a sham? Or does it suggest that the creator's purposes are sinister? Is our creator a "cosmic killjoy"? Has the creator purposefully set us up for disappointment, despair and resentment? These are possibilities. But they aren't the only possibilities. Nor are they the most desirable possibilities. Thankfully, they aren't the most reasonable possibilities either.

One might say that, if the foregoing evidence (evidence about the creator and designer of the universe, on the one hand, and evidence concerning the human predicament on the other hand) is all the evidence we have, then we should conclude that our creator is unworthy of our faith, loyalty and affection. Arguably that would be enough to disqualify the creator's claim to be God.[15] In a more charitable mood, we might exonerate the creator by attributing less power to the creator than we first thought appropriate. In that case, we might suppose that the creator is remote or aloof, not so much unconcerned as unaware of our plight.

But the evidence so far considered does not really justify any of these conclusions. If the evidences of earlier steps are all that we have, then perhaps we should remain agnostic about whether the creator is ultimately worthy of our commitment and worship. After all, it's *possible* that the creator has some ultimate purpose that is both good and consistent with the downside of human experience, but that we simply don't know what that purpose is. It's *possible* that the creator has provided a remedy for the human predicament, a remedy that has not turned up as such in any of the evidence *so far considered*.

Come to think of it, how could we perceive a remedy without first recognizing the need for one? But for most people, recognizing the need for a remedy is not going to be enough to support the conviction that there must be one. On the other hand, we might hope for one. And the ingenuity of the creator displayed in various ways set forth at earlier stages of our case should give us some hope that a remedy has been devised. Or perhaps we should say that the attributes of the creator surfaced at earlier stages encourage in us the expectation that a remedy exists.

It is at least as reasonable to suppose that the creator does have a plan for solving the problems of humanity as it is to suppose that the creator does not have such a plan. And it may turn out to be more reasonable to believe that the creator has a plan if we can devise a way to confirm the existence of such a plan. A revelation from God would be a helpful aid in our quest. Is that too much to ask?

Step three left us with a question: Is the creator on our side or even aware of our predicament and able to do something about it? By bringing this question explicitly before our minds in step four, we establish some basis for ex-

---

[15]For a helpful discussion of this point, see Jordan Howard Sobel, *Logic and Theism: Arguments For and Against Beliefs in God* (Cambridge: Cambridge University Press, 2004), pp. 9-11.

pecting the creator to intervene on our behalf, to set things straight. This expectation awaits confirmation by means that would lead on to other stages
in a cumulative case for God's existence.

Again, step three is stage-setting. In effect, it generates a question. That
question resolves itself into an expectation. And that expectation awaits confirmation. It is with step four that we come to realize this. So now we must
ask, how would the availability of a remedy be confirmed to us? That brings
us to step five.

Step five: The arena of religious traditions. If the human situation,
described in step three, indicates our need for a remedy prescribed by
our creator, and if, as we are led to expect by the evidence concerning
the creator at steps one and two, the creator has produced a remedy, then
it is to be expected that this would be manifest within the arena of human
experience in some way. This is the arena of religious belief and practice.
So the hypothesis that our creator has arranged for the human situation
to be healed may well be tested by examining appropriate religious perspectives. By "appropriate" I mean perspectives consistent with what we
have already understood to be the creator's nature and relation to the universe.

Suppose the creator has all the properties needed to explain all the phenomena so far considered. (This supposition is grounded in evidence developed in steps one and two.) And suppose the creator has prescribed a remedy for the human predicament. This supposition is our hypothesis, which
we seek to confirm or disconfirm. We have the basis by now for supposing
that confirmation of our expectation, generated in step four, will be found
in one of the great theistic traditions of the world.

It happens, perhaps not so coincidentally, that these three religious traditions—Judaism, Christianity, and Islam—all maintain that God has produced
a revelation. We should wonder whether any such revelation claim addresses precisely the expectation that has been generated in step four. Our
cumulative strategy has yielded a convenient means of narrowing the field
of religious options to those that are theistic.[16] The framework of each theistic tradition presents us with the means of conducting our search for confirmation.

In the next step we conduct this search. What do we find?

---

[16]If we fail in our quest to confirm the existence of God as described in theism, we may have
to return to the drawing board.

Step six: The evidence of miracles. Each of the theistic religions endorses a particular revelation claim. Jews historically affirm the divine authority of the Hebrew Scriptures. Christians claim that the Bible (Old and
New Testaments) is inspired by God. Muslims assert that the Qur'an is the
word of Allah. It is within their respective revelation claims that we are most
likely to discover confirming evidence for the hypothesis of a divine remedy
generated in step four. Or if not that, then clues to confirming evidence.
These distinct revelation claims might be compared, then, to see whether
any one of them emerges as the one that most adequately fulfills our expectation. We should also want to know whether a particular theistic tradition
enjoys superior evidential support.

It would be possible to examine each tradition simultaneously, one
alongside the others. This exercise is rendered more realistic now than ever
before by the close proximity of these religions to one another in our day
and by the comparatively greater availability of sacred texts and orthodox
statements for each tradition. But our examination procedure might proceed
chronologically instead.

There is good reason for conducting our inquiry chronologically, as it
were. If humanity is in need of a word from God (our hypothesis being that
our creator is God and has produced a revelation), then it is reasonable to
expect some fairly strong evidence of God's provision to meet the needs of
the human condition. Since this condition has been characteristic of the human situation as far back as our collective consciousness can reach, we
should also expect God's revelation to go very far back in human history.
The tradition with the longest history is Judaism, followed by Christianity as
more recent and then by Islam as most recent. Not only is the tradition of
Judaism the oldest, but it goes back, as documented in its Scriptures, to
Abraham. In fact, its Scriptures indicate a lineage going as far back as the
beginning of time and the creation of humanity.

Whatever one makes of Judaism on its own terms, one would do well to
suspend judgment about its successful confirmation of our hypothesis until
after examining the claims of Christianity and Islam. There isn't space here
for a full investigation along these lines. But the present cumulative case is
a case for *Christian* theism. So I'll restrict my remarks to the fortunes of
Christianity on this point. It will soon become obvious that Christianity sets
a very high standard for evidence needed at this stage in the case.

Christianity claims to be continuous with Judaism. Judaism, as rooted in
the Hebrew Scriptures, is very much a religion of anticipation, of unfilled

expectation. Christianity is a religion of fulfilled expectation, with the prospect of more and better things to come. The arrangements for healing the human condition as described in the Hebrew Scriptures appear to be provisional and temporary, proleptic of something more ultimate and satisfactory. Christianity maintains that this Jewish expectation is fulfilled in the person and work of Jesus Christ.

At any rate, sooner or later during step six, however one regards the relationship between Christianity and Judaism, Christianity will come under direct examination. And when it does, something remarkable and unique in the world of religions is presented as a means of testing the truth of its claims. Christianity purports to be evidentially grounded in a historical event, the resurrection of Jesus Christ. Such an event would, if it happened, be about the best candidate for a miracle one could imagine.

Historical support for the resurrection of Jesus would go a long way toward corroborating the claims of Christianity. For if it really happened, then it would seem that God—who alone may act in violation of the laws of nature—had something to do with it. And if God caused the miracle of the resurrection of Jesus, this would be evidence of God's endorsement of Jesus and his teaching.

In this stage-six examination of Christianity, several things come together at once.

First, at the heart of Christianity is a clear account of God's provision of a remedy. The Christian story, rooted in the New Testament and in deliberate connection with the Old Testament tradition, is a story of restoration of humanity by means of re-creation.

Second, this remedy is tied to the events leading up to and including the death of Jesus Christ, which in turn is directly associated with the most dramatic confirmation of Jesus' message, namely, his resurrection. The background evidence generated at stages one and two will prove relevant in our evaluation of the available evidence for the resurrection.[17]

Third, the occurrence of a miracle of this sort—supernatural if anything is, and so closely linked with the heart of the Christian message about human restoration—is new evidence for the existence of God. While this evidence may not be sufficient by itself to justify belief in God, it is new evi-

---

[17]See R. Douglas Geivett, "The Evidential Value of Miracles," in *In Defense of Miracles*, ed. R. Douglas Geivett and Gary R. Habermas (Downers Grove, Ill.: InterVarsity Press, 1997), pp. 178-95.

dence that tends to confirm the hypothesis of God's existence.[18]

Fourth, earlier evidence for the existence of a creator led to our expectation that some remedy for the human condition would turn up under this creator's initiative. If this expectation is fulfilled, then that, too, is an independent form of confirmation of the existence of just such a creator. The hypothesis of a creator was already strongly confirmed by stage one and stage two evidence. That evidence also supported the expectation of a remedy for the human condition. This expectation translated into a novel hypothesis: that the creator would provide a much-needed remedy and thus be worthy of human loyalty, affection and worship. The confirmation of this hypothesis would enrich our conception of the creator and at the same time increase the confirmation that had already emerged at earlier stages. The idea here is that the hypothesis of God's existence is initially confirmed to a strong degree by the evidence of steps one and two, that this hypothesis generated something tantamount to a prediction, and that the fulfillment of this prediction counts as new confirmation of the original hypothesis.

Of course, the availability of a revelation claim—in this case, the Old and New Testaments—could very well enrich our knowledge of the creator's nature and purposes. Such a revelation could thus be a source of evidence for theism.

Now none of this would be any more than a pipe dream if there were not sufficient evidence that the resurrection of Jesus actually happened. So step six must also include a development of the evidence for the resurrection. Such evidence consists especially in the fact that the early Christians came to believe with great conviction that Jesus was raised bodily from the dead. They believed this to be so on the basis of evidence they had: Jesus' tomb was found empty on the third day following his crucifixion, and he was seen alive again by numerous sane individuals who would have no difficulty recognizing Jesus.

How strong must this evidence be? It should be strong enough by historical standards to justify the conviction that the alleged historical events did take place. This does not mean that the case for the resurrection stands or falls on the historical evidence alone. Again, the theism indicated by the evidence that brought us to this point plays a valuable role. First, the conclu-

---

[18]I'm not here passing judgment on the claim that an argument for theism from miracles goes through on its own. I've explored that question in two other places; see "Evidential Value of Miracles," and pp. 56-59 in "Reflections on the Explanatory Power of Theism."

sion reached by the end of step two underwrites the *possibility* of miracles.[19] But by the time we come to step six, our hypothesis makes it *probable* that a miracle would take place as the most decisive corroboration that God's own remedy is truly his own and not a counterfeit.

Under normal conditions, historians can ignore these sorts of background considerations. Much of their work (but certainly not all of it[20]) is reliable whether they are naturalists or not. Metaphysical commitments make a difference to historical results. But I don't need a theist to tell me when and where Lincoln delivered the Gettysburg Address. In the case of the resurrection, though, conditions are not "normal." In this sort of case, one should not investigate the evidence within a metaphysical vacuum. A historian working from a position of metaphysical neutrality may get skewed results. A historian operating from a naturalistic commitment most certainly will.

Nevertheless, the evidence for the resurrection depends on conditions—an empty tomb, Jesus sightings and the remarkably uniform convictions of the earliest Christians—that can in principle be confirmed by historical investigation. Unfortunately, skeptical historians, theologians and philosophers stipulate standards of evidence here that are not required for comparable events or physical states. That is, after all, what we are talking about in the case of the empty tomb of Jesus and his postresurrection appearances to others. The only wrinkle is that the actual occurrence of these events, given the occurrence of certain other events—for example, the crucifixion of Jesus, equally well-attested historically—implies that a miracle occurred. But the earlier evidence of steps one and two in support of the theistic hypothesis greatly reduces the burden placed on historical evidence. On the evidence, the God of our theistic hypothesis has the power, ingenuity and motive to produce a miracle, both as the guarantee of the success of his intended remedy for the human condition and as evidence that this was his own remedy and not some counterfeit.[21]

---

[19]For my extended discussion of the possibility of miracles, see "Why I Believe in the Possibility of Miracles," in *Why I Am a Christian*, ed. Norman L. Geisler and Paul K. Hoffman (Grand Rapids: Baker, 2001), pp. 97-110.

[20]If the theism of our cumulative case is true, then a personal God who is actively interested in the human condition—as indicated by the resurrection, no less!—may well be much more of an agent in the historical process than most historians (naturalists and supernaturalists) have yet contemplated. Just to ensure the timely occurrence of the life of Jesus and his resurrection would take quite a lot of hands-on engagement with the historical process. But God's hand in the process may be discernible in any number of unexpected places, once historians have worked out a suitable "providentialist" conception of their discipline.

[21]Again, see Geivett, "Evidential Value of Miracles."

One might think that the cumulative case for God's existence has come to a fitting conclusion with the sort of confirmation produced at stage six. But it turns out there is more.

Step seven: Making the truth believable. Anyone who has reviewed the above sort of case and found it to be cogent may still find it difficult to believe. This difficulty, as Blaise Pascal suggested in the *Pensées,* has less to do with evidence and more to do with one's passional state in relation to evidence and the conclusion to which it points. Belief and disbelief have the aspect of *habit.* Coming to believe that Christian theism is true when one did not believe it for a prolonged period of time is tantamount to overcoming a long-established habit—call it a habit of belief. This reality produces a certain amount of inertia that evidence alone cannot cure.

The evidence developed in steps one through six can alert one to the need to "kick the habit" of disbelief. As with any habit one wishes to overcome, simple actions practiced on a regular basis can be an invaluable aid. And so it is with belief in God for anyone who has been in the habit of not believing in God.

Step seven addresses the means of overcoming the habit of disbelief by recommending what may be called a "devotional experiment." Armed with the hypothesis of Christian theism and all the weighty accumulated evidence in its favor, the would-be believer engages in an experiment. This person considers what it would mean, in terms of practical decisions and activities, for him or her to be a true believer. The person then seeks to orient his or her life in that way. The example and assistance of true believers will be a great aid at this stage.[22]

There's much to say in favor of this notion and about how to conduct such an experiment. The main thing to observe at this point is that such a practice often leads to bona fide belief in God. Sometimes it does so without fanfare. Sometimes the experiment culminates in a belief that is attended by a dramatic religious experience of some sort. In any case, there is often an experiential component that signals the achievement of reconciliation with God. It is within the laboratory of our own life at this stage that we may discover that our souls are so large that finite goods cannot fulfill our deepest

---

[22]See Carolyn Franks Davis, "The Devotional Experiment," *Religious Studies* 22 (March 1986): 15-28; Franks Davis, *The Evidential Force of Religious Experience* (Oxford: Clarendon, 1989); and my related article, "A Pascalian Rejoinder to the Presumption of Atheism," in *God Matters: Readings in the Philosophy of Religion,* ed. Raymond Martin and Christopher Bernard (New York: Longman, 2003), pp. 162-75.

IN DEFENSE OF NATURAL THEOLOGY

aspirations for happiness and peace.

Step eight: Religious experience. Experience of God deserves separate consideration in the final stage of this cumulative case for theism. While religious experience is sometimes offered as one of several supports for the claim that God exists, I believe an appeal to religious experience is often more persuasive within a context that has been prepared by earlier steps in this cumulative case. A person without the benefit of a thoroughly developed systematic case for the existence of God might well come to believe in God on the basis of a direct awareness of God. But for many Westerners today, both the opportunity and the need for prior preparation is very real.

For one thing, many are skeptical about the value of religious experience because they suppose that an experience of this type is conditioned by beliefs a person already has when the experience takes place. If a person has beliefs that are consistent with the idea of direct experience of God, then that person will tend naturally to frame his or her experiences in terms of those beliefs. An experience will be judged to be a genuine experience of God by those who have beliefs that enable them to make sense of their experience in those terms.

The cumulative case sketched here addresses this concern by exhibiting the rationality of such *framework beliefs* in advance of presenting the data of religious experience. Suppose it's true that an individual's experience is often interpreted in terms of that individual's conceptual framework. It may still be legitimate to regard that experience as an experience of God if the conceptual framework of theism is judged on independent grounds to be reasonable. A cumulative case for theism is sensitive to this when it introduces the "evidence" of religious experience as the culmination of the case for theism.[23]

In addition, the earlier stages in the cumulative case may be needed to prepare a person for religious experience. It may be that there is only a very low probability that a person will ever "experience God"—such that the person can recognize it as such—so long as that person adopts the attitude and

---

[23]Contrarian approaches to the data of religious experience have an equal opportunity to ground their assessments of that data in an independently supported conceptual framework. For example, one who favors a naturalistic explanation for the data of religious experience should have strong independent grounds for believing that naturalism is true. For a more developed account of the evidence of religious experience, see my chapter "The Evidential Value of Religious Experience," in *The Rationality of Theism,* ed. Paul Copan and Paul K. Moser (London and New York: Routledge, 2003), pp. 175-203, and the more concise comments in Geivett, "Reflections on the Explanatory Power of Theism," pp. 59-61.

behavioral stance of a resolute skeptic. But if this person can be persuaded to practice the sort of devotional experiment recommended in step seven, then this will likely lead to a new passional state that is more open and less skeptical. Such openness would likely increase the probability of an experience that the person could recognize as an experience of God. A devotional experiment places a person in a more auspicious position to experience God. Furthermore, conducting this sort of experiment is intellectually responsible if the conceptual framework of theism is itself well-supported by the evidence. At any rate, with any such experience there is an increase in the confirmation of theism.

HUME'S MISTAKE

This concludes my sketch of a cumulative case for theism. As I said earlier, it is a case for Christian theism, not just for some generic theism. In one sense, it is more difficult to argue for generic theism than it is to argue for Christian theism. That is because the hypothesis of theism in its most generic form enjoys less overall support than Christian theism does. Generic theism depends for its support on what we might call "nonspecifying evidence," since it does not specify a particular version of theism and *may* be compatible with any of the three major versions of monotheism in the world today—Judaism, Christianity and Islam. This nonspecifying evidence may be strong enough to justify theistic belief. I don't wish to suggest that it isn't. But Christian theism is a version of theism, and if it can be supported by additional "specifying evidence," that then counts as confirmation of theism more generally. So a complete cumulative case for God's existence will incorporate all the relevant evidence for God's existence, even if it tends to specify theism more precisely as the evidence is accumulated.

On the other hand, the situation may not be as neat as all that. As I've noted in my sketch of a cumulative case, what I'm calling "generic theism" may itself generate a prediction and thus subject itself to disconfirmation if the prediction is not fulfilled. But the fulfillment of the prediction that would confirm generic theism may take the form of specifying evidence, so that the seeds of a developed and more specified theism (like Christian theism) lie latent within generic theism and the evidence for it.

So there is good reason to make the case for theism a case for Christian theism. We have the added reason, noted earlier, that David Hume sought to undermine the theism of his Christian contemporaries and perhaps to influence subsequent generations to settle for something less "dubious."[24] And this chapter appears in a book devoted to answering Hume.

We come, then, to an important point about Hume's critique of natural theology. In his writings on religion, Hume neglected the complex relations that hold among various theistic evidences, and this prevented him from seeing the real strength of support for theism. But Hume erred in another respect as well. He restricted the focus of his critique while at the same time drawing a conclusion intended to have wider application. Let me explain.

In Hume's *Dialogues Concerning Natural Religion,* the term "natural religion" apparently refers to what I have called generic theism, a theism that is neutral with respect to Judaism, Christianity, Islam or what have you. This generic theism is Hume's ostensible target. That is how things seem initially. And yet, Hume's term "natural religion" correlates with a practice adopted by evidentialist theologians and philosophers of Christian persuasion who incorporated the evidence for theism into their overall case for Christianity. That practice has been called "natural theology." These Christian thinkers weren't particularly interested in defending generic theism. But Hume evidently had it in mind that if he could undermine the case for theism developed within the parameters of natural theology, then the effect would apply to any version of theism, however specified, including Christian theism. This was an egregious mistake. More egregious still is the fact that Hume's mistake has been repeated by many of his successors.

Other contributors to this volume on Hume have addressed specific arguments for the existence of God and have argued that Hume failed to undermine the best samples of such arguments. My objective in this chapter is different from that. I wish to expose a flaw in Hume's general strategy. The most basic statement of this flaw is that Hume attacks a piecemeal approach to natural theology that is to some degree artificial, with the result that his attack is ineffective against a cumulative approach like the one I outlined in the previous section.

Hume's strategy is artificial for a number of reasons. He conflates arguments that are radically different in kind. He sometimes reformulates arguments in ways that make it difficult to identify actual historical proponents of the arguments. I haven't attempted to support these charges here. But a more fundamental way his strategy can be seen to be artificial is that it pre-

---

[24]Many commentators have concluded that Hume was a deist, not an atheist. See especially Smith, Introduction, pp. 25-44. I think Hume was at best a minimalist deist.

tends to restrict the scope of argument to the lineaments of "natural religion" while drawing conclusions about every sort of theism.

To be clear, Hume's strategy is ineffective for two reasons, both relating to the greater viability of a cumulative case than the sort of case he attacks. First, each argument he addresses is interpreted as a stand-alone argument for the existence of God. Thus, if any such argument falters, it can play no constructive role in the case for God's existence. If the resources of a particular argument cannot fulfill its ambitions as a full-fledged argument for the existence of God, then it is of no use at all. Second, by restricting his critique to arguments on behalf of a generic sort of theism, he neglects the value of arguments that tend rather to specify theism more precisely. In fact, he doesn't even consider them.

These two problems are directly related, and they derive from a single assumption. Hume assumed that a refutation of generic theism is a refutation of any sort of theism one might describe. It's easy enough to see how someone might initially think such a thing. The reasoning process might go as follows: "If Christian theism is true (or reasonable), then theism is true (or reasonable); thus, if theism is not true (or reasonable), then Christian theism is not true (or reasonable)." The first statement seems true and the second statement seems to follow by *modus tollens*.[25] So how could Hume be mistaken?

Hume is mistaken because, in effect, he equates the term "theism" in these statements with "generic theism," and he equates "generic theism" with something very different from generic theism as I have described it— something I'll call "nonspecified theism." For Hume, "theism" and "nonspecified theism" are equivalent. But this is mistaken. Nonspecified theism is a form of theism that rules out any form of theism that is more specified than generic theism. Nonspecified theism rules out such specified theisms as Judaism, Christianity and Islam.

Now, let's substitute "nonspecified theism" for "theism" in the above *modus tollens* argument: "If Christian theism is true (or reasonable), then nonspecified theism is true (or reasonable); thus, if nonspecified theism is not true (or reasonable), then Christian theism is not true (or reasonable)." Since this is an instance of *modus tollens,* the argument is valid. But it isn't sound because the first statement is false. Strictly speaking, Christian theism

---

[25]*Modus tollens* ("the way of denial") is the name given to the valid deductive argument form *If P, then Q; and Q is false; therefore P is false.*

and nonspecified theism are mutually exclusive. They are different versions of theism. Assuming that theism entails monotheism, if one version of monotheism is true then the other version is false. After all, Christian theism is a specified theism. And if a specified theism is true, then any nonspecified theism is false. So, if Christian theism is true, then a nonspecified theism is false.

On the other hand, generic theism, as I'm using the terminology here, is a component of Christian theism; it is the *theism component* of Christian theism. But there is more to Christian theism than there is to theism in the generic sense. This use of terms entails a difference between "generic theism" and "nonspecified theism." Generic theism—with an important proviso—leaves open the question whether this or that specified theism (Christian theism, for example) is true. (I'll come back to the proviso in a moment.) But nonspecified theism does not leave open this question. Nonspecified theism and specified theism are mutually exclusive.

Generic theism and nonspecified theism have the same content, in the sense that "God" is conceptualized in the same way in both. But I've invented the term "nonspecified theism" in order to draw attention to an important distinction. Nonspecified theism is reductive; it stipulates that generic theism is the whole story about God. Or, rather, that the specifically theistic content of generic theism is the whole story. But "generic theism" itself (and here the conventional use of the phrase is on my side) is open to the possibility of more particular specification. And I wish to emphasize that evidence for theism has a tendency to specify theism beyond the conceptual content of generic theism.

This brings me back to the above-mentioned proviso. Recall the structure of the argument in my sketch of a cumulative case. The evidences for theism developed in the first two steps, combined with data concerning the human condition elaborated in step three, generate an expectation that some more specified form of theism is true. In this sense, a generic theism is supported to some degree in the way intimated in steps one and two. But this theism has the potential of mutating into something more specific. The generic theism that enjoys some initial support at stages one and two comes to enjoy greater support by evidence exploited at later stages; at the same time, this initial form of theism emerges as a more specified variety of theism.

Why think that the theism attacked by Hume was not the generic theism he thought it was, but nonspecified theism as defined above? Because generic theism begs to be developed into a more specified theism, when it is supported in the right way by means of a cumulative case argument. And

Hume neglects this possibility.

Even if Hume had refuted nonspecified theism, he would not thereby have automatically refuted specified theism. His refutation of nonspecified theism would be effectual against a specified version of theism (like Christian theism) *only if* (a) the arguments for nonspecified theism attacked by Hume were required in the case for the specified version of theism in question or (b) the best evidence for theism indicates a nonspecified version.

Hume repudiated theism (construed as generic) in favor of what I call "minimalist deism." But why? His argument, as I understand it, is that his minimalist deism is more plausible than the hypothesis of theism (again, in the generic sense). Hume seems (though this may just be Philo being disingenuous) to allow that generic theism (which is considerably more conceptually rich than his own minimalist deism) is consistent with the evidence explored in the *Dialogues*. But he reasons that his minimalist deism provides a better explanation for the evidence than the explanation provided by generic theism. But notice, that's only on the evidence that he considers in the *Dialogues*. Hume's deistic God takes no interest in the human condition and has done nothing to ameliorate the human predicament. Hume has some evidence for this minimalist deism. But he hasn't taken into consideration all of the relevant evidence. That's partly because he restricts himself to evidence for the merely generic theism of so-called natural religion.

I want to say that—even on the evidence of the *Dialogues*—Hume's conclusion is premature. The evidence considered there is, as he seems to allow, consistent with the hypothesis of generic theism.[26] So let us suppose that the hypothesis of generic theism is true. Then, so far as the evidence presented in the *Dialogues* is concerned, that hypothesis "predicts" a specified theism that would also be accompanied by special evidences. These special evidences would confirm some specified version of theism. But they would also confirm the lineaments of generic theism in virtue of fulfilling the prediction generated by the hypothesis of generic theism.

Hume hasn't investigated the special evidences that would confirm a specified theism implied by a viable generic theism. His survey of the evidence is truncated. It is unavoidably so, given his narrow preoccupation with the theism of "natural religion." He stops short of examining all the evidence that is relevant to the confirmation of the hypothesis of theism. By

---

[26]For that matter, it is consistent with some specified theism that includes a revelation claim. See *Dialogue* 12. I deal with the relevant passage more directly in the next section.

developing a cumulative case for theism that incorporates special evidences, a new hypothesis—the hypothesis of *Christian* theism—comes into view. Hume's minimalist deism must then be compared with the new hypothesis of Christian theism, relative to the full panoply of evidence sketched in the cumulative case. Relative to that evidence, Humean minimalist deism looks much less probable than Christian theism—and so, much less probable than theism. Minimalist deism is not clearly more probable than generic theism, even on the evidence of Hume's *Dialogues,* precisely because of the predictive power of that evidence if we assume that generic theism is true. I've argued that an evidentially fleshed out generic theism predicts a specified theism. If the prediction is fulfilled, then specified theism provides a better overall explanation than minimalist deism.

There is some irony in Hume's emphasis on the evidential argument from evil against theism. For if the logical argument from evil fails and there is only the possibility of an evidential argument from evil against theism, then it is reasonable to conclude that theism is false *only if* it is reasonable to conclude that God does not have a morally sufficient reason for permitting the evils there are. But one is in no position to draw that conclusion without reflecting on additional evidence, including the special evidences for Christian theism.

I accuse Hume of attacking nonspecified theism, even though he apparently thinks he is attacking generic theism. This is because his evaluation of the relevant evidence for theism is halting. It's made-to-order as a case for minimalist deism. Except for one thing: there is another hypothesis, one that takes us beyond generic theism to a specified theism, and that is compatible with the evidence he considers. The evidence examined in the *Dialogues* more strongly supports the hypothesis of generic theism, on the assumption that it can be converted into a more specified theism that will be accompanied by novel evidence. The evidence of the *Dialogues,* then, is not wide enough in scope to justify commitment to minimalist deism.

Bear in mind that if two arguments have different conclusions, then they are different arguments, even if they have the same premises. To illustrate, let's take a straightforward argument that Socrates is mortal:

> If Socrates is a human being, then Socrates is mortal.
> Socrates is a human being.
> Therefore, Socrates is mortal.

Now consider the following argument, which has the same premises but a different conclusion:

> If Socrates is a human being, then Socrates is mortal.
> Socrates is a human being.
> Therefore, Socrates will die by poisoning.

The first argument is valid, but the second is not. The first is an argument that Socrates will die. The second is an argument that Socrates will die by poisoning. Socrates did die by poisoning, but that is neither here nor there. The second argument does not make a good case for the fact that Socrates would die by poisoning. Different premises would be needed to justify that conclusion. On the other hand, the premises in these two arguments serve perfectly well as support for the conclusion in the first argument: Socrates is mortal.

Similarly, a theistic argument that isn't viable as a stand-alone argument for the existence of God may be a perfectly good argument for a more modest conclusion. And that argument might have an important function in a cumulative case for the existence of God. A conclusion might be "more modest" in one of two respects. It might be that there is some lower degree of probability that God exists. Or it might be that some being exists that could be God but also may not be God. In that case, additional arguments would be needed to draw the conclusion that this being is God.

HUME AND THE CUMULATIVE CASE ARGUMENT

I have argued that Hume's general strategy against natural theology is systematically misguided. It's time now to look more closely at particular Humean criticisms and ask how the cumulative case I've sketched holds up in response to these criticisms.[27]

Cosmological evidence. The argument I sketched in stage one of my cumulative case for theism may appear to be a cosmological argument for the existence of God. Certainly, that argument does make use of evidence featured in a version of the cosmological argument for the existence of God. But as used in step one, the cosmological evidence may be construed in one of two ways: as an argument that supports the hypothesis of theism to some degree of probability that perhaps needs buttressing by means of other arguments at later stages in the case, or as an argument that supports a part

---

[27]I regret that there isn't space here to deal more fully with each of these points, and especially the evidence of evil. Other sources referenced elsewhere in the notes for this chapter deal more extensively with specific points considered in this part of the chapter. See especially Geivett, *Evil and the Evidence for God.*

of theism, but not the whole, namely, that there is a being of great power and intelligence that may happen to have all the properties required for it to be God. In either case, it does not purport to be a stand-alone argument for theism that by itself fully justifies the theistic hypothesis.

What does Hume have to say about this argument? Not much of anything. The stage-one argument makes a posteriori use of cosmological evidence for a measured conclusion. The only thing resembling a cosmological argument in Hume's *Dialogues* is an argument introduced by Demea, who is a dubious advocate of natural theology, to say the least. His argument, which appears in part 9, is cast as an a priori argument for the necessity of God's existence.[28] Hume showed little interest in cosmological arguments. His fundamental objection is inspired by his general theory of causation, which is radically skeptical. Unfortunately, there isn't space here to deal with Hume's theory of causality.[29]

Design evidence. In contrast to Hume's insouciance towards cosmological evidence, he was almost obsessed with the evidence of design—the sort of evidence featured in stage two of my argument. This is reflected in the *Dialogues,* where Philo exhibits a keen interest in sorting out the nature of design evidence and its bearing on the question of God's existence. While Philo allows that there is evidence *of* design, he is skeptical about the possibility of inferring the existence of God (i.e., the God of religious practice) *from* design.[30]

In my argument, the evidence of design is sandwiched between the cosmological evidence of step one and data about the human condition brought into play in step three. The design evidence of step two plays a key role in the structural unity of the overall argument. It builds on the foundational evidence of step one and sets the stage for a consideration of other evidences at later stages. We must now consider how this characteristic of my argument relates to Philo's specific objections to the design argument for

---

[28]For an incisive examination of this peculiar argument, see Keith E. Yandell, *Hume's "Inexplicable" Mystery: His Views on Religion* (Philadelphia: Temple University Press, 1990), pp. 227-42. It is also helpful to consult David O'Connor, *Hume on Religion* (London and New York: Routledge, 2001), pp. 147-61.

[29]I warned early on that my comments on Hume would focus primarily on his *Dialogues.* For more on the challenge to the principle of causality, see Geivett, "The *Kalam* Cosmological Argument."

[30]It is now customary for philosophers of religion to distinguish between arguing *to* design and arguing *from* design. With many others, I recognize that Hume accepted an argument to design, but repudiated any argument from design to theism.

the existence of God.[31]

There are several Philonian objections to the design argument in the *Dialogues*. These have been individuated and grouped in various ways by different commentators and critics. For convenience, my response to these objections follows the fourfold grouping proposed by Hume scholar J. C. A. Gaskin.[32]

Restrictions on the conclusion.[33] This category includes three arguments that have this in common: they conclude that the richness of the theistic conclusion in the design argument far outstrips what can be said about God's nature on the available evidence from design.

Hume reasons that the evidence of design does not permit the ascription of omnipotence, omniscience and omnibenevolence (or moral perfection) to the agent responsible for design in the universe. He concludes, on the basis of an argument from evil, that the designer could not have the moral properties ascribed to God by theism. He also suggests that it is more likely that the "designer" is either a committee of designers, a bumbler disenchanted with a failed experiment or an absentee creator who left his universe to run of its own accord following its creation.

Steps one and two of my cumulative case reason that the designer will have that degree of power and intelligence needed, first, to create a universe from nothing, and second, to arrange for that universe to be a fit habitat for humanity and other living organisms. The creator's degree of benevolence will depend on his purposes in creating and his resources for achieving those purposes. At stage two in the cumulative case, this is not easy to discern. But the full panoply of design evidence relevant to step two suggests a remarkable measure of interest and concern for the welfare of human persons.

Step three explicitly acknowledges the reality of evil, among other noteworthy features of the human condition. These features, together with the evidences of cosmology and design, collectively generate a reasonable expectation that God would not permit the evils there are unless God has a morally sufficient reason for doing so. This is a specific dimension of the

---

[31]I have not done this elsewhere. For this reason, and also because the design argument is the major topic of the *Dialogues,* I take more time with this issue.

[32]See J. C. A. Gaskin, *Hume's Philosophy of Religion,* 2nd ed. (Atlantic Highlands, N.J.: Humanities Press International,1988), pp. 16-47. Gaskin asks, "How many criticisms of the design argument can be individuated in the *Dialogues* and the *Enquiry?*" He comes up with "ten interrelated criticisms," organized into four general groups (see pp. 16-17; cf. p. 47).

[33]See Gaskin, *Hume's Philosophy of Religion,* pp. 17-24.

expectation generated at step four, and it is subject to the sort of tests set forth in subsequent steps.

The evidence for the resurrection of Jesus is particularly relevant to Hume's allegations about the creator of the universe. For if Jesus was indeed raised from the dead, that event is a powerful and concrete indication of God's genuine interest in the human predicament and his intention to rescue humanity from its plight. According to Christianity, the inevitability of death is a singular symbol of all that is wrong in the world. But the resurrection of Jesus reveals God's radical defeat of this evil and is the ground of the Christian's hope that God's people may also look forward to deliverance on the day of their own resurrection.[34]

While the cumulative case as sketched above does not make explicit mention of the point, evil is itself evidence for the existence of God. First, this is suggested by the character of evil. Evil is a departure from the way things ought to be. But it could not be a departure from the way things ought to be unless there is a way things ought to be. If there is a way things ought to be, then there is a design plan for how things ought to be. And if there is such a design plan, then there is a designer.

Second, the significance of all the evil there is in the universe must be considered in light of all that is good about the created universe. From this point of view, our universe looks like an object of great value that has been broken and that its creator would most likely be able and desire to restore.

At most, the evil in our experience suggests only that if God exists, then God must have a morally sufficient reason for permitting all the evil there is. Apart from the evidence of my cumulative case, one might be justified in being agnostic about the goodness of the creator. But in light of the total available evidence, one can repose in the reasonable belief that God does exist and will conquer evil. The evidence of design, in particular, suggests that God does have a good purpose in creating, does care for his creatures, and knows what he's doing, despite anomalies generated by our experience of suffering.

The unique cause objection.[35] Here Hume levels an objection that can only seem cogent to one who is sympathetic with Hume's general skepti-

---

[34]For a thorough exposition of the theology of the resurrection and its place in God's solution to humanity's problems, see N. T. Wright, *The Resurrection of the Son of God* (Minneapolis: Fortress, 2003).

[35]Strictly speaking, this is one distinct argument, rather than a group of several arguments of a similar type. See Gaskin, *Hume's Philosophy of Religion*, pp. 24-27.

cism about causation. His point is that, as a one-of-a-kind object unlike any other object we have observed, the universe is such that we cannot observe the relation of causation to hold in its case. To infer a cause for our universe, it would be necessary that "we had experience of the origin of worlds," as Philo puts it (DNR 150). Of course, we don't.

In my cumulative case argument, the inference to a cause of the universe is not drawn from the evidence of design. To be precise, it is drawn from the evidence that the universe had a beginning. Granting the uniqueness of the universe under one description, it is not unique under *every* description. Experience, it would seem, does support the general claim that anything that begins to exist has a cause. The absolute origin of the universe is a special case of this type of event. Hence, it is reasonable to believe that the beginning of the universe was caused.

Weakness in the analogy.[36] Here, again, are three separable objections with something in common. We can treat them together, for they attack a common form of the design argument, namely, the analogical design argument. Hume's complaint is that the design argument depends on a dubious analogy between the universe and artifacts.

The trouble Hume raises for such an analogy is diminished if it is already known from step one that the universe, which shows so much evidence of design, was caused to exist by a personal agent. The creator of the universe and human artisans are alike in at least two respects: both are agents and both have produced objects that exhibit order. Step one of the cumulative case underwrites whatever analogy between the creator and human artisans, or between the order of the universe and the design of artifacts, is needed to make full use of design evidence at step two in explicating further what can be known about the creator and the creator's possible intentions in creating our particular universe.

Alternative explanations for order.[37] Finally, Hume suggests that there are alternative ways to explain the order of our universe. For example, there could be something intrinsic to the material of the universe that is "self-organizing," as it were. The details of his suggestions are anachronistic in light of modern science, but one can recognize the Humean impulse in contemporary claims that order in the universe could be the result of chance events.

---

[36]See Gaskin, *Hume's Philosophy of Religion*, 27-41.
[37]See ibid., pp. 41-47.

Again, step one provides important background evidence that should chasten excessive confidence in such "possibilities." The mere grounds that a hypothesis is logically possible is not an adequate basis for believing that it is true. Some logical possibilities are more plausible than others. If the universe depends for its existence on an agent of great power and intelligence, the evidence of design in our universe should most naturally be credited to the creator of the universe.

If it is suggested that the "chance hypothesis" works against the evidence in step one of my case, then it needs to be said that the term "chance hypothesis" used in this instance is an oxymoron. For chance, in total abstraction from concrete states of affairs, does not explain anything. Thus, it cannot count as the *explicans* in a hypothesis. Our ordinary application of the concept of *chance* serves us well in contexts pertaining to states already in existence (such as coins tossed into the air). But it cannot serve the same sort of purpose when it is the absolute origin of the universe that is in question. And even if it could, we should favor a hypothesis with rich explanatory power relative to a wide range of phenomena over the hypothesis of chance. Theism is just such a hypothesis.[38]

The argument in step two of my cumulative case is much more complex than anything Hume considers in the *Dialogues*. But the main thing to note is that his criticisms of the design argument have almost no direct bearing on my use of the design evidence in the cumulative case I have outlined. Again, the argument is treated by Hume in isolation from what comes before and what follows in my cumulative case. In my cumulative case for theism, the evidence for design is taken into account only after the stage has been set with the argument for the existence of a nonnatural being that brought the universe into existence. And the limited value and provisional force of the evidence of design is acknowledged when I suggest that on the basis of this evidence we get a modified hypothesis that includes the expectation that God would produce a remedy for the human condition and that this hypothesis needs further independent verification. This verification is looked for at subsequent stages of the cumulative case. And subsequent stages in the case provide additional resources for meeting Hume's challenge.

---

[38]It is difficult to imagine how the "hypothesis of chance" could be enriched with the same degree of conceptual content as the hypothesis of theism. But naturalism is such a powerful temptation that many find themselves in the grip of such a desperate proposal.

What does Hume say about these other elements of my cumulative case? In the *Dialogues,* precious little. He does seem, however, to recognize the temptation to carry the argument forward in approximately the way I have suggested in steps four and following.[39]

Desire and expectation. The final draft of Hume's Dialogues ends with Philo's confession of a mitigated deism: "The cause or causes of order in the universe probably bear some remote analogy to human intelligence" (DNR 227).

This confession is followed by an intriguing expression of desire and expectation:

> The most natural sentiment, which a well-disposed mind will feel on this occasion, is a longing desire and expectation, that Heaven would be pleased to dissipate, at least alleviate, this profound ignorance, by affording some more particular revelation to mankind, and making discoveries of the nature, attributes, and operations of the divine object of our Faith. A person, seasoned with a just sense of the imperfections of natural reason, will fly to revealed truth with the greatest avidity. (DNR 227)

This statement compares favorably with the expression of a similar desire and expectation in step four of my cumulative case. But the two expressions of a very natural intuition about what to expect, Philo's and my own, differ in significant ways. Philo's mitigated deism is severely truncated relative to the evidence elaborated at earlier stages. Our "profound ignorance" is the only feature of the human condition that Philo mentions in connection with this expectation. But a fuller explication of relevant features clarifies the scope of the human predicament and suggests more precisely the means of confirming the hypothesis that God would produce a remedy.

---

[39]This is not a big surprise, given Hume's acquaintance with the work of Samuel Clarke, Bishop Butler and others in the eighteenth century who developed a strategy similar to my own in opposition to deism. See Clarke's compendium of eight sermons (i.e, his Boyle Lectures) called *A Discourse Concerning the Unchangeable Obligations of Natural Religion and the Truth and Certainty of the Christian Revelation* (1705), and Butler's landmark work, *The Analogy of Religion* (1736). Clarke wrote: "Wherefore since those arguments which demonstrate to us the being and attributes of God, are so closely connected with those which prove the reasonableness and certainty of the Christian revelation, that there is now no consistent scheme of deism left . . . I thought I could no way better prevent their ill designs . . . than by endeavouring, in the same method of reasoning by which I before demonstrated the *Being and Attributes of God;* to prove in like manner, by one direct and continued thread of arguing, the reasonableness and certainty of the *Christian Revelation* also." I select Clarke for direct quotation because he published his system in the early eighteenth century and because he is not as well known now as Butler. Butler adopted a similar scheme and emphasized the probability of the Christian theistic hypothesis.

Finally, and most important, Philo does not seriously consider this to be a hypothesis subject to methods of confirmation and disconfirmation appropriate to the hypothesis. As Philo says next, "A person, seasoned with a just sense of the imperfections of natural reason, will fly to revealed truth with the greatest avidity. . . . To be a philosophical sceptic is, in a man of letters, the first and most essential step towards being a sound, believing Christian" (DNR 227). Reason, in other words, has run its course and left us with little more than a deism drained of religious value. In the end, we cannot be sure that Hume means for us to be taking Philo's "expectation" of revelation seriously. At best, Philo's expectation is grounded in sentiment rather than reason.

The evidence of miracles. Philo's "flight to revealed truth" beyond the limits of reason is premature. By stage four of the cumulative case, we have the basis for formulating a *reasonable* hypothesis that God would produce a remedy and thereby show himself to be actively concerned with the human predicament. This leads on to a delineation of methods for confirming or disconfirming this hypothesis. Notice, so far as Hume's *Dialogues* are concerned, there is no sustained argument against the possibility of formulating and testing this hypothesis.

Hume did famously object to the evidential value of miracles—relevant to step six in my cumulative case. But his critique of miracles appears in his epistemological treatise *An Enquiry Concerning Human Understanding*. Hume has nothing substantive to say about miracles in the *Dialogues,* where they might have some bearing on the question of God's existence. In the *Enquiry,* the evidence of miracles is evaluated in total isolation from the rich theistic evidence featured ahead of step six in my cumulative case. I've developed this point in some detail elsewhere.[40]

Hume's choice to deal in one volume with the evidence of design and in another volume with the evidence of miracles distracts attention away from the interconnection between these evidences. Hume's rationale for excluding the evidence of miracles in the *Dialogues* might be that such evidence falls outside the limited purview of "natural religion." That may be unfortunate for natural religion, but it's irrelevant to natural theology conducted in the service of a specified theism like Christian theism. What about Hume's rationale for omitting a general discussion of background evidence for theism in the midst of his critique of miracles in the *Enquiry?*

---

[40]See Geivett, "Evidential Value of Miracles."

It may be that Hume had already envisioned the demise of natural religion when he composed his piece on miracles.[41]

In any case, Hume assumes in his discussion of miracles that there is no adequate evidence for theism. And in his discussion of the evidence for theism, he is selective and insensitive to the structural relations that hold among evidences of different kinds. Hence, he fails to notice the natural bridge between the theistic evidence and the evidence of miracles. This bridge is a reasonable hypothesis about God's concern and likely remedy for the human condition. And it is a critical step in ratcheting up the case for theism.

The devotional experiment and religious experience. Since Hume does not recognize the possibility of generating a reasonable hypothesis that God has produced a remedy for the human condition, he has nothing to say about how this sort of hypothesis might be tested and confirmed. And so he has no inclination to address the relevance of conducting a devotional experiment and therefore no reason to assess the value of religious experience as possible confirmation to those who pursue a devotional experiment.

CONCLUSION

In the final analysis, Hume's most fundamental mistake is his failure to distinguish between generic theism and nonspecified theism. This accounts for his neglect of a much wider range of evidence for theism that is at the same time strong evidence for Christian theism. It falls to his philosophical heirs to correct Hume's error. They will no doubt mine Hume's writings on religion for bits here and there that can be used in a more satisfactory critique of theism. But to do critical justice to a cumulative case of the sort described in this chapter, there are few promising hints in Hume's writings. Critics of natural theology would do well to ignore Richard Gale's call for a return visit from Hume's Philo.

---

[41]Hume scholars have noted the oddness of locating a passage against miracles within the *Enquiry*, which treats more generally of epistemology. But if the reason, within the larger context of the *Enquiry*, had to do with the epistemology of testimonial belief, Hume's decision makes *some* sense. And if that is the explanation, then it probably would be a bit too much more of a detour for Hume to get involved there in lengthy assessment of theistic arguments.

CONTRIBUTORS

James F. Sennett

James F. Sennett (Ph.D. in philosophy, University of Nebraska) has taught at Pacific Lutheran University, Palm Beach Atlantic University, McNeese State University and Lincoln Christian College. He has written or edited three books and has published over twenty articles and many book reviews in numerous philosophical and theological journals, books and encyclopedias, including *Philosophy and Phenomenological Research, Faith and Philosophy, Religious Studies, Southern Journal of Philosophy, Philosophia Christi* and the *Cambridge Dictionary of Philosophy*.

Douglas Groothuis

Douglas Groothuis (Ph.D. in philosophy, University of Oregon) is professor of philosophy at Denver Seminary, where he has directed the Philosophy of Religion Masters Degree program since 1993. He is the author of several books, including two in the Wadsworth Philosophers Series: *On Jesus* and *On Pascal*. He has published over twenty articles in academic journals, including *Sophia, Inquiry, Religious Studies, Philosophia Christi* and *Research in Philosophy and Technology*.

Robin Collins

Robin Collins (Ph.D. in philosophy, Notre Dame) is professor of philosophy at Messiah College. He has published more than twenty journal articles and book chapters, many dealing with the relations between science and religion, and particularly with the "fine-tuning" argument for theism.

Paul Copan

Paul Copan (Ph.D. in philosophy, Marquette University) is the Pledger Family Professor of Philosophy and Ethics at Palm Beach Atlantic University, and has lectured at universities in the United States and other parts of the world. He is author and editor of numerous books, all in philosophy of religion or theology. He has published articles in *Philosophia Christi, Trinity Journal* and other professional journals. He is a regular reviewer for four philosophy and religion journals.

Garrett J. DeWeese

Garrett J. DeWeese (Ph.D. in philosophy, University of Colorado) is associate professor of philosophy and philosophical theology at Talbot School of Theology and Biola University. He is the author of *God and the Nature of Time* (Ashgate Press) and has published journal articles and book chapters in natural theology and the nature of God. His current research interests include the metaphysics of the Trinity and the incarnation.

Todd M. Furman

Todd M. Furman (Ph.D. in philosophy, University of California, Santa Barbara) is associate professor of philosophy at McNeese State University. He is the editor of two philosophy textbooks, including *The Canon and Its Critics,* and a highly acclaimed introduction to philosophy text, now in its second edition from McGraw-Hill. His research specialties include epistemology and applied ethics.

R. Douglas Geivett

R. Douglas Geivett (Ph.D. in philosophy, University of Southern California) is professor of philosophy at Biola University. He is the author of *Evil and the Evidence for God* (Temple University Press) and is coeditor of two critically acclaimed collections of essays in philosophy of religion. He has also published more than a dozen articles in philosophical and theological journals.

James D. Madden

James D. Madden (Ph.D. in philosophy, Purdue University) is assistant professor of philosophy at Benedictine College. He has published articles on early modern philosophy, omnipotence, intelligent design and Aristotle's epistemology in such journals as *The International Philosophical Quarterly, The*

Proceedings of the American Catholic Philosophical Association and *Perspectives on Science and Christian Faith*. In addition to his work in philosophy of religion, he is also engaged in research in philosophy of mind and ethics.

J. P. Moreland

J. P. Moreland (Ph.D. in philosophy, University of Southern California) is Distinguished Professor of Philosophy at Biola University in La Mirada, California, and director of Eidos Christian Center. He has authored, edited or contributed papers to twenty books with publishers ranging from Oxford University Press, Routledge, Wadsworth and Prometheus to InterVarsity Press and Zondervan. He has also published over sixty articles in academic journals, including *Philosophy and Phenomenological Research*, *American Philosophical Quarterly*, *Australasian Journal of Philosophy*, *Metaphilosophy*, *Pacific Philosophical Quarterly*, *Southern Journal of Philosophy*, *Religious Studies* and *Faith and Philosophy*.

Terence Penelhum

Terence Penelhum (B.Phil. in philosophy, Oxford) is Professor Emeritus of Religious Studies at the University of Calgary. His has authored dozens of journal articles and book chapters, and has written or edited many books, including *Religion and Rationality* (1971), *God and Skepticism* (1983), *Reason and Religious Faith* (1995), *Hume* (1975), *David Hume: An Introduction to His Philosophical System* (1993) and *Themes in Hume* (2000).

Joshua Rasmussen

Joshua Rasmussen (M.A. in philosophy, Talbot School of Theology) is a Ph.D. student in philosophy at the University of Notre Dame. He has published in the philosophy of religion in *Religious Studies* and *Philo* and has presented papers to the Society of Christian Philosophers and the Evangelical Theological Society.

Victor Reppert

Victor Reppert (Ph.D. in philosophy, University of Illinois) is adjunct professor of philosophy at Glendale Community College and Estrella Mountain Community College. He has published one book, *C. S. Lewis's Dangerous Idea* (InterVarsity Press) and numerous papers in academic journals, including the *International Journal for Philosophy of Religion*, *Philo* and *Metaphilosophy*.

Keith Yandell

Keith Yandell (Ph.D. in philosophy, Ohio State University) is Julius R. Weinberg Professor of Philosophy at the University of Wisconsin (Madison). He is author of five books and editor or coeditor of four others. He has published over seventy articles in academic journals and books. He is on the editorial board for *Sophia* and *International Journal for Philosophy of Religion* and is the editor of the First Books in Philosophy series for Blackwell Publishing.

Index